ABOUT THE AUTHORS

Margaret Drever

Margaret Drever FCPA BCom (UWS), Grad Dip Educ (UTS), MEc (UNE), PhD (UNE) is an accounting lecturer at Southern Cross University, Coffs Harbour. She is currently vice president of the Small Enterprise Association of Australia and New Zealand (SEAANZ) and a vice president of NSW CPA Australia with liaison for the SME committee and chairperson for universities liaison committee portfolios. She is also a member of the Institute of Chartered Accountants. Her research interests focus on small-business financial management issues, entrepreneurship and accounting education. At the yearly CPA Australia/Charles Sturt University's Accounting Educators' Forum, she has held workshops on accounting theory, mentoring and accounting issues. Before academe, Margaret worked as an accountant for Boral Ltd and was a director of a small engineering company.

Patricia Stanton

Patricia Stanton PhD (Newcastle), BComm (Hons 1, Newcastle), BA (Sydney) and DipEd (Sydney) is currently a senior lecturer in financial accounting at The University of Newcastle. She has published widely in international journals such as *Accounting Auditing & Accountability Journal, Australian Accounting Review,*

Corporate Communications: An International Journal and *Accounting History*. Two of her papers have won international best paper awards. Her current research interests are focused on the value of current reporting practices, including those of not-for-profits and government.

Sue McGowan

Sue McGowan BAcc (SAIT), MCom (UniSA), Grad Certificate in Higher Education (QUT) is currently an accounting lecturer at the University of South Australia in Adelaide. Her research interests focus on accounting education and internationalisation.

ABOUT THE CONTRIBUTORS

Jean Raar

Jean Raar BBus (GIAE), GDipEd (Vic Coll), MAcc, PhD (RMIT) is a senior lecturer in accounting in the School of Accounting, Economics and Finance at Deakin University, Melbourne. Her current teaching responsibilities and research activities are centred on environmental accounting, management accounting, accounting for small business and financial accounting theory.

Stella Sofocleous

Stella Sofocleous MAcc, PhD (RMIT) is a lecturer in the School of Accounting and Finance at Victoria University, Melbourne, where she was appointed after gaining experience as a public accountant and as a teacher of accounting at secondary schools. She has had extensive teaching experience at tertiary and postgraduate levels for more than 20 years, specialising in financial accounting, public practice and technology, taxation law and practice, and auditing. Dr Sofocleous has postgraduate qualifications in education, a masters in accounting from Victoria University and a PhD from RMIT University. Her doctorate provides an insight into specific sustainable forestry practices such as accounting, taxation and regulation. She is a fellow CPA with taxation specialisation, a fellow member of the Taxation Institute and a member of the Victorian Institute of Teaching. Dr Sofocleous has spoken at many conferences and seminars, published her research in Australia and internationally, and received awards for excellence in education.

Tom Ravlic

Tom Ravlic is policy adviser, financial reporting and governance at the National Institute of Accountants and has more than a decade of experience analysing and commenting on the accounting profession, the corporate environment and accounting standard setting.

CONTEMPORARY ISSUES IN ACCOUNTING

MARGARET
DREVER
Southern Cross
University

PATRICIA
STANTON
The University of
Newcastle

SUSAN
McGOWAN
University of
South Australia

WITH CONTRIBUTIONS FROM

JEAN RAAR
Deakin University

STELLA SOFOCLEOUS
Victoria University

TOM RAVLIC
National Institute of Accountants

BICENTENNIAL
1807
WILEY
2007
BICENTENNIAL

First published 2007 by
John Wiley & Sons Australia, Ltd
42 McDougall Street, Milton Qld 4064

Typeset in Palatino LT 9.5/13

National Library of Australia
Cataloguing-in-Publication data

Drever, Margaret.
Contemporary issues in accounting

Bibliography.
Includes index.
ISBN 978 0 470 80766 8 (pbk).
1. Accounting. I. Stanton, Patricia Anne. II. McGowan,
Susan (Susan C.). III. Title.

657

Cover and internal design images: © Fancy; ©PhotoAlto/Frederic Cirou;
© Image 100 Ltd
Wiley Bicentennial Logo: Richard J. Pacifico

Edited by David Rule

Printed in Singapore by
Mainland Press Pte Ltd

10 9 8 7 6 5 4 3 2 1

BRIEF CONTENTS

CONTENTS

PREFACE

Rationale for developing the text

Accounting and accounting education are changing. Given the increasing complexities of the business and social world, it is important that accounting education encourages and engages students to gain a better understanding of the world ahead of them. Rather than introducing various theories and research in accounting as in the traditional approach, this text considers these theories and associated research in the context of specific issues in financial accounting, so that when students finish their studies, they will have engaged in a current accounting information perspective in the context of specific issues.

Approach and application to business

This text takes a direction different from that of other accounting theory texts. The focus is on embedding theories and associated research in the current financial development era. In this, corporations and financial institutions are learning from international accounting standards, changing corporate governance and triple bottom line reporting. Because the text deals with, among other matters, international accounting standards, corporate governance and social and environmental issues, it is especially applicable to business.

Structure of content, extent of topics

While the structure of the content is unique, in that it covers a variety of topical issues, traditional subject areas such as the conceptual framework and measurement are included to ensure that students have an understanding of these topics, which underpin or influence accounting practices and debates relating to particular issues. In some ways, it is hoped that this text will help students in their professional and business life by giving them a better understanding of the business sector. The text deals with many areas that are unusual to accounting theory texts, including small-business entities, professional responsibility and speculation about the future directions of accounting.

The text provides a range of suitable learning tools for students to use: namely, mind maps, case studies, learning tips and review questions. Recognising the international nature of accounting, some of this material, especially case studies, relates to overseas issues, giving a multicultural dimension to the text.

Value to students

Students will be able to draw much from this text in relation to contemporary issues in accounting. The mind maps at the beginning of each chapter should help students understand the concepts in each chapter. Additionally, they will challenge accounting lecturers to use these as a tool both to motivate students and to link chapters to give a more complete picture.

Acknowledgements

We wish to thank the other authors who have given of their time to write this text, which has evolved over a couple of years to the final product.

The writing of this book for some has been very difficult and we, the authors, would like to thank John Wiley & Sons for their encouragement to venture into a text that is quite different. We acknowledge the role of Zoë Yule and Darren Taylor of John Wiley & Sons for their considerable persistence and enthusiasm.

All of the authors that have assisted in writing of this text are outstanding experts in their respective fields and provide authoritative reference to their chapters. Those authors are Jean Raar (Deakin University), chapter 7 'Environmental and Social Reporting and Accounting'; Stella Sofocleous (Victoria University), chapter 11 'Professional Responsibility'; and Tom Ravlic (National Institute of Accountants), chapter 8 'International Accounting'.

Without our families this text would not have been possible and their support and interest are greatly appreciated.

Margaret Drever
Patricia Stanton
Sue McGowan
April 2007

ACKNOWLEDGEMENTS

The authors and publisher would like to thank the following copyright holders, organisations and individuals for their permission to reproduce copyright material in this book.

Images

AASB: page **63** © 2006 Australian Accounting Standards Board (AASB). The text, graphics and layout of this publication are protected by Australian copyright law and the comparable law of other countries. No part of the publication may be reproduced, stored or transmitted in any form or by any means without the prior written permission of the AASB except as permitted by law. For reproduction or publication, permission should be sought in writing from the Australian Accounting Standards Board. Requests in the first instance should be addressed to the Administration Director, Australian Accounting Standards Board, PO Box 204, Collins Street West, Melbourne, Victoria, 8007. • ASB (UK): page **106** © Accounting Standards Board Ltd (ASB). Adapted and reproduced with the kind permission of the Financial Reporting Council. All rights reserved. • © The British Land Company PLC: page **209** • IASB: page **236** © 2007 International Accounting Standards Committee Foundation. All rights reserved. No permission granted to reproduce or distribute. • Australian Bureau of Statistics: pages **302–3** 'Small Business in Australia 2001' by Dennis Trewin, ABS Catalogue No. 1321.0, 2002. ABS data used with permission from the Australian Bureau of Statistics. • © Emerald Group Publishing Ltd: page **370** from 'Internal organisational factors influencing corporate social and ethical reporting: beyond current theorising' by Carol A Adams, *Accounting, Auditing & Accountability Journal*, Vol. 15, Issue 2, 2002, p. 246.

Text

IASB: pages **33, 37** and **39** © 2007 International Accounting Standards Committee Foundation. All rights reserved. No permission granted to reproduce or distribute. • CPA Journal: pages **34–5** reprinted from *The CPA Journal*, June 2006, copyright 2006, with permission from the New York State Society of Certified Public Accountants • Associated Press: page **41** 'Time Warner will restate earnings following accounting probe' by Seth Sutel, Associated Press Newswires, 18/08/06, reproduced with permission • *Accountancy Ireland*: pages **54–6** 'Code of ethics: IFAC issues revised code for professional accountants' by Richard George, *Accountancy Ireland*, Vol. 37, Issue 5, October 2005, p. 6 • CFO Publishing Corporation: pages **56–7** 'Reporting: one standard fits all?' by Lisa Yoon, CFO.com, dated 05/12/05 • © Mark Davis: pages **75–6** 'Treasury chiefs revolt over budget rules', *The Australian Financial Review*, 03/04/06, p. 3 • © 2006 PricewaterhouseCoopers Australia: pages **84–5** 'AIFRS: the complex issues and the way forward — a review of contemporary issues affecting our clients'. All rights reserved • © Leon Gettler: pages **86–7** 'Break for non-profit sector on onerous rules', *The Age*, 16/10/06, p. 3; page **146** 'NAB self-portrait less than flattering', *The Age*, 15/12/05, p. 4 • *Edmonton Sun*: pages **96–7** 'Metric mixup melted Mars probe' by Robyn Suriano, *Edmonton Sun*, 01/10/99, p. 65 • © *South China Morning Post*: pages **108–9**, 08/04/04, p. B2; pages **367–8**, 03/11/04, p. 17 • Elsevier: pages **114–16** reprinted from *Accounting, Organizations and Society*, Vol. 7, No. 3, C Harvey Rorke, 'An early pricing model regarding the value of a cat: A historical note', pp. 305–6. Copyright 1982, with permission from Elsevier • VNU Business Publications: pages **116–18** 'An end to the neo-soviet nightmare' by RA Rayman, *Accountancy Age*, 04/05/2006, pp. 22–3 • © Stuart Wilson: pages **130–1** 'Be kind to shareholders: keep it short, sweet and informative', *The Australian*, 09/06/06, p. 32 • © Australian Securities & Investments Commission: pages **142–5**, reproduced with permission, www.fido.gov.au • Torstar Syndication Services: pages **158–60** reproduced with permission. From an article originally appearing in *The Toronto Star*, June 2006 • © OECD: pages **163–7** from 'OECD principles of corporate governance', 2004 • CPA Australia: pages **163–7** from 'A guide to understanding corporate governance'. Copyright CPA Australia. Reproduced with the permission of CPA Australia. CPA Australia has used reasonable care and skill in compiling the content of these works. However, CPA Australia makes no warranty as to the accuracy or completeness of any information in these works. No part of these works are intended to be advice, whether legal or professional. As laws change frequently, all readers are advised to undertake their own research or to seek professional advice to keep abreast of any reforms or developments in the law; pages **374–5** Copyright CPA Australia Ltd 2004. Reproduced with the permission of CPA Australia Ltd. CPA Australia has used reasonable care and skill in compiling the content of these works. However, CPA Australia makes no warranty as to the accuracy or completeness of any information in these works. No part of these works are intended to be advice, whether legal or professional. These works feature references to ethical pronouncements that were current at the time of publication in the CPA Australia monthly magazine, *INTHEBLACK*. • © Stuart Lauchlan: pages **185–6** from 'Ethical Cleansing: companies on trial', *MIS Australia*, 01/11/03 • *The Asian Banker*: pages **187–8** 'S&P: Study shows Hong Kong companies' disclosure standards low', *The Asian Banker*,

30/09/04. Reproduced with permission. • Earthscan Publications Ltd: pages **196–7** from *The triple bottom line: does it all add up? Assessing the sustainability of business and CSR*, edited by Adrian Henriques and Julie Richardson, Earthscan, 2004, p. 38. Reproduced with the permission of Earthscan. • © Novo Nordisk A/S: pages **200–1** reproduced with permission • © The British Land Company PLC: pages **208–10** • © Accounting Standards Board Ltd (ASB): page **213** reproduced with the kind permission of the Financial Reporting Council. All rights reserved • Anthony Albanese MP: pages **221–2** 'Twenty years on: lest we forget the lessons from Chernobyl', *The Sydney Morning Herald*, 26/04/06, p. 13. Anthony Albanese MP is the Manager of Opposition Business in the House of Representatives and Shadow Minister for Infrastructure and Water. • © Richard Gluyas: pages **223–4** 'Banks set to go green', *The Australian*, 13/04/06, p. 7 • Commonwealth Copyright Administration: pages **251–2** letter — Adoption of the International Accounting Standards in Australia — from J Lucy and C Macek, 20/10/03, from www.frc.gov.au, copyright Commonwealth of Australia, reproduced by permission • © Tom Ravlic: pages **259–60** 'Politicians cast a shadow', *CFO*, 01/05/04, p. 30 • FASB: page **261–2** 'FASB and IASB agree to work together toward convergence of global accounting standards', News Release, 29/10/02. Extract reproduced with permission from the FASB and the IASB; page **269** 'The FASB and the Capital Markets' by John M 'Neel' Foster, FASB Report, June 2003. Portions of various FASB documents, copyright by the Financial Accounting Standards Board, 401 Merritt 7, PO Box 5116, Norwalk, CT 06856-5116, USA, are reproduced with permission. Complete copies of these documents are available from the FASB. • Copyright Clearance Center: pages **273–4** 'Is there no drop to Google stock?' by Michael Bazeley, *San Jose Mercury News*, Knight Ridder/Tribune Business News. Washington, 15/01/06, p. 1 © Knight Ridder Digital • © Ross Gittins: pages **279–81** 'Road to wealth may lie in marching out of step', *The Sydney Morning Herald*, 30/09/06, p. 38 • © Alan Kohler: pages **288–9** 'Rupert's shareholders lose out', *The Sydney Morning Herald*, 22/09/04, pp. 25–6 • © Anna Fenech: pages **290–1** 'Women take more risks when investing: survey', *The Weekend Australian*, 22/07/06, p. 40 • © 2005 Springer: page **297**, *Small Business Economics*, Vol. 24, No. 2, March 2005, p. 133, 'Gender discrimination, entrepreneurial talent and self-employment' by Rosti and Chelli, Table 1. With kind permission of Springer Science and Business Media • ICAA: pages **299–300** 'Tax guide' by Karen Smith, *Charter*, April 2006, Vol. 77, Issue 3, p. 54; pages **306–8** 'Help for NREs' by The Institute of Chartered Accountants Technical Standards Team, *Charter*, November 2005, Vol. 76, Issue 10, p. 68; pages **322–6** 'Spotlight on AASB 140' by Stephanie Kemp and Jeanette Dawes, *Charter*, April 2006, Vol. 77, Issue 3, p. 58. All © *Charter* • Europa: pages **316–17** 'Corporate governance and accounting — where we stand in the EU' by Charlie McCreevy, European Commission press release © European Communities 1995–2006 • Hardie Grant Magazines: pages **343–4** 'Best advice: "fess up" and stay out of jail' © Robert Richards, *INTHEBLACK*, July 2006, Vol. 76, Issue 6, pp. 68–9 • © Ben Wilmot: pages **388–9** 'Property bosses earn top dollar', *The Australian Financial Review*, 11/11/04, p. 54 • © Jimmy Chung: pages **389–90** 'New standards to lift investor confidence' by Jimmy Chung, *South China Morning Post*, 28/04/06, p. 4. Reproduced with permission.

Every effort has been made to trace the ownership of copyright material. Information that will enable the publisher to rectify any error or omission in subsequent editions will be welcome. In such cases, please contact the Permissions Section of John Wiley & Sons Australia, Ltd, which will arrange for the payment of the usual fee.

1 INTRODUCTION TO CONTEMPORARY ISSUES IN ACCOUNTING

LEARNING OBJECTIVES

After reading this chapter, you should be able to:

- define 'theory'
- explain the role of theory in financial accounting
- explain the differences between positive theories and normative theories
- understand the role of research in accounting.

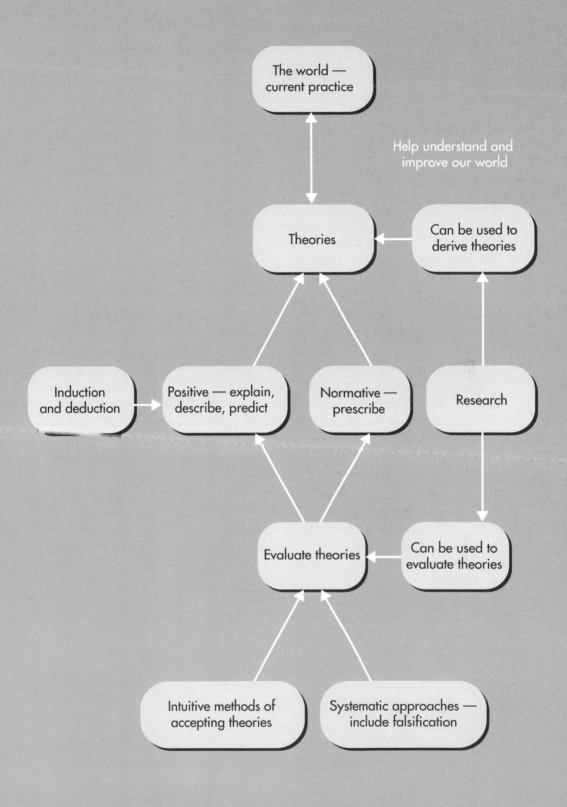

■ Introduction

This text considers some of the issues in financial accounting. **Financial accounting** can be defined as the regular reporting of the financial position and performance of an entity through financial statements issued to external users.

financial accounting: The regular reporting of the financial position and performance of an entity through financial statements issued to external users

This definition is relatively straightforward but financial accounting is neither straightforward nor simple. As this text shows, the influences on financial accounting are many and complex, and often the application of financial accounting principles and practices in specific contexts brings unique challenges. Although the basic building blocks of accounting — the debit and credit rules — have not changed for centuries, the world certainly has. Business activities and transactions are more varied and complicated, and increasingly more global; social expectations and priorities are changing; the scope and amount of regulation have increased. Accounting is often cited as the 'language of business', and financial accounting provides much of the public information about business (and non-business) entities that people rely on to make decisions. If the financial accounting information provided is not 'right', this can have significant adverse consequences; for not only shareholders, but also the public, the managers of businesses and accountants themselves. Even a brief look at business failures (such as Enron and WorldCom) confirms this.

Deciding what is to be reported and how to report in financial accounting is a complicated matter, influenced not only by political, financial and personal interests but also by accounting not being an exact science. At times there are no 'black and white' rules, and often alternative solutions may be offered to financial accounting problems. Chapters 2 to 5 of this text examine some general issues relating to, and influencing, financial accounting. The remaining chapters focus on financial accounting in specific contexts (such as its role in corporate governance, or small and medium enterprise accounting) and the distinct problems and approaches relevant to these contexts. You will see that financial accounting has come a long way from the simple and unproblematic application of debit and credit rules.

The examination of many of these issues in financial accounting, you will observe, often involves the use or discussion of theories and research. For example:

- The next chapter examines the conceptual framework in financial accounting, which is a type of theory.
- Agency theory is examined in chapter 6 to explain the components of executive payment packages.
- Various theories that explain why entities would provide disclosures about environmental or social performance are examined in chapter 7.

Before you consider the individual topics, it is useful to have some understanding of the nature and types of theories, and related research, and how these are used in accounting to solve or identify problems.

Accounting theory

Accounting is often viewed as a 'practical' discipline and much of your earlier studies may have been about learning *how* to apply accounting rules (such as debits and credits), often using computerised accounting programs. There seems to be little use for theory. This doubt about the relevance of theory is not limited to accounting students. Many people say that they do not need theories, that by definition theories are not practical or useful in the real world. However, theories are necessary for us to try to understand the world we live in. Theories provide a basis for decisions we make. Even though you may not yet have explicitly studied any accounting theories, you no doubt have used them. For example, when deciding whether to include an item in the financial statements, you may have applied the concepts of materiality and recognition criteria, such as relevance and reliability. These concepts are part of an accounting theory, referred to as the conceptual framework, which provides the basis for accounting standards. When choosing how to measure items in the financial statements (e.g. choosing between fair value and historic cost), you are applying measurement theory.

What theory is

There is no simple definition of 'theory'. In different circumstances, it can mean different things. People often use the word in common usage to mean a guess or their thoughts on something, such as 'I have a theory about why my friend is always late'. Or it is used to suggest an unrealistic or impossible ideal; such as '*In theory*, it should take one hour to get to work but the traffic always causes delays'. In this usage, a 'theory' is simply an opinion or explanation.

The following are dictionary definitions of what a theory is:

- a belief or principle that guides actions or behaviour (such as behavioural theories of positive reinforcement or theories in management about motivating employees)
- an idea or set of ideas that is intended to explain something (such as Darwin's theory of evolution)
- the set of principles on which a subject is based or of ideas that are suggested to explain a fact or event (such as economic theory or the laws of physics)
- more generally, a conjecture or an opinion (Macquarie, Concise Oxford and Cambridge dictionaries).

As these definitions show, theories can do different things: some describe and some explain what is happening. Some of these theories will also make predictions about what will happen. Other theories make suggestions or guide action (i.e. say what *should* happen). This text is not concerned with the 'opinions' that characterise the common usage of the term 'theory' but considers the more systematic theories. **Accounting theory** therefore means the following:

> **accounting theory:** Either a description, explanation or prediction of accounting practice or a set of principles on which to evaluate or guide practice

- 'A description, explanation or a prediction [of accounting practice based] on observations and/or logical reasoning' (Henderson et al. 2004, p. 4)

- 'Logical reasoning in the form of a set of broad principles that (1) provide a general framework of reference by which accounting practice can be evaluated and (2) guide the development of new practice and procedures' (Hendrickson as cited in Godfrey et al. 2003).

Before looking at the different types of theories, the next section considers why it is important to consider and know about theory.

Why theory is needed

In some civilisations, there was initially a theory that the world was flat. However, this theory was replaced by a new theory that the Earth was round. Let us consider how this 'round Earth' theory may have developed and the impact it may have had on people's views and actions. People would have sat on the shore and watched boats sail off, and will have seen the boats disappearing as they neared the horizon but always hull-first. Also, some stars disappeared from the sky if you travelled north or south. There may have been many individual observations of this happening. But without some explanation (some theory) about *why* the stars disappeared or why boats disappeared from view hull first, the observations were interesting but provided little useful information. Then a theory was formed that 'fitted' with the observations. *If* the world was round, then the stars disappearing as you travelled north or south or the boats disappearing hull-first on the horizon would be explained. It would 'fit' with what people had seen. This helped people understand their world and would of course influence their views and actions: if you believed this theory, then you would certainly not be concerned about travelling too far out in a boat thinking you would fall off the edge of the world. It also allowed people to *predict* what would happen to if you continued travelling in one direction; that is, you would end up where you began.

This example illustrates two different ways in which theories are useful:
- providing an explanation of what is happening
- helping us predict what will happen.

This example also demonstrates a further point. Just because there is a theory about something does not mean that that theory is correct. An important issue when learning about or using theory (including accounting theory) is to consider how the appropriateness of any particular theory can be assessed. Of course, we now know that the theory of the Earth being round is incorrect (it is not a true sphere), but to the people of the day, this theory was useful: it provided an explanation of how their world worked, so provided a basis for their actions and decisions.

Today, much of life is affected by theory. The end results of the application of theories only may be seen and the theories behind them may not be fully understood but theories are the driving force behind many of the things that affect our daily lives. For example:
- Governments make decisions about whether to increase or decrease taxes based on economic theories that explain and predict the impact rises or falls in tax will have on consumer behaviour, inflation, unemployment and national debt. These

decisions also take into account theories of social justice, which consider which groups in society should be helped or should bear the burden of higher taxes.

• There are theories about global warming and the impact of the use of resources on the environment. Some of these theories also make predictions about what will happen (such as the increase in temperatures to be expected and the impact this will have on climate in particular regions). Other theories suggest what *should* be done to reduce environmental damage. Our daily lives are witness to the result of these theories, reflected in recycling programs, reductions in certain chemicals in the petrol used in cars and in water restrictions.

These are only two examples but you should see that theory intrudes into our lives every day; from theories about the best way to treat diseases, theories about the best way to teach university students, to mathematically based theories that underlie the building of bridges and tunnels. These examples also illustrate two further things about theories:

• There are also theories that do not explain what is happening in the world but, rather, provide solutions or ways to improve the world.

• There are often different theories on the same topic. There are many alternative theories about the impact of global warming and what the best way to prevent it is. There are some theories that suggest that global warning is a natural cyclical event and that there is no need to do anything.

From this, you should see that theories are important. As noted, theories can do different things and in accounting there are many, some of which describe, explain or predict accounting practice and others that provide recommendations or suggestions about what accounting practice should be. Theories inform our everyday lives and provide important information that can be used in making decisions, such as whether to sail off into the horizon, or whether to recycle and reduce waste. Theories can provide the same benefits in accounting by:

• Describing and explaining current accounting practices. For example:
  – Capital-market theory describes how share prices react to accounting information.
  – Researchers investigating financial reporting failures (such as Enron) have after identifying factors that have contributed to these problems (e.g. lack of independence of auditors, rules-based accounting standards and share-based compensation payments) arrived at theories about why these failures have occurred.

• Predicting accounting practice. For example:
  – Agency or contracting theory, as well as explaining why managers may change the way in which they account (i.e. the accounting policies) for items in the financial statements, makes predictions about the accounting policies that will be chosen by managers in particular circumstances.

• Providing principles to take into account when taking action or making decisions. For example:
  – In management accounting courses you will have used theories of capital budgeting, which might involve calculating net present values of projects and payback periods, to help decide which projects to invest in.

- A theory of asset recognition helps to determine when and how assets should be included in the financial statements.
- Helping to identify problems and deficiencies with current accounting practice and improve accounting practice. For example:
  - The conceptual framework for accounting, by providing the basic principles on which to base accounting standards (the more detailed reporting rules), can make accounting practice more consistent.
  - Theories about how investors make decisions and what information they need and use can explain which accounting measures are most useful and suggest ways to improve the usefulness of financial statements (e.g. by increasing the use of fair values).
  - Theories about corporate responsibility can suggest that companies also need to provide information about environmental impacts of their activities.

Learning tips

Do you know...

1.1 *Accounting theory involves either a description, explanation or prediction of accounting practice or a set of principles on which to evaluate or guide practice.*

1.2 *Different theories do different things: some* describe, *some* explain, *some* predict, *some make suggestions about what* should *happen.*

Types of theories

Theories are often placed into two categories:
- positive theories
- normative theories.

Positive theories

This category is used to represent theories that are about the world as it is. **Positive theories** can:

positive theories: Theories that describe, explain or predict what is happening in the world (such as describing, explaining or predicting current accounting practice)

hypothesis: A tentative assumption or prediction of a theory

- *describe* what is actually happening
- *explain* what is happening
- make *predictions* about what will happen.
  Examples of positive theories are:
- theories of how contagious diseases are spread
- theories that explain why managers prefer or choose particular accounting methods or policies over others.

These theories are concerned with the world as it is, and help to make sense of what is happening. If a positive theory makes a prediction about what is happening, or is expected to happen, this prediction is often framed as a **hypothesis**. This hypothesis can then be tested to help decide whether the theory is correct. Positive theories are often referred to as 'empirical' theories. 'Empirical' means 'derived from or guided by experience or experiment' (Macquarie dictionary) and positive theories involve observations of the world, either direct or indirectly, either as a basis for its descriptions or explanations, and to test any predictions made. Most positive theories are developed from observation and by the process of induction and deduction.

Where positive theories come from

Let's consider a simple example of how a positive theory might be derived. A researcher observes a number of swans and notices that all swans she has seen are white. From this, the researcher arrives at the conclusion that it may be that all swans are white. This is a theory about swans. This process of moving from specific observations (particular instances) to a theory or conclusion is called **induction**.

induction: The process of inferring general principles from particular instances

deduction: The process of reaching a conclusion about particular instances from general principles

After the theory has been developed, it needs to be tested, which allows making predictions (a hypothesis) about the characteristics (in this case the colour) of swans. This process of developing predictions from theories is known as **deduction**. The researcher would then test the theory by making further observations of swans to see whether the observations agreed with its prediction (i.e. the hypothesis from the theory). This process is depicted in figure 1.1.

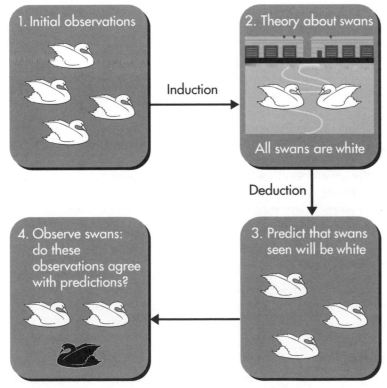

FIGURE 1.1 Scientific method

You should see that in this instance all of the observations do not 'fit' with the hypothesis because one black swan has been found, and so disproves the theory

'that all swans are white'. This process of beginning with limited observations, analysing them to derive a theory and then making predictions, which are tested by further observations, is often referred to as the **scientific method**. It is how positive theories commonly emerge.

Let's consider an example (based on Rivett 2000) of some positive research in accounting that illustrates a positive accounting theory and this approach.

Two accounting researchers, Hall & Stammerjohan (1997), arrived at a positive theory about influences on managers' choice of accounting policies and aimed to explain what accounting policy choices would be made by managers in particular circumstances.

This research considered the accounting policies of oil companies. You should know from your previous studies that managers often have a choice of accounting policies. For example, companies may value some assets at cost or fair value; depreciation is based on estimates of useful life of assets and probable resale value. In choosing different policies or methods managers can (without changing the actual and physical economic performance of the company) alter the financial statements significantly.

Initial observations

The researchers initially observed that in some companies in the oil industry, managers seemed to choose policies that reduced income or assets. This led the researchers to question the cause, and one of the other observations they make was that oil companies were often involved in litigation (e.g. being sued for environmental damage say from an oil tanker spill) and noticed that the damages awarded in these cases often seemed to be linked to the wealth of the company (in other words, 'richer' companies had to pay greater amounts in damages).

Conclusion: theory

Given these facts, the researchers theorised that where oil companies were being sued for damages, managers would chose accounting policies and methods to reduce profit and assets in an attempt to reduce the potential damages to be awarded. One of the choices available to managers in oil companies was how to report new discoveries or reserves of oil. The researchers arrived at several hypotheses, one of which was:

> [Oil] firms under-report reserves during periods in which they are defendants in litigation with high potential damages relative to other periods.

Testing the theory

The researchers tested this hypothesis by comparing how reserves were reported by managers of oil firms facing litigation and by those who were not. The researchers claimed that their observations of managers reporting of reserves were consistent with the hypothesis; that is, that firms facing litigation under-reported reserves compared with those not facing litigation, so the policy choices made by managers were consistent with the predictions of the theory, which may explain those choices.

This example also serves to illustrate some of the problems with accounting research and the testing of theories. In this case, the researchers did not directly research the motivations of the managers making the accounting policies choices but *inferred* them from two sets of facts: litigation and under-reporting of reserves. The researchers theorised that they were connected: that the litigation *caused* the managers to under-report reserves. The researchers themselves identify as one of the limitations of the research that there may be other reasons (other than litigation) that influenced the managers accounting policy choice.

Normative theories

Normative theories do not describe, explain or predict what *is* happening, but rather make suggestions or recommendations as to what *should* happen or what 'ought to be'. In other words, they prescribe. The prescriptions or recommendations of these theories aim to achieve some goal or objective. For example:

normative theories: Theories that provide prescriptions about what *should* happen

- There are theories about what *should* be done to reduce greenhouse gas emissions with the aim of reducing the rate of global warming and the environmental damage it results in.
- There are theories in accounting that propose that fair values *should* be used to measure assets in the financial statements with the aim to ensure that more relevant information is provided to users of financial statements.

This does not, however, mean that observations or facts about, say, current accounting practice are not considered in the development of normative theories. Indeed, it is often a result of considering positive theories and research in relation to these that normative theories evolve.

Let's consider an example.

Goal: what we are trying to achieve

People may believe that we should prevent further environmental damage. So the goal is to reduce the impact of our activities on the environment.

Premises

There may be evidence that one of the largest impacts on the environment comes from the generation of power. Research may confirm that using fossil fuels (such as coal) in power generation produces large amounts of greenhouse gases. There may be theories that suggest that greenhouse gases are a major cause of global warning and temperature change and these damage the environment. There may be evidence that nuclear power generation results in much less production of greenhouse gases.

Conclusion: Prescription

Given the goal and the premises, it would be suggested that nuclear reactors should replace power generation facilities that rely on fossil fuels.

Do you think everyone would agree with this conclusion and prescription? The answer is no. Many people are opposed to nuclear reactors because of the potential for environmental damage from accidents and the radioactive waste products from this method of power generation. These concerns may require the addition of further premises to consider (such as there being evidence that waste products from nuclear power generation can cause environmental damage or of the magnitude and nature of damage to the environment from potential accidents at nuclear power generation facilities). The inclusion of these premises may cause the conclusion and prescription to change.

Some of the normative accounting theories that suggested that fair values should be used came about by identification of problems with the measurements (mainly historic cost) being actually used in accounting, combined with research that indicated that many of the current accounting measures may have limited usefulness for users.

The nature of the conclusion of a normative theory is a prescription (it is a *recommended* course of action) and this factor needs to be considered when looking at how to test normative theories. The conclusion of a normative theory cannot be tested by seeing whether it actually happens: the theory is not saying this is *what* actually happens but what *should* happen.

Evaluating and testing theories

There are many theories, in some cases alternative theories, about the same topic or area. In financial accounting, for example, there are alternative theories about how items should be measured. Just because there is a theory about something does not mean that it is correct. So how can it be decided whether a theory should be accepted? How do people decide that they believe a particular theory is true? In practice, various ways are used to make judgements about theories. These range from simple (often intuitive) approaches, to more systematic and scientific approaches. People accept theories every day that they may not fully understand (such as theories of global warming; the theory of relativity and theories about how certain diseases are spread).

There are a number of reasons theories might be accepted without 'first hand' or direct knowledge, including the authority of the source of the theory, whether the theory makes sense and fits with our own experiences and beliefs, and also whether other people accept the theory. If you are a researcher or professional in a particular discipline, it would be expected that more legitimate, independent and justifiable methods would be applied in assessing and evaluating theories. These would include examining the logical construction of the theory and considering evidence that confirmed or refuted the theory. It is generally accepted that theories cannot be proven true. This is because regardless of how many observations 'fit' or confirm a theory, it can never be certain that there are 'enough'. Relating back to the swans example, how many observations of white swans would prove that the theory was true? However, a theory can be proven incorrect by just one observation that does not fit with the theory (e.g. finding one black swan would establish that the theory that all swans are white is wrong). Therefore, the rational way to use observation to test a theory is not to try to find observations that confirm the theory but to search for instances that do not fit with the theory, which disprove it. This is referred to as **falsification**.

> **falsification:** The method of testing theories by attempting to find observations that conflict with the conclusions or predictions of the theory

This book does not consider in further detail the specific ways in which theories are tested and you should refer to more detailed texts that specifically focus on accounting theories if you wish to consider this issue further. The testing and evaluation of theories will usually involve research, although this is not the only reason for the latter. The following sections consider accounting research because the specific issues in financial accounting this text goes on to consider all involve or are influenced by research.

What research is

As outlined, an accounting theory is either a description, explanation or prediction of accounting practice or a set of principles on which to evaluate or guide practice. According to the Macquarie dictionary, **research** is the 'diligent and systematic enquiry or investigation into a subject in order to discover facts or principles'. Research is often repeated and adjusted, which means that later studies build on earlier ones, so that knowledge about a particular aspect of accounting is expanding.

> **research:** Diligent, systematic enquiry into a subject to discover facts or principles

Most research studies will not provide definitive answers to the problem examined, but by searching over and over again, each study should contribute to our understanding of the issue.

Relationship between theory and research

The relationship between theory and research is complex. **Empirical research** is essentially concerned with observation; although this may not be observation of the 'real' world. For example, researchers may conduct experiments and use the results (observations). Research is not categorised in the same way as theories, as either positive or normative. Research is an activity that is undertaken, and it can be associated with both positive and normative theories. For example:

> **empirical research:** Research based on observation or experience

- Research may be conducted using an experiment in which the relative usefulness of historic cost and fair value measures are considered and it is found that better decisions are made using fair values. This may suggest a normative theory that fair value should be used as the measure for items in the financial reports.

- There may be a positive theory that explains the relationship between the accounting methods a manager chooses and the compensation package of the manager. This could predict that if a manager's bonus is related to the accounting profit, the manager will choose accounting methods that increase reported profits. Research could test whether this actually happens by examining the bonus plans of managers and the accounting choices they make.

As you can also see from these examples, research can come *before* a theory is formed or *after* it is formed.

You should note that positive and normative accounting theories are intertwined and accounting research and solving accounting problems will often consider and involve both types of theories. For example:

- There is positive research on conceptual framework projects (which is a normative theory) such as that undertaken by Ruth Hines, whose theory provides an alternative explanation for why conceptual frameworks are developed.
- When considering alternative measurements of assets, positive research can be used to inform whether existing measures are useful (e.g. through capital-market research) or which measures would be preferred by management (e.g. through accounting policy choice research).

Because accounting is a human activity, the object of the accounting research extends beyond the economic events, the procedures for recording and the methods of reporting them, to the uses made of accounting products and the users and their interests in accounting information. That accounting is a human invention also means that research (and related theories) can be categorised in two ways, although these can overlap.

Research *of* or *about* accounting

This considers the role of accounting itself (the 'bigger' picture) at the macro level and considers questions such as what is the role of accounting, is accounting information useful in investment decisions, should accountability or decision usefulness be the key goal of accounting, what impact does culture have on accounting, what role has accounting played in the rise of capitalism or environmental degradation?

A developing research area here is critical accounting. Critical accounting aims to develop:

> A critical understanding of the role of accounting processes and practices and the accounting profession in the functioning of society and organisations with an intention to use that understanding to engage (where appropriate) in changing these processes, practices and the profession (Laughlin 1999, p. 73).

The two abstracts in the In Focus vignette opposite represent examples of critical accounting research. You can see that this type of research considers the social context of accounting. Such research often challenges and questions the current state of accounting and in particular the relationships (and relative power or influence) of the participants.

Abstracts from critical accounting research studies

Within recent years, financial statement users have been accorded great significance by accounting standard-setters. In the United States, the conceptual framework maintains that a primary purpose of financial statements is to provide information useful to investors and creditors in making their economic decisions. Contemporary accounting textbooks unproblematically posit this purpose for accounting. Yet, this emphasis is quite recent and occurred despite limited knowledge about the information needs and decision processes of actual users of financial statements. This paper unpacks the taken-for-grantedness of the primacy of financial statement users in standard-setting and considers their use as a category to justify and denigrate particular accounting disclosures and practices. It traces how particular ideas about financial statement users and their connection to accounting standard setting have been constructed in various documents and reports including the conceptual framework and accounting standards.

Source: Abstract of article 'Making up users' by Joni J Young, *Accounting, Organizations and Society*, vol. 31, iss. 6, Aug 2006.

The complex relationships unfolding as people flow across borders in the 20th and 21st centuries hold infinite possibilities for research. In this work, we consider one aspect of our contemporary global economy — US immigration policy and its relationship to accounting disclosure. We review the processes of social discourse and accounting myth making in general, and provide a context of immigration policies in the US. Our concern, that the accounting profession presents a particular reality, focuses on how it obscures significant relationships between immigrant employment and financial reports and thus our observed muddled meaning to profit — 'the bottom line'. Conventional accounting rhetoric suggests that the bottom line represents appropriate business transactions, successful performance, and a basic 'stewardship contract' fulfilled, and recent debates regarding 'earnings management' lament the affront of these obligations. Yet, this conventional view obscures complex social relationships, one being the use of immigrant labor in achieving these results, and we provide evidence of some of those most deleterious effects.

Source: Abstract of article 'The bottom line' by Cheryl R Lehman, *Critical Perspectives on Accounting*, vol. 17, iss. 2–3, Feb–Apr 2006.

Research *in* accounting

This focuses at the more micro level on issues within accounting and considers questions such as: what measurements are being used, what measures should be used, what impact do changes in specific accounting policies have on share prices?

An analogy would be medicine. To research *about or of* medicine would be to consider what is the role of medicine. For example, should a holistic approach be taken, which considers lifestyle, cultural context, personal preferences and choices and so on, or should the role be to treat physical health only? Whereas research *in* medicine would be at a more micro level, such as considering different approaches to treating a particular disease or impacts of particular drugs. Within both of these categories, there may be normative or positive theories and associated research.

Research areas in accounting

Financial accounting has a wide range of theories and research. Examples of some are described in the following.

Capital-market research

The first research was undertaken by Ball & Brown (1968) and Beaver (1968), which began the positive research stream known as capital-market research, which investigated the use (and impact) of accounting information by capital markets. Given that a key role identified by normative researchers in the previous period had been that accounting information should be useful to investors, this research provided descriptions and explanations of market behaviours and reactions to accounting information.

Accounting policy choice research

Another major school of accounting research is accounting policy choice research (this is often known by the title as simply 'positive accounting theory' because of its domination of research for a significant period), which began with Watts & Zimmerman (1978). This research attempted to explain the motivations behind the accounting choices made by managers and its significant position continues. Agency (or contracting) theory, which underlies much of this research, is considered in chapter 6.

Accounting information processing research

Given that the objective of financial accounting is to provide information to aid decision making, this research investigates the use (and users) of information in the decision-making process, often using theories and models from psychology. One example here is the Lens model, which can be used to examine how specific types of information are used in making, for example, investment decisions by a particular user of financial accounting information (say an investor).

Critical accounting research

As discussed, this considers the role of accounting in society and its social context. It can adopt a social welfare perspective or rely on philosophical perspectives and theories (e.g. those of Marx, Habermas or Foucault).

International accounting research

With increasing calls for more uniform accounting standards worldwide and effort towards harmonisation of financial accounting, this research area grew in the second half of the twentieth century. This has included research into differences in accounting practices and also considered contextual and cultural influences on financial accounting.

There are of course other areas of research (such as those specifically relating to auditing and also accounting history). Research about an issue in accounting can involve many types of research and research areas. For example, the issue of environmental accounting and disclosures could involve the following research:

- documenting the environmental disclosures made by companies and evaluating the quality of these disclosures
- determining whether environmental disclosures have been used in decisions. This could involve information processing research and trying to identify how decision makers have used this information or could involve capital-market research by examining market reactions to the disclosure of such information.
- examining the motivations behind companies' disclosure (or nondisclosure) of environmental information
- examining the impact that accounting's focus on measurable financial costs (rather than externalities such as environmental costs) has on environmental impacts made by companies; so taking a more critical approach.

Learning tips

Do you know...

1.3   Positive theories describe, explain or predict what is happening in the world; they are derived from observation combined with the process of induction and deduction to test a hypothesis.

1.4   Normative theories provide prescriptions and recommendations about what should happen.

1.5   Accounting research involves diligent and systematic enquiry or investigation into a subject to discover facts or principles.

Overview of chapters in this book

This book examines issues related to financial accounting. Many of these involve consideration of associated theories and research, although the extent will vary. There are many issues in and influences on financial accounting and it is not possible to consider all of these in one book. So the text is selective and chooses issues to consider based on their significance and prevalence. The topics chosen should provide you with an understanding of a range of issues and influences confronting financial accounting that will help you understand the implications and rationales behind some of the decisions, changes and developments in the accounting arena. The following is an overview of the chapters considered in this book.

Chapter 2: Conceptual framework

This is a normative theory that you should already be familiar with, at least in part, from your previous studies in accounting. Conceptual frameworks have been dominant in the normative theories of accounting both locally and internationally for the past 20 years. The text looks at the theory itself, by looking at the international conceptual framework, which specifies the purpose of financial reporting, the nature and qualities of information to be included in financial reports. The chapter also considers the alternative reasons and rationales for having such a normative theory as the conceptual framework and looks at some specific criticisms of these.

Chapter 3: Standard setting

This chapter examines the application of the conceptual framework in its practical form: accounting standards. It considers the process of setting accounting standards, and examines the structure of this procedure in Australia in more detail. It also considers the benefits and disadvantages of rules- over principles-based standards, and examines several theories of regulation that attempt to explain the purpose of standards in accounting. Finally, it examines the political nature of the standard-setting process, and looks briefly into the program to harmonise international standards.

Chapter 4: Measurement

This chapter follows from the examination of the conceptual framework. The conceptual framework, in its recognition criteria, requires that items reported in the financial statements be measured. However, the conceptual framework does not specify *how* the items are to be measured, except to require that the measurement method or basis used must be reliable. This chapter considers the alternative measurement bases that could be used and some of the considerations in measurement and also whether there is any real 'theory' of measurement currently used in accounting.

Chapter 5: Products of financial accounting

The products of financial accounting include general purpose, special purpose and voluntary reporting practices. This chapter considers some of the ways these accounting products are manipulated (both legally and illegally) and undertakes an examination of the purpose of reported disclosures. It looks closely at the value of disclosures not required by law, and the methods open to entities to manage the image of their firm through voluntary, nonregulated disclosure. It also examines some theories of management motivation, which attempt to explain why firms supply voluntary information in the first place.

Chapter 6: Corporate governance

Corporate governance is concerned with how companies are managed and controlled. Financial accounting plays a key role in ensuring good corporate governance, which this chapter discusses. There are positive theories of accounting that support the introduction of corporate governance practices and may provide explanations for some financial reporting problems (such as accounting policy choice research). Furthermore, it briefly considers the role of ethics in corporate governance and accounting practices.

Chapter 7: Environmental and social accounting

Social and environmental accounting is concerned with the impact of a firm's activities on society and the environment in more general terms than are usually reported by law. This chapter looks at the difficulties firms face when attempting to measure the effects of their activities accurately, and the various international guidelines that provide some methods for comparing and analysing this kind of nonfinancial information. It also considers some of the theories that attempt to explain the value of nonfinancial disclosure, and how accountants are required to make assessments of this value.

Chapter 8: International accounting

The most significant development to arise in the accounting profession in Australia in past few years has been the adoption of the international accounting standards laid down by the International Accounting Standards Board. This chapter examines in detail the processes involved in developing a single set of international standards, and the importance of an independent and transparent structure. It then goes on to look at the impact of the adoption process on the Australian standard-setting environment, and the impact on the business community in Australia so far.

Chapter 9: Capital markets

Capital-market research considers the relationship between security (share) prices and accounting information. Given that investors are often seen as the traditional users of accounting reports it makes sense to see how much share prices reflect and are affected by accounting information. The research in this area considers such questions as whether the accounting information provided was useful, and also examines the effect that changes in accounting policies have on share prices

Chapter 10: Small and medium-sized entities

Small and medium-sized entities (SMEs) are the largest group of business entities in the world, and their accounting needs are unique and sometimes challenging. This chapter examines the characteristics of SMEs, focusing on the differences between their stakeholders and those of larger entities. The information needs of sometimes less sophisticated users means that SME reporting regulations require careful consideration. The chapter reflects on several regulatory procedures, both at an international and Australian level, and discusses the ongoing deliberations from standard setters and researchers around the world.

Chapter 11: Professional responsibility

This chapter examines the meaning of professional conduct, and considers in detail the code of professional and ethical conduct imposed on professional accountants. It looks at several specific areas of practice with significant and unique responsibility requirements, including taxation, and examines the need for quality control procedures, particularly in regards to the preparation of financial, compilation or special purpose reports. Finally, it considers new areas of practice, in which accountants may not be aware of their duties and professional responsibilities.

Chapter 12: Future directions

The final chapter examines some of the new directions of subjects covered in earlier chapters, such as in international convergence, the strengthening of the global economy, creative solutions to the crisis in accountability in the profession and some of the aspects of social corporate responsibility that are changing the way accountants of the future will run their practices.

The accounting practice is changing as rapidly as the world around it, and it is important that accounting professionals continue to maintain their level of understanding of new areas of accounting, of exciting and fundamental changes to the way in which accountants work, and of the continuing effort to maintain the reputation of accounting as a profession.

Summary

Define 'theory'.

- There is no one definition of theory because theories can do different things; they can describe, predict, explain and prescribe.
- Accounting theory in this text is defined as either a description, explanation or prediction of accounting practice or a set of principles on which to evaluate or guide practice.

Explain the role of theory in financial accounting.

- In financial accounting, theories can help the understanding of current accounting practice and also provide the means to improve it by:
  - describing and explaining current accounting practice
  - providing principles on which to base actions and decisions in financial accounting
  - identifying problems and deficiencies with current accounting practice
  - providing suggestions for change.

Explain the differences between positive theories and normative theories.

- Theories are often identified as positive or normative. Positive theories in accounting are theories about accounting practice as it is and may describe or explain what is currently happening or predict what will happen. Normative theories in accounting are not concerned with accounting as it is practised, but make prescriptions (recommendations) on how it should be practised.

Understand the role of research in accounting.

- Research is an activity that involves investigation. Research can be used to test or to derive theories. Various types of research are undertaken in financial accounting, which contribute to knowledge of financial accounting issues and can also result in changes to financial accounting practice and development.

Key terms

accounting theory   5
deduction   9
empirical research   13
falsification   13
financial accounting   4
hypothesis   8
induction   9
normative theories   11
positive theories   8
research   13
scientific method   10

Review questions

1.1   Define what is meant by 'theory' and explain how theory is useful. Do you think theory needs to be considered in financial accounting?

1.2   Explain what is meant by positive theory.

1.3   Explain what is meant by normative theory.

1.4   Explain what is meant by induction and deduction.

1.5   It has been stated that 'many people accept theories without justification'. Identify reasons people may accept theories. Provide examples of theories that you accept or believe although you may not have direct knowledge in the area.

1.6   Identify a positive theory (this can be about any area; e.g. global warming). Consider how you would test whether this theory was true. Do you think you could prove it?

1.7   What is your understanding of the term 'research'?

1.8   Explain the role of research and how this relates to theory.

1.9   Is the following statement correct: 'Empirical research is only related to positive theories.'?

1.10   Research can be classified in several ways. Outline them.

Recommended readings

For more detail about the history of the accounting theory the following are recommended:

Gaffikin, MJR & Aitken, MJ 1982, *The development of accounting theory: significant contributors to accounting thought in the 20th century*, Garland Publishing, Inc., New York and London.

Previts, GJ & Merino, BD 1979, *A history of accounting in America*, Ronald Press, John Wiley & Sons, New York.

For an overview of Karl Popper and falsification refer to:

Magee, B 1974, 'Karl Popper: the world's greatest philosopher?' *Current Affairs Bulletin*, 1 January, pp. 14–23.

For more detail about the testing of the accounting theory, the following is recommended:

Godfrey, J, Hodgson, A & Holmes, S 2003, *Accounting theory*, 5th edn, John Wiley & Sons, Brisbane.

References

Ball, R & Brown, P 1968, 'An empirical evaluation of accounting income numbers', *Journal of Accounting Research*, vol. 6, no. 2, pp. 159–78.

Beaver, WH 1968, 'The information content of annual earnings announcements', *Journal of Accounting Research*, supplement, pp. 67–92.

Godfrey, J, Hodgson, A & Holmes, S 2003, *Accounting theory*, 5th edn, John Wiley & Sons, Brisbane.

Hall, SC & Stammerjohan, WW 1997, 'Damages awards and earnings management in the oil industry', *The Accounting Review*, January, p. 47.

Henderson, S, Pierson, G & Harris, K 2004, *Financial accounting theory*, Pearson Education Australia, Sydney.

Laughlin, RC 1999, 'Critical accounting: nature, progress and prognosis', *Accounting, Auditing & Accountability Journal*, vol. 12, no. 1, pp. 73–8.

Leo, K & Radford, J 1999, *Financial accounting issues*, 2nd edn, Jacaranda Wiley, Brisbane.

Rivett, D 2000, *Issues in accounting theory study guide*, University of South Australia.

Watts, R & Zimmerman, J 1978, 'Towards a positive theory of the determination of accounting standards', *The Accounting Review*, vol. 53, no. 1, pp. 112–34.

2 THE CONCEPTUAL FRAMEWORK IN FINANCIAL ACCOUNTING

After reading this chapter, you should be able to:

- explain what a conceptual framework is

- understand the history and evolution of the accounting conceptual framework

- outline the structure, approach and components of the international conceptual framework

- explain the purpose and possible benefits of a conceptual framework

- explain the problems and criticisms of the conceptual framework in accounting.

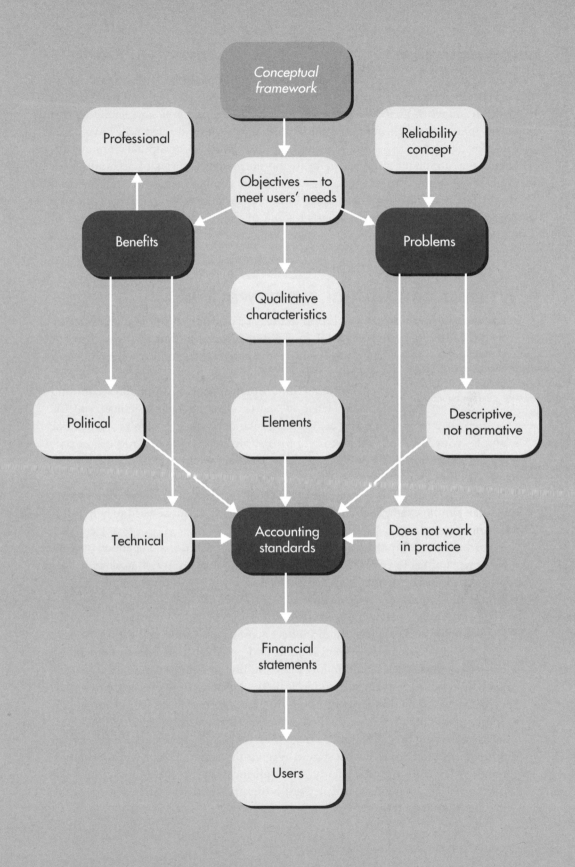

Introduction

From your previous accounting studies, you will already be familiar with some parts of the accounting conceptual framework, although you may not have looked at the framework itself. For example, the definitions of assets and liabilities that are in many of the accounting standards that you have studied will have come directly from an accounting conceptual framework. Conceptual frameworks have been dominant internationally in the normative theories of accounting for the past 30 years. This chapter considers the conceptual framework for financial accounting that has been developed by the International Accounting Standards Board (IASB). In addition, it looks at some of the reasons for having a conceptual framework in accounting and some of the criticisms of and problems with the current framework.

What a conceptual framework is

A **conceptual framework** is a group of ideas or principles used to plan or decide something. It can be seen as a set of guiding principles; that is, those ideas or concepts that influence and direct decisions being made in a particular area.

> **conceptual framework:** A set of broad principles that provide the basis for guiding actions or decisions

Conceptual frameworks are not only found in accounting but are used in many areas to help establish specific guidelines, to help make decisions or solve problems. For example, your lecturers will use a set of principles relating to the purpose of professional education and principles of adult learning when deciding what assignments or other assessment tasks to set students.

Before examining the accounting conceptual framework in detail, this section looks at a simple example of how a *set of guiding principles* can be used to help influence and direct decisions.

Governments and judges need to set rules and make decisions about punishments or penalties to be applied when people are found guilty of a crime. In this simple example, the guiding principles (the underlying concepts) may be:

- All people should be treated fairly.
- The community's safety must be ensured.
- Punishments and penalties should reflect community values and expectations.

Any actual decisions about punishments and penalties to be imposed should be consistent because they should follow these guiding principles. Of course, the decisions would not necessarily all be identical. The guiding principles are very broad. Specific decisions could vary because of different interpretations. For example:

- Some people may interpret the first principle (that all people should be treated fairly) as saying that all should be treated identically. So, for example, any person who steals food from a shop should receive the same penalty or punishment. Others may interpret 'treat fairly' as requiring them to take into account the particular circumstances, so if it were a hungry child who stole the food, the penalty would be less.

- Values and expectations will vary from community to community, often because of cultural, religious and even economic influences. This can be seen in the different types of punishment imposed for the same crimes in various countries. So one community may impose heavier penalties for a behaviour than do others. Also, community values and expectations may change over time.

Conceptual frameworks being made of broad principles is an advantage because it means that these principles can be used as a basis for making decisions across a wide range of situations or circumstances. However, the principles' breadth also has disadvantages; it is usual for more specific guidelines (consistent with them) to be established to ensure their clearer and more consistent application in particular circumstances. In accounting, these specific rules are found in the accounting standards and interpretations, and the conceptual framework contains the guidelines to accounting standards.

Conceptual framework theory

The conceptual framework is a normative theory. It prescribes the basic principles that are to be followed in preparing financial statements. So an **accounting conceptual framework** can be described as: a coherent system of concepts, which are guidelines to the accounting standards used for financial reporting.

> **accounting conceptual framework:** A coherent system of concepts that underlie financial reporting

Normative theories are normally thought of as including terms such as 'should' or 'ought to'. The accounting conceptual framework studied here makes statements such as:

> The objective of financial statements is to...
> An asset is a resource...
> To be useful, information must be relevant...

Although it does not use the terms 'should' or 'ought to', it is outlining the concepts that should be used in preparing financial statements.

How a conceptual framework differs from an accounting standard

As noted, the principles in the conceptual framework are general concepts. These are designed to provide guidance and apply to a wide range of decisions relating to the preparation of financial reports. Accounting standards provide *specific* requirements for a *particular* area of financial reporting.

For example:
- The conceptual framework defines what an asset is and when it should be included in the financial statements.
- The accounting standard on leases (e.g. IAS 17 or AASB 117) contains detailed requirements and guidance on when an asset is to be included if there is a lease. This standard requires an asset be recognised if the risks and benefits associated

with ownership have been transferred (and provides detailed guidance to help determine whether it has) and also requires these assets to be measured using present or fair value.

You should see that accounting standards apply to a much narrower area of financial reporting (in the example given, the accounting standard only applies to leases) and include more detail, allowing less scope for different interpretations. Furthermore, accounting standards go beyond areas that the conceptual framework has considered. For example, this standard requires that leased assets be measured at present or fair value, whereas the conceptual framework does not require any particular measures for assets. Another difference is that generally accounting standards must be complied with (this varies between countries but can be required by law or the professional accounting bodies). The principles in the accounting conceptual frameworks may not though be mandatory (although it is often recommended that they are used for guidance) and if they conflict with a requirement of an accounting standard, the latter must be followed (IASB 1989, para. 3).

History and evolution of the conceptual framework

The conceptual framework studied in this text is the *Framework for the preparation and presentation of financial statements* (known as 'the Framework') issued by the IASB. This Framework was initially issued in 1989 and has been adopted, or is used as the basis for, the conceptual framework in several countries, including Australia, Hong Kong and Singapore, and is similar to the conceptual frameworks in the UK and the United States. The European Union has not formally endorsed the Framework but the adoption of the international accounting standards as the basis of its own standards will mean that the Framework will be influential, because the international accounting standards are themselves based on concepts drawn from the Framework. Parts of the Framework have also been incorporated in the *Accounting standard for business enterprise: basic standard* in China (MOF 2006).

Although the Framework was issued less than 20 years ago, the idea of a set of principles in accounting has been around for much longer. From about the 1920s and 1930s, there were attempts to draft statements of principles to guide accounting. The need for them was often a response to reporting failures; in particular, the problems in the financial statements of some large companies. As well as leading to accounting regulation (such as the requirement for audits of particular companies), these failures often led many to question current practice and argue that unless accounting was based on a set of fundamental principles, these reporting failures would continue. Several sets of principles were proposed in the period; for example, in 1936, the American Accounting Association issued a *Statement of accounting principles*. In 1959, the American Institute of Certified Public Accountants created the Accounting Principles Board to, in part, establish a set of basic principles on which accounting standards could be based, and in 1962, published *A tentative set of broad accounting principles for business enterprises* by Sprouse and Moonitz.

Principles suggested in this period ranged from restating the principles used in current practice to proposing radical change to current practice, especially in the area of measurement. The development of more comprehensive and formal conceptual frameworks begins in the 1970s, again following company failures in the 1960s and criticisms of financial reporting, although work on these was relatively slow and intermittent. In the United States, the Financial Accounting Standards Board (FASB) published six concept statements between 1978 and 1989. This first US framework project was influential, and all future conceptual frameworks have followed it substantially in approach and in some degree of detail (Rutherford 2003). During this period the UK, Canada and Australia also worked on developing their own conceptual frameworks. The IASB's Framework is drawn directly from these previous conceptual framework projects.

Currently, the IASB and FASB are undertaking a project to develop a common conceptual framework. This has in part resulted from the decision by the FASB to adopt a principles-based (rather than rules-based) approach to standard setting. The initial stages of the project are generally consistent with the current IASB Framework.

The structure and components of the current Framework

Figure 2.1 provides an overview of the parts of the current conceptual framework in accounting. The Framework can be seen as providing answers to questions that you need to answer when preparing financial statements such as:

- What is the purpose of financial statements?

- Who are they prepared for?

- What are the assumptions to be made when preparing financial statements?

- What type of information should be included?

- What are the elements that make up financial statements?

- When should the elements of financial statements be included?

You should see that the Framework moves in what is essentially a series of steps or levels. It begins with principles that consider broader questions, such as those relating to objectives, and moves to more narrow and specific issues. The approach or answers to the broader (initial) questions provide direction and influence subsequent principles. For example, the decision about the nature of information included in financial statements (e.g. understandability and relevance) is influenced directly by the prior principle that financial statements are prepared to provide information for users to assist in decision making. The 'initial' principles determine and influence the principles included later in the Framework, so that all parts of the Framework are linked in a hierarchy.

FIGURE 2.1 Overview of the IASC Framework

Questions that the Framework answers	Approach in the Framework
What statements are we considering?	General purpose financial statements
Who are the financial statements for?	For a wide range of users (including investors, employees, lenders, customers, public)
Why report? What is the purpose of the financial statements?	The key objective is to meet the *common* information needs of users for decision making.
What are the assumptions to be made when preparing financial statements?	The two underlying assumptions are: • accrual basis • going concern.
What type of information should be included?	To be useful to users, information should have a balance of the following attributes: • understandability • relevance • reliability • comparability. These are subject to two constraints: • timeliness • cost versus benefit.
What are the elements that make up financial statements?	Five elements are defined: • assets • liabilities • equity • income • expenses. These definitions identify the *essential* features of each element. For example, an asset is defined as a: *resource controlled by the enterprise as a result of past events and from which future economic benefits are expected to flow to the entity.*
When should these elements be included?	There are two criteria required to be met before an element can be included in the financial statements. These are known as recognition criteria. These relate to: • probability • ability to measure reliably.

continued

FIGURE 2.1 *continued*

Questions that the Framework does not answer	
What measurement basis should we use?	It is noted that different bases are used to measure (including historic cost, present value, current cost, realisable value). No particular measurement base is recommended.
What capital concept should be used?	It is noted that either a financial or physical capital concept can be used but none in particular is recommended.

Source: Adapted from Sutton, T 2003, *Corporate financial accounting and reporting*, 2nd edn, Prentice Hall, London.

Purposes of the Framework and the objectives of financial statements

The purposes of the Framework itself are discussed under the section in this chapter relating to benefits of conceptual frameworks. Before looking at the objectives of financial statements as outlined in the Framework, this section considers the Framework's scope.

Reporting focus

The Framework states that it is concerned with **general purpose financial statements**. These can be defined as financial reports intended to meet the information needs common to users who are unable to command the preparation of reports tailored to satisfy, specifically, all of their information needs (AASB 101, AUS 11.1).

> **general purpose financial statements:** Financial reports intended to meet the information needs common to users who are unable to command the preparation of reports tailored to satisfy, specifically, all of their information needs

For example, if a person owns a few shares in a large company (in Australia, this could be the communications company, Telstra, or in Hong Kong, the transport provider, MTR), even though that shareholder is a part owner of the company, he or she could not ask the company for a report containing exactly the information he or she needs to decide whether he or she will continue to hold the shares in that company. The only information such small shareholders would have access to would be the annual reports that companies provide publicly. An annual report is an example of a general purpose financial statement.

The Framework does not need to be applied in the preparation of *special* purpose financial statements, which are statements prepared to meet the needs of particular users. These normally contain specialised information designed for users who have the power to ask for the information they need. For example:

- Some lenders can require, as part of the terms for granting a loan, that reports be prepared with specific information.

- Taxation authorities can require specific reports.
- Management would require, and be able to obtain, more detailed reports.

Entity focus

The Framework applies to general purpose financial statements prepared by commercial, industrial and business reporting enterprises. A **reporting enterprise** is 'an entity for which there are users who rely on the financial statements as their major source of financial information about the entity' (para. 8).

The Framework is not aimed at financial statements prepared by not-for-profit entities. Some countries have made changes to the Framework so that the principles also apply to them.

The Framework does not set out which entities must actually prepare financial statements. Which entities must prepare general purpose financial statements (such as annual reports) is decided by the specific laws and custom of particular countries. In its role as an international accounting body, the IASB does not have the authority to demand that particular entities prepare financial statements.

The Framework uses the term 'enterprise'; many of the other standards and frameworks in other countries use the term 'entity'. These terms are often used interchangeably.

Learning tips
Do you know...

2.1 A conceptual framework provides a broad statement of principles that standard setters use to guide their decisions when designing specific standards.

2.2 The IASB conceptual framework has been modified and updated continually since its inception in 1989, and is currently under review by the IASB in conjunction with the US body, the FASB.

2.3 The Framework outlines the purpose and end-user requirements of financial statements, the assumptions made during preparation of statements, what type of information should be included and the elements that make up statements.

▪ The objectives of financial statements

There are broadly two views of what should be the objectives of financial statements. These are:
- stewardship or accountability
- decision usefulness.

Stewardship or accountability focuses on the duty of the managers of an entity. They are entrusted with the resources of the entity. Stewardship requires the managers to provide a report to the providers of the resources to explain how well they have managed them. Historically, this was the main purpose of financial statements and accounting.

The current Framework adopts a decision-usefulness approach and states:

> The objective of financial statements is to provide information about the financial position, financial performance and cash flows of an entity that is useful to a wide range of users in making economic decisions (para. 12).

Under this objective, the financial statements should provide information that is useful to users in making decisions. This requires considering *how* information is used in decision making. In models of the decision process, information is needed to:

- *Help us predict what may happen in the future.* This does not mean, however, that financial statements necessarily provide forecasted or future-oriented information. However, the information provided should help users make these predictions.
- *Provide feedback on previous decisions.* Information can help in deciding whether past decisions, and the information used to make them, were correct, and can help in making better decisions in the future.

It is also assumed financial statements that provide information useful for decision making will also provide the information needed to assess accountability:

> Financial statements also show the results of the stewardship of management, or the accountability of management for the resources entrusted to it (para. 14).

Users and their information needs

It is important to consider *who* the users are and what information they need, given that the purpose of financial statements is to provide them with useful information. The Framework identifies a range of users of financial statements. They include:

- investors
- employees
- lenders
- suppliers and trade creditors
- customers
- governments and their agencies
- the public.

This is a very wide range of users, and the Framework acknowledges that not all the information needs of all of them can be met by general purpose financial statements.

The aim is to provide information where users' needs overlap or are shared; to meet the information needs that are *common* to these user groups.

Although diverse groups of users are identified, the Framework takes the view that if the information needs of investors are met, this will meet the information needs common to other users:

> As investors are providers of risk capital to the enterprise, the provision of financial statements that meet their needs will also meet most of the needs of other users that financial statements can satisfy (para. 10).

The primacy of the investor is a common position taken in many of the accounting conceptual frameworks and reflects that historically these frameworks have been developed in countries where the capital markets and the related protection of investors have been key influences on accounting developments and regulation (Street & Shaughnessy 1998).

The information in financial statements is limited mainly to *financial* information. This is normally in the form of a balance sheet, an income statement, a cash flow (or funds) statement and associated notes.

The financial statements provide financial information about the *past* transactions and events of the entity. As noted, users will also need information about the future to help them make their decisions.

Many users will need and place importance on nonfinancial information. Many investors, for example, consider ethical issues (such as the nature of the product, the environmental impact of the entity or the entity's treatment of its employees) when making investment decisions. This type of information is not intended to be provided by the financial statements and would be part of the information needs that the Framework acknowledges are not met by financial statements.

The In Focus vignette that follows considers some of the issues with users' information needs, and how far these are met by current financial reports.

 ## infocus *The usefulness of financial reporting*

FASB Concepts Statement 2 states that, to be useful, financial information must be both relevant and reliable. Although much has been written about the importance of the reliability of financial information following the high-profile corporate scandals of Enron, WorldCom, and others, comparably little attention has been given to the relevance of the financial information presented. Because of the litigious nature of our society, many accountants prefer to provide more information, rather than less, sometimes without considering its relevance or usefulness.

So how do we determine what information is relevant? Simply put, relevant information enhances the user's ability to make an informed decision. Accordingly, relevant information is not limited to numbers. For example, if a technology company hires one of the best minds in the field, would that information be an important factor in making an informed decision about the company's future economic prospects? Or if a bioengineering company lost its most productive R&D scientist, might that information influence stake-holders' decisions?

In our knowledge-based society, many business entities derive much of their value from intangible assets; yet many intangibles, such as human capital, ideas, and innovations, are nowhere to be found on the balance sheet. The real value of these companies may not be accurately reflected in their financial reports. Although these economic resources may be difficult to quantify, to ignore them would not fairly represent the financial and business position of the company. Furthermore, assumptions and estimates in financial reporting will never be perfect, and there will always be some companies that go to great lengths to manipulate the numbers through aggressive, misleading, or even fraudulent application of the rules. If we're going to limit ourselves to counting beans, our value in the business reporting process won't be worth a hill of them.

Source: *The GAAP between Public and Private Companies* by Mary-Jo Kranacher. Reprinted from *The CPA Journal*, June 2006, copyright 2006, with permission from the New York State Society of Certified Public Accountants.

Underlying assumptions

The Framework requires the financial statements to be based on two underlying assumptions. These are:

- the **accrual basis**. 'The effects of transactions and other events are recognised when they occur (and not as cash or its equivalent is received or paid) and they are recorded in the accounting records and reported in the financial statements of the periods to which they relate' (para. 22).

accrual basis: Where the effects of transactions and other events are recognised when they occur (and not as cash or its equivalent is received or paid) and they are recorded in the accounting records and reported in the financial statements of the periods to which they relate

- the **going concern basis**. 'The financial statements are normally prepared on the assumption that an entity is a going concern and will continue in operation for the foreseeable future' (para. 23).

going concern basis: Where the financial statements are normally prepared on the assumption that an enterprise is a going concern and will continue in operation

The reason for the application of the accrual concept is to provide better information to users. Using the cash basis for financial statements would restrict the information provided to those transactions and events involving cash receipts or payments. For example, sales made on credit, for which payments had not yet been received, would be excluded from the financial statements. This does not mean that information about cash flows is not important or useful to users. The Framework identifies as a normal part of the financial statements a statement of cash flows or its equivalent (para. 9).

The going concern assumption has a direct impact on both the recognition and measurement of items in the financial statements. If the entity is not expected to continue in business, then the economic benefits in particular items, such as prepaid insurance, would no longer be expected to be received, so they could not be recognised as assets. The reported values of assets would also need to be reconsidered. For example, if the business is to close, inventory may not realise its 'normal' selling price. Where the assumption that the entity is a going concern is inappropriate, this basis should not be used and this would need to be disclosed.

Fundamental properties of reporting information

Having decided that the role of financial statements is to provide information useful to users for making decisions, the Framework then identifies the properties that information must have to be included in the financial statements. These are known as qualitative characteristics and the aim is to ensure that the information provided is of adequate quality to help users make decisions. There are four main qualitative characteristics. These are:

- understandability
- relevance
- reliability
- comparability.

Understandability

Unless a person can understand information they cannot use it. **Understandability** deals with this issue but it does not require that the information be simplified so that anyone can understand it.

Relevance

The **relevance** characteristic aims to ensure that only information that could make a difference in decisions be included.

understandability: The quality of the information that means it is readily understandable by users

relevance: The quality of information when it influences the economic decisions of users by helping them evaluate past, present or future events or confirming, or correcting, their past evaluations

materiality: The quality of information if its omission or misstatement could influence the economic decision of users taken on the basis of the financial statements

reliability: The quality of information when it is free from material error and bias and can be depended upon by users to represent faithfully that which it either purports to represent or could reasonably be expected to represent

This qualitative characteristic outlines why the information is needed. It is linked directly to the purpose of financial statements: to provide information useful to users in making decisions. Clearly, if the information cannot be used either to help make predictions or to provide feedback, it is not useful to users, so would not be relevant and should not be included in the financial statements. For these reasons, relevance is often the first 'test' applied to information.

A component of relevance is **materiality**. This is the quality of information if its omission or misstatement could influence the economic decision of users taken on the basis of the financial statements (para. 30).

Some information is relevant because of what it is about – its nature. For example, regardless of its size, information relating to loans to directors of the company may be considered material and important to users because of the position of directors in the company, even if these loans are relatively small. In other cases, you may need to consider the size or amount of the item to determine whether it is material, and so is relevant. For example, in a manufacturing company, you would not normally need to provide specific information about individual expenses, such as costs of postage, unless these items were large. Of course, for a mail order company, postage costs would be material in amount and also would be relevant because of the company's nature.

Reliability

The purpose of the **reliability** characteristic is to make sure that users have confidence in and can 'trust' the information that is provided.

Five components need to be considered in determining the reliability of information.

Faithful representation

This requires making sure that what is shown in the financial statements corresponds to the actual events and transactions that are being represented.

Substance over form

This requires items to be accounted for and presented in accordance with their substance and economic reality and not merely their legal form. For example, if a financial instrument is described in legal documents as a preference share, but the actual terms indicate that the instrument is in the nature of debt, it should be recognised as a liability.

Neutrality

For information to be neutral, it must be free from bias (para. 36). This component of reliability aims to ensure that there is no attempt to promote any particular view; that the financial statements provide an impartial description of the events and transactions.

Prudence

'**Prudence** is the inclusion of a degree of caution in the exercise of the judgements needed in making the estimates required under conditions of uncertainty, such that assets or income are not overstated and liabilities or expenses are not understated' (para. 37).

When assets or liabilities are either understated or overstated, the financial statements are not neutral, so the information is not reliable. Prudence acknowledges that particular care must be taken when there is uncertainty.

prudence: The inclusion of a degree of caution in the exercise of the judgements needed in making the estimates required under conditions of uncertainty, such that assets or income are not overstated and liabilities or expenses are not understated

Completeness

Users require *all* relevant information to be included in the financial statements, if these are to be useful for decision making. Good decisions cannot be made on the basis of incomplete information. However, the requirement to provide specific information in the financial statements is subject to certain restrictions. These are timeliness and the benefit versus cost constraints on the provision of relevant and reliable information that are discussed later in this chapter.

Comparability

When comparing financial statements over time and between entities, users need to be able to determine the reasons for changes or differences. An important aspect of comparability is that it requires the accounting policies used in the preparation of the financial statements to be disclosed, so that users are able to understand whether changes or differences are caused by variations in accounting policies or actual economic conditions.

Comparability would generally be achieved with consistent measurement and presentation of items over time and between entities. However, the Framework acknowledges that this may not be possible or even desirable. The need to ensure comparability does not justify the use of a particular accounting policy if more reliable or relevant information could be provided with an alternative policy or measure.

Determining the relative importance of qualitative characteristics

Ideally, the information provided should have all of these qualitative characteristics. This may not always be possible in practice and there will often be a need to 'trade off' to determine which should be given more importance. This is a matter of professional judgement and will depend on the particular circumstances. For example:

- Historic cost is often the most reliable measure for assets. However, this may not be as relevant to users as other measures such as present or fair value. In some cases, it may be decided that the other measures are too unreliable, so historic cost is used. In other cases, it may be decided that relevance should override the reduction in the reliability, so other measures are provided.
- You cannot leave out relevant information on the basis that it is very complex and may be difficult for some users to understand. This means you may need to reduce understandability to ensure relevance.

Although the Framework states that there are four primary qualitative characteristics, it indicates that the need to ensure the understandability and comparability of information should not be used as a reason to reduce the relevance or reliability of information. This suggests that the qualitative characteristics of relevance and reliability are of the highest importance.

Constraints on information

Although the Framework states that information that is relevant and reliable and passes the test of materiality should be included in the financial statements, it acknowledges that two constraints may limit the ability to provide information that is relevant and reliable. These are:

- _Timeliness._ Users need information on a timely basis. Although delaying the issue of the financial statements may improve the quality of some information, it is likely to reduce its usefulness to users. For example, it may be that the entity has been found liable to pay damages but the amount has not yet been decided by the courts. Waiting until it is decided would make the information more reliable but the delay in issuing the financial statements would make them less useful overall. In this case, the issue of timeliness would override considerations of reliability.
- _Benefits versus costs._ This constraint relates to the general economic principle that the benefits of an action should outweigh the costs. The analysis for financial

statements would include the costs in preparing the statements and the benefits to users from better decisions. However, there are potentially more indirect costs and benefits that relate to the economic consequences of providing information. The concept of economic consequences is discussed later in this chapter. The Framework recognises that this constraint is applied subjectively.

The elements of financial statements

The Framework provides definitions for the five essential elements of the financial statements: assets, liabilities, equity, income and expenses. These definitions are:

- 'An **asset** is a resource controlled by the enterprise as a result of past events and from which future economic benefits are expected to flow to the entity' (para. 49).
- 'A **liability** is a present obligation of the enterprise arising from past events, the settlement of which is expected to result in an outflow from the enterprise of resources embodying economic benefits' (para. 49).
- '**Equity** is the residual interest in the assets of the enterprise after deducting all its liabilities' (para. 49).

The definitions of the elements relating to financial performance are:

- '**Income** is increases in economic benefits during the accounting period in the form of inflows or enhancements of assets or decreases of liabilities that result in increases in equity, other than those relating to contributions from equity participants' (para. 69).
- '**Expenses** are decreases in economic benefits during the accounting period in the form of outflows or depletions of assets or incurrences of liabilities that result in decreases in equity, other than those relating to distributions to equity participants' (para. 69).

You will notice that these definitions do not refer to legal form but to economic benefits. This reflects the substance over form approach required by the Framework. This has a significant impact on the financial statements. For example, you do not need to have a legal debt or obligation for an item to meet the definition of liability; an item does not need to be owned by the entity for it to meet the definition of an asset. The Framework also provides rules, known as recognition criteria, for deciding when these elements may actually be included in the financial statements.

The Framework adopts what is known as the 'balance sheet' approach to defining the elements of the financial statements. This approach places most importance on the definitions of assets and liabilities. The other elements of financial

asset: A resource controlled by the enterprise as a result of past events and from which future economic benefits are expected to flow to the entity

liability: A present obligation of the enterprise arising from past events, the settlement of which is expected to result in an outflow from the enterprise of resources embodying economic benefits

equity: The residual interest in the assets of the enterprise after deducting all its liabilities

income: Increases in economic benefits during the accounting period in the form of inflows or improvements of assets or decreases of liabilities that result in increases in equity, other than those relating to contributions from equity participants

expenses: Decreases in economic benefits during the accounting period in the form of outflows or depletions of assets or incurrences of liabilities that result in decreases in equity, other than those relating to distributions to equity participants

statements (equity, income and expenses) are defined in terms of assets and liabilities. For example, the definition of an expense given in the Framework includes a requirement to identify a decrease in economic benefits 'in the form of outflows or depletions of *assets* or incurrences of *liabilities*'. This means that before it can be determined whether an item is an expense, the definitions of assets or liabilities or both must be applied. The identification of balance-sheet items (i.e. assets and liabilities) determines whether the definitions for the other items in the financial statements are met. The In Focus vignette opposite illustrates how the application of the accounting definitions and recognition criteria of items can affect the financial statements.

Recognition criteria

Having met the definition of a financial statement element, an item must meet two further tests, known as recognition criteria, before it can be recognised in the financial statements.

---

recognition: The process of incorporating an item in the balance sheet or income statement. It involves depiction of the item in words and by a monetary amount and that inclusion of that amount in the balance sheet or income statement totals.

Recognition is the process of incorporating an item in the balance sheet or income statement. It involves depiction of the item in words and by a monetary amount and that inclusion of that amount in the balance sheet or income statement totals (para. 82).

The Framework states that an item that meets the definition of an element should be recognised if:

(a) it is probable that any future economic benefit associated with the item will flow to or from the enterprise; and
(b) the item has a cost or value that can be measured with reliability (para. 83).

So the two tests to be met for recognition relate to the following.

Probability

The probability test takes into account there being some uncertainty about many items in the financial statements. The flow of benefits should be more likely rather than less likely (usually interpreted as more than 50 per cent (Henderson & Pierson 2002)).

Reliable measurement

To be included in the financial statements, the item needs to be measured; to determine a monetary amount for that item. In many cases, measuring an item will require the use of estimates but the use of estimates does not mean that a measure is unreliable. This test also requires *either* a cost *or* value to be able to be measured with reliability. If you cannot reliably measure the benefits, there may still be a cost (e.g. historic cost) that can be measured; alternatively, simply because a particular item has no cost does not mean it cannot be measured with reliability.

Elements that meet both of the recognition criteria *should* be recognised; elements that do not meet both of recognition criteria *cannot* be recognised, although information may be disclosed in notes to the statements where this is useful to users.

 ## Earnings restatement

Media conglomerate Time Warner Inc. on Thursday said it would restate earnings as far back as 2000, based on the findings of an independent examiner assigned to look through AOL transactions following a previous settlement with securities regulators.

The findings conclude a two-year probe by the U.S. Justice Department and the U.S. Securities and Exchange Commission into accounting at AOL. The review, which began in June 2005, had focused on about $584 million in advertising revenue from deals with 17 companies.

Time Warner said the restatements would reduce net income by $1 million in 2000 and by about $161 million in 2001. They also will increase reported net income by about $62 million in 2002, by $18 million in 2003, by $30 million in 2004, by $16 million in 2005 and by about $15 million for the first half of 2006.

The deals that led to the restatements were primarily transactions, called round-trip deals, in which AOL secured online ad commitments from another party at the same time that it entered into deals with those companies to purchase products or services or make investments.

Round trip deals were common during the hey days of the Internet stock market boom of the late 1990s, but were frowned upon by regulators as they artificially boosted financial results.

Pending a restatement Time Warner said financial statements related to the affected time periods should not be relied upon.

Source: Extracted from an article from Reuters News.

 ## *Learning tips*
Do you know...

2.4   The Framework aims to provide information that is useful to the users in decision making, and that, as a consequence, ensures stewardship or accountability.

2.5   The Framework requires statements to be based on accrual (all transactions are reported when they occur) and going concern (if the entity will continue) bases.

2.6   To ensure it is useful, information provided in financial statements must be understandable, relevant, reliable and comparable.

2.7   *Financial statements are composed of assets, liabilities, equity, income and expenses, and the Framework provides detailed definitions of each of these elements.*

The benefits of a conceptual framework

It is claimed benefits may arise from a conceptual framework in accounting. These can be arranged into three categories:

- technical
- political
- professional.

Technical benefits

If you think of 'technical' improvements, you think of changes that make something work or function better. A key argument for a conceptual framework in accounting relates to technical benefits. As stated by Rutherford, the principal attraction of a conceptual framework in accounting:

> is argued to be the improvement in the quality of standards that would follow because they would rest on more solid ground; other less elevated, attractions include the contribution it can make to the technical consistency and speed of development of standards and the effectiveness with which standards can be defended (2003, p. 377).

So the main benefit of having a conceptual framework is to improve accounting itself, to improve the practice of accounting and to provide a basis for answers to specific accounting questions and problems. It is stated that the Framework does this in two ways:

- by providing a basis and guidance for those who set the specific accounting rules (such as accounting standards or interpretations)
- by helping individuals involved in preparing or auditing or using financial statements.

The role of a conceptual framework in setting accounting standards

For many years, accounting standards were set without a conceptual framework. This was referred to as a 'piecemeal' approach, because of the slowness of the process and because the rules within some standards were incompatible with those in others.

In the Framework itself an important purpose is to:

> assist the Board of the IASC in the development of future International Accounting Standards and in its review of existing International Accounting Standards (para. 1 (a)).

The conceptual framework provides a set of established and agreed principles. 'The key measure of the success of a standard is its acceptance. An important prerequisite for gaining acceptance is a language common to all parties involved. An agreed upon set of concepts and principles provides this language' (Xiao & Pan 1997, p. 285). Having a conceptual framework means that when determining the accounting rules or standards for specific events or transactions, the focus is on deciding how to apply the principles already in the conceptual framework. For example, when deciding on how to account for money spent on creating and maintaining websites, the issue considered is whether the costs should be recognised as an asset or expense, *given* the definitions and recognition criteria in the conceptual framework. This approach focuses the discussion on how to apply the principles in the framework to website costs. It also helps to ensure that the recognition of any assets, for example, is consistent with the recognition of assets in other circumstances. As Foster & Johnson (2001) state, the conceptual framework:

> provides a basic reasoning on which to consider the merits of alternatives. Although it does not provide all the answers, the framework narrows the range of alternatives by eliminating some that are inconsistent with it. It thereby contributes to greater efficiency in the standard setting process by avoiding the necessity of having to redebate fundamental issues such as 'what is an asset?' time and time again.

Of course, using the conceptual framework as the basis for setting specific accounting rules does not mean there is no room for debate or disagreement. There may be different interpretations of the definition of assets or expenses in the conceptual framework. This problem with the current framework is considered later in this chapter. Also, in particular cases, standard setters may deliberately depart from the principles in the conceptual framework for other reasons (such as concerns over abuse of accounting requirements or political influences).

Benefits to preparers and users

Consider what would happen if you are preparing the financial statements but have a particular case for which there are no specific standards or rules. How do you decide how to account for it? One way is to go to the basic principles in the conceptual framework and use them as a guide to help you make your decision.

Also, standards based on a conceptual framework should be more easily understood and interpreted by users. This is because:

- Users can refer to the principles in the conceptual framework to understand the basis for the specific accounting rules.
- The accounting rules should be more consistent because they are based on the same underlying principles.

Political benefits

A further benefit of a conceptual framework is to prevent political interference in setting accounting standards. To understand this benefit, you need to be aware of the political nature of accounting. Many accounting students view accounting standards as boring and uncontroversial. However, remember that financial statements provide information on which people base their decisions. Therefore, if the information in these statements changes, it is likely that the decisions based on this information will also change.

Decisions made by users, such as where to invest, whether to continue to supply goods to a company or even whether to buy the products of a company or work for an entity, could change. Decisions by the management of the entity could also change. For example, when the accounting standard was introduced that required an asset and liability for finance leases to be included in financial statements, some companies stopped using finance leases. In the United States, when the accounting standard was introduced that required companies to include health benefits to be provided to employees as a liability, some companies ended these health benefit schemes to employees (Baker & Hayes 1995). These decisions have a real economic impact, and affect the wealth and welfare of particular individuals, entities and industries.

Political pressures and potential economic consequences

Of course, it is natural for people to try to look after their own interests and this leads to attempts to influence accounting requirements. For example, when the international accounting standard setters proposed that share-based payments made to employees be included as an expense in the financial statements, some argued that requiring recognition of these payments would have unfavourable economic impacts discouraging entities from introducing or continuing employee share-based share plans. This would in turn:

- disadvantage employees
- harm the economy because share option schemes are needed to attract employees
- harm young, innovative companies that did not have cash available to offer equivalent alternative payment
- place companies in countries that required these expenses to be recognised at a competitive disadvantage.

These potential impacts of changes in accounting standards are known as 'economic consequences'.

Political pressure takes the form of individuals or groups trying to influence the standard setters (by a range of methods including lobbying standard setters directly, as noted, or by lobbying governments; see Georgiou 2004 for further examples) to make sure that the resulting accounting standards best meet their own preferences and do not result in unfavourable economic consequences that would 'disadvantage' them.

Political interference

The conceptual framework provides some defence against 'individual interests' and claims of economic consequences. Standard setters can argue the theoretical correctness of their decisions by referring to the principles in the conceptual framework.

It is more difficult for individuals to argue for their own preferred way of accounting for events if this is inconsistent with the principles in the Framework. As Damant states: 'Individual standards cannot be attacked unless the principles on which they are based are attacked' (Damant 2003, p. 11).

A conceptual framework cannot guarantee freedom from political interference. In some cases, proposed accounting standards have been either changed or not introduced because of political pressures (see for example Zeff 2002). In addition, there is still debate as to whether economic consequences should be considered when deciding on accounting standards. Some argue that the cost–benefit constraint within the Framework itself justifies taking into account the economic consequences when deciding on accounting requirements (see for example Leo & Hoggett 1998).

Professional benefits

An alternative reason for having a conceptual framework is the benefit it may provide to the accounting profession itself. The argument here is that conceptual frameworks exist not to improve accounting practice, but to protect the professional status of accounting and accountants.

This argument (summarised from Hines 1989a) is based on the following line of reasoning:

- Professional status is valuable. People and groups that are members of professions generally have more influence and status, and receive higher rewards (payments) than do those who are seen as nonprofessionals.
- A profession has a unique body of knowledge; it has expertise in an area that other groups do not have.
- The historical 'knowledge base' of accounting is double-entry bookkeeping. However, this, at least in a simple form, is practised widely in the general community. Other problems with accounting's knowledge base cited include the influence of political pressure, accounting failures (Enron and WorldCom represent examples of these), and inconsistencies in standards.
- Because of the problems with the historical knowledge base of accounting, the conceptual framework has been developed to establish a unique body of knowledge of accounting.

This argues that although the accounting profession may state that the reason for conceptual frameworks is to improve accounting (i.e. to achieve the technical benefits discussed), the true reason is to provide the appearance of having a unique body of knowledge so that it can maintain its status as a profession and so that its members can gain the benefits of professional status.

However, others have questioned this theory and argue that:

- The professional status of accountants has been developed and maintained through 'social' actions of accounting bodies, such as creating barriers to entry to the profession, and legislation restricting certain activities (such as some auditing and taxation functions) to those with specialised qualifications. (West, as cited in Staubus 2004, p. 141).

- The theory does not explain why some countries in which accounting rules are regulated by the government (such as China) have, at least in some way, adopted parts of the conceptual framework (Xiao & Pan 1997).

Problems with and criticisms of the conceptual framework

Although benefits are claimed for having a conceptual framework in accounting, there are also some problems with and criticisms of the current Framework. The criticisms are either:

- caused by the nature of a conceptual framework as a set of general guiding principles. These criticisms would apply to many conceptual frameworks, not only the accounting conceptual framework.
- relate to specific parts of the current Framework in accounting.

This chapter considers three main criticisms or problems with the current Framework:

- that it is ambiguous and open to interpretation
- that it is too descriptive
- that the meaning of reliability is problematic.

You should remember some of the key benefits of the conceptual framework in accounting were to improve the quality of accounting rules by providing guidance, in the form of general principles, to standard setters and individuals. This would also help ensure consistency. However, some features of the current Framework suggest that these benefits may not occur.

The Framework can be ambiguous

The principles in the Framework are intended to provide a 'common language'. However, the principles and definitions in the Framework are broad and individuals may interpret them differently. Much of the debate about some recent issues in financial reporting relates to the exact meanings of the definitions in the current Framework. For example, some have argued that share options to employers did not meet the definition of an expense. Although the international standard setters interpreted these options as meeting its definition of an expense, it noted:

> However, given that some people have arrived as a different interpretation of the Framework's expense definition, this suggests that the Framework is not clear (IASCF 2002, p. 12).

A common criticism of conceptual frameworks in general is that the principles are often too vague, leaving too much room for alternative interpretations. Therefore, the ability to provide practical guidance, and in particular consistent application of the principles, is limited.

Balancing the desired attributes of information

The current Framework lists qualitative characteristics for information and also identifies some constraints on the ability to provide information or to ensure that these qualities of information are met. These qualities and constraints require those deciding on the information to be included in the financial statements to balance or weight these issues. In the Framework there is no clear guidance on how to make these decisions — such as how much importance to give to reliability and how much to relevance — and so the decisions will be subjective.

Adjusting for deficiencies in the guidance

A major criticism of the current Framework is that it does not provide guidance for all of the important aspects of and decisions relating to financial statements. In particular, that it provides no definite answers to the question of how to measure the items to be included in financial statements is seen as a barrier to achieving high-quality, consistent and comparable financial statements. Measurement is perhaps one of the most controversial areas in financial reporting. It can be argued that decisions relating to it can be guided by other principles in the current Framework (such as considering the reliability and relevance of alternative measures for particular items). However, this does not provide straightforward or clear guidance on what choices should be made for measuring particular financial statement items. The incompleteness of the current Framework in this regard is seen by many as a major weakness.

The Framework is descriptive not prescriptive

A further complaint is that some see the current Framework as simply reflecting and giving approval to *existing* accounting principles and practices. In other words, the Framework simply describes accounting principles as currently practised and applied, rather than being prescriptive (normative) and trying to improve practice. This criticism is often based on two arguments. These are:

- The current Framework includes many of the concepts used in accounting practice historically. This argument, however, assumes that these concepts must be incorrect or defective. On the contrary, it could be argued that the current Framework includes 'old' assumptions and principles because these are the appropriate ones to use in preparing financial statements.
- People do not agree with the principles included in the current Framework. For example, some argue that stewardship or accountability is a more appropriate primary objective for financial statements than the objective of providing information useful for decision making.

The concept of reliability in the current Framework is inappropriate

A further criticism made of the current Framework relates to the use of reliability. In particular, one component of reliability, representational faithfulness, is considered to misunderstand the nature of accounting (based on Hines 1989b).

Let's consider the meaning of represent faithfully. To represent can be seen as meaning to 'portray' or 'describe'. Faithful can be seen as meaning 'true' or 'accurate'. When thinking of the accuracy, one thinks of how close one is to the correct answer. Consequently, many interpret the requirement for financial statements to represent faithfully the transactions and other events to mean that the aim is to provide as accurate a report or description of the financial position and performance of the entity as possible. This implies that there is a single correct financial position and performance measure for an entity. The financial statements that correspond closest to this correct position or measure will be the most accurate and consequently the most reliable.

But is there one 'correct' financial position or performance measure in accounting? Take, for example, the final profit figure for an entity.

The following events and transactions have occurred in the financial year:
- The net profit before depreciation is $250 000.
- The company has the following noncurrent assets:
  - Building A cost $600 000 five years ago. It has a fair value of $1 000 000 and a further useful life of five years.
  - Building B cost $300 000 20 years ago. It has a fair value of $2 000 000 and a further useful life of ten years.

In one set of financial statements, the accountant uses the cost basis; in another, the fair value basis is used. Both are acceptable according to the conceptual framework and current accounting standards. The financial performance of the entity under each basis is shown in table 2.1.

TABLE 2.1 Reporting profit using cost basis and fair value basis

	View 1 (at cost)	View 2 (at fair value)
Net profit before depreciation	250 000	250 000
Depreciation building A	60 000	200 000
Depreciation building B	10 000	100 000
Final net profit (loss)	180 000	(50 000)

Which profit figure is correct and represents the 'true' measure of the entity's performance? Both are correct in the sense that they follow generally accepted accounting principles. But how can this be? One view shows the company making a profit, the other a loss.

The problem that many argue here is that the concept of faithful representation treats accounting as similar to a 'hard' science. In science, there is generally one correct objective measure. For example, scientists can measure the distance between the Earth and the moon at a particular point in time. There would only be one correct distance and the most accurate measure (the measure closest to the true distance) would be the one that represents this faithfully. This view of the world as having one single set of objective facts to be discovered is often referred to as the 'realist' perspective. Applying this view to accounting:

> Financial statements... are representationally faithful to the extent that they provide an objective picture of an entity's resources and obligations – a reality that exists in the physical world (Monson 2001, p. 278).

not a fact

An alternative perspective, known as the 'materialist' or 'social constructionist' view, argues that accounting cannot be viewed as a science whose aim is to discover objective facts that simply exist in the world. Although the underlying events and transactions do exist (such as the purchase of a particular asset or the sale of goods to a customer), the accounting measures that are reported (such as income or net assets) are created by accountants and do not exist independently of them. If this approach is accepted, then the concept of faithful representation does not really fit. The question to be decided when preparing the financial statements is not which view represents most faithfully the events and transactions (as the reliability characteristic asks us to do) but how to *choose* among the possible views that could be used to represent them. This choice does not involve considerations of accuracy (which view is the most 'correct') but would need to consider the question of which is the *preferred* view to be represented in the financial statements.

This criticism of the conceptual framework challenges the very nature of accounting. From these arguments, it should be obvious that the principles in any conceptual framework for accounting are not unchangeable or unchallengeable. Principles in accounting are not like the 'laws' in science or mathematics (such as the law of gravity, or $E=mc^2$). Principles, such as the definition of an asset, are decided on by debate and agreement. There will always be alternative views and those who disagree.

Summary

Explain what a conceptual framework is.
- A conceptual framework is a set of guiding principles.
- It is a normative theory that sets out the basic principles to be followed in preparing financial statements.
- You should see that it has broad principles, whereas accounting standards relate to a narrow and specific area of financial reporting.

Understand the history and evolution of the accounting conceptual framework.
- The conceptual framework examined is the Framework issued by the IASB, which derives from conceptual frameworks developed in several countries over the past 30 years.

Outline the structure, approach and components of the international conceptual framework.
- The Framework comprises a series of concepts. These relate to the objectives of financial statements, underlying assumptions, qualitative characteristics, definitions and recognition criteria for the elements that make up the financial statements. When complete, it is expected that this will also include principles relating to measurement and presentation of the financial statements.

Explain the purpose and possible benefits of a conceptual framework.
- There are three potential benefits of a conceptual framework in accounting. These are:
  - *technical:* to improve the quality of financial statements by providing guidance to standard setters and for users and preparers
  - *political:* to reduce political interference in the setting of accounting requirements
  - *professional:* to provide a claim of a body of knowledge to ensure the professional status of accountant is maintained.

Explain the problems with and criticisms of the conceptual framework in accounting.
- Three criticisms of the conceptual framework are discussed. These are:
  - The conceptual framework does not work in practice because the principles are too unclear to provide adequate guidance, that guidance in applying the principles is inadequate and that the current framework is incomplete.
  - The current framework describes current practice, so is mainly descriptive, not normative.
  - The concept of representational faithfulness in the reliability characteristic misunderstands the nature of accounting.

Key terms

Review questions

2.1   What is a conceptual framework in accounting?

2.2   What is the difference between the conceptual framework in accounting and accounting standards?

2.3   Outline the technical benefits of a conceptual framework in accounting. What problems could occur if accounting standards were set without a conceptual framework?

2.4   How can the conceptual framework help users and preparers understand accounting requirements and financial statements?

2.5   What is the objective of financial statements according to the Framework?

2.6   How is the decision-usefulness approach reflected in the Framework?

2.7   The Framework states that 'financial statements do not provide all of the information that users may need to make economic decisions' (para. 13). What information is not provided and why?

2.8   What are the underlying assumptions to be applied in preparing financial statements according to the Framework? How do these assumptions affect the financial statement items?

2.9   Identify the qualitative characteristics of information in the Framework. How are these related to the objectives of general purpose financial statements?

2.10 Not all relevant and reliable information will be included in financial statements due to the materiality test and other constraints identified in the Framework. Outline the materiality test and the other constraints on the provision of relevant and reliable information. Can you think of any problems in applying these constraints?

2.11 What is the difference between recognition and disclosure in accounting? According to the Framework, when should an item be recognised in the financial statements?

2.12 Why is accounting said to be 'political' in nature? How can a conceptual framework help in the setting of accounting standards in a political environment?

2.13 It is claimed by some that the reason for conceptual frameworks in accounting is to protect the accounting profession rather than improve accounting practice. Explain the basis for this claim.

2.14 Some people argue that the conceptual framework is acceptable in theory but in practice it does not work. Explain possible problems with and criticisms of the current Framework. Do you think these problems exist and criticisms are valid?

2.15 Explain why some people believe that the concept of faithful representation in the Framework is incorrect.

Application questions

2.16 As a group, identify two or three general principles to help guide the making of more specific rules in relation to a particular area, context or task. For example:

- It may be that a group of students is planning on sharing accommodation (such as an apartment).
- You may be required to undertake a group assignment.

Once you have agreed on the two or three principles, use these to form more specific rules in relation to the context or task. Then consider the following questions:

- How easy was it to agree on the basic principles?
- Are all the rules consistent with these principles?
- Have any members interpreted the principles differently?
- How useful were the principles in helping establish more specific rules?
- Were there any problems with using principles as a basis for setting the rules?

2.17 Look at the accounting standards. Then:

(a) Find examples of how parts of the conceptual framework (e.g. the definitions, recognition criteria, qualitative characteristics) have been included in them.

(b) Identify any inconsistencies between the requirements in accounting standards and the conceptual framework. Why do you think these occur?

2.18 Find the comments letters received on a current exposure draft or proposal. (These can be found from the websites of most standard-setting organisations, such as IASB, AASB or FASB.) Read a sample of comments from a range of respondents (e.g. from accounting bodies, industry, company or corporate bodies) and answer the following questions:

(a) Is there agreement among the various groups?

(b) If there are any concerns or objections, are they based in conceptual issues, practical issues or potential economic consequences? Does this vary among groups?

(c) Have any of the comments letters referred to the conceptual framework as a basis to support their views?

(d) Do the comments letters suggest that there is support for the current conceptual framework?

2.19 The following information is provided for two items of property for a company.

Property A was purchased five years ago for $400 000. It was intended to be used to build another factory but the company has now reorganised its original factory and it is no longer required. The company now intends to sell it. The current property market has dropped but is expected to rise when interest rates fall. If sold now, the property is expected to realise $360 000. Real estate experts have predicted that if the company waits for the property market to recover, it could realise $450 000.

Property B is the current factory. It was purchased ten years ago for $200 000. If sold now, it would be expected to realise $380 000 (and $500 000 if the property market recovers). The company has various estimates about its contribution to the profit of the company. Using current interest rates and various assumptions about future sales and costs, the property is calculated to have a present value (in terms of future cash flows) of $900 000. It is insured for $600 000 because this is the cost required to rebuild it.

The company has always recorded property using the historic cost basis. Other companies in the same industry have traditionally used the same basis, although about 40 per cent now use the fair value basis.

(a) For each of the properties identify which cost or value would best meet each of the four qualitative characteristics of:
- understandability
- relevance
- reliability
- comparability (consider each qualitative characteristic separately).

(b) For each of the properties, choose which cost or value should be stated in the financial statements. Explain why you have chosen it and how you balanced the qualitative characteristics.

(c) Do you think everyone would agree with your choices?

Application of definitions and recognition criteria in the Framework

The following questions (2.20–2.22) require you to apply the definitions and recognition criteria in the Framework to specific cases. After you have answered these questions, compare your answers with those of other students. Do your answers differ? How did using the Framework help you to make your decision?

2.20 A company has a copper mine in South Africa. It purchased the mining rights ten years ago for $20 million and has been operating the mine for the past ten years. It is estimated that there are about 8 million tons of copper in the mine. Because of a fall in world copper prices, the company has closed the mine indefinitely. At current world copper prices, the mine is uneconomic because the costs involved in extracting the copper are greater than the selling price. If copper prices rise by more than 25 per cent, the company has stated that the mine would be reopened.

Applying the principles in the Framework, explain whether this mine would:

- meet the definition of an asset
- pass the recognition criteria.

2.21 The company is currently growing and it is expected that in five years an additional factory will need to be built to meet product demand at a cost of $500 000. The directors wish to recognise an expense of $100 000 and a liability (provision for future expansion) for each of the next five years.

Applying the principles in the Framework, explain whether:

- the definition of a liability or expense is met.
- the recognition criteria for a liability or expense are met.

2.22 The company has recently issued some preference shares. The terms of these shares are:

- A fixed dividend of 3 per cent is payable each year. If no profit is available to pay dividends in one year, these will be back-paid in future years.
- The preference shares will be redeemed (bought back) by the company in three years at their issue price.

Applying the principles in the Framework, explain whether these preference shares should be considered as equity or a liability.

---

case**study**   2.1

The following article from Accountancy Ireland, *'Code of ethics: IFAC issues revised code for professional accountants', discusses the revised code of ethics issued by the International Federation of Accountants (IFAC) for professional accountants.*

IFAC's recently released Revised Code of Ethics applies to all professional accountants — whether you work in practice, in industry, in academe, or in government. It is effective from June 30, 2006.

This article is about ethical matters and the activities of the IFAC Ethics Committee. Besides ethics, IFAC Boards and Committees develop international standards on auditing and assurance (ISAs), on education and on public sector accounting. Each of the member bodies of IFAC — there are 163 currently from all parts of the globe — undertakes to use its best endeavours, subject to national laws and regulations, to implement the standards issued by IFAC in each of these fields.

Fundamental principles

The fundamental principles are:

- Integrity

  An accountant should be straightforward and honest in all professional and business relationships. For example, accountants should not be associated with information which they believe contains a false or misleading statement.

- Objectivity

  An accountant should not allow bias, conflict of interest or undue influence of others to override professional or business judgements.

- Professional Competence and Due Care

  An accountant has to maintain professional knowledge and skill at the level required to ensure that a client or employer receives competent professional service. This requires accountants to act diligently and in accordance with current technical, professional and legislative requirements when engaged in professional activities.

- Confidentiality

  An accountant should respect the confidentiality of information acquired as a result of professional and business relationships and should not disclose any such information without proper and specific authority unless there is a legal or professional right or duty to disclose.

- Professional Behaviour

  An accountant should comply with relevant laws and regulations and should avoid any action that discredits the profession.

  Where accountants consider that any proposed professional activity might compromise compliance with these fundamental principles they are required to put safeguards in place to mitigate the threat or, where they cannot do so, to desist from the proposed activity.

Threats

The threats identified in the Code are:

- Self Interest Threat

  May occur as a result of a financial or other interest held by the accountant or a family member.

- Self Review Threat

  May occur when a previous judgement needs to be re-evaluated — you cannot audit your own work.

- Advocacy Threat

  May occur when an accountant promotes a position or opinion to the point where subsequent objectivity may be compromised.

- Familiarity Threat

  May occur when, because of a close relationship, the accountant becomes too sympathetic to the interests of others.

- Intimidation Threat

  May occur when an accountant may be deterred from acting objectively by threats — actual or perceived.

  The Code contains many examples of situations that may be faced by accountants and of possible safeguards that could mitigate the threats. In some cases, the code makes clear that no safeguard could adequately address the perceived or actual threat to the fundamental principles — for example, the threat to objectivity (or independence) if an auditor held shares in his audit client — and, in such cases, the only option is to walk away, to resign or to refuse the assignment. However, the Code clearly states that the examples are not all inclusive and that the obligation is on the accountant to identify and assess any threats that might arise in the particular circumstances faced — and then to address them appropriately in accordance with the framework approach set out in the Code.

Conceptual framework advantages

The advantages of this conceptual framework approach are that:

- the principles-based standards set out in the Code are robust and can be applied to the diverse and varying circumstances faced by professional accountants;
- it avoids technical evasion of detailed rules;
- it is appropriate for global application; and
- it continues to be applicable in a rapidly changing environment.

Source: Extracted from an article that appeared in *Accountancy Ireland*.

1. Can you identify any potential problems or criticisms of the principles outlined in the conceptual framework in the case?
2. Do you think using these principles would be interpreted and applied consistency between the accountants in determining whether an action is ethical?
3. How effective do you think such a framework is in (a) ensuring accountants act ethically and (b) enforcing or penalising unethical behaviour?
4. Would a set of specific rules about what constitutes ethical and unethical behaviours in specific circumstances be more or less useful than the principles in the code of conduct outlined?

case**study**   **2.2**

This extract discusses in part whether the principles in the conceptual framework for financial reporting for business entities are appropriate for other contexts, such as small business or the public sector or not-for-profit entities.

FASB and IASB say rules for clarity of financial reporting should be no different for smaller businesses than for their larger peers.

The fourth meeting of the Financial Accounting Standards Board's Small Business Advisory Committee, on November 30, dealt with uncertain tax positions, changes in accounting for postretirement benefit obligations including pensions, and the joint conceptual framework project of FASB and the International Accounting Standards Board.

Of these, the last topic got the most attention from the committee members. The joint conceptual framework project involves discussions on the objectives of financial reporting and the qualitative aspects, such as faithful representation and understandability, of accounting data. At the October joint meeting of FASB and IASB, the two boards determined it unnecessary to modify the objective or qualitative characteristics of financial reporting information for different types of companies — including smaller and non-public businesses.

Several reasons contributed to that conclusion. True, most of the users of financial reporting by smaller and non-public companies — such as bankers, rating agencies, and owners — have the ability to require the financial information they want from the company, rather than merely relying on what management gives them. But these users generally have the same informational needs as parties who don't have that ability.

As for the six qualitative characteristics of financial reporting identified by FASB and IASB — relevance, faithful representation, understandability, comparability, materiality, and cost-benefit considerations — understandability drew special attention. Users of smaller-company reporting, the boards observed, often are less financially sophisticated and find some data or presentations too complicated. To address this gap, many smaller companies simplify their reporting and present information in a way more easily understood by their users.

However, committee members noted that it's important to clarify what 'simplifying' means. To FASB board members, it doesn't mean dumbing down information for accountants; simplifying should be about presenting information so it's clearer and more useful to users who make financial decisions. Ways to achieve this, asserted the board, include eliminating smoothing of costs over time, avoiding accounting jargon, and choosing the most cost-effective means of applying accounting methods.

FASB and IASB have yet to discuss the applicability of cost-benefit considerations for all sizes of companies, but board members indicated that it's likely they will conclude that cost-benefit considerations are equally important in financial reporting for both small and large companies.

Source: Extracted from an article that appeared in *CFO.com*.

1. Do you think the objectives in the Framework equally apply to small or not-for profit or public-sector entities?
2. Do you think the same qualitative characteristics would be equally important and appropriate to small or not-for profit or public-sector entities?
3. Are separate and distinct conceptual frameworks needed for different entities or areas of financial reporting?

Recommended readings and websites

For updates on the Conceptual Framework — Joint Project of the IASB and FASB: www.fasb.org or www.iasb.org.

For more detail about the nature of accounting and the economic consequences of accounting:

Leo, KJ & Hoggett, JR 1998, 'Standard-setting reform: neutrality, economic consequences and politics', *Accounting Forum*, vol. 22, no. 3, pp. 330–51.

Hines, RD 1989b, 'The sociopolitical paradigm in financial accounting research', *Accounting, Auditing and Accountability Journal*, vol. 2, no. 1, pp. 52–62.

For more detail about the role of conceptual works in maintaining professional status:

Hines, RD 1989a, 'Financial accounting knowledge, conceptual framework projects and the social construction of the accounting profession', *Accounting, Auditing and Accountability Journal*, vol. 2, no. 2, pp. 72–92.

References

Baker, C R & Hayes, RS 1995, 'The negative effect of an accounting standard on employee welfare: the case of McDonnell Douglas Corporation and FASB 106', *Accounting, Auditing & Accountability Journal*, vol. 8, no. 3, pp. 12–33.

Damant, D 2003, 'Accounting standards — a new era', *Balance Sheet*, vol. 11. no. 1, pp. 9–20.

Foster, JM & Johnson, LT 2001, *Understanding the issues: why does the FASB have a conceptual framework?*, FASB.

Georgiou, G 2004, 'Corporate lobbying on accounting standards: methods, timing and perceived effectiveness', *Abacus*, vol. 40, no. 2, pp. 219–37.

Henderson, S & Pierson, G. 2002, *Issues in financial accounting*, 10th edn, Prentice Hall, Sydney.

Hines, RD, 1989a, 'Financial accounting knowledge, conceptual framework projects and the social construction of the accounting profession', *Accounting, Auditing and Accountability Journal*, vol. 2, no. 2, pp. 72–92.

—— 1989b, 'The sociopolitical paradigm in financial accounting research', *Accounting, Auditing and Accountability Journal*, vol. 2, no. 1, pp. 52–62.

International Accounting Standards Board (IASB) 1989, *Framework for the preparation and presentation of financial statements*.

Leo, KJ & Hoggett, JR 1998, 'Standard-setting reform: neutrality, economic consequences and politics', *Accounting Forum*, vol. 22, no. 3, pp. 330–51.

Ministry of Finance (MOF) 2006, *Accounting standard for business enterprises: basic standard*, 15 February, MOF, China.

Monson, DW 2001, 'The conceptual framework and accounting for leases', *Accounting Horizons*, vol. 15. no. 3, pp. 275–87.

Rutherford, BA 2003, 'The social construction of financial statement elements under Private Finance Initiative schemes', *Accounting, Auditing & Accountability Journal*, vol. 16, no. 3, pp. 372–96.

Staubus, GJ 2004, 'On Brian P. West's professionalism and accounting rules', *Abacus*, vol. 40, no. 2, pp. 139–56.

Street, DL & Shaughnessy, KA 1998, 'The quest for international accounting harmonization: a review of the standard setting agendas of the IASC, US, UK, Canada and Australia, 1973–1997', *The International Journal of Accounting*, vol. 33, no. 2, pp. 179–209.

Sutton, T 2003, *Corporate financial accounting and reporting*, 2nd edn, Prentice Hall, London.

Xiao, Z & Pan, A 1997, 'Developing accounting standards on the basis of a conceptual framework by the Chinese government, *The International Journal of Accounting*, vol. 32, no. 3, pp. 279–99.

Zeff, SA 2002, '"Political" lobbying on proposed standards: a challenge to the IASB', *Accounting Horizons*, vol. 16, no. 1, pp. 43–54.

3 STANDARD SETTING

After reading this chapter, you should be able to:

- understand the institutional framework of Australian accounting standard setting
- explain and define an accounting standard
- distinguish principles-based from rules-based standards
- define regulation and explain the reasons the production of accounting information is regulated
- understand why standard setting is a political process
- explain the process of harmonisation of accounting standards.

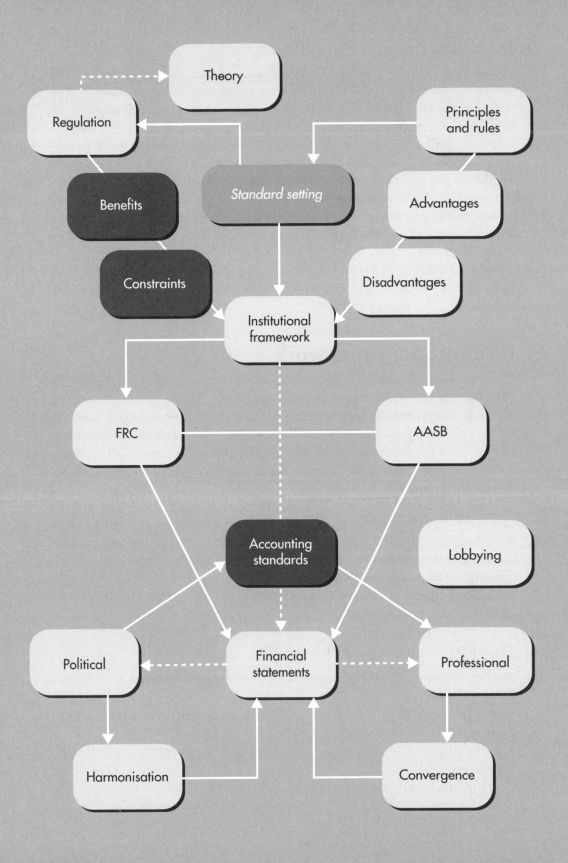

Introduction

Chapter 2 shows that conceptual frameworks are broad principles used to guide accounting standards setters by providing a base for considering the merits of alternative methods. In contrast, accounting standards provide specific requirements that must be complied with.

However, some aspects of conceptual frameworks are also pertinent to standards, particularly the question whether they should be rules or principles based, as well as the potential influence of political pressures on the standard-setting process. This chapter considers these points and examines the most significant standard-setting development in Australia in recent times: the harmonisation of Australian accounting standards with those issued by the International Accounting Standards Board (IASB).

Before examining the issues, however, the chapter considers the context in which the Australian accounting standards are set, and the institutional framework that underlies the Australian regulator.

Institutional framework

The Australian Accounting Standards Board (AASB) was established under the *Australian Securities and Investments Commission Act 1991* (ASIC Act), and was designed to improve the quality and independence of the accounting standard-setting process in Australia. Previously, accounting standards were developed and administered by the accounting profession through various professional bodies, particularly the Institute of Chartered Accountants in Australia and Certified Practising Accountants Australia.

The AASB is designed as a neutral, independent body, with full legislative backing to enforce the standards it publishes. It is overseen by the Financial Reporting Council (FRC) and is aided in its work by several advisory groups, including interpretations advisory panels and user groups. The structure of this institutional framework is shown in figure 3.1.

Each component of this structure is discussed in further detail in the following sections.

The FRC

The FRC is a statutory body operating within a framework set out in the ASIC Act. It is responsible for:

- broad oversight of the standard-setting process, including the strategic directions of the AASB and the Australian Auditing Standards Board.
- monitoring the development of international accounting and auditing standards
- monitoring the effectiveness of auditor independence requirements
- advising and supplying reports to the minister on these matters.

The FRC also appoints the members of the AASB, other than the chairman who is appointed by the minister. The act prohibits the FRC from being involved in the technical deliberations of standard setting, ensuring the independence of the standard setter from its overseer.

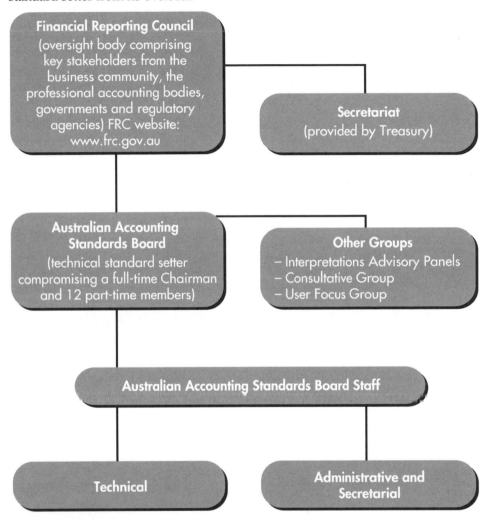

FIGURE 3.1 Australian accounting standard setting: structure of institutional arrangements
Source: Australian Accounting Standards Board, www.aasb.com.au.

The AASB

Under the ASIC Act, the functions of the AASB are to:

• develop a conceptual framework for the purpose of evaluating proposed accounting standards and international accounting standards
• make accounting standards for the purposes of corporations legislation
• formulate accounting standards for other purposes, including not-for-profit entities

- participate in and contribute to the development of a single set of worldwide accounting standards.

In performing its functions, the AASB must pay attention to the objectives of part 12 of the ASIC Act:

(a) to facilitate the development of accounting standards that require the provision of financial information that
   (i) allow users to make and evaluate decisions about allocating scarce resources;
   (ii) assists directors to discharge their obligations in relation to financial reporting;
   (iii) is relevant to assessing performance, financial position, financing and investment;
   (iv) is relevant and reliable;
   (v) facilitates comparability;
   (vi) is readily understandable;
(b) to facilitate the Australian economy by
   (i) reducing the cost of capital;
   (ii) enabling Australian entities to compete effectively overseas;
   (iii) having accounting standards that are clearly stated and easy to understand; and
(c) to maintain investor confidence in the Australian economy.

Since 2002, the AASB has been pivotal in mediating the transition from Australian standards to the adoption of IASB standards (known as International Financial Reporting Standards, or IFRSs). This involved the alignment of Australian standards with IFRSs as they were produced by the IASB, as well as adjusting for any unique Australian regulatory conditions. The entire suite of IASB standards came into effect in Australia on 1 January 2005.

Interpretations

The Urgent Issues Group (UIG) was a committee of the AASB before 2006. Its members were appointed by the AASB, with the approval of the chair of the FRC. The role of the UIG was to provide timely guidance on urgent reporting issues identified by its members and observers. These issues were those likely to receive divergent or unacceptable treatment in the absence of authoritative pronouncements. In doing so, the UIG attempted to avoid developing divergent or unsatisfactory practices in areas not dealt with in accounting standards. The accounting issues tackled by the UIG also included those considered by the International Financial Reporting Interpretations Committee (IFRIC).

With the implementation of IFRSs, the role of the UIG was reassessed, resulting in a new interpretations model, which was implemented in 2006. This model returned the interpretations role directly to the AASB, replacing the UIG. Under the model, an Interpretations Advisory Committee (IAC), formed of members of the AASB, considers IFRIC proposals and interpretations and advises the board on a recommended course of action. The AASB may then elect to appoint an advisory panel to consider specific issues that arise and provide further alternative views and advice for the board. Members of advisory panels are drawn from a register of potential members, composed of preparers, users, auditors and regulators. Appointment to a particular advisory panel is made on an individual basis, depending on the topic of discussion, to ensure a balance of expertise and experience. The AASB is also helped by other groups in its standard-setting role.

Other groups

Two other groups provide advice and assistance to the AASB in formulating standard-setting priorities and revising and improving disclosure processes. The first is the AASB User Focus Group. This is composed of eight to ten members of a significant group of users of financial reports, particularly the professional investment community. These may include 'investors and investment professionals, equity and credit analysts, credit grantors and rating agencies'. The AASB sees the role of this group as to raise awareness and provide feedback on how financial reports are used, and whether standards achieve the information disclosures needed by the sector.

The second group, the AASB Consultative Group, is a broad collection of interested parties, drawn from preparers, users and regulators of financial reports, both national and international. The purpose of the group is to provide the AASB with views representative of these groups in relation to the board's work program and technical activities, and to provide feedback on the project priorities and due processes of the standard setter.

▪ Accounting standards

The process of standard setting is designed to produce *quality financial reporting*. To ensure that financial reports are of a high quality, accounting standard-setting boards produce 'standards'. The most appropriate definition of a standard from the Macquarie dictionary is: 'anything taken by general consent as a basis of comparison'. It was in this sense that guides to selecting accounting treatments were referred to as Generally Accepted Accounting Principles, or GAAP. When those principles receive authoritative backing from a body such as the Australian federal government, they are referred to as **accounting standards**. Their purpose is to provide guidance to preparers of financial reports so that the information contained in those reports permits users to make useful decisions about the allocation of resources based on it.

accounting standards:
Authoritative statements that guide the preparation of financial statements

Australia's first accounting standards were issued in 1946. They were not mandatory. Since then, accounting standard-setting boards such as the AASB have been established to issue standards guiding the preparation of financial statements. Recently, the surprise collapse of many prominent corporations has prompted questions about the quality and enforceability of those standards. Developments in the United States, Australia and Europe, after the high-profile collapses of Enron, WorldCom, Parmalat, HIH and others, have resulted in questioning the very basis on which standards are developed: rules-based or principles-based platforms.

Rules-based versus principles-based standards

Rules-based standards are filled with specific details to meet as many potential contingencies as possible. Supposedly, rules-based standards are a result of preparers demanding them (Maines et al. 2003).

rules-based standards: Standards that contain specific details and mandatory definitions that attempt to meet as many potential contingencies and situations as possible

principles-based standards: Standards that contain a substantive accounting principle that focuses on achieving the accounting objective of the standard. The principle is based on the objective of accounting in the conceptual framework.

Principles-based standards are based on a conceptual framework that provides a broad basis for accountants to follow instead of a list of rules (Shortridge & Myring 2004). Principles-based standards focus on the economic substance of a transaction, engaging the professional judgement and expertise of those preparing financial reports.

Rules are sometimes unavoidable. The intent of principles-based standards is not to provide specific guidance for every possible situation but is directed to the principles of the conceptual framework.

The IASB follows a principles-based approach to standard setting. In the United States, the Financial Accounting Standards Board (FASB) and the Securities and Exchange Commission are agonising over the benefits and disadvantages of both rules-based and principles-based standards.

The differences between rules-based and principles-based standards can be illustrated. For example, a rules-based standard for depreciation might say:

> Annual depreciation expense for all depreciable assets is to be 10 per cent of the original cost of the asset, until the asset is fully depreciated.

In contrast, the principles-based standard might say:

> Depreciation expense for the reporting period should reflect the decline in the economic value of the asset being depreciated over the period.

You should see that the rules-based standard is very prescriptive in its directions, whereas the principles-based standards is much more broad. The following In Focus vignette demonstrates the flexibility of a principles-based approach.

 Rules-based versus principles-based standards

Four students from an accounting theory class were given the assignment of explaining the difference between principles-based standards and rules-based standards to their student peers. They had a 50-minute class in which to do so. Other than being provided with some readings on the topic, they were given little direction but encouragement to be creative.

Their presentation commenced with the four presenters dividing the class into two groups: the principles group and the rules group. Both groups were supplied with large sheets of white, blank butcher's paper and drawing implements. An ice-age-type scene, an environment of a deep wide valley filled with snow, with its sides covered in tall tress to the tree line and a lot of snow above the tree line, was projected onto the wall of the classroom. This provided the context of their exercise.

The students were then asked to develop a design for a village in that environment: one that would provide its inhabitants with the basic needs of shelter and protection. The principles group was unrestricted in the ideas that they could use. Their task was to design a village based on the principle that the village would provide shelter and protection for its inhabitants in that environment. The rules group was limited in its choices by many rules that kept changing marginally. The only possible outcome was to build igloo housing and a protective wall of ice bricks!

When each group had completed its task, the environment changed. Global warming set in, increasing temperatures so that the snow melted. Of course, the igloo village was doomed. The principles group had used what was available in the environment to achieve the objective of shelter and safety: timber, a moat outside the timber protective wall and timber and brush houses. Their village, with a few modifications, still satisfied the principle despite the increase in temperatures.

The move away from rules-based standards is related to the problems generated by their misuse in many of the high-profile accounting scandals associated with the collapse of Enron and others. This misuse is related to the disadvantages of rules-based standards, which are outlined in the following section.

Disadvantages of rules-based standards

Rules-based standards have some significant disadvantages, mostly related to the attempt to cover all contingencies. The diversity of entities, and the many unique situations covered by the reporting system, give rise to some particular problems.

- Rules-based standards can be very complex, and complexity can allow confusion and even manipulation.
- Spelling out rules for every potential situation results in companies being able to structure transactions to circumvent unfavourable reporting. Enron is a good example, in that special-purpose entities were used to mask the unfavourable financial position it faced.
- Detailed standards are likely to be incomplete or even obsolete by the time they are issued.

- Manipulated compliance with rules makes auditing more difficult because managers can justify their manipulations as compliance. Compliance with the letter of the law may nonetheless be contrary to the spirit of that law.

In contrast, the literature currently finds little to disagree with in relation to *principles-based standards*, and much to recommend them. However, Maines et al. (2003) stress that the tension between companies and their auditors, investors and regulators is not specific to the nature of standards as principles based or rules based. Standards cannot solve the conflicts between reporting entities and their auditors and other stakeholders.

Advantages of principles-based standards

Principles-based standards reflect a more consistent application of the underlying conceptual framework than do rules-based standards. After investing heavily in a conceptual framework, the accounting profession would not like to see it undermined. This framework provides the basis for the consistency and flexibility inherent in a principles-based system.

- Principles-based standards should be simpler than rules-based standards. The examples given illustrate how simple a standard can be when based on a principle rather than many rules.
- They supply broad guidelines that can be applied to many situations.
- Broad guidelines may improve the representational faithfulness of financial statements.
- Principles-based standards allow accountants to use their professional judgement in assessing the substance of a transaction. Using their judgement is the service that accountants offer to their clients, so principles-based standards highlight their professionalism.
- Evidence suggests that managers are less likely to attempt earnings management when faced with principles-based standards (Nelson et al. 2002). With rules-based standards, structuring transactions a particular way is 'black or white'. The use of principles makes the structuring more difficult to justify. Auditors are less likely to permit earnings management when standards are principles based.

Disadvantages of principles-based standards

Despite these positives, all standard systems have inherent disadvantages. The inherent latitude of principles-based standards is a 'double-edged sword' (Maines et al. 2003) in that managers are able to select treatments both that reflect the underlying economic substance of a transaction and that do not. Managers, audit committee members and auditors must have the desire for unbiased reporting and the expertise to achieve treatments that reflect the underlying economic substance. Even when unbiased reports are produced, the judgement and choice involved in many of the decisions mean that comparability among financial statements may be reduced.

In Australia, the standard-setting process is governed by an independent government-controlled process with legislative backing. Corporate failures such as those of HIH and One.Tel have focused unwelcome negative attention on this process, and, in response to society demand, the government has moved to increase its regulatory role in the procedures further. Government intervention now extends to legal enforcement of financial reporting and audit independence. The purpose of regulation in the standard-setting arena is discussed in the next section.

Learning tips
Do you know...

3.1 *Accounting standards in Australia are set by an independent board, the AASB, in conjunction with the Interpretations Advisory Committee, the Consultative Group, and the User Focus Group.*

3.2 *Standards can be either rules based or principles based.*

3.3 *Rules-based standards are prescriptive and complex, and can allow manipulation.*

3.4 *Principles-based standards are flexible and consistent but are also open to manipulation, and may not be comparable even when accurate.*

Theories of regulation

'Information is the oil that lubricates markets' (Staubus 1995). Without accurate and useful information, the market cannot function. Because accounting information is argued to be a public good and is likely to be underproduced without some form of regulation, the production of accounting information and financial statements should be regulated. Others argue that regulation is needed because without it, information would not be produced at all. Ross (1977) disagrees: '[D]isclosure regulations are generally neither required nor desirable, since left on their own, firms will have incentives to report accurately.' The theories behind the justification for regulation fall roughly under several theoretical umbrellas: signalling theory, public interest theory, capture theory and 'bushfire' theory. Before discussing each theory in turn, it is useful to provide the analysis with some definitions and scope.

What regulation is

The Macquarie dictionary's pertinent definition of the act of **regulation** is to control or direct by rule, principle or method. Regulation is a rule or order, as for conduct, prescribed by authority. Mitnick (1980) defines regulation neutrally, extending the concept to self and governmental regulation:

> **regulation:** The policing, according to a rule, of a subject's choice of activity, by an entity not directly party to or involved in the activity

> [R]egulation is the policing, according to a rule, of a subject's choice of activity, by an entity not directly party to or involved in the activity.

According to these definitions, the elements of regulation are:

- *an intention to intervene.* Throughout the history of standard setting, some body, initially the accounting profession, sought to intervene in the production of financial information by reporting enterprises.
- *a restriction on choice to achieve certain goals.* Accounting standards restrict choices of accounting methods by directing which are to be used.
- *an exercise of control by a party at least nominally independent of those directly involved in the activity.*

The control through an accounting standards board is at least nominally independent of those being regulated, although capture theory (outlined later) suggests otherwise. First, however, the next section considers signalling theory.

Signalling theory

Signalling theory holds that a reporting enterprise can increase its value through financial reporting. If an enterprise fails to disclose, it will be identified by interested parties as merely an average enterprise among all 'tightlipped' (Hakansson 1983) or nondisclosing enterprises.

This gives above-average enterprises the motivation to show, through financial reports, that they are better than the non-reporting entities. The remaining firms are perceived as of even poorer quality than before, causing them to wish to better their reputation by implementing financial reporting themselves. Consequently, signalling theory is virtually a self-regulating system, in which almost every enterprise has a reason to issue financial statements to lower its cost of capital.

Public interest theory

Although signalling theory is acclaimed as a self-perpetuating process, it relies on the function of a perfect, free-market economy. Economic markets are, however, rarely perfect or free, and are instead subject to various imperfections and inefficiencies. Public interest theory holds that regulation is supplied in response to the demands of the public for the correction of these inefficient or inequitable market practices (Posner 1974, p. 335).

The theory is based on two assumptions:

- Economic markets are fragile so that they are likely to operate inefficiently or inequitably if left unregulated.
- Regulation is virtually costless.

In this theory, accounting standard setting is a response to an inefficient market for financial (or accounting) information. The quantity and quality of an item such as financial information in an unregulated market differ from the social optimum because financial information has the characteristics of a public good. A public good is one for which those who bear the costs of producing it do not capture its benefits. The inefficient market for financial information is reflected in its either under- or overproduction.

Capture theory

Capture theory attempts to build on the evidence that interest groups are intimately involved in regulation. Capture theory holds that regulation is supplied in response to the demands of interest groups trying to maximise the incomes or interests of their members. It is based on the assumption that people seek to advance their self-interest, and do so rationally. You should note the similarity of this assumption and that underlying positive accounting theory.

The theory is also based on two insights:

- The first is that the coercive power of government can be used to give valuable benefits to particular groups, such as the accounting industry. By making adherence to accounting standards mandatory, government is bestowing benefits on the accounting profession, particularly auditors. One of the early problems for standard-setting bodies was the lack of adherence to standards. Government backing for standards largely eliminates this problem.
- The second important insight is that regulation can be viewed as product that is governed by the laws of supply and demand. This insight means that attention is focused on the value and cost of regulation to particular groups. Economics tells us that a product will be supplied to those who value it the most, a value that will be weighed against the cost of obtaining the regulation.

Staubus pointed out that management is the interest group which lobbies most on proposed standards. As a producer of financial information, management can afford to invest more than users in lobbying for their point of view. As a result, standards are more likely to reflect benefits for the reporters of financial information than for users of that information (Staubus 1995, p. 207).

'Bushfire' theory

Bushfire theory highlights the political and public nature of regulatory influences by attempting to take into account the reactions of users, and society in general, to 'failures' of regulatory processes. Regulations tend to arise from crises such as the collapse of Enron, WorldCom and HIH. These crises tend to occur regularly, although always unexpectedly, and are often spectacular in their explosion. They highlight the shortcomings in accounting, so that the media cries out, 'Where were the auditors?'. Media attention results in solutions that are not necessarily of any use to solve the perceived crisis but are understandable to the layperson. The resulting rules do not necessarily deal with the issues that caused the crisis.

According to Watts & Zimmerman (1986), the resulting rules and regulations are designed to gain media exposure so that politicians and their bureaucrats are more likely to gain re-election.

After the recent unexpected collapses of high-profile companies, many legislative initiatives occurred worldwide, including the Corporate Law Economic Reform Program (CLERP) 9 in Australia and the Sarbanes–Oxley Act in the United States. The proposed answer to the crises caused by these collapses is to base standards on principles rather than rules.

Advantages and disadvantages of regulation

There has been much debate about the benefits and costs of regulation. Those in favour promote its benefits; those against tend to emphasise its costs. The commonly offered benefits are listed here, followed by the commonly offered costs.

Advantages of regulation

Proponents of regulation in the standard-setting environment believe in the need for correction of imperfect and inefficient market systems. The nature of accounting information as a free public good means that normal market-pricing mechanisms are unable to operate. Similarly, the company is solely responsible for the release of internal information, and self-interest suggests significant incentives to under-produce. Regulation intervention is therefore needed to protect the public interest, and to increase the production of useful information. The benefits of regulation can be summarised as follows:

- *Increased efficiency in allocating capital.* Information is needed to ensure efficient allocation of capital. Perfect competition requires perfect information. In the absence of a compulsory disclosure system, some issuers of financial reports may conceal or misrepresent information relevant to decision making. Mandatory disclosure should increase the quantity of information communicated — information that should be accurate because the costs of verification are borne publicly by oversight bodies such as Australian Securities and Investments Commission.
- *Cheaper production.* Mandatory disclosure reduces the redundant production of information because without it, users must produce their own information. If several users produce the same information, too much has been produced. Mandatory disclosure also reduces the search costs of users because they know where to find the information and should understand the form in which it is supplied.
- *Check on perquisites.* In the absence of mandatory disclosure, underwriting costs and management salaries (including perquisites) will be excessive because with no checks on them, shareholders have to pay heavily to monitor them. Recent publicity given to executive compensation casts some doubt on this particular benefit.
- *Public confidence.* Mandatory disclosure increases public confidence because it substantially limits a company's ability to remain silent, and controls the time, place and manner of disclosure.
- *Standardisation.* Regulation will result in the standardisation of accounting, which will reduce ambiguity in accounting reports. With it, users will be able to make comparisons among reporting entities. Without regulation, incentives do not exist for preparers to conform to any particular model of accounting. Remember that comparability and understandability are two of the qualitative characteristics of the conceptual framework that are enabled by standardisation.
- *Public good.* As a public good, information has to be regulated to correct market imperfections.

Disadvantages of regulation

Most opponents of regulation argue that free-market mechanisms would generate enough information to reach a socially acceptable level at which the costs of providing that information are equalled by the benefits. Furthermore, it is often argued that users, who mostly bear very little of the cost of providing information, are the most vocal in demanding increased regulation. If this demand is acceded to, it is argued, overregulation could have significant consequences. Some of the arguments against regulation are summarised as follows.

- *Various problems arise when using regulation to achieve efficiency and equity.*
  - Because regulation can benefit some stakeholders to the detriment of others, those with an interest in financial reporting are likely to lobby standard setters, an exercise that can be costly.
  - Problems emerge for regulators from lack of disclosure by regulated enterprises. The corporate collapses of 2002 illustrate these. Despite many accounting and auditing standards, these firms collapsed without much warning. Regulators are seen to be failures in these situations, losing prestige and legitimacy.
  - What will be disclosed? What will not be disclosed? The regulator declaring in the pertinent international accounting standard that expenditures on intangibles must not be capitalised created difficulties for enterprises with many intangibles.
  - What or who governs the regulators? The move towards principles-based standards partly answers this question. The conceptual framework should govern decisions made by the standard setters.
- *Determining the optimal quantity of information is problematic.* The public-good argument is unable to determine the optimum amount of information. At what point do users of financial information face information overload?
- *Regulation is difficult to reverse.* Once an accounting standard is in place, considerable time elapses before it is revised or withdrawn.
- *Communication is restricted.* By reducing ambiguity, regulation also reduces the means of communicating information as well as stifling innovation in ways of presenting financial information.
- *Reporting enterprises are different.* Regulation of financial reporting on a standardised basis forces different cases into the same mould: regulation does not allow for differences among entities. The arguments against the extension of accounting standards to the public and not-for-profit sectors illustrate the difficulties some reporting enterprises have with some standards.
- *There is lobbying.* Certain interest groups seek and gain economic rents by investing resources in the pursuit of favourable regulations.
- *Contracts.* Because users can write contracts with management stipulating the provision of information to them, regulation is not needed.

Despite these arguments, it is unlikely that regulatory bodies will relinquish their control over the current standard-setting process. However, it is also impossible to remove the regulatory bodies and their functions from the social and political environment in which they operate.

Users are the focus of standards designed to produce general purpose financial reports with all the information required for decision making. As pointed out, there is always inherent tension between reporting enterprises and their auditors, investors, regulators and other interested parties. Standards cannot resolve these conflicts, nor can the development of a conceptual framework. Because of this tension, standard setters are constantly subject to political pressures.

Learning tips
Do you know...

3.5   *Signalling theory relies on the value of voluntary reporting functioning in a perfect free-market economy.*

3.6   *Public interest theory operates on the assumption that market economies are inherently imperfect, with inefficiencies that disadvantage society, requiring government regulation to intervene in the public interest.*

3.7   *Capture theory maintains that regulation has been 'captured' by the accounting profession to preserve its control over the standard-setting process and its associated benefits.*

3.8   *Bushfire theory argues regulation is the result of public pressure mediated through media sensationalism, designed to benefit politicians and bureaucrats seeking re-election.*

3.9   *Each of these theories has benefits and disadvantages.*

▪ The political nature of setting accounting standards

In most democratic countries, there is some mix of public and private participation in the standard-setting process. For example, standard setting in Australia was initially in the hands of the profession but many factors, especially the difficulty of enforcing private standards, led to a public–private partnership. Acceptance of the process by which standards are set does not mean that those on whom they are imposed will necessarily accept them. They are controversial.

Why are standards controversial? Various corporate collapses in many countries have caused a legitimacy crisis in the accounting profession for both financial reporting and auditing (Guthrie & Parker 2003). Whenever a crisis occurs, someone or something has to take the blame. Earlier crises in the corporate world resulted in accounting being blamed. To restore confidence in accounting, the conceptual framework was developed.

In the aftermath of the most recent corporate collapses, many things have been blamed, including auditor–client relationships, corporate governance structures, corporate legislation and accounting standards. The number and size of the collapses and their impact on stakeholders show that accounting does count. However, the losses that society has suffered have further undermined its confidence in accounting and auditing (Guthrie & Parker 2003).

The various parties that have an interest in reporting enterprises and in accounting standards often have conflicting interests. As outlined in previous chapters, users, particularly investors and creditors, are the group whose needs will be taken into account by standard setters. But this is not the only group with an interest. Company accountants and management do too because their performance is often tied to the financial performance of the firm. Auditors do because they must enforce the rules generated by accounting standards. Governments and governmental agencies do, particularly in seeing that standards are enforced.

Two points here are relevant:

- *The interests of these groups often conflict.* Management is likely to want accounting choices that allow it to produce as favourable a picture of its performance as possible. Shareholders are likely to want to know the 'real' performance of management and the enterprise under its control.
- *Auditors like auditability, which often translates into objectivity.* However, management never likes having its choices limited (Staubus 1995, p. 192).

Remember that standard setting aims at increasing the amount of information available about a reporting enterprise. Information is said to be the oil that lubricates markets. A perfect market would require perfect information. Given this, what should the goals of those setting standards be when they have to make a choice among different methods and among ways of reporting information? The conceptual framework is designed to provide guidance, and hopefully to reduce the tension among parties interested in the outcomes delivered by standards.

Lobbying

Accounting standard setting is a political process because accounting standards can transfer wealth from investors to creditors, from investors to employees, from present investors to future investors and so on. As a result, those affected by regulation in the form of accounting standards have an incentive to lobby standard setters to achieve a favourable outcome. The standard-setting process offers several opportunities and means by which those affected by the resulting standards can influence the outcomes of the standard setting process (Sutton 1984; Georgiou 2004). The following In Focus vignette demonstrates the lobbying power of stakeholders, in this case, government bureaucrats themselves.

 infocus *Treasury chiefs revolt over budget rules*

Federal and state treasuries are demanding that Australia's main accounting standards body rewrite a sweeping overhaul of the rules that governments must follow when they present their annual budgets and financial reports.

Federal Treasury secretary Ken Henry and the head of the Department of Finance and Administration, Ian Watt, have written to the Australian Accounting Standards Board to say that its proposed new standard for government financial reporting would make budgets unwieldy, confusing and complex.

The AASB is due to meet this week to consider the backlash from governments over its exposure draft of a new standard for financial reporting, which was issued last year in an attempt to harmonise the two existing sets of accounting rules for government budgets.

Sources believe the AASB may give ground on some of the issues raised by the treasury chiefs, in particular a plan for budgets to include a complex, multi-column format for their operating statements, balance sheets and cash-flow statements.

However fresh divisions have emerged on a separate but critical issue: whether to force governments to produce consolidated financial reports, including information about public corporations in their bottom lines, rather than confining their financial reports to the general government sector.

The chairman of the AASB, professor David Boymal, told *The Australian Financial Review* that if the debate about consolidation could not be resolved, then the whole project to produce a harmonised accounting standard for government reporting could collapse.

The disputes have been triggered by a direction from the Financial Standards Council asking the AASB to produce a single accounting standard to replace two existing sets of accounting rules for governments in Australia.

The two sets of rules are the government finance statistics framework produced by the Australian Bureau of Statistics based on International Monetary Fund requirements and existing Australian accounting standards based on generally accepted accounting principles.

The attempt to harmonise these rules into a single standard is the biggest shake-up for government financial reporting since the move from cash-based reporting to accrual accounting in 1999–2000.

It had been anticipated that the AASB would resolve these differences by adopting one treatment for areas where the standards diverge.

However the draft leaves several issues unresolved and suggests instead that financial statements include four columns showing GFS and GAAP results as well as the size of the resulting 'convergence differences'.

In their letter to the AASB, Dr Henry and Dr Watt said they had strong reservations about whether harmonisation had been achieved under this approach.

Source: This article appeared in *The Australian Financial Review*.

Those affected by the decisions in the accounting standard-setting process have several decisions of their own to make (Walker & Robinson 1994):
- *Whether they should lobby*. Sutton (1984) suggests that self-interest and choice govern lobbying behaviour. In deciding whether to lobby, a potential lobbyist will weigh the costs against the benefits.
- *Which method of lobbying they should use*. Lobbying methods are classified as either direct or indirect. Direct methods involve lobbying the standard setter by communicating with members of the standard-setting board. Indirect methods involve communicating with a member of the board through a third party regarded as

influential over him or her. Indirect methods often leave little or no evidence. Which method is chosen will depend on its relative cost effectiveness (Georgiou 2004).

- *When they should lobby.* Sutton (1984) suggests that the most effective time to lobby accounting standard setters is at an early stage in the development of the standard. Standard setters' thoughts at this stage are likely to be just crystallising. Because of this, the probability of influencing the outcome is high.
- *What arguments they should use to support their position.*

Lobby groups

The standard-setting environment is different in the United States from that in Australia. Nonetheless, lobbying is a force in almost all standard-setting environments. Any individual, business, professional association or regulator with an interest in the direction of the standard-setting process can become a lobbyer but some of these are more involved, and more successful, than others.

Reflecting on standard setting by America's FASB, Staubus (1995) offered valuable insights into the competition among interest groups for the control of an activity in which more than one group has an interest. (Remember that multiple interest groups have been identified as having an interest in standard setting.)

The conceptual framework's mission of decision usefulness makes end-users the fundamental group when listing those with an interest in the products of the financial reporting process. However, users are not a homogeneous group. Staubus divides users into two groups:

- casual, nonprofessional users
- full-time professional users.

Casual, nonprofessional users have difficulty defining what information they require, making them a weak constituency, rarely motivated to lobby on proposals of standards setters. For example, the harmonisation of accounting standards was a major step for Australian accounting standard setting. The move was promoted by the CLERP. User groups failed to provide input into the debate about the international harmonisation of Australia's accounting standards. Not one user group lodged a written submission to the CLERP (Collett et al. 2001, p. 179).

In contrast, full-time professional analysts spend much of their time seeking pertinent information to give them a comparative advantage over their competitors. Large institutional investors have specialist staff that focus on particular industries. They jealously guard the information they obtain through their efforts and skills, so they do not respond to exposure drafts in case the resulting standard may undermine their efforts.

Similarly, auditors respond but their views are sometimes criticised for not being independent in the standard-setting process.

Academics also come under criticism for their lack of comment on exposure drafts. This is attributed to the research process by which academics are rewarded by other academic scholars rather than by involvement in professional activities, including responding to exposure drafts.

Because financial reports are to managers what marks are to students, managers are more willing to lobby accounting standard setters. They are regarded as far more motivated than are members of any other group.

Staubus views the standard-setting process as dominated by managements. This phenomenon is known as 'regulatory capture', which is discussed further in the section on theories about regulation.

The Australian situation

In Australia, the history of standard setting includes many instances demonstrating the influence of political lobbying by various groups to achieve change. The demise of the Accounting Standards Review Board (ASRB) is an obvious example. The ASRB was a standard-setting board established by the federal government in 1984 to be independent of the accounting profession (the precursor to the AASB). The ASRB lasted only one term, forced out by pressure emanating from the various professional bodies, which lamented their loss of control over the standard-setting process (Collett et al. 2001).

Individual standards themselves have been vulnerable to the lobbying process as well, most noticeably, the mandatory status of Statement of Accounting Concepts (SAC) 4, part of Australia's original conceptual framework, which was withdrawn after influential lobbying by the G100, a group that represents corporate Australia.

More recently, reforms of Australia's corporate legislation led to the decision to adopt IFRSs rather than harmonise AASB standards with international ones. Although the original reform paper (CLERP paper no. 1) stated that international accounting standards (IASs) were not of a quality that Australia could adopt, it was nevertheless directed to work towards replacing its own standards with international ones.

This was despite opposition from the G100, from the big accounting firms, the professional accounting bodies, the major banks and academics. The impetus to adopt rather than harmonise seems to have come from the Australian Securities Exchange (ASX). It was the only organisation (other than the International Accounting Standards Committee, IASC) to make a written submission supporting the adoption of IASs. At the time, the ASX was planning its float as a public company. 'Through standard-setting reforms that reduce reporting requirements, it is likely that the ASX sought to facilitate offshore listings. Increased listings and easier access to offshore capital would boost the value of the Exchange and the success of the initial public offering' (Collett et al. 2001, p. 180).

Greater insight into the political machinations associated with Australian accounting standard setting can be obtained by reading Walker and Robinson's (1994) analysis of the introduction of cash flow reporting in Australia.

Harmonisation

One of the functions of the AASB is to participate in and contribute to the development of a single set of worldwide accounting standards. The concept of international **harmonisation** is much older than the AASB. The idea can be traced to the 1972 World Accounting Congress, held in Sydney. It was at this conference that the concept of an IASC was developed.

harmonisation: The adoption of the content and wording of IASB standards, except where there is a need to change words to accommodate Australia's legislative requirements

Australia embarked on its international harmonisation program because benefits were expected from reducing diversity in international accounting practice (Collett et al. 2001).

Three main benefits were identified:

- International comparability of financial statements would increase, which should encourage the flow of international investment and increase the international markets' operational efficiency.
- The cost of capital should decrease because the risk associated with not fully understanding the financial reports of enterprises produced under a different accounting regime is reduced.
- By removing the need for enterprises to produce two or more financial reports to comply with differing standards, listing rules or regulations, reporting costs should be lowered.

Australia and the European Union (EU) adopted IFRSs on 1 January 2005. This means that approximately 90 countries have adopted IFRSs or have based their national standards on them. Within Asia, China, Japan, Thailand, Hong Kong and Singapore have also adopted the international standards, although the details of their standards reveal differences from IASs (Quinn 2004).

The outcomes for national standard setters

The adoption of IASs has implications for standard setters in Australia, the EU and many countries in Asia. The main ones are discussed in the following sections.

National standard modifications

Australia's approach has been to adopt the content and wording of IASB standards. Words are changed only when there is a need to take account of the Australian legislative environment. For example, there is a need to include references to Australia's *Corporations Act 2001*. Similarly, the Malaysian Accounting Standards Board sees its role as screening each IFRS to ensure that it complies with Malaysia's legislation (House 2004).

Additionally, in its quest to provide high-quality financial reporting, the AASB may require additional disclosures in adopted IFRSs or may limit the number of optional treatments and disclosure requirements. These changes do not affect the ability of an Australian reporting enterprise to comply with international standards.

International accounting standards focus on for-profit enterprises. The AASB has responsibility for setting standards for all reporting enterprises, including the government and not-for-profit sectors. The AASB must therefore include additional text in international standards to deal with situations applicable to not-for-profit enterprises and governmental entities. The AASB also writes separate standards for these entities if there are important issues peculiar to that sector that are best dealt with in separate standards.

Technical input and regional insight for the IASB

The IASB's constitution requires that it shares research and standard-setting projects with its seven 'liaison' standard-setting boards: Australia, the UK, the United States, Germany, France, Japan and Canada. Australia, in its role as a liaison board, also represents New Zealand.

During the transition to IFRSs, many international standard-setting boards expressed concern that they would become 'rubber stamps' for standards in which they had not been involved (House 2004). The EU has ensured that its national boards are involved in the standard-setting process by using the European Financial Reporting Advisory Group to canvass member countries about particular standards. Concerns are then channelled to the IASB.

Asian accounting standards boards also worry about the lack of opportunities for communicating with the IASB (House 2004). Resources, or the lack thereof, are a problem for Asian boards, which must screen IFRSs to ensure their compliance with national legislation.

To overcome these difficulties, each member of the IASB has liaison responsibilities for some certain countries within regions. Those members are expected to organise regional meetings and to create regional associations between national standard-setting boards. Of particular value, the expertise of lesser-developed countries is used on issues relevant to hyperinflation and the small enterprise project.

Summary

Understand the institutional framework of Australian accounting standard setting.

- The FRC is the oversight body. It appoints the standards setters other than the chair of the AASB. The AASB is responsible for:
  - developing a conceptual framework
  - making accounting standards
  - contributing to a set of worldwide standards.
- The IAC is a committee of the AASB. It monitors the work program of the International Financial Reporting Interpretations Committee (IFRIC) and makes recommendations to the AASB.

Explain and define an accounting standard.

- Accounting standards are authoritative statements that guide the preparation of financial statements.

Distinguish principles-based from rules-based standards.

- Principles-based standards are based on a statement of accounting principle that is consistent with the objective for accounting as outlined in the conceptual framework. The standard derives from, and is consistent with, that conceptual framework.
- Principles-based standards should not allow exceptions.
- Principles-based standards require professional judgement.
- Rules-based standards are characterised by quantitative tests, exceptions, a high level of detail and, often, internal inconsistencies.
- Rules-based standards minimise the use of professional judgement.

Define regulation and explain the reasons the production of accounting information is regulated.

- Regulation is the intervention in an activity by a party nominally independent of those engaged in the activity. Signalling theory disputes whether accounting information needs to be regulated because reporting enterprises have incentives to distinguish themselves from other reporting enterprises. The cost of capital for a reporting enterprise provides the incentive to provide accounting information.
- Public interest theory says that accounting is regulated to correct inefficient or inequitable market practices. Accounting information is a public good so, without regulation, it is either under- or overproduced.
- The 'bushfire' approach says that accounting is regulated to overcome the stigma for accounting created by crises such as unexpected corporate collapses.
- Capture theory says that interested bodies 'capture' the regulatory process The incentive to capture the regulatory body is to claim for those doing the capturing the valuable benefits created through regulation.

Understand why standard setting is a political process.

- Various parties have conflicting interests in reporting enterprises. Standards result in wealth transfers among these parties. Incentives differ between these parties to participate in the standard-setting process. Society must bear the losses that unexpected corporate collapses impose on it. Society, through the media, usually blames accounting for these collapses.

Explain the process of harmonisation of accounting standards.

- Australia embarked on its international harmonisation program because of the perceived benefits in doing so:
  - international comparability of financial statements
  - reduced cost of capital
  - eliminating redundant reporting.
- Australia adopts the content and wording of international standards, although some changes may be made. It also provides technical input and regional insight into the international standard-setting process.

Key terms

accounting standards   65
harmonisation   79
principles-based standards   66
regulation   69
rules-based standards   66

Review questions

3.1   In what sense are accounting standards 'standards' in the general meaning of the word?

3.2   How do principle-based standards differ from rules-based standards?

3.3   What are the functions of accounting standards?

3.4   What do you think the standard-setting process should achieve?

3.5   Justify Australia's approach of imposing its set of accounting standards on all reporting enterprises, irrespective of whether they are profit seeking.

3.6   Outline the functions of the FRC, AASB and IAC.

3.7   Define regulation.

3.8   In what ways does accounting standard setting conform to your definition?

3.9   If the standard-setting process should achieve better information, what criteria would identify better information?

3.10   Is the setting of accounting standards desirable for society? If so, who should set standards?

3.11   How does good financial reporting add value to companies?

3.12   Are interested parties behaving ethically when they try to influence the standard-setting process?

3.13   Explain the statement that 'information is the oil that lubricates markets'. How can this statement be used to justify the regulation of accounting information?

3.14   In your opinion, do the benefits from regulating accounting information outweigh the costs? Justify your answer.

3.15 How do you reconcile the 'adoption' of international accounting standards with the process of 'harmonisation'?

3.16 With particular reference to the following opinion expressed by Watts and Zimmerman, discuss whether accounting standards setting is a 'two-edged sword':

> Regulation affects the nature of the audit. It expands the audit...
> [R]egulation provides the auditor with the opportunity to
> perform additional services and lobby on accounting standards
> on clients' behalf. Regulation also provides the auditor with
> the opportunity to lobby for increasing accounting complexity
> because of its audit fee effect (Watts & Zimmerman 1986).

3.17 Drawing on your knowledge of the conceptual framework and of principles-based standards, discuss the following statement:

> Ultimately, it is the underlying economic substance that must
> drive the development of the scope of standards, if... standards
> are to remain stable and meaningful (US Securities and Exchange
> Commission, www.sec.gov).

3.18 Sutton (1984) states that accounting standard setting is a political lobbying process, and as such offers several opportunities and means for interested parties to influence its outcomes. What are the opportunities that Sutton mentions? What methods do lobbyists employ to influence the outcomes? How will Australia's adoption of international standards effect lobbying activity by interested parties?

Application questions

3.19 *The Australian* newspaper reported in October 2004 that many Australian companies would be affected by the new standards (IAS 32) for 2005 in relation to reset preference shares (hybrids). These hybrids had a unique debt and equity mix: although they were borrowings, they were classified as equity, not debt; they delivered franking credits to investors and were paid out of profits.
   (a) Refer to chapter 2 on the conceptual framework. How does the framework distinguish liabilities from equity?
   (b) What advantages might the hybrids classified as equity deliver to a company issuing them?
   (c) Reporting on the substance of a transaction has long been important in accounting. Speculate on how Australian companies have been able to include hybrids as equity rather than liabilities.

3.20 Coca-Cola Amatil conducted a campaign against Australia's adoption of IFRSs in 2004. The company lobbied against requirements that meant Coca-Cola Amatil's balance sheet values would have to be written down by as much as $1.9 billion.

(a) What is meant by the term 'lobbying'?

(b) Who would be likely targets of Coca-Cola Amatil's lobbying activities?

(c) Why would adoption of international standards so heavily affect Coca-Cola Amatil?

(d) What other companies might have lobbied against the adoption of the intangibles standard?

3.21 ResMed, a sleep disorder specialist company, is listed on both the New York Stock Exchange and the ASX. The introduction of international accounting standards meant that the company was thinking of delisting from the ASX. The company's chief financial officer said that adoption meant that 'we're about to enter a whole new field of quicksand' (Charles 2004).

(a) International accounting standards would move Australia's standards closer to those of the United States. Why then would ResMed consider delisting after their introduction?

(b) What are the difficulties of listing on two exchanges in different countries?

(c) Speculate on the reasons ResMed's chief financial officer would say that the introduction of international accounting standards was a 'field of quicksand'.

3.22 During 2004, much publicity was given to the move by James Hardie Industries to transfer its domicile to The Netherlands, and to move its asbestos liabilities to a foundation separate from the company. One of the reasons touted for these moves was the impending introduction of an accounting standard that would have required the company to include the present value of all likely future asbestos liabilities in its accounts.

(a) What is the definition of a liability?

(b) What are the recognition tests for the inclusion of liabilities in the financial statements?

(c) How does the long gestation period of diseases resulting from exposure to asbestos complicate the calculation of future liabilities for James Hardie?

(d) Debate the role that the public backlash against James Hardie's moves played in subsequent changes to the foundation holding asbestos liabilities.

(e) Debate whether the executives who made the decisions could have behaved more ethically.

case**study**   **3.1**

AIFRS: the complex issues and the way forward — a review of contemporary issues affecting our clients

This article highlights a number of issues covered in the PwC publication 'AIFRS: the complex issues and the way forward — a review of contemporary issues affecting our clients'. The text has been taken from this publication. For more information on these and other issues, please refer to the publication, which is available on the PwC Australian IFRS website: www.pwc.com/au/ifrs.

Since the introduction of IFRS and Australian equivalent to International Financial Reporting Standards (AIFRS) on 1 January 2005, the reporting landscape has changed significantly. And as can be expected with a change of this scale, concerns have arisen. Many of our clients are questioning not only the technical reporting challenges that the new standards present, but also the broader overarching issues. Most notable is the perception that AIFRS has overcomplicated our accounting.

AIFRS was heralded as bringing the advantage that information would be more easily understood and interpreted by users of financial statements. Yet it is well known that AIFRS financial reports are longer than those prepared under AGAAP. Companies could be forgiven for thinking that such voluminous information might have the opposite effect on users.

We are encouraging the IASB to consider developing a disclosure framework to guide it when mandating disclosures so that financial reports are not cluttered with information that obscures what is most important to users. This would involve establishing criteria:

- to identify disclosures that provide limited value and drop them from the standards
- that new disclosures must meet to be mandated.

Achieving a single set of high-quality, understandable and enforceable global accounting standards is the 'holy grail' of accounting — with its aim of overcoming the costs and inefficiencies that stem from differences in accounting methods.

The IASB is working towards that end with the US Financial Accounting Standards Board (FASB). Their first step is to improve certain standards, which is expected to overcome the need for companies with secondary listings in the US to prepare two sets of financial reports or to reconcile their reports to US GAAP by 2009.

Although only a few Australian companies fall into that category, all Australian reporting entities will be affected by the outcome. It is therefore not surprising that some disquiet has emerged — sometimes expressed as 'We signed up to adopt IFRS, not US GAAP'.

We are encouraging the IASB to obtain the SEC's commitment to discourage its staff from insisting on the application of US GAAP guidance when reviewing IFRS filings.

The IASB has recognised that companies are still finding the transition challenging. Although it will continue to develop, amend and potentially issue new standards and interpretations, adoption will not be mandatory until 2009. The next few years of stability will be a welcome chance to come to grips with the standards currently in place.

Source: This article appeared in *The Australian.*

1. PWC is concerned with the overregulation of standard setting in Australia. Explain its perspective in terms of public interest theory.
2. How can PWC encourage the IASB to consider its complaints?
3. Who does PWC claim to represent in lobbying the IASB for change?
4. Before harmonisation, interested parties wishing to influence outcomes of standard setting would lobby the AASB or its members. Debate whether lobbying activity after harmonisation should be directed at the AASB or the international standard-setting body or its members.
5. How are the US reporting standards more prescriptive than the current Australian IFRSs? Why would United States – IASB convergence be a cause of nervousness among Australian companies?

case**study** 3.2

Break for non-profit sector on onerous rules

Charities, private schools and sports clubs will be given some relief from the convoluted and meaningless agonies of preparing their accounts to meet international accounting standards.

Australia's accounting standard setters plan to introduce a special set of rules that effectively quarantine the non-profit sector from the International Financial Reporting Standards, which came into force last year.

The changes are also expected to insulate the public sector from IFRS.

Small business might also get some relief from next year, with the London-based International Accounting Standards Board preparing a special tier of accounting rules that small and medium enterprises can use.

Non-profit organisations claim the new standards are designed for listed companies but not for charities and community associations.

Problems include the relevance of bottom-line reporting when for non-profit organisations, the issue is more about whether the services are adequate.

The international standards also have no provision for placing a value on voluntary assistance, which is the lifeblood of non-profit organisations.

And then there is the problem with balance sheets. Whereas balance sheets for a listed company have details about liability, assets and equity, most non-profit organisations have no equity. And while donations for charities and cricket clubs come in on an annual or irregular basis, receiving money in one period and not spending it immediately does not make for a surplus.

Non-profit organisations raised these concerns at a meeting last week with the Australian Accounting Standards Board and the Financial Reporting Council.

AASB chairman David Boymal said the complaints from non-profit organisations were much the same as those raised by government agencies and SMEs. The AASB will develop a set of rules to suit the needs of the non-profit sector.

'You mightn't call them international any more but you might have variations on the international theme that would better suit their sector,' Professor Boymal said.

'The sort of topics they highlighted are not impossible to fix. It's just a matter of finding out exactly what their issues are and tackling them.

'There is really a strong push that says IFRS might be fine if you are a listed entity but what about the rest of us? The standards are regarded as overly complex, overly detailed, and there are additional complications and added detail that don't seem to produce any more meaningful information for these entities.'

Source: This article appeared in *The Age*.

1. How are current accounting standards regarded as inappropriate for not-for-profit entities?
2. Research the IASB policy on the reporting of intangibles. How might the IASB approach affect non-profit organisations and their reporting requirements?
3. The AASB publishes exposure drafts and standards on its website (www.aasb.com.au). Research the exposure drafts or standards relevant to the non-profit sector. How are they different from the reporting requirements for the private sector?
4. The AASB is responsible for standard setting for non-profit and government sectors, as well as the private sector. What are the Australian requirements for government departments and statutory bodies, and how are they different from general purpose financial statements?
5. The IASB is considering alterations to IFRSs for small and medium enterprises. Research the changes proposed. What, if any, input have the AASB and other Australian organisations had into this process?

Recommended readings

Collett, PH, Godfrey, JM & Hrasky, SL 2001, 'International harmonisation: cautions from the Australian experience', *Accounting Horizons*, vol. 15, no. 2, pp. 171–83.

Walker, RG 1987, 'Australia's ASRB: a case study of political activity and regulatory "capture"', *Accounting and Business Research*, vol. 17, no. 67, pp. 269–86.

—— & Robinson, SP 1994, 'Competing regulatory agencies with conflicting agendas: setting standards for cash flow reporting in Australia', *Abacus*, vol. 30, no. 2, pp. 119–37.

Watts, RL & Zimmerman, JL 1978, 'Towards a positive theory of the determination of accounting standards', *The Accounting Review*, vol. LIII, pp. 112–34.

—— 1979, 'The demand for and the supply of accounting theories: the market for excuses', *The Accounting Review*, vol. LIV, pp. 273–305.

References

Charles, M 2004, 'Resmed loses sleep over listing', *Herald Sun*, 29 April, p. 29.

Collett, PH, Godfrey, JM & Hrasky, SL 2001, 'International harmonisation: cautions from the Australian experience', *Accounting Horizons*, vol. 15, no. 2, pp. 171–83.

Georgiou, George, 2004, 'Corporate lobbying on accounting standards: methods, timing and perceived effectiveness', *Abacus*, vol. 40, no. 2, pp. 219–37.

Guthrie, J & Parker, L 2003, 'Editorial introduction: AAAJ and accounting legitimacy in a post-Enron world', *Accounting, Auditing & Accountability Journal*, vol. 16, no. 1, pp. 13–18.

Hakansson, NH 1983, 'Comments on Weick and Ross', *The Accounting Review*, vol. 58, no. 2, pp. 381–4.

House, J 2004, 'Financial reporting: national standard-setters — endangered species', *Accountancy*, vol. 133, no. 1327, pp. 86–7.

Maines, LA, Bartov, E, Fairfield, P, Hirst, DE, Iannaconi, TE, Mallett, R, Schrand, C & Vincent, L 2003, 'Evaluating concepts-based vs rules-based approaches to standard setting', *Accounting Horizons*, vol. 17, no. 1, pp. 73–90.

Mitnick, BM 1980, *The political economy of regulation*, Columbia University Press, New York.

Posner, RA 1974, 'Theories of economic regulation', *Bell Journal of Economics*, pp. 335–58.

Quinn, LR 2004, 'What's the state of international standards?', *Strategic Finance*, vol. 85, no. 10, pp. 35–40.

Ross, SA 1977, 'The determination of financial structure: The incentive signalling approach', *Bell Journal of Economics*, vol. 8, pp. 23–40.

Shortridge, RT & Myring, M 2004, 'Defining principles-based accounting standards', *The CPA Journal*, vol. 74, no. 8, pp. 34–8.

Staubus, GJ 1995, 'Issues in the accounting standards-setting process', *Accounting theory, a contemporary review*, ed. by Jones, S Romano, C & Ratnatunga, J, Harcourt Brace, Sydney, pp. 189–215.

Sutton, TG 1984, 'Lobbying of accounting standard-setting bodies in the UK and the USA: a Downsian analysis', *Accounting, Organizations & Society*, vol. 9, no. 1, pp. 81–95.

Walker, RG & Robinson, SP 1994, 'Competing regulatory agencies with conflicting agendas: setting standards for cash flow reporting in Australia', *Abacus*, vol. 30, no. 2, pp. 119–37.

Watts, RL & Zimmerman, JL 1979, 'The demand for and the supply of accounting theories: the market for excuses', *The Accounting Review*, vol. LIV, pp. 273–305.

—— 1986, *Positive accounting theory*, Prentice Hall, Englewood Cliffs, New Jersey.

4 MEASUREMENT AND ITS PROBLEMS

After reading this chapter, you should be able to:

- understand why measurement is needed in financial reporting
- explain what measurement is and what is involved in measuring
- identify and explain the problems with measurement in accounting
- identify and apply a range of attributes that could be measured and explain the advantages and problems with these
- be aware of the range of measurements currently used in accounting and the influences on choices of measures.

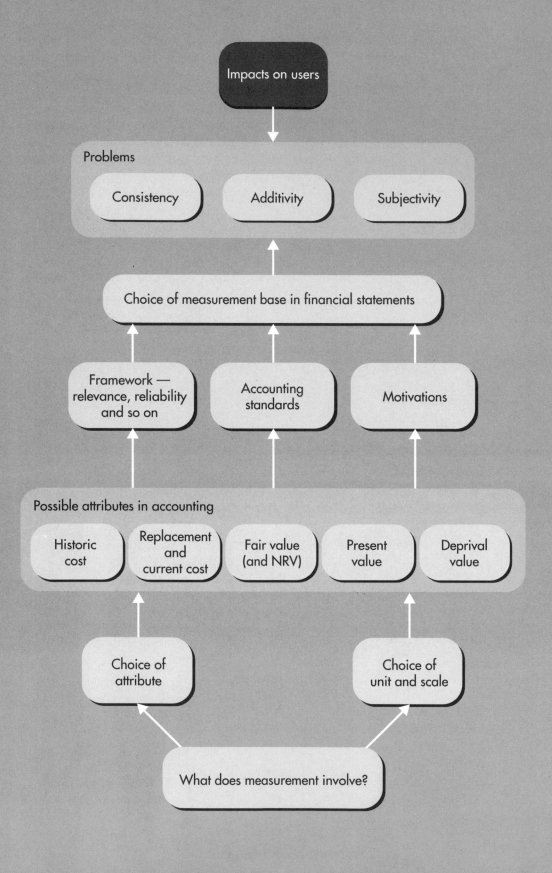

Introduction

Measurement is perhaps the most controversial issue in financial accounting. From your previous studies in accounting, you will have noticed that different items are measured in different ways (e.g. present values are used to decide the amount of finance leases; the lower of cost or net realisable value is used to measure inventory), or a choice is given how to measure financial statement items (e.g. property can be measured at either cost or fair value). This chapter considers the process of measurement, and some of the reasons for and issues and problems with the different measures used in financial statements. In addition, specific measures are examined.

The need for measurement in financial reporting

The next section considers what measurement means and involves in more detail. We can think of measurement in financial reporting as simply choosing and placing a money amount (i.e. a number of dollars) against an item in the financial statements (such as an asset or revenue). Imagine if these items were not measured. Can you think of a balance sheet or income statement with just a list of items, such as different types of expense, with no numbers attached? How would you assess financial performance or position, or compare over time or even among entities? These statements would be of little use to anyone. The usefulness of financial statements depends on two key decisions made by accountants and standard setters:

- What items should be included or excluded from the financial statements?
- How should the items that are included be measured?

Furthermore, some items are defined in terms of increases and decreases in other items. For example, the definition of income requires us to identify if there has been an increase in assets or a decrease in liabilities (IASB 1989, para 69). 'But whether there has been an increase in the stated amount or value of assets and or a reduction of liabilities depends on how assets and liabilities are measured' (Loftus 2003, p. 306).

So you should see that the definition and recognition of financial statement items, and the usefulness of these statements, depend on measurement.

What measurement is and what it involves

Dictionary definitions are:

- **measurement** is the act (Macquarie dictionary) or process (Cambridge dictionary) of measuring
- a **measure** is defined as:
  - the quantity, weight, height and so on of something
  - a unit used for stating the size, weight and so on of something
  - an agreed unit of this quantity (Heineken dictionary)
  - the extent or dimensions of a thing as determined by measuring (Oxford dictionary).

> **measurement:** The act or process of measuring

> **measure:** The quantity, weight, height and so on of something or a unit used for stating the size, weight and so on, of something or the extent or dimensions of a thing as determined by measuring

These definitions show that measurement is a process that involves two steps: deciding *what* to measure and then *how* to measure it.

Deciding *what* to measure: attributes

The first step requires identifying an attribute (some dimension or quality or characteristic) of an item to measure. For a person, this could be height, weight, age, intelligence or health. For a building (which would usually be an asset as defined in accounting), it could be the height, floor space, the cost, the cash flows it will generate or its selling price. You should see usually several possible attributes could be measured and there is a need to choose which to measure. The choice will depend on the reason or need to measure in the first place: what you are trying to achieve by measuring and how the measure will be used. For example, a bank would not find the measure of floor space for a potential borrower's property particularly useful; the important measure for the bank is the property's selling price, to ensure that it is sufficient if the loan is not repaid (although a valuer trying to estimate the selling price would use floor space as one of the measures in estimating the value of a property in most cases). The selling price is an example of a financial attribute. In financial accounting the focus is on *financial* attributes that can be expressed in terms of money — such as costs or values — not on physical attributes.

Deciding *how* to measure: scale and unit

Once the attribute is chosen, the second step in the process of measurement is to decide *how* that attribute is to be measured: which amount is to be used to describe or express the attribute. This involves choosing a scale and a unit.

For example, in measuring a person's size you could use alternative scales.

- One scale would be using clothes or dress sizes, such as size 12 or 14. This is a type of *interval* scale. An interval scale represents the characteristic or attribute at different levels but the levels progress at equal distances and represent similar changes. Another example of an interval scale is temperature.
- Another way of measuring size would be to measure weight (say as 65.32 kg). This is an example of what is called a ratio scale. You should see that with a scale such as kilograms, the scale measures the attribute 'exactly' and provides more information about the attribute than a simple interval scale in which the interval (such as the dress size) must be chosen that is closest to what is being measured. Ratio scales have a 'true' zero. This enables better comparisons among items and allows mathematical analysis. For example, if one person weighs 50 kg and another 75 kg, it is known that the second person weighs 50 per cent more than the first. The same assumptions cannot be made if measures are compared on an interval scale; for example, a person with a dress size 12 is not necessarily 50 per cent bigger than a person with a dress size 8. Furthermore, there is no 'true' zero; although the United States has a zero dress size, this does not mean that the dress has 'no' size.

In financial reporting, money amounts are used (in Australia, dollars) as the scale of measurement. This is a ratio scale.

The unit of measurement

A unit of measurement also needs to be chosen. Given the choice of dollars as the scale, there is a choice between two different units. The scale means that the number of dollars (the amount of money) is measured but which dollars? There are essentially two alternatives:

- The unit is simply the quantity or number of physical dollars involved or transacted. This is usually referred to as nominal dollars. For example, if you purchased a piece of inventory and paid $1000 for it, the nominal dollars are simply the number of dollars involved in the transaction (i.e. $1000).
- The alternative choice of unit views dollars not as simply physical quantities (i.e. the number of dollars) but recognises that dollars represent purchasing power. The value of a particular unit of money (such as a dollar) changes over time. For example, if you spent $10 000 to buy a piece of land ten years ago, would you expect to be able to purchase the same land today for $10 000? The answer would normally be no. Why is this?
  - Changes in the general price of goods and services (such as those caused by inflation) often mean that the value of a dollar (in terms of what you can buy with it) reduces over time.
  - The price of particular items changes over time. For example, in Australia the value of land has increased over the past five years by more than 30 per cent. Other items (such as DVD players and digital cameras) have had decreases in price over this period.

Because of these factors, an alternative unit is *constant* dollars. This uses the number of dollars involved in a transaction but then adjusts or measures these in terms of equivalent purchasing power *now*, so is measuring the underlying value of the money (dollars) involved in the transactions, not simply the physical quantities of money involved.

Which unit to use

In practice, financial accounting traditionally uses nominal dollars in measuring many items, although constant dollars have been used under some current-cost accounting systems (usually these were additional financial statements) and you should see that measuring the present values takes into account the time value of money. Which unit should be used depends on the purpose and your objective in measuring the items. Some of the problems and criticisms of current accounting practice relate to the use of nominal dollars but there are also problems with measuring constant dollars.

A simple example can illustrate this point. Assume two entities that have only one asset each (an item of land). These entities generate revenues by renting their land. Entity 1 purchased its land 15 years ago for $50 000. It has generated a profit of $10 000 in the past year. Entity 2 purchased its land five years ago for $100 000. It has also generated a profit of $10 000 in the past year.

To assess the profitability of an entity, the profit is usually compared with the resources (assets) used to generate it. By this measure, Entity 1 is twice as profitable as Entity 2, despite generating the same profit from the same asset. If the asset was not land, and it was depreciated, this difference would be even more extreme, because Entity 1 would have lower depreciation expenses (because it paid less for the asset than Entity 2), so its profit would be higher.

One of the arguments against the use of nominal dollars as the unit of measurement is that it results in this type of comparison.

If constant dollars are used as the unit, what information does this provide? Assume the following:

- Over the past 15 years, the overall increase in prices (such as inflation estimated by a consumer price index) was 20 per cent, and 2 per cent over the past five years (in other words, the purchasing power of the dollar has decreased by these amounts over these periods).

If the cost is measured in terms of constant dollars, then the $50 000 that Entity 1 spent on the land is equivalent to spending $60 000 today; the $100 000 that Entity 2 spent is the equivalent to spending $102 000 today. But what does this mean? It does not necessarily represent the change in the cost of land; the price of land on average could have increased or decreased very differently from the general price changes; furthermore, the price of the particular items of land held by Entity 1 or Entity 2 may have changed differently from the average. So the usefulness of this type of unit in measurement is also questionable.

Learning tips
Do you know...

4.1   *Measurement is a process that involves deciding what to measure (the attribute) and how to measure it (the scale and unit).*

4.2   *The attribute and scale chosen will depend on the purpose of measurement.*

4.3   *In practice, the unit used in financial accounting is nominal dollars.*

■ Issues and problems with measurement in accounting

A person asks three others what is 2 + 2? The first person, a mathematician, says I can prove in two hours that the answer is definitely 4. The second person, a statistician, says it lies between 3.999 and 4.001. The accountant answers, 'What would you like it to be?'. This is an old joke about accountants that you may have seen before but today the joke is still appropriate. Why? There are two key reasons the measures in accounting are potentially as flexible as the joke suggests. First, there is still no agreement on which measures should be used. This allows a choice (often even within accounting standards) of a range of possible measures for the same items and different measures for different items. Second, there is often subjectivity involved in the actual measurements. As noted, measurement involves putting numbers against the items in the financial statements. A 'number' looks very precise and seems to present a view of an item that is definite and beyond question. As Margenau stated, 'the trouble with the idea of measurement is its seeming clarity, its obviousness, its implicit claim to finality in any investigative discourse' (1959, p. 163, cited in Hampton & Bishop 1998, p. 44).

Before considering specific measures that could be used, this section looks at some of the issues and problems that cause measurement in accounting to be less precise or exact than it would seem.

Requirements and guidance for measurement in accounting

The Framework requires that for an item that meets the definition of an element to be included in the financial statements, it must have *a cost or value* that can be measured *reliably* (para. 83(b)). But the Framework does not require or even recommend any particular measurement basis, and many items may have alternative costs or values (attributes) that can be measured reliably. Chapter 2 noted that this is seen as one of the major weaknesses of the current Framework.

However, the choice of *which* reliable measure to use can be guided by other principles in the Framework (such as the objectives and qualitative characteristics of relevance, reliability, understandability and comparability).

The role of objectives and qualitative characteristics

The information in financial statements is provided to help users make decisions. The Framework identifies a very broad group of users, and the range of decisions they make is also very wide. Users may need different information for these different decisions. For example:

- In decisions concerning the ability of an entity to pay its debts, users may prefer measures that reflect the amount that could be obtained from assets if these were sold.
- In decisions relating to future profitability, measures that reflect the future cash expected to be generated from assets may be more useful.

Consider how well the guidance in the framework helps to answer questions such as:

- What minimum level of each characteristic is required?
- How can one choose between a very reliable measure that is less relevant and a more relevant measure that is less reliable?
- How can one choose between a measure that is very relevant to some users but not as relevant as an alternative measure is to other users?
- To aid comparability, should how other entities measure items be considered, even if the measure is less relevant or reliable?

It is likely that individual accountants will answer these questions differently. Furthermore, it has been argued that without details of the decision-making context (i.e. the specific decision that is being made) and the preferences of decision makers, it is impossible to use abstract set of criteria (such as relevance or reliability) to make choices between alternatives (Liang 2001, p. 231).

The role of subjectivity

As noted, applying the objectives and qualitative characteristics in the conceptual framework when making decisions about measurements involves judgement and thus makes these decisions subjective. Indeed, if the need to make judgements about other principles (apart from measurement) such as the definitions of items, or the use of estimates, is considered, the possible variations in accounting practice are enormous. Subjectivity also affects other aspects of the financial statements.

Given the complexities of modern-day business, and the differences between the circumstances of one entity and another, it is preferable to allow flexibility so that accounting choices and measurements can be made that best reflect the economic substance of the entity concerned. However, flexibility also allows opportunistic accounting choices, in which the accounting methods and measures are chosen to reflect a biased picture of the financial performance and position of an entity. Recent examples of accounting failures (such as Enron, WorldCom and HIH) have brought this to the forefront. The opportunistic measurement of financial statement items in particular can mislead users.

The focus on individual items and a system of measurement

One criticism of measurement in accounting is that it is not holistic. An ideal system of measurement chooses attributes, units and scales that best meet the objectives and purpose of the measurement. The argument is that you need some coherent system of measurement — the measures of identical parts need to be consistent and fit together — to make any sense or provide useful information. The following In Focus vignette illustrates the problem when there are inconsistencies in the measurement system.

 Metric mixup melted Mars probe

An error with metric measurements caused NASA to send a $125-million Mars probe on a kamikaze dive into the planet's atmosphere last week, agency officials said yesterday.

Controllers thought they were getting navigation information about Mars Climate Orbiter in metric units. Instead the data was in English standard units.

As a result, engineers sent the probe on a course that took it too deep in the Martian atmosphere, where it burned up while attempting to settle into orbit.

Deeply embarrassed NASA officials don't know why the mistake was not caught during the probe's nine-month, 670-million-km flight to Mars.

'The failure here was not that human error occurred,' said Carl Pilcher, science director for solar system exploration at NASA headquarters in Washington, D.C.

'Human error occurs all the time. But even so we have a tremendous success rate because we have systems that detect and correct the errors. The problem here is that our system failed to do that.'

NASA officials said the orbiter's sistership — Mars Polar Lander, currently en route to Mars — is not in danger.

'Even if the same thing is going on with Mars Polar Lander, there's absolutely no problem in correcting it' in time to ensure a safe arrival, said Tom Gavin, deputy director for space and earth science at NASA's jet propulsion laboratory in Pasadena, California.

The two spacecraft are part of a joint, $356-million mission to search for water on Mars.

Climate Orbiter's job was to track water vapour in the atmosphere, while Polar Lander is to land near the Martian south pole and dig for ice.

Mars Climate Orbiter's flight to Mars began in December with a launch from Cape Canaveral Air Station. Polar Lander followed with a January liftoff.

Climate Orbiter's journey appeared trouble-free.

As planned, engineers periodically fired the spacecraft's smaller thrusters in brief bursts to keep it properly pointed.

But it was those manoeuvres that caused the problem.

To carry out the firings, NASA controllers relied on data supplied by the spacecraft's manufacturer, Lockheed Martin Astronautics in Denver, Colorado.

Lockheed Martin engineers provided the information in the English measurement of pounds.

But NASA controllers mistakenly believed the data was in metric units called newtons.

By the time the orbiter reached Mars last week, the bad numbers had put the spacecraft on its catastrophic path into the atmosphere.

Source: This article appeared in the *Edmonton Sun*.

The accounting Framework requires measurement to be primarily (or at least initially) considered at the level of *individual* items (or elements). Whether *an* item (i.e. an individual asset or liability for example) has a cost or value that can be measured reliably is looked at to determine whether it can be included in the financial statements.

At a practical level, because there is no explicit framework to consider measurement in relation to the financial statements as a *whole*; measurement tends to be considered in the context of the individual parts or elements of the financial statements. Accounting standards do tend to reduce some variation, in the sense that these often require the same types of assets to be measured in the same way (e.g. if you use fair value to measure an item of property, all items in that class of property must also be measured at fair value) but these requirements only reduce inconsistencies within classes of items and not among classes and not necessarily among entities.

It has been argued that accounting has no 'system' of measurement and there is no real *overall theory* of measurement in accounting; rather, there are just alternative methods of measurement. An opposing view is that there can be no 'one' measurement basis because of the broad range of users and their decisions and the variety of items to be measured.

The issue of additivity

Although individual items are measured in the financial statements, mathematical calculations are then done using the measures. For example:

• In the balance sheet, totals for assets, liabilities and net assets are calculated.
• In the income statement, totals for revenues and expenses are calculated and deducted to arrive at the final profit amount.

But given the range of different attributes that are measured in accounting, many argue that these types of mathematical computations cannot legitimately be used; that the financial statements cannot, or should not, be added up.

Mixing attributes

A simple example illustrates this criticism. Assume for three people, Peter, Kevin and Susanna, various attributes are measured using the unit centimetres and arrive at the following measurements: Peter's height is 156 cm; Kevin's waist is 85 cm; Susanna's head is 32 cm around.

Now put these in a list and add them:

Peter	156
Kevin	85
Susanna	32
Total	**273**

What does this 'total' mean? Is it correct to add the measures of these different attributes? How useful is the information provided by this total? You may think this is a ridiculous example, but in effect this is what is often done in accounting. If from a number of assets, some are measured at cost, some at present value and some at fair value, what does 'total assets' mean?

Mixing times and units

Measurement also needs to be undertaken within some temporal conditions. For example, if for all the 'people' in the example given, the same attribute, height, was measured, it would be expected perhaps that the individuals' heights would be measured at either the same age or the same point in time.

A criticism in accounting is that even if the same attributes are used, they are not always measured at consistent 'times'. Measures such as fair value do measure all items at one point in time but historic cost does not. Think also of the problems if different units are used (such as inches and centimetres or kilograms and pounds) and tried to add these or calculate ratios. Many argue that this is what is done in accounting by mixing past with current dollars.

Measures used in accounting

This section identifies and discusses the range of measures that are used, or have been suggested, in accounting and evaluates them by considering their advantages and disadvantages. Financial accounting currently uses what is called a mixed attribute model; in other words, different attributes are measured. Most can be seen as trying to measure different attributes relating to either costs or values.

The meanings of cost and value

Cost can be defined as the price paid to acquire, produce, accomplish or maintain anything (Macquarie dictionary); or something that is given, needed or lost to obtain a particular thing (Cambridge dictionary). Cost is normally

> **cost:** Something that is given, needed or lost to obtain a particular thing

thought of in terms of amounts of money but it also involves time, services, giving up of other assets and even other opportunities. The cost of education not only involves the direct costs of payment of fees but also the cost of the student's time, which could be spent working and earning money or enjoying him- or herself. These latter costs are referred to as opportunity costs, although these are not generally measured in financial reporting. You may find costs referred to as 'entry prices' because costs represent the amount that would need to be paid for an item (such as an asset) to be brought into the entity.

Value can be defined as the importance or worth of something for someone; utility or merit (Cambridge dictionary). Value is concerned with benefits. While cost represents some sacrifice made for obtaining an item, the

> **value:** The importance or worth of something for someone; utility or merit

value is what you get, or expect to get, from an item. People obtain value in many ways from different items; for example, a souvenir that reminds people of a memorable holiday has value to that person; a favourite DVD provides value through enjoyment. You should see that in these examples value is subjective. The souvenir will only be valuable to that particular individual; other people may not like that DVD, so it has no value to them. What makes something have value is its usefulness or worth to the particular individual (in economics, this is often referred to as its utility).

How items have value for businesses

Business entities, however, do not obtain satisfaction in terms of personal enjoyment but from cash flows. The value of something to a business entity is in its ability to provide or contribute to the generation of cash flows for the entity. An entity can benefit from an item in two ways, either:

- From *using* the item. For example, a building may be used as sales rooms to help generate sales revenue or rented out to provide cash flows from rent payments. Benefits from using an item are often referred to as the **'value in use'** of an item.

> **value in use:** The benefits from using an item, usually considered as the present value of the future cash flows associated with the item

• From *selling* the item. For example, inventory provides benefits when it is sold and generates sales revenues: an investment in gold will provide benefits when that investment is eventually sold. Benefits from selling an item are often referred to as the '**value in exchange**' of an item.

Of course, some items will have both a value in use and a value in exchange. An office building can be used by an entity or it could be sold. The entity will decide *what* to do with an individual item (whether to use it or sell it) by considering what provides the *most* benefits.

Deciding whether to use cost or value

The Framework allows an item to be measured at a cost *or* value. It has been argued that, conceptually, an item does not need to have a cost to be an asset so why then would cost be measured? That items are defined in terms of economic benefits suggests that values are more appropriate to measure. However, the decision whether to use a cost or value depends on considerations of the usefulness of the measure in terms of:

• relevance to particular decisions for particular users
• the relative reliability of different costs and values.

Specific costs and values

This section briefly looks at alternative costs and values that may be used in financial accounting, and consider the reasons for using these, and the issues and problems with each. The use of these costs or values primarily for measuring assets is illustrated but the principles and issues apply equally to the measurement of other items in the financial statements.

Historic cost

Historic cost is the amount of money (dollars) or equivalent sacrificed or given up to obtain an item. This is the traditional measure used in accounting, and is usually measured in nominal dollars — *in face* simply the number of dollars involved in the original transaction — although it can also be measured in constant dollars. *not change*

The main advantage of historic cost is its reliability. The amount paid for an item can usually be proved by documentation. It is an objective measure, usually easy to establish and understood by users.

Issues, disadvantages and criticisms

Despite, or even because of, its reliability and stability, historic cost has key issues associated with its use, including its relevance, its reliance on a stable monetary unit, its subjectivity and its exclusion of some intangibles. *limitation*

Relevance

The key criticism of this attribute is its relevance. Historic cost is a 'sunk' cost and cannot be changed by any future decision or actions. For example, if you purchased *sunk in the water* land 50 years ago for $20 000, how relevant is this cost for any decisions you need to make now? Once you have acquired an item, the amount you have paid for it (its historic cost) should not rationally influence decisions. *(not)*

The usefulness of historic cost is also questionable if you believe that users need information about the value of items. Cost can be an indicator of the *minimum* value ☆ you expected to get from an item *at the time* you purchased the item. We have all bought something thinking it will be useful and then found that it is not as suitable, or as useful, as we had thought. So after purchase, the historic cost may give no indication even of the minimum value of an item. *Maybe not useful for operating anymore after purchased!*

not show

Assumption of a stable monetary unit

As noted, the value of money changes. Some argue that because historic cost using nominal dollars does not account for this, it does not show the 'true' cost of an item. The cost of buying our piece of land 50 years later would be much higher than $20 000. Alternatively, if the land turns out to be contaminated, the cost of cleaning it up before using or selling it could be even higher.

Subjectivity

In practice, although historic cost is the basis for measurement, the measure that is reported in the financial statements is written-down historic cost (historic cost less accumulated depreciation). Depreciation involves using judgement to make decisions about how to allocate this historic cost over the period that the asset will generate benefits for the entity. This could provide opportunities for inconsistencies or manipulation, and threaten reliability. *it shows diff't aspects* { *cost* & *depreciation* }

Exclusions

The use of historic cost does restrict the recognition of some items. What if you have an item donated at no cost to the entity? What about items that are not purchased but are internally generated within the entity, such as goodwill? For many intangibles (such as internally generated brands) that are said to be of greater value and importance in the knowledge economy, it is difficult to establish the historic cost.

Replacement cost and current cost

An alternative cost that can be used in measurement is the cost to replace resources now. There are two different ways to measure the cost of replacing resources. The **replacement cost** of an item is the amount that would be paid at the current time to acquire an identical item. The focus here is on the cost of exactly the same item in the same condition as the one the entity currently holds. Sometimes this is calculated by using the replacement cost for a new item but adjusting it (by depreciation) to reflect the item's age. The **current cost** of an item is the lowest amount that would be paid at the current time to provide or replace the future economic benefits expected from the current item. This recognises that an entity may be able to obtain the same benefits from

> **replacement cost:** The amount that would be paid at the current time to acquire an identical item

> **current cost:** The lowest amount that would be paid at the current time to provide or replace the future economic benefits expected from the current item

different items, particularly with technological change. A simple example illustrates the differences between these two costs.

Assume that an entity uses a small loader or forklift to shift items in its warehouse to the delivery area. The loader originally cost $50 000 and is six years old.

To purchase a second-hand loader of the same type and age now would cost $30 000. This would be the *replacement cost* of the loader.

Alternatively, the entity could install a conveyer belt to move the items to the delivery area. This would cost $25 000. This would be the *current cost* of the loader. Although the item is not the same in form as the current item, it provides the same services or future economic benefits.

Why choose replacement or current cost?

Businesses need to consider the *current* cost of replacing resources (not what they originally paid for these resources). If resources are replaced, businesses then will need to pay the current prices for these, which may be quite different from historic cost if inflation is high or relative prices are changing. The second reason for using current cost is that it seems to be a compromise. As Ravlic sates it 'sits comfortably between the two extremes [of historic cost and fair value] and is able to cope with a greater range of accounting problems.' (1999, p. 40). Current cost also deals with the problem of how to value assets that have no resale value (so no fair value) but are used by an entity to provide future economic benefits. Current cost is also reliable in the sense that the use of market prices to determine the current cost is more objective, and is less open to manipulation and influence by management.

Issues, disadvantages and criticisms: relevance

Because the entity already has the item, the decisions open to it are either to continue to use the item or to sell it, rather than replacing it. Replacement cost may also have no connection to value. For example:

- An entity could have a machine that provides benefits greater than the cost of replacing it.
- Alternatively, an entity may have a machine that would cost far more to replace than the value it generates for the company.

These criticisms of current cost relate to current cost and replacement cost using market prices and not being entity specific. This and many of the criticisms relating to the use of current and replacement costs are similar to criticisms made of fair values. These are discussed in the next section.

Fair value and net realisable value

Two alternative exit values are used in accounting. An exit value is the value that an entity would get from the item leaving the entity (by selling it).

The two exit values are fair value and net realisable value. Both of these values assume normal sale conditions; so, for example, it is not the price you would receive if you needed to sell an item quickly. **Fair value** is 'the amount for which an item could be exchanged between

fair value: The amount for which an item could be exchanged between knowledgeable, parties in an arm's length transaction

knowledgeable, willing parties in an arm's length transaction' (para. 6 AASB 116). **Net realisable value** (sometimes referred to as net selling price) is fair value less the
costs of sale or disposal. You should realise that both of these values reflect market
prices. This is both a key advantage and a key disadvantage.

Fair value

If fair value is considered against the qualitative characteristics required in the
Framework, its advantages are that it is:

- *Reliable.* Assuming fair value can be found, it is a market price, set by forces
  outside the entity (such as supply and demand), so it is considered a reliable
  measure in the sense that it is neutral: it is not biased by subjectivity or judgement and cannot be manipulated or influenced by an entity's management.
- *Relevant.* For many decisions, it is argued that fair value is useful. If you are considering either purchasing or selling an item, clearly the amount you will need to
  pay or will receive is relevant and will help to assess the liquidity of an entity.
- *Understandable and comparable.* Fair value is an easy concept to understand for all
  users — simply the amount to be received if the item was sold — and given that
  fair value is determined at the same point of time, then valid comparisons among
  entities can be made.

Issues, disadvantages and criticisms

These advantages, in particular their perceived relevance and reliability, are key
reasons there is a trend towards the use of fair values in financial accounting.
However, there are arguments against.

Relevance

It can be argued that fair value ignores the assumption made in accounting that the
entity will continue in business (i.e. is a going concern) and effectively measures value
as though the entity was to liquidate (Al-Hogail 2001). However, the value that an
entity receives from items 'necessarily depend[s] on the circumstances (including,
but not limited to, current market circumstances)' (Horton & Macve 2000, p. 33).
What of a specialised asset, such as a machine specially built for a company to use
in its factory? Even though the item provides future economic benefits to the entity
from its use, this item may have no value to any other entities, apart from the scrap
value, so it would have no, or minimal, fair value. Also, the fair value is measured
at the current date. Many investments, or items held for sale, may be held for long-
term gain. Short-term fluctuations in fair value may not be relevant.

Subjectivity

A key advantage of fair value is that it is independent from management and determined by market forces. This is the case *if* there is an active market; that is, where
there are regular sales of the item, so the market price can be easily measured.
However, not all items are regularly traded. For these, an *estimate* needs to be made
of the fair value.

Market prices

That fair values are market prices, so cannot be influenced by management, is claimed to be an important advantage of fair values. However, there are two arguments against the use of market prices. These are:

- Market prices represent the expectations of the buyers and sellers in the market. These expectations are based on predictions, which may not be correct. There is often volatility in market prices and sometimes this is caused by market 'corrections', in which past prices were considered to be too high or too low.
- Some question whether accounting should use prices at all. This is based on the belief that part of the role of accounting information is to assess the validity of prices. As Penman (2003) notes:

> if accounting is to challenge price bubbles, it must not be influenced by bubble prices. Investors look to financial reports to assess whether stocks are fairly priced and thus want measures that are independent of prices (p. 85).

Present value

The **present value** of an item is the present discounted value of the future net cash flows associated with that item. This involves:

---

present value: The present discounted value of the future net cash flows associated with an item

---

- identifying and estimating the future cash flows (both inflows and outflows) that are linked to an item
- deciding on an appropriate discount rate. The discount rate recognises that an amount of money received in one year does not have the same value as the same amount of money received today. This is not only because of changing prices but also because money received today can be invested and earn a return. It is intuitively understood that when you receive or pay cash (i.e. the timing of cash flows) is important. Imagine if someone offered to pay you $1000 now or $1000 in two years. Which would you prefer? Present value reduces the nominal amounts of cash flows from the future and restates these in terms of their value now (i.e. their present value).

The key argument is that present value is conceptually consistent with the definitions of the elements of the financial statements. For example, assets are defined in terms of future economic benefits, and present value measures those, whereas 'cost is backward looking and based upon the sacrifice made; it is not future-benefit based' (Hampton, 1999, p. 25). Given that the value of items for businesses comes from the cash flows those items generate, present value directly measures the actual value (i.e. the future economic benefits) because it measures cash flows. Furthermore, because it requires them to be discounted, it takes into account the time value of money. For these reasons, present value is often considered the 'ideal' measure. It directly measures the future economic benefits (the real value) of items in a unit that represents that value at the same point in time, enabling comparisons.

Issues, disadvantages and criticisms

Although these rationales for the use of present value appeal, the use of present values has problems in practice.

Estimates, subjectivity and uncertainty

Present value requires us to identify and estimate cash flows in the future. In some cases, this is relatively simple. However, for other items, this will involve predicting benefits expected, the timing of the cash flows and future operating costs. Furthermore, which discount rate to use needs to be decided. This has a major impact on the present value measure. A range of discount rates may be chosen from, including interest rates, cost of capital and market rates. These factors mean that the reliability of present value may be questionable. Comparisons may not be valid if differences among values are caused by subjectivity in estimating cash flows and variations in discount rates chosen.

Difficulties in determining cash flows for items

Present value requires identifying the cash flows that are linked to an item. But some items do not result in specific direct cash flows because they are used in combination with other resources to produce cash flows for the entity.

- How much of the revenue (cash flows) of a car manufacturer belongs to the spray-painting equipment used to paint the vehicles?
- What cash flows does a building used as a head office of a company result in?

In these cases, it is impossible to identify the cash flows that result from the particular item. The only way to measure these at present value is somehow to measure the present value of the entity as a whole and allocate it to the items. This is arbitrary and subjective.

Using present value to assess managers

A further problem with using present value is that it is based on expectations and *management's* predictions about cash flows. Yet an important decision made by those using financial statement information is an assessment of how well the managers of the entity have performed. A simple analogy will perhaps help identify the problem here: your lecturer (say in an accounting course) needs to provide a grade for a student. A grade is a measure of performance. What if the lecturer decided to base the grade on how the student *thought* they would perform in the final exam? Do you think the student would say that he or she did not believe he or she would pass the exam?

Present value is based on what managers think will happen. But if their performance is assessed on such a measure, their own opinions are in effect being used to measure their performance. This is not an objective way to assess performance.

Deprival value

Deprival value is an alternative measure that has been used in accounting. This is neither a particular cost nor value but instead it compares cost and values to arrive at a measure. It is also often referred to as 'value to the owner' but this can be confusing because although the deprival value may in some cases be the value that the owner will get from an item, this is not necessarily the case.

Deprival value of an asset is the loss that a rational businessman or businesswoman would suffer if he or

deprival value: The loss that a rational businessman or businesswoman would suffer if he or she was deprived of the asset

she was deprived of the asset (Alexander & Britton, cited in Schneider 1998, p. 31).

To decide the deprival value of an item, the action to be taken *if* the item currently held by the entity was lost needs to be considered. The entity could either:

- *Do nothing.* In this case the entity has lost the value it would have received from the asset. This will be either present value (if the asset was held for use) or net realisable value (if the asset was held for sale).
- *Replace the item* (or the services that it would have received from the item). In this case, the entity would have to pay the current cost of the asset (and this would be the loss because of the asset being taken away).

Deprival value assumes that the entity will take the action that results in the lowest cost or loss (see figure 4.1). A simple example can illustrate this concept.

Company ABC, a removalist, owns a truck used in its removal activities. The truck was purchased by the company some years ago at a cost of $60 000 and is expected to contribute $190 000 (in terms of present value dollars now) to the company if it was used to the end of its useful life. To replace the existing truck would cost $84 000. If the truck was sold by ABC, it would expect to realise $70 000. What would the deprival value be for this asset?

In this case, if deprived of the truck, ABC can either:

- *Do nothing.* The loss suffered is the value that would have been obtained from the truck. In this case, the asset is held for use (because it receives more value from using the truck than it would from selling it) and the value it would have received from the asset is $190 000. This is what it would lose if it did nothing and did not replace the truck.
- *Replace the truck.* In this case, the loss incurred would be the replacement cost of $84 000.

The deprival value in this case is the replacement cost, because rationally ABC would replace the truck (so this is the loss it would suffer) and by doing so the company would be able to obtain a value higher than the replacement cost, so the company is restored to its original position.

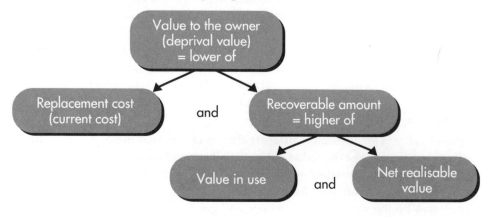

FIGURE 4.1 Deprival value

As with replacement and current cost, deprival value was introduced to meet concerns about the need to reserve funds for asset replacement, particularly in times of increasing costs (Clarke 1998). The advantage of deprival value over replacement or current cost is that it takes into account the entity's circumstances and whether the asset will actually be replaced. It has been used widely in the past in The Netherlands (Camfferman 1998) and also in the public sector in Australia (Clarke 1998).

Issues, disadvantages and criticisms

Is deprival value relevant, given that the entity has not been deprived of the asset? Also, because deprival value can result in a range of values being measured (such as replacement or current cost, present value or net reliable value), many of the criticisms of these measures are relevant (e.g. difficulties in measuring cash flows for determining present values).

Learning tips
Do you know...

4.4   *There is a range of possible attributes to use to measure items in financial accounting, including historic cost, replacement cost and current cost, fair value and net realisable value, present value and deprival value.*

4.5   *Each of the possible costs or values has advantages and disadvantages.*

4.6   *The usefulness of alternative measures will vary between entities and items.*

▪ Measurement in practice: trends and influences

Current accounting standards allow a range of measures to be used in financial statements but three dominate. These are:
- historic cost
- fair value (or net realisable value), although this is often restricted to cases where there is an active market
- present value, although its use is usually limited to cases in which cash flows are easily measured (such as finance leases, provisions relating to employees and deferred sales revenues).

Although it is expected that a range of measures will continue to be used, accounting standard setters worldwide seem to be moving towards a preference for current values (in particular, fair value) and often assume that such values are more relevant than alternatives (Kirk 1991). 'The idea of a mixed measurement system has taken hold and, spurred by the widely accepted decision-usefulness objective of financial reporting and changes in the business environment, standard-setters and regulators seem determined to replace historical costs with current values whenever they are sufficiently reliable' (Miller & Loftus 2000, p. 4).

The trend towards fair value in practice is less certain. Although the use of fair value is allowed, some accounting standards do not require its use but rather allow a choice (often between fair value and historic cost). Why allow a choice? Of course, some of the problems with fair value have been considered in this text (such as that for some items fair value may not be able to be obtained, so not to allow a choice would mean that these items could not be recognised). However, the choice is often allowed even for items for which fair value can usually be reliably obtained and would be relevant (e.g. for investment property). Evidence suggests (see for example Carlin 2000; Miller 2000) that companies are often choosing historic cost, and that where this is a choice allowed, movement away from historic cost has been piecemeal and limited (Carlin 2000, p. 67).

Influences on the choice of measurement basis

Ideally, you would wish the choice of the measure used for an item in the financial statements to take into account:

- the measure best meeting the needs of users
- practical issues. Some of the difficulties in determining specific measures have been noted.

However, a further influence on the choice of the measures used is the impact particular measures may have on the financial statements. This is especially the case if the measure may change from period to period. Apart from historic cost, it is likely that all measures will change from period to period. Take, for example, the fair value of an item of property of $400 000. In the next period, the fair value may be $450 000. If measures change from period to period, how to account for the change needs to be decided. The changes in values or costs may be:

- treated as reserves (current accounting standards require this for items of property held for use and measured at fair value if the value increases)
- treated as a gain or loss (current accounting standards require an expense for items of property held for use and measured at fair value if the value decreases, and an expense or revenue for investment property measured at fair value).

The following In Focus vignette illustrates the effect of changes in values and costs.

 HKSA backs adoption of controversial accounting rule

The Hong Kong Society of Accountants (HKSA) is proposing adoption of a controversial international accounting standard that property companies say could inject more volatility into their bottom lines.

The accountants' guild will float a consultation document to its members next month calling for the introduction of International Accounting Standard (IAS) 40 from January next year, saying that Hong Kong must conform to inter national accounting standards to protect its status as a global financial centre.

The rule would require companies to reflect property valuation swings on profit-loss accounts. At present, property fluctuations are placed in balance-sheet reserves.

The society abandoned a similar consultation two years ago amid vigorous opposition from property developers. Some feared the rule would force them to book substantial losses during property downswings. They pointed to the inherent volatility in the market, and noted property holdings are key assets in many listed companies.

In March 2002, London-listed Hongkong Land reported a US$416 million loss under the standard, after including a $600 million property valuation deficit in its profit-loss account.

Wilson Fung, deputy chairman of HKSA's financial accounting standards committee, said Hong Kong needed the rule to enhance market transparency, as some firms were using their reserve to hide massive valuation deficits. 'Hong Kong will lag behind international practice without the change. Europe, Australia and Singapore will all introduce IAS 40 from January next year,' Mr Fung said. 'Failure to adopt the rule could affect Hong Kong's role as an international financial centre.'

The opposition to IAS 40 has been a key impediment to attempts to bring the local accounting regime in line with global rules set by the International Accounting Standards Committee. Similar efforts are under way in Singapore, Europe, and Australia to encourage international transparency and cross-border listings.

Observers say the opposition to IAS 40 is likely to be muted this time, thanks to a firmer property market and a desire to attract international portfolio investment.

'Many local developers need to issue bonds in international markets to raise funds,' said Herman Fung, managing director at developer Hon Kwok Land. 'If we are not following international accounting rules, it might prove difficult to attract international investment.'

Gilbert Cheung Yik-cho, director of Hung Sing Securities, thinks market conditions will dissuade any opposition to change.

'Local property prices are rising, and developers' profit will be higher under the proposed rule,' Mr Cheung said.

Source: This article appeared in the *South China Morning Post*.

As you can see, changes in values and costs could significantly affect the profit (or loss) and balance sheet amounts and increase their volatility. Also, if the measures are based on market prices (such as fair value or replacement cost), management will have limited ability to influence the amounts recorded in the financial statements.

So a range of incentives (apart from meeting users needs) that can influence the choice of measures is used, and it has been argued that opposition to particular measures is often a result of self-interest and other motivations related to the potential impacts on financial statements (see for example Schneider 1998; Carlin 2000).

Conclusion

Measurement remains the most controversial and incomplete issue in financial accounting. Getting measurement 'right' determines the essential usefulness of financial accounting, yet it is not an easy task. Alterative measures each have their own advantages and disadvantages, and these relative qualities vary depending on the nature of the item being measured and the context. Although there is a trend towards the use of fair value, this is not without its problems and it is likely that financial accounting will continue to use a range of attributes despite the internal inconsistencies that the multiattribute model necessarily involves. It is also expected, given practical and political considerations, that choices may still be allowed that will leave measurement open to possible manipulation.

Summary

Understand why measurement is needed in financial reporting.

- Items need to be measured in the financial statements to make the latter useful to users for assessing the performance and position of entities, and for making comparisons. The ability to measure reliably also decides whether items can be included in financial statements.

Explain what measurement is and what is involved in measuring.

- Measurement involves a choice of deciding what to measure (i.e. choosing an attribute) and of how to measure this attribute (i.e. choice of unit and scale). In the financial statements costs or values, which are financial attributes, are measured.

Identify and explain the problems with measurement in accounting.

- There are several issues and problems with measurement in accounting, in particular:
  - The conceptual framework allows a range of measures to be used, and the guidance provided through the qualitative characteristics is open to interpretation, so requires subjectivity.
  - There is no one system of measurement; rather, the measurement of items is considered on an individual or class basis.
  - The range of alternative attributes measured in accounting leads to the problem of additivity.

Identify and apply a range of attributes that could be measured and explain the advantages and problems with these.

- The possible costs and values measured in accounting are historic cost, replacement cost, current cost, fair value, net realisable value, present value and deprival value. Each of these attributes has particular advantages and disadvantages.

Be aware of the range of measurements currently used in accounting and the influences on choices of measures.

- Several measures are currently used in accounting, although it is apparent that regulators and standard setters have moved towards preferring fair values.
- The choice of measures in accounting is subject to a range of influences.

Key terms

cost   99
current cost   101
deprival value   105
fair value   102
historic cost   100
measure   91
measurement   91
net realisable value   103
present value   104
replacement cost   101

value   99
value in exchange   100
value in use   99

Review questions

4.1   Explain the need to measure in accounting and what measurement involves.

4.2   Explain the difference between cost and value.

4.3   Explain the advantages and disadvantages of using historic cost as a measure.

4.4   Explain the difference between current and replacement costs.

4.5   Explain the advantages and disadvantages of using current or replacement cost as a measure.

4.6   Explain the advantages and disadvantages of using fair value as a measure.

4.7   Explain the advantages and disadvantages of using present value as a measure.

4.8   Explain what is meant by deprival value.

4.9   What role does judgement have in measuring items in the financial statements?

4.10 Some argue that we should use a system of measurement in accounting rather than a range of attributes. What would be the advantages and disadvantages of this?

Application questions

4.11 Obtain the annual reports of a range of companies (these are normally available from their websites). Answer the following questions (the notes to the financial statements will be helpful):

(a) What range of measures is used in the reports of individual companies? Do you think it is valid to add the measures used? How could you interpret the total assets in these financial statements?

(b) Compare the measures used by different companies. Are there any inconsistencies in how similar items are measured by different companies?

4.12 Find the comments letters received on a current exposure draft or proposal. (These can be found from the websites of most standard-setting organisations.) Read a sample of comments from a range of respondents (e.g. from accounting bodies, industry, companies or corporate bodies) and answer the following questions:

(a) Have any of the comments letters referred to measurement issues?

(b) Is there agreement among the various groups on the appropriate measurement to be used?

(c) If there are any concerns or objections relating to measurement, do you agree or disagree with the comments?

4.13 Company X currently has one factory and is considering building another to undertake identical activities to its existing one but in a different location. Explain which of the three costs (i.e. the historic, replacement or current cost) of the existing factory would be the most *relevant* in making this decision. Justify your choice.

4.14 Company ABC buys and sells antique furniture. One piece of furniture was purchased at auction for $6000 about six months ago. To replace (repurchase) this piece of furniture now would cost $8000 because demand for furniture like it has increased. If this piece of furniture was sold by ABC Company, it would be expected to receive $14 000. The company has no alternative use for this piece of furniture.
Calculate the deprival value for the piece of furniture

4.15 Assume that an entity has an item of inventory that it bought for $10 one year ago. To purchase it now would cost $12. The change in general prices over the year is 10 per cent.
(a) Which of the following measures is most relevant?
  • Historic cost at nominal dollars
  • Historic cost in constant dollars
  • Replacement cost
(b) How could we account for the difference of $2 between the original cost and the current replacement cost, if we increase the measure for the inventory to its replacement cost of $12?

4.16 A company owns an office building. Half of the building is rented out on a long-term contract. The other half is used by the company as its head office. Explain the issues and problems in calculating the present value of this office building.

4.17 Obtain the annual reports of two companies in the same industry (these are normally available from company websites) and consider the items of property, plant and equipment. Answer the following questions (the notes to the financial statements will be helpful):
(a) What range of measures is used for these items in the reports of individual companies? Do you think it is valid to add the measures used? How could you interpret the total amount of this class of assets in these financial statements?
(b) Compare the measures used by different companies for similar items. Are there any inconsistencies in how similar items are measured by different companies?

4.18 Obtain the annual report of a company in property investment. The accounting standard *AASB 140 Investment property* allows a choice of measuring investment property at either cost or fair value. If fair value is used, any changes in value are recognised in the profit and loss. Review the annual report and answer the following questions:
(a) How is investment property measured by this company?
(b) Is this choice justified by the company?

(c) Look at the changes in fair value for investment property (if fair value is not used the company must still disclose this in the notes). Do you think changes in fair value should be included in the profit or loss? How would this affect the volatility of the reported profit?

4.19 The following information is provided about a specialised machine that is used by a company in its operations.

The machine originally cost $50 000 and it would cost $120 000 now to replace this machine.

The company expects to receive (discounted to present value) $98 000 by using this machine over the next five years. If sold now, the machine would bring in $60 000.

Consider how useful each of these measures is to the following users:

- shareholders
- creditors
- managers.

4.20 Examine the requirements for measuring assets at fair value in the following accounting standards:

IAS 116/AASB 116 Property, plant and equipment

IAS 138/AASB 138 Intangible assets

(a) How can fair value be determined in each of the standards?

(b) What impact would the differences in the methods allowed to determine fair values have on the financial reports?

(c) Do you think the requirement for an active market in relation to intangible assets is justified? What problems could occur if the active market requirement was not included for intangible assets?

casestudy 4.1

An early pricing model regarding the value of a cat: A historical note

Have you ever worried about how much your cat was worth? The ancient Welsh had a formalized system for cat valuation. This system, however, illustrates that the Welsh recognized and faced many of the same vexing problems facing today's valuation theorists.

Geoffrey Ashe (1971) reports to us that early in Welsh history (10th century) cats were considered a valuable asset as they were effective in protecting granaries from the ravages of mice and rats. Presumably the theft of cats from royal granaries was a common enough occurrence that the punishment for such a crime became a part of the written legal codes. The thief was to be fined the value of the cat.

This clearly requires a valuation formula and the following relationship was defined:[1]

Its head is to be held downwards on a clean level floor, and its tail is to be held upwards; and after that, wheat should be poured over it until the tip of its tails is hidden, and that is its value.

Further, the law, recognising that the original cat was not always available (perhaps deceased) suggested that in its absence a substitute could be used:

It should be perfect to ear, perfect to eye, perfect of teeth, perfect of claw, without marks of fire, and it should not go caterwauling every new moon.

Although ancient, this pricing model indicates that our forefathers were troubled about many of the same issues that are troubling today.

To start with, apparently the ancient Welsh had little faith in currency (perhaps they too had rampant inflation) so chose to value cats in terms of a real commodity — wheat. If you wish, wheat was used as the numeraire in a partial equilibrium model. One wonders whether such a cone of wheat represents the true opportunity cost of the marginal cat. This could, however, only be determined by identifying the number of mice a cat could be expected to catch over its lifetime and then discounting to the present the expected losses of wheat that could be expected from each mouse. The identification of an appropriate discount rate is, however, troubling as I suspect that capital markets were much less perfect than today so that risk adjusted discount rates might be hard to identify. The Welsh did not expand on these topics.

This ancient economist did, however, face up squarely to the problem of missing observations which is so prevalent in empirical research. Recognizing that the original cat might not be available (perhaps deceased) a proxy cat was proposed. However, this proxy cat is defined in not only physical and esthetic dimensions but in moral as well. This perhaps indicates that the ancient Welsh economists were of a sterner breed than the modern variety who tend not to include moral dimensions in either theoretical or empirical work.

There is, however, one crucial aspect to this model which does disturb me. In particular, it is not absolutely clear that the price of a cat is determinate.[2]

At issue is the stickiness of the wheat. If the wheat is frictionless then an infinite quantity of wheat could be poured over the long suffering feline with no resolution of its value. A wheat farmer friend of mine has assured me that in fact wheat will form a cone but that the size of the cone may well depend upon the grade of wheat used and whether it has been properly dried. Clearly much work remains to be done on this aspect of the model because it is currently underspecified.

Finally, while one applauds the Welsh for their model, it seems that the value of the cat is in fact simply the difference between the volume of the cone of wheat and the volume of the cat. It seems that one could easily invoke separability so that the two volumes could be separately determined. Frankly, I have some doubts about the willingness of the feline in question to submit to the proposed experiment. Simpler volume measures could, I suspect, be devised.

In conclusion, then, it seems that the current explosion of literature in accounting and finance on the question of valuing assets (for both theoretical and balance sheet purposes) is directed toward a very old problem. Societies, both ancient and modern need methods for valuing capital assets.

BIBLIOGRAPHY

Ashe, Geoffrey, The Quest for *Arthur's Britain* (Paladin, 1971).

---

[1] Ashe (p.168) is quoting from the earliest available written record of Welsh Common Law. The record is known as the Laws of Hywel Dda. It purports to be a compendium of earlier (now lost) Welsh legal codes. It is reported as being written in the 10th century.

[2] I would like to thank Dr. Elroy Dimson for discussing this problem in detail with me. His comments on the nature of cats and on the likelihood of finding a determinant price are greatly appreciated.

Source: This article appeared in *Accounting, Organizations and Society.*

---

1. What is the purpose of the measurement?
2. What is the measurement unit or scale proposed?
3. What attributes are to be measured?
4. How reliable do you believe the proposed measurement method would be?
5. What is the 'true' value of a cat?
6. Do you think the measurement method proposed is appropriate? Can you suggest any others?
7. If cats were assets today, how do you think accountants would measure them?

case**study**   4.2

An end to the neo-soviet nightmare

There is an old saying that those who fail to learn from history are condemned to repeat it. Thirty years ago, the great inflation accounting debate was in full swing. Its most striking feature, however, was not the rich variety of alternatives on offer, but the neo-soviet tactics adopted by the inflation accounting experts in order to impose their views on the profession.

The various rival systems were compared on the basis, not of the quality of the information they provided to the consumer, but of the alleged superiority of the techniques by which they were produced. In typical neo-soviet fashion, the inflation accounting experts refused to consider the obvious question: will the accounts present a 'truer and fairer view' of a company's return on capital — which is number one on the ASB's recent list of 'key performance indicators'.

Thirty years on, and the IASB seems intent on thrusting its 'fair value' wonder-drug down the throats of its patients — again without conducting any clinical tests.

Yet even the simplest test is sufficient to show that fair value accounting can have lethal results: fair value gains can be reported even when the returns from the firm's assets fall; fair value gains can be reported even though the firm's credit-rating is downgraded; the accounts of firms generating higher actual returns for investors can indicate lower fair value returns than the accounts of firms generating lower actual returns.

Since the IASB can hardly claim ignorance, the question arises of the criminal liability of its members under section 17 of the Theft Act 1968 on false accounting.

Insofar as fair values represent market opportunities at the balance sheet date, their disclosure is a development to be welcomed. The objection is to the treatment of changes in fair value as 'gains' or 'losses'. The very fact that an item appears on a balance sheet proves that it has not been exchanged at the balance sheet date. The fair value therefore represents an opportunity that has been rejected — a transaction that could have taken place but did not in fact do so. Nowhere does the IASB provide any argument to support its requirement in IAS 39 that the difference between two non-existent transactions 'shall be recognised in profit or loss' as a gain or a loss.

The IASB has been remarkably successful in conveying the impression that it occupies the 'theoretical high-ground'. From time to time, there are hints at consistency with concepts like economic income, business income, and deprival value.

Despite their distinguished pedigree, however, these sacred academic cows are riddled with fundamental theoretical flaws. It is not simply that they do not work in practice — they do not work even in theory.

Consequently, the existing conceptual framework is liable as a matter of normal routine to produce serious errors in the calculation of the return a company obtains on the resources it controls — not only in retrospect (financial reporting) but also in prospect (investment analysis).

Perhaps the most astonishing aspect of modern investment theory is the prevalence of the neo-soviet assumption that the directors of public companies (described by Adam Smith as 'the managers rather of other people's money than of their own') should act as enlightened central planners, not in their own self-interest, but altruistically in the interests of a multitude of investors whose (often conflicting) preferences and opportunities they cannot possibly know.

Standard textbook theory typically involves a discussion of the relative merits of net present value and the internal rate of return as techniques of appraising investment projects. But, even in an ideal world where everything turns out according to plan and the cost of investors' capital is known, investment projects that are acceptable by both conventional DCF criteria can actually make investors worse off.

The conventional wisdom is therefore fundamentally flawed in two crucial areas. Discounted cash flow analysis is liable to generate the wrong choice of investment projects even in perfect conditions where everything goes according to plan. The error is then liable to be covered up by an accounting system which cannot by its very nature be relied upon to give a 'true and fair view' of the results.

The IASB's claim that such information 'is useful to a wide range of users in making economic decisions' can only widen the 'expectation gap' between what the public commonly considers the auditors' report to represent and what it actually does represent.

Irresponsible claims and the use of labels like 'fair value' are contributing to the perception of auditors as 'insurers of last resort'. The audit fee is regarded as an insurance premium against business risk, and, if things go wrong, anyone who suffers damage feels entitled to compensation from the auditor.

What investors are entitled to expect is reasonable protection against the risk of fraud and error. What they are not entitled to expect is protection against business risk. That is something the auditor does not provide, cannot provide, and, above all, should not provide. It is, after all, the acceptance of business risk that makes the economic world go round.

A company's assets are, to some extent, lottery tickets in the game of business. It is the auditor's duty to verify the existence of the tickets, not to give a guarantee that they will be winners.

In 1976, the US Financial Accounting Standards Board launched its conceptual framework project with the express instruction that there should be a fresh start without preconceptions. The project was almost immediately derailed by powerful vested intellectual interests within a small section of the academic establishment. For the past thirty years the main effort has been concentrated on patching up the accounting system in order to protect the existing conceptual framework. The result is a bureaucratic nightmare of regulations and an inexorable drift towards Sarbanes–Oxley type legislation.

The neo-soviet trend needs to be reversed. That means refusing to tolerate the neo-soviet attitude of standard-setters who impose their products without regard to their customers; the neo-soviet presumption that corporate management can measure economic advantage on behalf of investors instead of providing information to enable them to do so for themselves; and the neo-soviet proliferation of regulations so complex that no-one can understand the results.

In its draft of proposed amendments to IAS1 presentation of financial statements, the IASB states that its purpose is 'to enhance comparability both with the entity's financial statements of previous periods and with the financial statements of other entities'. It also states that the proposed amendments 'affect the presentation (but not) the recognition, measurement or disclosure of specific transactions and other events required by other standards and interpretations'.

How does the board expect to achieve its stated purpose by amending the presentation, when the real problem is the content?

What is needed is an alternative conceptual framework combined with recognition that the only feasible route to effective corporate governance is, not by regulation, but by market forces. There is, however, an essential precondition: the discarding of old academic baggage.

Source This article appeared in *Accountancy Age*.

1. What are the arguments for using fair values for assets and liabilities?
2. What are some of the arguments against using fair values from a theoretical perspective?

3. What impact does using fair value have on a company's 'return on capital' compared to other measures such as historic cost? Do you think fair value risks presenting a true and fair view?
4. What is the basis for the article claiming that fair value accounting can have 'lethal' results? How do you think changes in fair value for items such as non-current assets should be accounted for?

Recommended readings

Chambers, RJ 1991, 'Metrical and empirical laws in accounting', *Accounting Horizons*, vol. 5, no. 4, pp. 1–15 for a discussion of the problems with and application of laws of measurement in accounting.

Financial Accounting Standards Board 2006, *Statement of financial accounting standards; fair value measurements*, no. 157, September, for a discussion about fair value.

References

Al-Hogail, AA 2001 'Raymond J Chambers' contributions to the development of accounting thought', *The Accounting Historians Journal*, vol. 28, no. 2, pp. 1–30.

Beaver, WH 1991, 'Problems and paradoxes in the financial reporting of future events', *Accounting Horizons*, vol. 5 no. 4, pp. 122–35.

Camfferman, K 1998, 'Deprival value in the Netherlands: history and current status', *Abacus*, vol. 34, no. 1, pp. 18–27.

Carlin, TM 2000, 'Measurement challenges and consequences in the Australian public sector', *Australian Accounting Review*, vol. 10, no. 2, pp. 63–72.

Clarke, FL 1998, 'Deprival value and optimised deprival value in the Australasian public sector: unwarranted drift and contestable serviceability', *Abacus*, vol. 34, no. 1, pp. 8–17.

Hampton, G 1999, 'The role of present value-based measurement in general purpose financial reporting', *Australian Accounting Review*, vol. 9, no. 1, pp. 22–32.

Hampton, G & Bishop, T 1998, 'Measurement and the Australian conceptual framework', *Australian Accounting Review*, vol. 8, no. 1, pp. 42–53.

Horton, J & Macve, R 2000, '"Fair value" for financial instruments: how erasing theory is leading to unworkable global accounting standards for performance reporting', *Australian Accounting Review*, vol. 10, no. 2, pp. 26–39.

International Accounting Standards Board (IASB) 1989, *Framework for the preparation and presentation of financial statements*.

Kirk, DJ 1991, 'Commentary on completeness and representational faithfulness of financial statements', *Accounting Horizons*, December, pp. 135–41.

Liang, PJ 2001, Recognition: An Information Content Perspective, Accounting Horizons, vol. 15, no. 3, pp. 223–42.

Loftus, JA 2003, 'The CF and accounting standards: the persistence of discrepancies', *Abacus*, vol. 39, no. 3, pp. 298–309.

Miller, M 2002, 'Editorial measurements in the third millennium: perspectives, problems and prospects', *Australian Accounting Review*, vol. 10, no. 2, pp. 2–3.

Miller, MC & Loftus, JA 2000, 'Measurement entering the 21st century: a clear or blocked road ahead?', *Australian Accounting Review*, vol. 10, no. 2, pp. 4–18.

Penman, SH 2003, 'The quality of financial statements: perspectives from the recent stock market bubble', *Accounting Horizons*, vol. 17, supplement, pp. 77–96.

Ravlic, T 1999, 'Measure for measure; new issues or old problems?', *Australian CPA*, vol. 69, no. 2, pp. 39–41.

Schneider, D 1998, 'German reflections on asset valuation', *Abacus*, vol. 34, no. 1, pp. 31–5.

5 PRODUCTS OF THE FINANCIAL REPORTING PROCESS

LEARNING OBJECTIVES

After reading this chapter, you should be able to:

- appreciate the role alleged manipulation of reported earnings plays in the production of financial information

- appreciate the debate surrounding the exclusion of intangibles and intellectual capital from the financial reporting process

- explain the options available to companies reporting voluntary disclosures

- appreciate the debate surrounding the length and frequency of reporting periods

- identify three theories that explain the motivation for voluntary disclosures in annual reports.

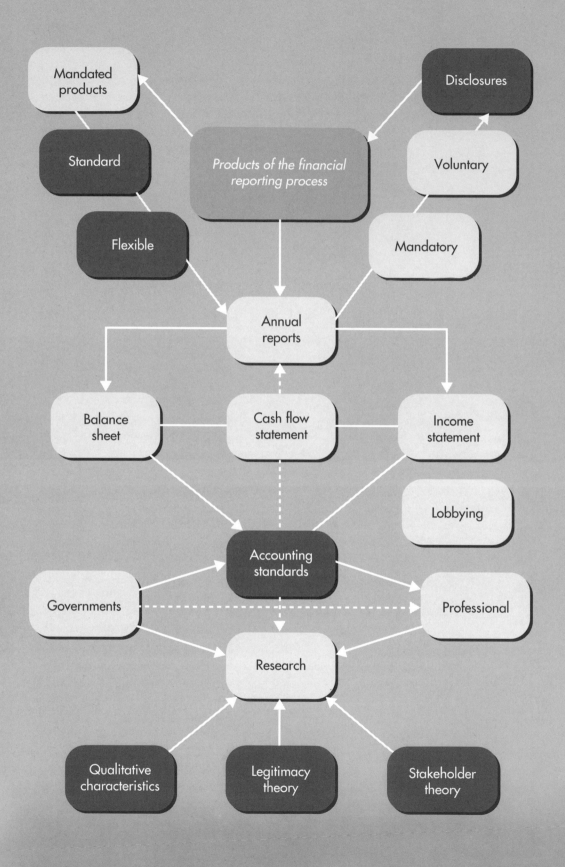

Introduction

The delivery of financial accounts in the form of financial statements, attested to by a public accounting firm, is highly valued by society because the financial statements impart a sense of reliability and credibility. It is through these accounts (statements) that claims about economic responsibility, agency and accountability are made. They are the means by which others judge those claims.

Economic responsibility is commonly judged by performance and wealth. The profit and loss statement represents the claims by the reporting entity about its economic performance. The balance sheet is the dated statement about its wealth.

Accounting regulations are like a straitjacket: what is reported is only one dimension of the reporting entity. In generating its wealth and performance, an entity will engage in activities that are not captured by the accounting process. Many enterprises will give an account of these activities within their annual reports and elsewhere. Back in the 1970s, proposed conceptual frameworks for accounting were in favour of reporting all activities. The *corporate report* was notable for exploring these issues. More recently, calls for innovation in financial reporting have advocated the inclusion of information apparently relevant to the decisions of users as well as the adoption of new technologies.

Increasingly, accounting's 500-year-old system is being questioned because its methods are seen to be out of touch with the needs of twenty-first-century investors and shareholders (Boerner 2005). Critics of accounting say it needs to explore financial reporting that will restore investor confidence. The issues discussed in this chapter relate to some of these criticisms. They are:

- the alleged manipulation of reported earnings
- the exclusion of certain activities from the financial reporting process
- how these activities are reported
- where they are reported, including the adoption of new technologies
- when they are reported.

Alleged manipulation of reported earnings

While the Enron affair in particular has highlighted it, concern about manipulation of reported profit or of the balance sheet is not new, and researchers and the media have highlighted it since the 1970s. Although both the income statement and the balance sheet are manipulated, focus is mainly on income and its manipulation.

Why does management manipulate the accounts? The main reason suggested relates to the desire to influence wealth transfers among the various stakeholders, including management, controlling shareholders, other shareholders and potential shareholders.

Why are accounts open to manipulation? Managers and controlling shareholders take advantage of the information asymmetry between themselves and existing and potential shareholders (Stlowy & Breton 2004). Accounting is seen as the tool for manipulation.

Manipulation is defined as the:

use of management's discretion to make accounting choices or to design transactions to affect the possibilities of wealth transfer between the company and society (political costs), funds providers (cost of capital) or managers (compensation plans) (Stlowy & Breton 2004).

manipulation: The use of management's discretion to make accounting choices or to design transactions to affect the possibilities of wealth transfer between the company and society (political costs), funds providers (cost of capital) or managers (compensation plans)

Manipulation that is within the law is called earnings management, which includes income smoothing, big bath accounting and creative accounting. Manipulation that is outside the law is fraud. Often the difference between the two is narrow.

Earnings management

Calculated income (or profit), commonly referred to as 'the bottom line', has become the most widely used indicator of an enterprise's performance. Financial analysts spend a lot of time analysing corporate performances, and issue predictions about upcoming performances. These predictions have become so important in some capital markets that it is thought that management 'cook the books' to present as favourable a performance as possible. 'Cooking the books' is a term used in the media; in the accounting literature, the term used is **earnings management**. The investigation of whether earnings management takes place is currently a hot topic, especially after the world-famous corporate collapses of Enron, WorldCom and others.

earnings management: A manager's use of accounting discretion through accounting policy choices to portray a desired level of earnings in a particular reporting period

Earnings management depends on the timing differences that arise between accrual accounting and cash accounting. Although there are customary ways to treat these differences, earnings management generally brings revenues into the year of 'need' and postpones expenses into the next or subsequent years. Creative compliance is a form of earnings management. It uses schemes to circumvent the law. Lawyers are used to ensure that those schemes are defensible. As a consequence, creative compliance is costly.

Because the measure of corporate success has become whether a corporation has reached its earnings predictions, the temptation for management is to 'manage' earnings to match analysts' forecasts. In this process, as outlined by Macintosh et al. (2000), accounting earnings do not reflect the outcomes of an enterprise's strategic decisions. Instead, analysts' predicted earnings determine the strategy of an enterprise to satisfy the prediction. This means management may take predictions about earnings as targets, and select investments that are likely to produce reported income equal to or exceeding the analysts' forecasts. Meanwhile, the market incorporates analysts' earning forecasts into share prices. In this way, share prices, analysts' forecasts and reported income all relate to each other but not to 'true' or underlying income.

Parfet (2000), a representative of preparers of financial reports, defends earnings management by differentiating 'bad' from 'good' earnings management. The bad involves intervening to hide true operating performance by creating artificial accounting entries or by stretching the estimates required in preparing financial statements beyond reasonableness. This, he points out, is the realm of hidden reserves, improper revenue (income) recognition and overly aggressive or conservative accounting judgements.

Good earnings management, on the other hand, involves management taking actions to try to create stable financial performance by acceptable, voluntary business decisions in the context of competition and market developments. The market tends to reward corporations that achieve stable trends of growing income. Good earnings management involves spotting the most beneficial use for the corporation's resources and quickly reacting to unforeseen circumstances. Parfet declares earnings management not to be a bad thing but a reflection of expectations and demands, both inside and outside a business, on the part of all stakeholders in the capital market.

Income smoothing

The good earnings management discussed in the previous section is more commonly known as income smoothing. Management artificially manipulates earnings to produce a steadily growing profit stream: above-normal profits in good times are artificially reduced by certain provisions and are called upon in not-so-good times to inflate the reported profit figure. Management can only smooth income when the entity is making sufficient profits to allow it. Commentators believe management indulges in income smoothing to increase its remuneration, while for controlling shareholders, the benefits lie in transferring wealth to themselves from new shareholders (Stlowy & Breton 2004).

The situation in which current income is reduced by a new management team by using as many income-decreasing accruals as possible is known as 'taking a bath' or 'big bath accounting'. The aim is to reduce current income so that reported low income levels may be blamed on the previous management team, as well as providing a reduced basis for future comparisons. Because the future income stream is free of these charges, improved earnings are more likely, and targets within management compensation schemes can more easily be achieved.

Pro-forma reports: massaging earnings

Pacific Brands, an Australian enterprise listed on the stock exchange in 2004, in its first annual report reported **pro-forma results** for the year to balance date as well as a pro-forma review of financial performance. Pro-forma results are primarily used to show 'as though' results; for example, in the case of Pacific Brands, the enterprise had not been operating for a full 12 months so the results and review of operations were 'as though' the company had

pro-forma results: Financial statements for a period prepared before the end of the period, which therefore contain estimates

been operating for 12 months. Pro-forma figures have been used to show the effect of an accounting change for the previous year's results so that the previous year provides a proper comparison with the current year's figures.

However, the use of pro-forma financial statements to exclude one-time or unusual items from earnings has generated intense debate between supporters and critics of the practice (Bhattacharya et al. 2004), particularly in the United States. Supporters argue that pro-forma earnings clarify complex accounting disclosures, so providing a clearer picture of *core earnings* expected to continue in future periods. Critics claim that pro-forma reporting is being used to turn a loss under the Generally Accepted Accounting Principles (GAAP) into a profit under pro-forma reporting, and that pro-forma earnings are not comparable across reporting entities or across reporting periods.

It is this aspect of pro-forma reporting that worries critics such as Brody and McDonald (2004), because most of the pro-forma results released in the United States reflect higher income levels than if the financial statements were prepared according to accounting standards or GAAP. More than 300 firms in the S&P 500 excluded some expenses in the operating earnings released to analysts and investors as pro-forma reports (Brody & McDonald 2004). Accounting regulations do not extend to such releases of financial performance. Brody and McDonald find it disquieting that enterprises are reporting earnings outside of the financial statements in the annual report in any way they want.

Another study of pro-forma reporting (Bhattacharya et al. 2004) found that it is used by less profitable firms with higher debt levels than other firms in their industry, and that these firms are more likely to release the pro-forma reports when their share price and earnings decline. Firms tend to use them to meet analysts' expectations, and to downplay bad earnings news.

Exclusion of activities from the financial reporting process

Although management can manipulate approved methods of accounting for certain activities or exclude expenses to massage their earnings, accounting regulations themselves may result in inaccurate company assessments because they do not allow certain items to be reported. Currently, this issue centres on the tighter rules relating to the reporting of intangibles, especially the reporting of intellectual capital. 'As much of two-thirds or three-fourths of the real value of the company is based on intangibles, and investors are not getting the information they need to make decisions' (Lev, cited in Boerner 2005). Another issue has been the reporting of social and environmental activities of corporations.

To overcome accounting regulations, firms make voluntary disclosures. These are increasing, particularly among larger companies undertaking to fill the void between what can be reported within accounting rules and the drivers of value generation within firms (Hunter et al. 2005). Disclosures also seem to be included as corporate management responds to media attention. Disclosures may relate to human resources, the environment, or community, although environment disclosures are the most researched (see chapter 7).

Intangibles

Although accounting authorities have no difficulties in including physical assets in balance sheets, irrespective of whether they have been purchased or internally generated, the rules for intangibles are different. Traditional accounting systems are not able to provide information about corporate intangible assets. This, according to a Securities and Exchange Commission official (Dyckman & Zeff 2000), consigns the balance sheet to the status of an antique.

Investment by global manufacturers in intangible assets such as research and development, brand building, or employee training, is approximately equal to the total investment of these manufacturers in physical assets (Lev & Daum 2004). For example, Coca-Cola's brand name was valued in 1992 at approximately US$25 billion, which is more than the value of the company's tangible assets (Dyckman & Zeff, 2000). Intangibles are identified as the value and growth creators in almost all industries (Lev & Daum 2004). More and more resources are being put into research and development, brand building, customer relationships, employee training and education, supply chain networks and information technology structure.

Intangibles are seen to be the reason the book value of corporations has been shrinking in relation to market value (Lev & Daum, 2004). The difference is regarded by capital markets as the value of a corporation's intangible assets. Between 1982 and 1992, the value of intangibles increased by 38 per cent to 62 per cent of market value, with book value decreasing from 62 per cent to 38 per cent. Currently, financial statements do not give an overview of all value-creating activities, so that investors and other stakeholders are unable to properly assess the potential of a reporting entity as well as its ability to achieve sustainable results.

The treatment of intangibles is outlined in the following to show why information about them is limited in financial reporting. This treatment has sparked debate about whether intangibles should be treated differently from other assets. The conceptual framework was supposed to overcome differing treatments that cannot be substantiated. Intangibles should be treated similarly to any other tangible asset (Lev & Zarowin 1999) because they are no less assets just because they lack physical substance (Hendriksen & van Breda 1992). There can be no asset unless there is an expectation of future benefits.

Intangible assets are defined as *identifiable* nonmonetary assets without physical substance (IAS 38, AASB 138). The international (and Australian) standard (IAS38/AASB138) declares that identifiable intangible

intangible assets: Identifiable nonmonetary assets without physical substance

assets should only be recognised when it is probable that the future economic benefits generated by them will flow to the reporting entity, and when these benefits can be reliably measured. However, the insertion of *identifiable* into the definition means that to be recognised, an intangible asset must be able to be separated from the reporting entity or have arisen from contractual or other legal rights. This means that internally generated intangibles such as brands, mastheads, publishing titles, customer lists and the like are not recognised, but expensed. Expenditure on research is to be expensed when it is incurred. Any intangible asset arising from development expenditure can be recognised only if criteria relating to the technical and commercial feasibility of the development project are met.

Any recognised intangibles are subject to the impairment test. Revaluations are restricted to those intangibles for which there is an active market. An **active market** (AASB 138, para. 8) is one in which all of three conditions exist. Those conditions are:

active market: A market in which the items traded are homogeneous, willing buyers and sellers can be found at any time and prices are available to the public

- The items being traded in the market are homogeneous.
- Willing buyers and sellers normally can be found at any time.
- Prices in the market are available to the public.

There are not many assets, physical or intangible, that would comply with this test. Yet the test is applied only to intangibles.

Arguably, contractual provisions, particularly those governing the payment of dividends or the issue of additional debt, have generated strong corporate resistance to any changes in the definitions of assets and liabilities, despite the importance of intangibles to the modern organisation (Dyckman & Zeff 2000). The basic financial statements of balance sheet, income statement and cash flow statement are not up to the task of providing users with the contextual information necessary for understanding the complex financial affairs of a reporting entity. Consequently, voluntary disclosure is entities' answer to the lack of comprehensiveness of financial statements. The In Focus vignette that follows discusses the state of corporate accounting systems.

 infocus *Are corporate accounting systems out of date?*

In an address to a 2005 conference entitled 'The Future of Financial Reporting', Professor Baruch Lev noted:

> The research and development (R&D) pipeline of a major pharmaceutical marketer is an important determinant of future value. Today, as R&D is expensed, the real value of a potential drug, including a 'market blockbuster' is not transparent to investors. We know that if a drug is approved by regulators at the end of Phase I trials, it has a 25 percent chance of making it to market. We know that by the end of Phase III trials, those odds move to 75 percent favorable. This movement has a direct impact on top and bottom lines. Nowhere in the present accounting information do we find guidance on these important drivers of values.
>
> There is a cause-effect, input-output linkage with training and turnover. Is a firm doing more or less training? Is there a direct link to employee

turnover?... Most executives don't know the costs of training, or the real value of alliances (and the average large company has 30 or more), or the asset value of the firm's intellectual property, or the contribution of these and other factors to either cost savings or earnings.

Source: This extract appeared in *Corporate Finance Review.*

Intellectual capital

Voluntary disclosures in annual reports focus on matters neglected by financial reporting, so that they are concerned with environmental and social activities, employees and *intellectual capital*.

Within the debate about intangibles, there is another debate about the reporting and measurement of **intellectual capital**. The term was first used in one of Skandia's annual reports about a decade ago. It is an umbrella term that refers to:

- capital created by employees or purchased, such as patents, computer and administrative systems, concepts, models research and development
- relationships with customers and suppliers that consist of brand names, trademarks and the like
- capital embedded in employees, such as through education, training, values and experience.

> **intellectual capital:** An umbrella term encompassing capital created by employees (such as patents), relationships with customers and suppliers (such as brands, trademarks) and capital invested in employees (such as in training or education)

Accounting has adopted a conservative approach to intangibles. Under accounting's rules, only intellectual capital that has been purchased will be recognised in the financial statements. Knowledge organisations' assets are their employees. Because of this, corporations have been voluntarily disclosing information about intellectual capital in annual reports. The trend in these disclosures has been towards the score card approach (Hunter et al. 2005). The problem that arises is that scorecards do not measure monetary allocations to intellectual capital. However, they do make intellectual capital visible. Nonetheless, comparisons among reporting entities suffer from a lack of standardisation of disclosures.

Hunter et al. (2005) point out that it is fundamental to an understanding of value creation within firms that users be informed of the categories of expenditures that generate value-creation processes. The rate of return to intellectual capital investment can be determined only through an analysis involving original expenditure data. Management intent at the time of investment should determine whether expenditure on intellectual capital is an asset.

Learning tips
Do you know...

5.1 *The line between legal earnings manipulation and fraud is very thin. Earnings management, income smoothing and pro-forma reporting can all be used to manipulate the bottom line reporting of an entity, but there is still considerable debate over whether these are legitimate management options.*

...nting regulations do not allow the reporting of unidentifiable intan-
...so firms resort to voluntary disclosure of valuable nonfinancial assets
...brands, mastheads and research.

...embedded in employees and invested in relationships with customers
...pliers is referred to as intellectual capital, and is not recognised by
financial statements unless sold on the open market.

■ Where voluntary disclosures are reported

The traditional, statutory formal communication vehicle between a reporting entity and its interested constituencies is the annual report. Its dominance as a communication device is shown by the many variations in its structure, content and presentation. Annual reports comprise quantitative information, narratives, photographs, tables and graphs. They are commonly divided into two sections, with the required financial statements usually assigned either to a rear section or to a separate volume. Voluntary disclosures are made in the larger 'up-front' section of an annual report. The glossy overlay of this front half is seen as being capable of overriding the numerical and other statutory messages relegated to the rear (Stanton & Stanton 2002).

Annual reports provide management with a unique opportunity to achieve certain purposes. They are a means to communicate with customers, shareholders, employees, suppliers, media and government. The annual report's role as a communication tool generates controversy because it can be used as a marketing tool as well as a conveyor of a particular organisational image to its readers. These uses of annual reports are controversial because the annual report's credibility lies in the inclusion of audited financial statements. The In Focus vignette that follows considers this issue further.

 Be kind to shareholders: keep it short, sweet and informative

The annual report is the single most important document a company sends to its shareholders.

It is also an ever-evolving form of communication, with a phenomenal amount of change in the past few years and some of the biggest improvements expected over the next few years.

Recent years have seen the expansion of the annual report with the introduction of the Corporate Governance and Remuneration Reports as well as the introduction of the International Financial Reporting Standards.

A strongly supported initiative is the 'shareholder friendly report', a concept produced by the Australian Institute of Company Directors and PricewaterhouseCoopers. While it isn't a perfect replacement for a concise annual report (for instance it omits far too many director disclosures), it is a serious attempt to condense a company's annual activities and results into a brief document, and is an initiative to be encouraged.

Some of the key features of the Shareholder Friendly Report include key performance indicator reporting, achievements versus targets and disclosure of new targets for the next year, as well as an overall outlook in the CEO's review of operations, where sensitivities and critical success factors are outlined. Financial statements include an explanation of terms and an elaboration of the data.

The reporting includes the figures for the past five years and the data tie back to the full report to encourage reference to the full document. Shareholder-friendly reporting encourages the company to provide greater interpretation of data. These don't always appear in annual reports, but are considered to be of great value to owners.

A recent survey from Chartered Secretaries Australia suggests that fewer shareholders are reading annual reports. It may be that many are becoming too long, providing information with too much corporate spin or too diverse, or simply incomprehensible to the average person. It may also be that many shareholders own shares in both their own name and their superannuation fund, and have requested only one annual report.

The Shareholder Friendly Report concept also seeks to address the problem that far too many annual reports, including the concise variety, have become overly lengthy. Of course, there are a lot of disclosure requirements these days, however there remains a great deal of wastage, with superfluous photographs and over-the-top graphic design.

Given that the annual report is the most important communication provided by companies to shareholders, it is irksome to see it laden with expensive bells and whistles, while at the same time its creators bang on about how cost-conscious the firm has been over the prior year.

It is essential, therefore, that the board of directors and senior executives maintain control of its content and production, rather than the all too frequent occurrence of letting it get hijacked by the public relations team and graphic artists.

All too often, when a company's performance has been disastrous, it is often described as merely disappointing, or if a good spin doctor has edited the report, mixed. There is, on the other hand a plethora of superlatives for a successful year. If only the chairman actually wrote the chairman's report rather than some lower-level flak.

There are many annual reports that are readable, easily understood and to the point. Let's hope that number continues to grow, and that in the event the economy's dream run starts to fade companies will be as forthcoming about their failings as they have been about their successes.

Source: This article appeared in *The Australian*.

Annual reports

Annual reports increasingly report voluntary, largely narrative disclosures, which consign the statutory financials to the rear. These narrative disclosures provide the means by which management can report corporate achievements, particularly those excluded by accounting standards from the financial statements. An added advantage is that these disclosures can influence and mould readers' expectations about the reporting corporation. Whether the information provided is credible is contestable. Increasingly, this reporting is viewed as an exercise in obfuscation.

Annual reports generally seek images that have positive expected values, while negative images are avoided. Different 'impression management' strategies are adopted for different stakeholders but how powerful a stakeholder group is will influence how much attention they receive (Lee 1994).

Impression management is said to be 'proactive' when it is designed to improve a corporation's image. The strategic purpose is to build an image of the corporation that ingratiates it with its stakeholders, to gain their approval (self-promotion). Alternatively, impression management is said to be 'control protective' when it is used to protect an established image under threat as a result of a predicament. The purpose is self-serving. The strategy may be either to admit fault or to deny responsibility by way of excuses, justifications and apologies, disclaimers, self-handicapping and denouncement. Within the annual report, language is used to blur distinctions about the causes of poor performance, presenting the company in a positive light. Interestingly, the annual reports of good performers are easier to read than those of poor performers because they use 'stronger' writing.

Language can be used to blur or bias culpability. This is where responsibility and accountability is said to take on a 'hedonic bias': a general tendency to attribute anything negative to external, environmental causes ('it's not my fault') and to attribute favourable outcomes to internal dispositional factors ('it's all thanks to my abilities'). Additionally, negative results are explained in technical accounting terms (Aerts 1994) or in convoluted language (Jones 1996) while positive performances are explained in strict, simple cause-and-effect terminology so that management's responsibility for them is clear (Aerts 1994).

Imagery in annual reports displays similar patterns. Symbols are used to guide interpretation to particular outcomes. Financial graphs are frequently distorted to improve perceptions of management performance (Beattie & Jones 1992, 1997, 1999; Mather & Story 1996), so that graphs are more likely to heighten good news, while minimising bad news (Beattie & Jones 1999).

Internet reporting

Reporting entities are adopting the Internet as a means of communication with parties interested in information about them. Both financial and nonfinancial information is being disclosed on reporting entities' websites. In contrast to the annual report that places the reader in a passive role as the receiver of information in a form or manner that the reporting entity deems useful, Internet reporting can be far more interactive. Visitors to websites are often given audio or video downloads, email alerts and links to related sites. Users are able to interpret and analyse the information provided by using spreadsheets and graphical tools. Internet reporting gives users a wide range of options in relation to the types of information presented as well as the delivery method.

Lack of standardisation in Internet financial reporting arising from such options worries many accounting commentators (Seetharaman, Subramanian & Shyong 2005). Particularly worrying is the possibility that users believe all information accessed through a reporting entity's website is audited. The annual report in Internet reporting does not provide the boundary that the physical copy gives to disclosed information. Internet users can unknowingly leave the audited sections. Also, forward-looking statements are provided without adequate disclaimers.

Another worry is the potential for fraudulent information releases. Some American companies have been subject to damage from such releases. Bloomberg News broadcast fraudulent news that resulted in a company's share price falling from $103 to $45 in 15 minutes (Seetharaman et al. 2005).

The International Accounting Standards Board has developed a code of conduct for Internet reporting. Among the guidelines are that:
• Boundaries of financial reports should be clear.
• The content of financial reports should be the same as the reporting entity's paper-based reports.
• Financial reports should be complete, clearly dated and timely.
• Information provided should be user friendly and downloadable.
• Information should be appropriately secured to ensure reliability.

Some of these problems are forecast to be overcome by new technology, particularly the rise of extensible business reporting language, or XBRL (see the In Focus vignette that follows).

infocus *Standardised business language cuts operating jargon confusion*

One of the big issues in financial data reporting is the use of different terms to identify the financial information provided by companies in their reports. This makes for a confusing lack of consistency and transparency for users — from laypeople to business data analysts. To rectify the problem, a consortium of international government agencies, business organisations and major corporations has developed a computer-based language that converts business and financial data to a standardised form.

Extensible business reporting language, or XBRL, uses XML tags, similar to those used in spreadsheet software such as Microsoft Excel, to identify data. This allows the data to be easily shared and analysed without the need to rekey it. The XBRL consortium has developed a dictionary of commonly used financial reporting terms, and uses it to assign common tags to relevant data. For example, cash and cash equivalents are assigned the same tag, regardless how they are calculated or reported. This means that the need for longhand identification by a skilled specialist is eliminated. The data can then be analysed automatically through software systems.

XBRL is expected to be particularly useful to large, publicly listed companies, with an eventual flow-on effect to medium-sized businesses. However, some commentators believe small businesses could benefit most from XBRL, since capital markets will have increased access to their information.

In the United States, XBRL is also expected to ease the burden of financial reporting analysis by the SEC, as required under the Sarbanes–Oxley Act of 2002. Currently, the law mandates the SEC undertake analysis of a certain percentage of the reports it receives, a tedious and labour-intensive process under current practices. XBRL-tagged reports would make this analysis simpler and far more cost-effective.

Companies such as Edgar Online Inc., based in Norwalk, Conn., which provides normalised data to analysts, are also expected to use XBRL to their advantage. Despite the ability of XBRL to make financial data easily accessible and interchangeable without the need for specialised data processing, Liv Watson, Edgar Online's vice president of XBRL, believes the company will be able to provide intelligent analytical tools, which will further simplify the process. Currently, Edgar Online devotes 80 per cent of its time to mechanically converting data into a searchable and analysable form. Watson expects XBRL will enable the company to focus instead on ways to make this information more marketable.

Source: This article appeared in the *New Orleans CityBusiness.*

When information is reported

The practice of closing reporting enterprise ledgers each year and producing annual balance sheets and profit and loss (income) statements is well established. International accounting standards require financial reports to be presented at least annually. Annual balancing and closing of accounts have been common in Europe for about 500 years. It was useful in providing arithmetic accuracy (Luther 2003). Also, the balance sheet was useful in providing a summary of the financial position to owners who did not manage their businesses. Despite these advantages, many firms did not embrace regular 12-month accounting periods. The introduction of income tax, the separation of ownership from control and the monitoring concerns of shareholders are thought to be responsible for the universal adoption of the annual accounting cycle (Luther 2003).

This practice — of producing annual accounts — is so well established that little thought has been given to the possibility of other time periods, other than that of shorter ones. In many countries, listed companies are required to produce interim financial accounts. Real-time reporting, such as with XBRL, opens up the possibility of nonstandardised reporting periods, so that uniformity is surrendered for flexibility.

The practice of producing annual accounts was a response to the continuing nature of reporting entities. The closing of accounts at the completion of a venture was not applicable for continuing enterprises. The idea of an accounting period was to mimic a completed venture. Profit determination for the period represents the liquidation proceeds at the end of a venture. The balance sheet imitates the distributions at the end of the venture.

After a series of high-profile corporate collapses, Australia's *Corporate Law Economic Reform Program Act 2004* aimed at restoring public confidence in corporate Australia by requiring better disclosure in both the annual and half-yearly financial reports and in the continuous disclosure regime for Australia-listed companies. Australia-listed companies also comply with Australian Securities Exchange listing rules, which require them to disclose share-price-sensitive information immediately the company becomes aware of it.

Arguments for standardisation of reporting periods

The four main arguments for standardisation of the accounting cycle into a 12-month reporting period are briefly outlined in the following.

- The standardisation of reporting periods allows investors to compare and evaluate the relative effectiveness of managements of different companies or reporting entities.
- The shareholder requirement for dividends makes it necessary to close the books, calculate profits and declare a dividend based on those profits. English law requires companies to pay dividends only out of profits, so their calculation is integral to paying them.
- Various company acts require entities that they cover to supply shareholders with annual balance sheets and profit and loss accounts.
- Before the twentieth century, stewardship was more important than measuring a rate of return on capital (Luther 2003). Accounts were seen as control mechanisms rather than measuring rate of return. Control needed standardisation of the reporting period.

Arguments for a more flexible approach to reporting periods

There are several arguments given to support a more flexible approach to reporting periods. For example, any standardised period cuts across many uncompleted transactions. Standardisation may result in accountants apportioning unfinished operations and allocating assets to an arbitrary accounting period of 12 months.

Chambers (cited by Luther 2003) argued that the appropriate accounting period is determined by the nature of the firm, so that it should reflect the earnings cycle of the reporting entity. This view was supported by the American Institute of Certified Public Accountants in 1973.

Johnson & Kaplan (1987, cited by Luther, 2003) argue that standardisation puts pressure on managers to produce profits over short-term periods. Luther (2003) quotes several authors who argue that to overcome the problems created by standardisation, annual accounts should have a cumulative component because they are tentative and conjectural statements, the truth of which cannot be verified until the reporting entity has run its entire course.

Interim reporting

Reports issued between annual reports are called **interim financial reports** to distinguish them from annual reports. There is an accounting standard (AASB 134/ IAS 34) for interim financial reports but it does not mandate their preparation. Nor does the standard mandate their frequency or how soon after the end of an interim period they should be completed. However, if interim reports are prepared, they must, at a minimum, have the following components:

interim financial reports: Reports issued between annual reports

- condensed balance sheet
- condensed income statement
- condensed statement of changes in equity
- condensed cash flow statement
- selected explanatory notes determined by what is needed to give the user an understanding of the report.

Additionally, comparative information should be supplied.

XBRL

As discussed, continuous disclosure by reporting entities is being made possible by XBRL. It is becoming an important means of putting data and their associated figures or numbers in a uniform electronic format. The growth of this technology may see the advent of real-time financial reporting from corporations, allowing virtually instantaneous analysis and comparisons.

Learning tips
Do you know...

5.4 *Traditionally, voluntary disclosures are presented in the first half of the annual report, in which they are often manipulated as a marketing tool. Increasingly, voluntary disclosures are being made on company websites, which are interactive, but are not subject to the same regulatory controls as the annual report.*

5.5 *Through company law regulations, reporting periods are traditionally standardised to 12 months, allowing for better comparability and analysis.*

5.6 *Arguments supporting a more flexible approach to reporting periods see this as an arbitrary line, which may result in inaccurate reporting of incomplete transactions and create a short-term view.*

5.7 *Voluntary interim financial reporting is used by some companies in an attempt to provide a more accurate financial statement, and XBRL may allow for real-time reporting in the future.*

■ Why entities voluntarily disclose

Accounting authorities talk of the need to supply information useful for financial decision making, particularly to investors, yet current standards prevent the recognition of many assets that contribute to the market value of the reporting enterprise. Linked with this lack of recognition is the view, shared by many accounting commentators, that information should be available to groups other than investors. According to Deegan (2002), those who advocated such socially related disclosures, or who researched nontraditional disclosures, were regarded as both radical and critical, because they were explicitly or implicitly criticising the current structure of the discipline: historical financial accounting reports for shareholders and creditors.

However, much research was engendered by an early interest by some professional accounting bodies in widening the focus of financial accounting. *The corporate report*, published in 1975 by English accounting authorities, was notable for its concern for stakeholders and its growing anxiety about business ethics and corporate social responsibilities. The basic philosophy recognised that an entity has multiple responsibilities extending beyond its legal obligations. Public accountability derives from the reporting entity's existence being dependent on the approval of the community in which it operates. It also derives from the special legal and operational privileges afforded these entities by society, their use of manpower, materials and energy resources and community-owned assets, and the belief that the maximisation of shareholders' profits is not the only legitimate aim of business. *The corporate report* advocated the need for new accounting methods, such as social audits.

Studies of annual reports show that these reports contain a variety of information, not necessarily all financial. This means that they contain two antithetical forms of accountability: dialogue and accounting.

Management motivation to disclose

Because annual reports contain a great deal of information not required by any authority, researchers have speculated about the motivation that drives management to voluntarily disclose information. Many, such as Beckett & Jonker (2002), attribute the motivation to accountability. In contrast, Deegan (2002) speculates that there is a desire by managements to legitimise various aspects of their respective organisations. Accountability implies a responsibility to disclose information to those with a right to know, reflecting the philosophy of *The corporate report*.

Deegan (2002) lists ten reasons management might voluntarily disclose information in annual reports:
- to comply with legal requirements
- because of economic rationality arguments
- because of management's feeling that it is accountable to stakeholders
- because of borrowing requirements
- to comply with community expectations
- to ward off threats to organisational legitimacy
- to manage powerful stakeholders
- to forestall regulations
- to comply with industry requirements
- to win reporting awards.

O'Donovan's (2002) research suggests that management discloses environmental information in annual reports to:

- align management's values with social values
- pre-empt attacks from pressure groups
- improve corporate reputations
- provide opportunities to lead debates
- secure endorsements
- demonstrate strong management principles
- demonstrate social responsibilities.

Research into annual reports

If you compare the two lists given, you will find factors common to each. Researchers have taken some of these common threads to build theories about why management chooses to disclose certain information in the front half of annual reports. The collective name given to this theorising and its associated research is **corporate social responsibility** (CSR). In the accounting literature, it is called corporate social reporting.

corporate social responsibility: Term referring to management's choosing to voluntarily disclose noncompulsory information in the front section of annual reports

Big business is always a target for criticism: the food industry is accused of contributing to obesity, supermarkets are criticised for impoverishing farmers, banks are criticised for closing branches and retrenching staff, chemical manufacturers are criticised for air pollution and so on. The recent high-profile collapses of corporations such as Enron, WorldCom and HIH have added corporate governance to the list of grievances associated with the world's corporations. CSR refers to these and other impacts of corporations on society and the need to deal with these impacts in relation to stakeholders. These are generally identified as shareholders, creditors, suppliers, employees and the community.

The main idea underlying CSR is that companies will build shareholder value by engaging nonshareholder stakeholders and by taking account of the companies' impacts on society. This view is in contrast to that which states that businesses should concentrate on what is good for their owners. CSR does not advocate that companies should forgo profitable opportunities, unless they will threaten future profitability by increasing risks or costs, by threatening revenues and access to capital or labour (Hopkins & Cowe 2004).

The most common theories about why management would want to disclose its actions in annual reports are accountability theory, legitimacy theory and stakeholder theory.

Accountability theory

Accountability theory views corporations, through their management, as reacting to the concerns of external parties. Accountability involves the monitoring, evaluation and control of organisational agents to ensure that they behave in the interests of shareholders and other stakeholders (Keasey & Wright 1993).

There are two interpretations of this concept. The narrow one deals with the relationship between the company and its shareholders so that the primary focus is on financial information within the annual report. The second interpretation deals with the relationship between a corporation and its stakeholders so that its focus may be any disclosures within an annual report. Because accountability focuses upon the *relationship* between the corporation and users of its annual reports, information transmission between them depends upon the terms of that relationship (Owen et al. 1987). Management is monitored, evaluated and controlled to ensure that it behaves in the interests of shareholders and other stakeholders (Keasey & Wright 1993).

Legitimacy theory

Both Deegan and O'Donovan identify the need to align management's values with social values as a motivation for disclosure. The annual report is a tool with which management signals its reactions to the concerns of particular stakeholders. The underlying assumption is a social contract between society and organisation. Because corporations only exist because society has provided them with the means to do so, they have obligations to society.

An organisation's survival will be threatened if society perceives that it has breached its social contract. Consequently, reporting entities are controlled by community concerns (Brown & Deegan 1998) and values. Values change over time, and reporting entities need to respond to that (Dowling & Pfeffer 1975). Successful legitimation depends on reporting entities convincing society that a congruency of actions and values exists. Management will react to public concern over corporate actions by increasing the level of corporate disclosures in annual reports if it perceives that its legitimacy is threatened by that public concern (Brown & Deegan 1998).

Researchers using this perspective have been concerned largely with environmental issues. There is mounting evidence that managers should adopt legitimising strategies (Deegan 2002).

Stakeholder theory

Stakeholder theory is actually two theories: an ethics-based theory and a managerial- or positive-based theory. The ethics-based theory largely prescribes how organisations should treat their stakeholders, emphasising the organisations' responsibilities. The managerial-based theory emphasises the need to manage particular stakeholder groups, especially powerful ones. Some stakeholders are powerful because they control resources needed by the organisation's operations and for its survival. For example, lenders, suppliers, regulators and consumers are powerful for this reason.

Information is an important part of the strategy of managing valuable stakeholders. Management informs them of the reporting enterprise's activities through means such as the annual report. In many ways, stakeholder theory is not unlike legitimacy theory. However, while legitimacy theory is concerned with the community as a whole, stakeholder theory is concerned with only those stakeholders powerful enough to endanger the organisation in which they have a stake.

Summary

Appreciate the role alleged manipulation of reported earnings plays in the production of financial information.

- Accountants take advantage of the information asymmetry between themselves and external stakeholders to manipulate the image and financial performance figures of the company.
- Legal manipulation, or 'earnings management', involves the management of revenues and expenses to match analysts' earnings forecasts for the company.
- Income smoothing involves the management of earnings and expenses to provide a stable financial performance. Pro-forma reporting, generally used to estimate a recently listed entity's performance before listing, can also be used to exclude one-off or unusual items from earnings as atypical.

Appreciate the debate surrounding the exclusion of intangibles and intellectual capital from the financial reporting process.

- Accounting regulations exclude the reporting of intangibles in annual reports, resulting in a disparity between the reported and market value of entities. To overcome this, firms make voluntary disclosures, which may relate to human resources, the environment or community activities of the firm.
- The treatment of intangibles by accounting standards requires them to be identifiable. This means they must have been generated separately from the company, excluding internally generated intangibles such as brands, mastheads, customer lists and research, which are expensed, despite any market value they may generate.
- Intellectual capital refers to the capital created by employees, invested in employees and invested in relationships with customers and suppliers. Only intellectual capital that is purchased is recognised in financial statements. This can create significant issues for knowledge-based organisations.

Explain the options available to companies reporting voluntary disclosures.

- Traditionally, voluntary disclosures are made in the first half of the annual report. This section of the annual report can create controversy because it can be used as a marketing tool to manipulate the image of the organisation.
- New technological innovations have resulted in an increase in reporting disclosures made on company websites. The Internet provides increased flexibility and interactivity for the reader but it is not subject to the same auditing requirements as the physical annual report and information cannot be monitored to the same extent. The development of XBRL is designed to resolve this.

Appreciate the debate surrounding the length and frequency of reporting periods.

- Arguments for the standardisation of reporting periods to 12 months claim that it allows better comparability between companies, more accurate calculation of dividends, continued compliance with company law and better stewardship.
- Arguments supporting a more flexible approach to reporting periods claim that standardisation creates an artificial and arbitrary halt that may cut across

incomplete transactions, be contrary to an entity's internal earnings cycle and put pressure on managers to take a short-term view.

- Some of these issues are overcome by the provision for voluntary interim financial reporting, while the advent of XBRL may eventually allow for real-time reporting and analysis.

Identify three theories that explain the motivation for voluntary disclosures in annual reports.

- The theoretical basis for voluntary disclosure is based on CSR research, which aims to identify the motivations for companies to make voluntary disclosures about nonfinancial aspects of the business.
- Accountability theory involves the control and regulation of relationship between a corporation and its stakeholders, whether shareholders or a wider community, mediated through the disclosures made by the company.
- Legitimacy theory assumes a social contract between society and the organisation, using the annual report as a tool in which management can demonstrate its fulfilment of its obligations to meet community concerns and values.
- Stakeholder theory emphasises the ethical responsibilities of organisations to their stakeholders, and in particular, the need for management of relationships with smaller, more powerful stakeholder groups.

Key terms

active market 128
corporate social responsibility 138
earnings management 124
intangible assets 127
intellectual capital 129
interim financial reports 136
manipulation 124
pro-forma results 125

Review questions

5.1 Why does accounting have regular reporting periods?
5.2 Consider the arguments for and against standardised reporting periods. Do you agree that accounting periods should be more flexible? Give reasons for your answer.
5.3 What are the perceived purposes of an annual report?
5.4 Why are financial statements 'highly valued'?
5.5 What do you understand by the term 'fair presentation'? Give an example to support your answer.
5.6 Financial reports have been criticised for their lack of completeness. In what ways do financial reports fail the completeness test?
5.7 Defend the stand taken by accounting authorities in AASB 138/IAS 38 in relation to the treatment of intangible assets.

5.8   Define 'earnings management'. Do you consider it to be good or bad? Why?

5.9   Why are annual reports so well regarded?

5.10   Researchers speculate that management is motivated to disclose information voluntarily either because it feels accountable or because it wishes to legitimise its activities. Which do you think is the more likely reason and why?

5.11   Debate whether management should solely pursue profits.

5.12   What factors appear to instigate voluntary disclosure by management in annual reports?

5.13   Why should management explain poor performance in technical accounting terms?

5.14   Why do you think environmental disclosures are more researched than other social disclosures?

Application questions

Obtain a copy of an annual report and answer the following questions.

5.15   What do you think is the message being conveyed? For example, is management optimistic about profitability in the forthcoming financial year?

5.16   How long is the report in pages?

5.17   Where are the financial statements located in the report?

5.18   Is the company doing well financially? How do this year's results compare with previous results?

5.19   How many pages do the financial statements occupy?

5.20   How much of the report is devoted to nonverbal forms of communication?

5.21   Are there photographs in the report? If so, what do they depict? Do they reflect the message being conveyed in the report?

5.22   Are there graphs in the report? If so, what has been graphed?

5.23   What voluntary social disclosures are made in the report?

5.24   What is your overall impression of the annual report? Does it make you want to buy shares in the company? If you already own shares in the company, does it confirm that you have made a good decision in buying them?

case**study**   **5.1**

Reading the annual report: ten issues to consider

The ASIC website publishes a range of information designed to allow amateur investors to avoid the pitfalls of making ill-informed decisions when investing. These tips include advice on the best way to use a company's annual report to make an assessment of its financial performance. They include the ten issues detailed in the following.

There are lots of matters you can check in the annual report. Here are 10 issues you should consider, grouped into three areas:

• Operational and strategic activities of the company: The year's highlights

- Financial results
- Future strategic directions and performance: Looking ahead to next year

The year's highlights

1. Are the activities reported by the Chairman and Managing Director the same as the activities the company said it was going to do either in its prospectus or last annual report?

Any prospectus the company issued may have included information about markets the directors were aiming to penetrate and the products the company planned to produce. The company may also have made statements in the annual report or announcements to the market about new or different activities it is going to pursue.

Ask:

- Is the company doing the same things shareholders expected it to be doing, for example, was it going to build websites whereas now it is selling computer hardware?
- If it was going to sell products — is it selling the *same* products?
- If there has been a change in the activities, this may mean the company's prospects are significantly different. There may be different cost structures associated with the different activities and they may require different amounts of development or capital expenditure. There may be differences in the amount and timing of revenue for the company.

2. Is the current business strategy the same as that described in the prospectus or last annual report? If it has changed, how will it affect the performance of your investment?

Business strategy can be described in various ways — future directions, strategic objectives, business plans, corporate goals and vision statements. What are the ultimate goals of the company? Are the company's activities moving towards these goals? For example, did the company say it would develop e-commerce software applications for the banking industry, and now it is considering biotechnology products for the medical industry?

3. If strategic acquisitions were made during the year, how did they add value to the company?

Many companies make strategic acquisitions in other companies. For example, they purchase a substantial shareholding in another company. This company may be complementary because it sells key products to your company or it may provide access to additional markets, new technologies or new products.

Such investments may or may not generate a direct dividend/revenue stream for the company. Where investments like these have been made, how will these acquisitions help the long-term future of the company? Will the investment assist the company in achieving its short and long-term objectives? For example — if the company's strategy is to establish a significant market presence in Australia, how does acquiring a business in Brazil help achieve this objective?

4. **Has a tangible result been achieved from any money spent on research and development activities, such as developing high technology products or software applications?**

Companies may spend significant resources on areas described as research and development, product development and intellectual property development. These activities generally aim, among other things, to develop new products, improve existing products and help a company stand out in the market. Such expenditure will not always produce immediate results, but it is important for you to understand the size and purpose of that expenditure and any results that have been achieved.

A tangible result is something like the first sale of a software application or starting production of a high technology product or entering into a technology licence agreement for another business to use the technology developed by the company.

Financial results

5. **Did the company receive any revenue from its business activities? If it didn't, did the directors explain why not?**

In last year's annual report or a recent prospectus, the company may have expected to generate a certain amount of revenue in the coming year. These expectations may have depended on the types of revenue, some of which may be more sustainable over the longer term, and the amount of that revenue.

When reviewing the financial results, look at the actual revenue of the company and where it came from against these expectations. For example, did it come from selling software products or licensing technology rights to another business?

6. **Did the company make a profit or a loss? If it was a loss, did the directors explain why?**

Many companies during their 'start-up' phase do not make a profit. If this is the case, the directors may indicate in the annual report when they expect the company *will* make a profit. If this is not discussed in the report, ask the directors at the AGM. You should also consider the factors that will or may affect whether this profit forecast is achieved.

7. **How did the company fund its activities during the year? Did the company generate its own cashflow from its business activities or did it merely rely on funds from other sources such as funds raised from shareholders, debt financing and asset sales?**

In reviewing the Statement of Cashflows in the financial report, consider the source of the company's cash for the year.

For example, has the company only used the money raised from the issue of shares or has it borrowed additional funds through loans or by issuing convertible notes (these are debt securities than can be converted to shares at a later stage)? If the company has issued more shares during the year, have these diluted existing investors' shareholdings?

Be aware that Statement of Cashflows normally has three sections: operating activities, investment activities and financial activities.

Looking ahead to next year . . .

8. Is the company going to change its activities or business strategy for next year?

Companies operating in a competitive environment have opportunities for the future, and risks or hurdles that must be overcome to achieve success. Think about the key factors that will affect future performance and how the company plans to address these — making the most of the opportunities and minimising the risks.

9. How long can the company last at its current 'cash-burn' rate? If it looks like it might run out of cash during next year, what is the company proposing to do about this?

'Cash-burn rate' usually refers to the rate at which the company is using its cash reserves. Where the company is not yet generating cash from its operations, see where cash is being spent and the rate at which it is being spent. Many high technology companies lodge cashflow statements with the ASX at the end of each quarter. You may want to ask for a copy of the company's last couple of cashflow statements.

Where a company is not yet producing revenue but is still using cash to fund its operations, you should assess whether the company will have enough cash on hand until revenue begins to be generated. If it won't, how will the company meet its requirements — will it try to raise more funds? Or will it borrow the money?

10. Is the company going to make a profit next year? How?

You should get an idea of what the directors expect for the coming year. If a product is still in the development phase, the directors may think that the company will continue to run at a loss. However, if the company is beginning to develop markets for its product, expectations may be more positive.

You should also distinguish between *possible* developments, customers and contracts, and those prospects that are more certain.

Source: This article appeared on www.fido.asic.gov.au.

---

1. Obtain a copy of an annual report issued by a listed company.
2. Follow the suggestions of the corporate regulator, and analyse the annual report:
   (a) Examine the figures in the financial statements to get an overall impression of the financial performance of the company.
   (b) Note which figures you think are important to an understanding of the financial performance of the company you have chosen.
   (c) Read what management has to say about these figures in the front half of the report.
   (d) Return to the financial report and examine the figures again, taking into account what management has said in the front half. Has your assessment changed in any way? How?
3. Write a short assessment of the company as a potential investment.

NAB self-portrait less than flattering

In an attempt to repair the culture of the bank that resulted in the $360 million foreign exchange loss and the traumatic upheaval of its board and management, Australia's biggest bank is aiming to show it is more transparent and accountable.

This time, it's trying to do it with a comprehensive index on how well it reports on the Global Reporting Initiative 2002 Sustainability Reporting Guidelines, an internationally recognised de facto standard for the triple bottom line requirements, which take into account social and environmental factors as well as economic ones.

While the index shows that the bank is complying with requirements such as anti-discrimination policy, assets under management with a high social benefit, equal opportunity and corporate community investment, the report shows gaps in such areas as biodiversity and client engagement on environmental issues.

The report says the bank has beefed up its whistleblower guidelines with workshops, a staff awareness campaign, and training of senior managers to understand it.

It has also promised to align next year's CSR report with financial reporting processes used in the annual report. The aim here would be to provide a more comprehensive and robust picture on where the bank stood on CSR issues.

NAB's total expenditure on 'corporate community investment', which includes charitable gifts, volunteering, and commercial initiatives in the community, totalled $17.74 million, compared with $12.76 million in 2004.

Chairman Michael Chaney and chief executive John Stewart, in their statement in the report, said that the experiences of the foreign currency losses showed the value of 'taking a balanced and more focused approach to stakeholder engagement'.

Source: This article appeared in *The Age*.

1. Milton Friedman once said that the social responsibility of business is to increase its profits. How can you reconcile this statement with the issue of CSR reports?
2. How could the independent verification of CSR reports dispel the image that they are self-congratulatory?
3. Do you think that shareholders would react differently from other stakeholders to the CSR report?
4. Download National Australia Bank (NAB)'s CSR report from its website (www.nabgroup.com) and read the chairman and managing director's statement. How do the NAB directors describe their motivation for the disclosures made in the CSR report? Discuss their statement in relation to accountability theory, legitimacy theory and stakeholder theory.
5. Research the CSR reports of ANZ Bank, Westpac and the Commonwealth Bank of Australia. How does NAB's CSR performance compare with that of other Australian banks?

Recommended readings

Beattie, V & Jones, MJ 1999, 'Australian financial graphs: an empirical study', *Abacus*, vol. 35, no. 1, pp. 46–76.

Stanton, PA & Stanton, PJ 2002, 'Corporate annual reports: research perspectives used', *Accounting, Auditing & Accountability Journal*, vol. 15, no. 4, pp. 478–500.

Walker, RG & Robinson, SP 1994, 'Competing regulatory agencies with conflicting agendas: setting standards for cash flow reporting in Australia', *Abacus*, vol. 30, no. 2, pp. 119–37.

Wright, S 2004, 'Accounting for intangible assets in Australia: exposure draft 109', *Accounting Research Journal*, vol. 17, no. 1, pp. 32–42.

References

Aerts, W 1994, 'On the use of accounting logic as an explanatory category in narrative accounting disclosures', *Accounting, Organizations & Society*, vol. 19, nos 4/5, pp. 337–53.

Australian Accounting Standards Board (AASB) 2004, *AASB 101 Presentation of financial statements*, Australian Accounting Standards Board, Melbourne.

—— 2004, *AASB 118, Revenue*, Australian Accounting Standards Board, Melbourne.

—— 2004, *AASB 138, Intangible assets*, Australian Accounting Standards Board, Melbourne.

Beattie, V & Jones, MJ 1992, 'The use and abuse of graphs in annual reports: theoretical framework and empirical study', *Accounting and Business Research*, vol. 22, no. 88, pp. 291–303.

—— 1997, 'A comparative study of the use of financial graphs in the corporate annual reports of major US and UK companies', *Journal of International Financial Management and Accounting*, vol. 8, no. 1, pp. 33–68.

—— 1999, 'Australian financial graphs: an empirical study', *Abacus*, vol. 35, no. 1, pp. 46–76.

Beckett, R & Jonker J 2002, 'AccountAbility 1000: a new social standard for building sustainability', *Managerial Auditing Journal*, vol. 17, nos 1/2, pp. 36–43.

Bhattacharya, N, Black, EL, Christensen, TE & Mergenthaler, RD 2004, 'Empirical evidence on recent trends in pro-forma reporting', *Accounting Horizons*, vol. 18, no. 1, pp. 27–44.

Boerner, H 2005, 'Are corporate accounting systems out-of-date?', *Corporate Finance Review*, vol. 10, no. 2, pp. 35–41.

Brody, RG & McDonald, R 2004, 'The next scandal: the undisciplined use of pro-forma financial statements', *American Business Review*, vol. 22, no. 1, pp. 34–8.

Brown, N & Deegan, C 1998, 'The public disclosure of environmental performance information — a dual test of media agenda setting theory and legitimacy theory', *Accounting and Business Research*, vol. 29, no. 1, pp. 21–41.

Deegan, C 2002, 'The legitimising effect of social and environmental disclosures: a theoretical foundation', *Accounting, Auditing & Accountability Journal*, vol. 15, no. 3, pp. 282–312.

Dowling, J & Pfeffer, J 1975, 'Organizational legitimacy: social values and organizational behaviour', *Pacific Sociological Review*, vol. 18, no. 1, pp. 122–36.

Dyckman, TR & Zeff, SA 2000, 'The future of financial reporting: removing it from the shadows', *Pacific Accounting Review*, vol. 11, no. 2, pp. 89–96.

Hendriksen, ES & van Breda, MF 1992, *Accounting theory*, 5th edn, Irwin, Homewood, Illinois.

Hunter, L, Webster, E & Wyatt, A 2005, 'Measuring intangible capital: a review of current practice', *Australian Accounting Review*, vol. 15, no. 2, pp. 4–21.

Jones, MJ 1996, 'Readability of annual reports', *Accounting, Auditing & Accountability Journal*, vol. 9, no. 2, pp. 86–91.

Keasey, K & Wright, M 1993, 'Issues in corporate accountability and governance: an editorial', *Accounting and Business Research*, vol. 23, no. 91A, pp. 291–303.

Lee, T 1994, 'The changing form of the corporate annual report', *The Accounting Historians Journal*, vol. 21, no. 1, June, pp. 215–32.

Lev, B & Daum, JH 2004, 'The dominance of intangible assets: consequences for enterprise management and corporate reporting', *Measuring Business Excellence*, vol. 8, no. 1, pp. 6–17.

Lev, B & Zarowin, P 1999, 'The boundaries of financial reporting and how to extend them', *Journal of Accounting Research*, vol. 37, pp. 353–83.

Luther, R 2003, 'Uniform accounting periods: an historical review and critique', *Accounting History*, vol. 8, no. 2, pp. 79–100.

Macintosh, NB, Shearer, T, Thornton, DB & Welker, M 2000, 'Accounting a simulacrum and hyperreality: perspectives on income and capital', *Accounting, Organizations and Society*, vol. 25, pp. 13–50.

Mather, P, Ramsay, A & Serry, A 1996, 'The use and representational faithfulness of graphs in annual reports: Australian evidence', *Australian Accounting Review*, vol. 6, no. 2.

Owen, D, Gray, R & Maunders, K 1987, 'Researching the information content of social responsibility disclosures: a comment', *British Accounting Review*, vol. 19, no. 2, pp. 169–75.

Parfet, WU 2000, 'Accounting subjectivity and earnings management: a preparer perspective', *Accounting Horizons*, vol. 14, no. 4, pp. 481–9.

Seetharaman, A, Subramanian, R & Shyong, SY 2005, 'Internet financial reporting', *Corporate Financial Review*, vol. 10, no. 1, pp. 23–34.

Stanton, PA & Stanton, PJ 2002, 'Corporate annual reports: research perspectives used', *Accounting, Auditing & Accountability Journal*, vol. 15, no. 4, pp. 478–500.

Stlowy, H & Breton, G 2004, 'Accounts manipulation: a literature review and proposed conceptual framework', *Review of Accounting & Finance*, vol. 3, no. 1, pp. 5–69.

6 CORPORATE GOVERNANCE

LEARNING OBJECTIVES

After reading this chapter, you should be able to:

- understand what corporate governance is and why good corporate governance systems are needed

- outline the role of the following concepts in agency theory: agency contract; monitoring costs; bonding costs; residual loss

- explain the nature of manager–shareholder agency problems: risk aversion; dividend retention; horizon disparity, and derive the bonus plan hypothesis

- understand the key areas involved in corporate governance and the alternative approaches

- understand the role and impact of accounting in and on corporate governance

- understand the role of ethics in corporate governance.

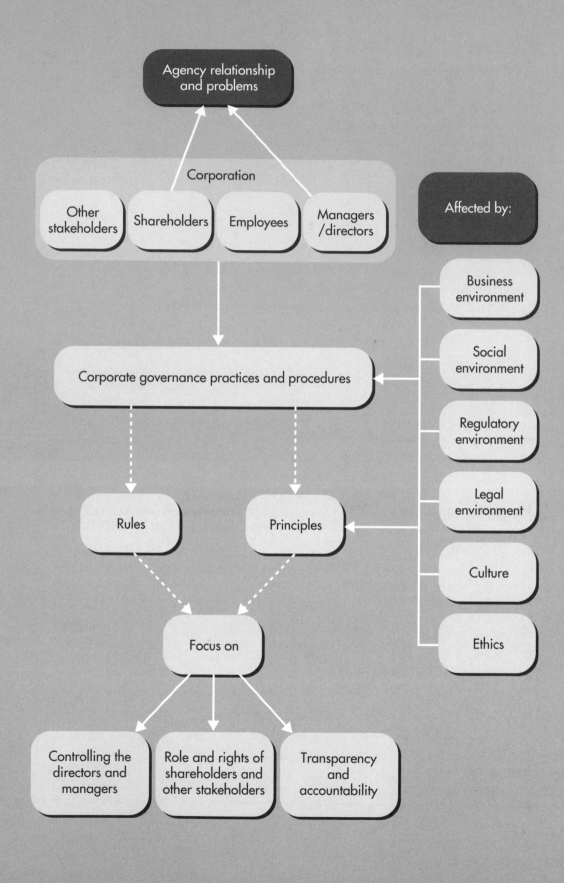

Introduction

How corporations are managed affects all our lives. They control a large part of the resources of this planet and are increasingly the dominant form of economic organisation. Clearly, decisions made by the people who run corporations affect the prosperity of individuals directly involved with the particular corporations (such as their shareholders and employees) but their decisions also have a much wider impact. In many instances those running companies have abused their positions and corporations have been found wanting: the collapses of Enron and WorldCom in the United States, and companies polluting the environment are examples. Yet we want those in positions of responsibility in companies to run them properly and to make the 'right' decisions. How can we try to make sure that companies do act appropriately?

'Corporate governance' is the term used to cover the series of principles, mechanisms or procedures developed for this end, and this chapter focuses on some of the underlying causes of corporate governance problems and the role of accounting in effective corporate governance. It must be remembered, however, that decisions are made by people, and so there is a need to consider the behaviour of individuals in companies; this involves us looking at the role of ethics in corporate decision making.

The growing interest in corporate governance

In the past decade, interest in corporate governance practices has increased as a direct result of highly publicised cases of corporate misconduct and concerns over the management of corporations. There is also a growing realisation that good corporate governance can not only help in avoiding problems but also provide other advantages. Although the corporate structure has many advantages (such as facilitating capital investment and limiting some risk, through the limited liability afforded to shareholders), the separation of the management of the corporation from those who contribute resources (such as shareholders) can lead to problems. So what can go wrong?

Problems with the management of corporations

Recent examples show what type of problems may occur:
- Those managing a company may use the resources to benefit themselves (rather than shareholders). Often this can involve fraud, as, for example, in the case of Parmalat, where documents were forged to hide debt and flows of cash to family members (*The Economist* 2004). However, it is often more subtle, and in many corporate scandals it has been argued 'false' reporting has sometimes been motivated by the desire to maintain the value of benefits provided to corporate managers (such as the value of share options).

- Corporations may take actions that shareholders (or society) may not consider desirable. For example, Mitsubishi in Japan failed to inform customers of potential safety problems with vehicles or recall the vehicles for repair, which it is claimed led to accidents, including one resulting in the death of the driver (*Asahi Shimbun* 2004)
- Corporations may 'hide' or provide 'false' information to shareholders to avoid consequences. For example, Enron failed to inform shareholders of the true level of debt, and WorldCom incorrectly recorded expenses as assets to increase reported profits.
- In recent times a disparity (a 'mismatch') has been perceived between the payments received by the managers of corporations and their performance, with directors and executives of corporations receiving massive payments and benefits even when corporate performance is poor or declining.

For an insight into just one of the highly publicised scandals, consider the example in the In Focus vignette that follows.

 ## infocus *Boss of 'Australian Enron' jailed*

The former boss of insurance firm HIH, Raymond Williams, was sentenced to four-and-a-half years in jail in April 2005, for his involvement in the collapse of Australia's second-largest insurer. The collapse of the company in 2001, with debts of $5.3 billion, affected tens of thousands of policyholders, leaving many uninsured or out of pocket. The scandal precipitated an industrywide crisis.

The company aggressively pursued an increased share of the insurance market by reducing premiums dramatically, leaving it without adequate funds to cover future claims. Senior executives were found to have manipulated accounts to cover the extent of the financial consequences, which were exacerbated by ill-advised and inadequately financed forays into the US and UK markets.

Williams, one of nine former executives charged over their involvement in the collapse, admitted to misleading and reckless corporate behaviour. During his trial, details of his extravagant spending sprees were revealed, with thousands spent on jellybeans, cigars and jewellery. Williams was also accused of providing large loans to friends and workers, all funded by the company coffers.

Source: Information from an article that appeared in *Investments Magazine*.

Although these examples may be the focus of media attention, high-profile corporate scandals and misconduct are not recent occurrences. Of course, it could be argued that the problems mentioned are inevitably part of the risks of 'doing business', and the history of corporations for more than the past 100 years is associated with regulations to protect the public, usually in response to corporate scandals or failures. These have included the need for financial reports and audits.

However, good corporate governance practices go beyond reporting and regulations. Furthermore, the risks in not having good corporate governance practices are high — not only to individuals who may be directly involved with specific corporations, but to business and the economy in general. For an individual company, the failure to assure others that it has good governance practices can reduce its value; for the economy, a lack of public confidence in corporations can result in reduced economic growth. Given the key role that financial reporting and auditing play in corporate governance, failures or poor corporate governance also risks a loss of confidence in the position of the accounting profession itself.

Advantages of good corporate governance

Companies that can demonstrate good corporate governance practices have advantages. With the increasing globalisation of business and competition for capital, companies that can provide assurances that the company is being appropriately managed can gain a competitive edge. Reducing perceived risks to investors can reduce the cost of capital. Furthermore, the expansion of company shareholdings to a broader base (in many countries, small shareholders are becoming increasingly common, either by direct investment or indirectly through their superannuation plans), combined with more organised and active shareholders lobby groups, is placing more scrutiny on company management.

A key reason for the interest in corporate governance, and many of the current prescriptions for best practice, is that they are needed for an efficient market and to facilitate economic growth:

> The presence of an effective corporate governance system, within an individual company and across the economy as a whole, helps to provide a degree of confidence that is necessary for the proper functioning of a market economy. As a result, the cost of capital is lower and firms are encouraged to use resources more efficiently, thereby underpinning growth (OECD 2004, p. 11).

▪ What corporate governance is

Corporate governance in very simple terms is 'the system by which business corporations are directed and controlled' (Cadbury, cited in Cowan 2004, p. 15). A 'good' corporate governance system ensures that the corporation sets appropriate objectives and then puts systems and structures in place to ensure that these objectives are met, and also provides the means for others, both within and outside of the corporation, to control and monitor the activities of the corporation and its managers.

corporate governance: The system by which business corporations are directed and controlled

Corporate governance stakeholders

The determination whose interests are to be protected and what are 'appropriate' objectives of the corporation is a central question and will influence the related corporate governance systems. The traditional view of the role of the corporation is best stated by Milton Friedman, who argued that: 'corporate governance is to conduct the business in accordance with the owner or shareholders' desires, which generally will be to make as much money as possible while conforming to the basic rules of the society embodied in law and local customs' (cited in India Info Line 2005).

This view that corporate governance relates to ensuring that the interests of the key providers of capital to the corporation (the shareholders) are met underlies many of the current requirements and practices in corporate governance. This view is referred to as the 'Anglo-Saxon' model and is the basis for many corporate governance models currently, including, increasingly, in Asia, where there is convergence on this model (Allen 2000). This approach views a key role for corporate governance as enabling the efficient use of resources by helping financial markets to work properly and gives priority to shareholder value (Cornford 2004, p.10). The Anglo-Saxon model tends to focus on the problems caused by the relationship between managers and owners (because of the agency relationship discussed in the next section) and often takes a control-orientated approach, concentrating on mechanisms to curb self-serving managerial decisions and actions.

A wider view and more pluralist model that is increasingly being supported is that the responsibility of corporations goes beyond the narrow interests of shareholders and should be extended to a wider group of stakeholders. For example, German models of corporate governance emphasise multiple stakeholders; other European countries have more focus on employees. Corporate governance systems are more and more considering stakeholders beyond the traditional shareholder groups, and a range of models exists with varying emphases on stakeholders and views of corporate responsibility. This extension of corporate responsibility is also discussed in chapter 7 with relation to social and environmental accounting. Before considering what is involved in practicing good corporate governance, and briefly examining current guidelines, the next sections consider why there may be a problem with corporate governance and one dominant positive theory in accounting linked to this.

The need for corporate governance systems

Corporate governance rules and prescriptions are needed because of the nature of the company structure. This, at least for all but small family companies, means that the people who have provided the resources to the company (the shareholders and lenders) do not actually run the company directly. These capital contributors need to rely on managers. This separation between capital contributors and management is the source of many issues and problems relating to corporate governance. It could be argued that if managers behaved properly (i.e. acted as though they had contributed the capital), there would be no difficulties. Alternatively, people could opt not to contribute capital to companies; rather, they could only invest in businesses that they themselves manage. A dominant positive accounting theory, agency theory, provides an explanation why these things do not happen and why managers may 'bias' or distort the financial statements. This stream of accounting theory and associated research is referred to as accounting policy choice research and is based on agency theory. It is often referred to simply as 'positive accounting research' because it has been the prevalent positive paradigm in accounting research for more than 30 years.

Separation of management and capital providers

The beginning of this research derives from contracting theory. As noted, many problems with corporate governance are caused by the separation of management and the owners of capital. So why have this separation? Contracting theory explains this by arguing that the arrangement is efficient. The alternative is managing everything oneself. This of course would not be possible: imagine trying to organise a concert on your own!

The solution is for firms or companies to be formed to produce and provide goods and services efficiently. These firms can be viewed as a network of contracts or agreements that determine the relationships with and among the various parties involved in the firm: suppliers, employees, distributors, shareholders, lenders and so on. One important relationship is that between the managers and the capital contributors. The latter, such as shareholders, authorise the managers to make the key business decisions. This is a form of agency relationship.

◾ Agency theory and the nature of the agency relationship

An **agency relationship** by definition has two key parties:

- a principal who delegates the authority to make decisions to the other party
- an agent who is the person given the authority to make decisions on behalf of the principal.

agency relationship: A relationship in which a principal delegates decision-making authority to an agent

An agent is considered ethically and often legally to have a fiduciary duty. This means that the agent (i.e. the manager) is placed in a position of trust and assumes a duty to act in good faith and should act in the best interests of the principal (i.e. the shareholder).

However, a common assumption in economic theory is that if individuals are rational, they will act in their own best interests. Therefore, although managers should supposedly make decisions that are best for the principals, in some instances they will make decisions that maximise their own wealth, rather than the principals'. Principals are also rational and will expect the managers not always to act in the shareholders' interests. Jensen & Meckling (1976) identified that the existence of this agency relationship, although put in place for efficiency reasons, had disadvantages, and identified three costs that were incurred in the agency relationship. These are outlined overleaf.

Monitoring costs

Given that the shareholders cannot completely 'trust' the manager to act always in their best interest (it would be expected that the manager would act in his or her own interest), there needs to be some mechanism to monitor the manager's actions, which will involve **monitoring costs**. These include the costs in preparing financial reports, which can advise principals of the result of man-ager's decisions, and the cost of employing an auditor to certify the accuracy of the financial statements.

monitoring costs: Costs incurred by principals to monitor the behaviour of the agent

Bonding costs

Given that principals will expect managers to act in their own interests, it is likely that what the manager will receive in terms of rewards for managing the company will be less to reflect expectations of self-interested behaviour. However, if the manager (the agent) can provide some assurance that he or she will not act against the principal's interests, then the remuneration will not be reduced as much. One way to provide this assurance is to bond the interest of the manager to that of shareholders (i.e. to make what is in the interests of shareholders also in the best interest of the manager). This can be done, for example, by linking the payment made to the manager to the profit of the company. In this case, the manager is also interested in achieving as high a profit as possible. However, this costs the manager by restricting his or her actions. If the manager would have preferred taking expensive business trips, this will reduce the profit and, given the payment arrangements, will also reduce the payment to the manager. This 'loss' of choice for the manager, because of limiting or restricting his or her behaviour, is an example of **bonding costs**.

bonding costs: The restrictions placed on an agent's actions deriving from linking the agent's interest to that of the principal

Residual loss

Monitoring and bonding activities will never be complete. They are also limited because some of these activities may cost more than the expected benefits. So sometimes the decisions made by managers, despite monitoring and bonding, are not in the interests of the principal, and the value of the principal's investment is not optimised. This cost (i.e. the reduction of wealth because of less than ideal behaviour on the part of the manager) is known as the **residual loss**.

residual loss: The reduction in wealth of principals caused by their agent's non-optimal behaviour

Agency theory suggests that in an ideal world these costs will actually be paid by the manager. This is because, given that principals will expect managers to act in their own self-interest, they will 'pass' these costs on to managers through, for example, lower salaries. Therefore, the incentive is for managers to try to minimise these costs. However, to be able to pass on all these costs would require that principals could perfectly estimate the impact of managers' behaviour.

Agency problems

What could managers do that would be against shareholders' interests? The most obvious action would be that managers could use the funds of the business for their own personal use. For example, they might take the company's money and purchase a boat or property for themselves or for their family. This has occurred in several cases and involves deception and often fraud. In these cases, managers are acting outside the authority given to them by shareholders and often illegally. However, managers can use more subtle means to make decisions that benefit them, at the expense of shareholders. These do not involve fraud or deception but making business decisions (i.e. of the type they are authorised to make) that still result in less than optimal results from the perspective of the principal.

The literature identifies different types of problems between managers and principals. Furthermore, agency theory suggests that some of these potential problems can be reduced by contracting with managers. These contracts then 'bond' the interests of managers with those of principals. As noted, principals in this relationship can be either shareholders or lenders but this text is restricted to the relationship between managers and shareholders.

Risk aversion

This problem is caused by the relationship between risk and return. In economic theory it is generally accepted that the higher the risk, the higher is the potential return. Shareholders often diversify their investments, and any particular company may only be one investment in a portfolio of investments. Thus shareholders can manage risk by diversification. Managers are primarily concerned with the risk of the particular company because that is normally their key source of income, so managers will take less risk than shareholders might prefer. If managers continue to take lower-risk projects, this will be expected to lead to lower profits, which is not in the interest of shareholders. One way of encouraging managers to undertake more risk (and consequently earn greater potential returns) is to provide a bonus to the manager linked to profits.

Dividend retention

Managers, compared with shareholders, prefer to pay out less of the company's earnings in dividends This may allow the company to expand further (and the managers' interest is in the company growing) or allow even more funds for them to use for their own salaries and benefits (big offices, expensive business trips). Shareholders usually prefer more in dividends. This provides them with disposable income and also provides the ability to invest further (either in this company or other investments).

Horizon disparity

This problem relates to the differences in timeframes. Because the value of the company (and the share price) theoretically reflects the long-term value of the company, shareholders want managers to make investments and decisions that are best for the long term. However, managers are concerned with the performance of the company while they manage it. After they leave, they will have no interest in the company. This is particularly a problem if the manager expects to stay with the company for a relatively short time. Examples of the types of actions managers could take that reflect a short-term view but are detrimental in the longer term to the company might be to:

- *Reduce money spent on research and development.* This often involves higher current expenses but the benefits are not realised until later.
- *Delay or fail to undertake maintenance or upgrades.* This will reduce expenses now but in the long term could result in greater expenses (or reduced productivity) for the company.

You should see that these are actions that affect economic wealth (they affect the *cash* inflows and outflows for a company due to investing in less profitable projects, or paying less in dividends, or investing less in research, which will reduce profitability); these are not *accounting* adjustments.

Avoiding agency problems

Agency theory explains that these problems can be reduced by linking management's rewards to certain conditions. This in effect 'bonds' the interests of the managers to those of the shareholders. The mechanism to do this is by contracting with the managers, through a bonus plan that specifically deals with each of these problems. For example:

- To reduce the risk aversion problem, part of the manager's bonus is linked to the profit of the company. This provides an incentive for managers to invest in more risky projects that have the potential to earn higher profits, and consequently provide a larger bonus to the manager.
- To reduce the dividend retention problem, part of the bonus can be tied to profits (because the higher the profits, the less able are managers to justify reductions in dividends) or more directly to a dividend payout ratio. Also, because share prices are affected by dividend payments, a bonus may be linked to share price.
- To ensure that the manager takes a longer-term view and to avoid the horizon problem, it is common either for manager's bonuses to be linked to share price or for part of the manager's rewards to be in the form of shares or share options.

The In Focus vignette that follows discusses executive compensation, showing how the propositions from agency theory are often reflected in this context.

 Not regulators' role to cap CEO salaries

Bill Holland's pay was near the bottom in a ranking of the 100 most highly paid CEOs last year. As chief executive of CI Financial Inc., he collected $600 000 in gross salary, $600 000 in bonuses, cashed in $1.9 million worth of stocks and received stock options valued at $1.5 million.

What's interesting about Holland's hefty pay is not that it's low compared to his peer group, it's that investors can even decipher how much he was paid.

David Wilson, chairman of the Ontario Securities Commission, recently weighed in on the increasing complexity of understanding how much business leaders are paid.

'Executive compensation is getting tougher for investors to understand,' he told an audience at the Canadian Club in Montreal last week. 'It seems like no one is just paid a straight salary any more.'

The other issue surfacing about the pay packets for business leaders is the basis on which they're determined. A study released last week by the Ontario Teachers Pension Plan found no correlation between executive compensation and shareholder returns, including share price appreciation and dividends.

It's no surprise the issue of executive compensation is coming under increasing scrutiny...

The sheer amount CEOs are paid is coming under fire, leading North American regulators to push for more transparent disclosure requirements for all forms of executive compensation — stock options, pension benefits, use of company assets such as airplanes and severance allowances, including golden handshake payments...

As CEO pay packets become ever more complex, disclosure becomes all the more important, critics say.

Historically, CEO pay was based on what chief executives at comparable companies were paid, Slipp says. But there is growing sentiment that pay should be related to a company's performance.

Increasingly, compensation is based on evidence of performance, such as current and recent years' financials. Bonuses tend to be based on short-term indicators, such as earnings and revenue growth, Slipp says, not longer-term ones like shareholder return.

Another way of determining compensation would be to examine the underlying performance of the company by looking at earnings growth, stock price or rate of return on equity, says Crawford.

However, since what happens may not necessarily be directly attributable to a CEO, Crawford suggests that a compensation committee would need to scrutinize each individual situation. For instance, oil shortages, not savvy CEOs, have driven oil stocks up recently.

Alternatively, 2005 was a record year for Home Depot's earnings per share, gross and operating margins and sales. Yet its stock fell 12 per cent — more than its peers or the 5 per cent the S&P 500 index declined. This is an example of a company whose underlying value has improved but whose external value hasn't, says Crawford. So the CEO should not be penalized for the stock's dismal performance.

In asking for increased disclosure, regulators are seeking a better explanation from boards on what the executives did well, what targets were met, where the executive succeeded and where he or she failed. After all, boards ultimately approve a CEO's pay.

Current compensation systems provide too many 'free passes,' says Holland...

Holland says executive compensation should be based on a number of measures and not just a 'formula that makes corporate governance experts happy'. If a company's stock price rises 15 per cent while the overall market jumps 35 per cent, it's no reason to celebrate.

'It's quite trendy to talk about how much they make versus why they make as much as they do,' says Holland.

At CI, Holland's compensation is set by the board, which uses several measures to determine his total pay, including changes in mutual fund operating expenses, retail managed assets, net income and operating efficiencies. Holland says his pay is among the lowest of his peers, even though shareholder returns are among the best.

Source: This article appeared in *The Toronto Star.*

■ The implications and predictions of bonus plans

A key implication of agency theory is that it provides a reason and explanation for the need for accounting reports: to help monitor and control the activities of managers. This would explain, for example, why accounting reports were prepared even before required by regulation.

Furthermore, the theory considers the interaction of two factors:

- to avoid the potential problems identified, a manager's bonus will be linked to particular accounting measures (such as profit)
- the assumption that individuals act in their *own* interest.

It would be expected that managers try to ensure that the accounting profit is as high as possible to increase their bonus. This leads to a prediction (known as the bonus plan hypothesis) about the accounting policy choices a manager will make in such circumstances. The **bonus plan hypothesis** states that if managers' remuneration is tied to accounting profit through a bonus plan, they will adopt accounting policies that shift reported income from future periods to the present period.

bonus plan hypothesis: A prediction of agency theory that if managers' remuneration is tied to accounting profit through a bonus plan, they will adopt accounting policies that shift reported income from future periods to the present period

For example, managers need to make choices about whether to expense or capitalise certain expenditures, or at what rate to depreciate certain assets. The hypothesis predicts that generally managers will make the choices that increase the current year's accounting profit to increase their bonus. In other words, the accounting profit reported is influenced not just by the actual economic circumstances or success of the company, but also by how managers decide to account for transactions and events that have occurred in the period. In this sense, it means that the accounting reports are biased because managers are trying to influence (or manipulate) the profit figure to benefit themselves.

Whether bonuses that are linked to share price also create these incentives for managers is debatable. This depends on whether managers believe that the market is efficient. Market efficiency is discussed in chapter 9 on capital market research. If the manager does not believe that the changes in reported profits caused by changes in accounting policies would affect the share price (i.e. the manager does not believe that the market is efficient), then such a bonus plan would create no incentives. However, some commentators have suggested that in some of the more recent reporting failures that the manipulation of accounting results has, at least in part, been caused by managers' attempts to maintain share prices.

Research support for agency theory

Intuitively, this theory appeals because it makes sense that managers would try to increase their bonuses where possible. The research generally confirms the bonus plan hypothesis and the principles of this theory also appear to be reflected in the types of bonus packages often offered to managers.

Figure 6.1 summarises the key principles of the shareholder–manager relationship in agency theory.

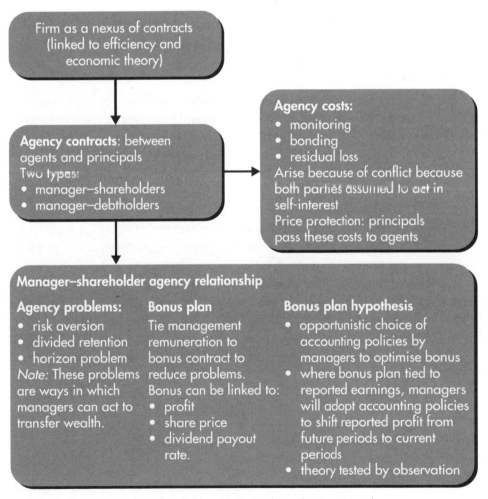

FIGURE 6.1 Overview of the shareholder–manager relationship in agency theory

Learning tips

Do you know...

6.1 Corporate governance refers to the series of principles, mechanisms and procedures by which a corporation is managed and controlled. The objective of corporate governance is to ensure that the interests of corporate stakeholders are met.

6.2 The separation of ownership and managements, which is a feature of the structure of corporations, result in an agency relationship between managers and shareholders. Agency theory identifies three types of problems that occur because of the differing interests of managers and shareholders.

6.3 To deal with the agency problems, bonus plans are commonly implemented to align managers' interests with those of shareholders. This predicts that managers are likely to try to use accounting policy choices to increase their payments under these bonus plans.

◾ Corporate governance guidelines and practices

As noted, corporate governance involves ensuring that the decisions made by those managing the corporation are appropriate, and providing a means to monitor corporate activities and the decision making itself. It is primarily concerned with managing the relationship between the shareholders, the key managers of the corporation (usually the board of directors), other senior managers within the corporation and other stakeholders. Many countries have developed suggested (and sometimes required) lists of rules or descriptions of the types of practices that should be included in corporate governance systems. However, it is generally acknowledged that there is no 'one' system of corporate governance. The practices and procedures required or desired will be affected by:

- *The nature of the particular corporation and its activities.* For example, in some companies there are dominant shareholders, whereas in others shareholding may be more widely spread.

- *The environment in which the corporation operates.* This will include the legal, regulatory and social environment. For example, in some countries, employees have particular legal rights to information and board representation; in others, directors are individually responsible for decisions, whereas in others, the members of the board of directors may have joint responsibility under law. The *legal* status and enforcement of particular corporate governance systems and procedures will also affect actual practice. In some countries, particular practices (such as requirements for an audit committee or disclosures of remuneration of directors) will be required by law. In other countries, these may not be legally required, although they may be recommended practice.

Elements of corporate governance

Table 6.1 contains summaries of codes of good corporate governance as outlined by the Organisation for Economic Co-operation and Development (OECD), the Australian Securities Exchange (ASX) and the China Securities Regulatory Commission. You should review these summaries now.

TABLE 6.1 Various codes of good corporate governance

Summary of OECD's 6 Principles of Corporate Governance	Summary of ASX 10 Principles of Corporate Governance	Overview of Code of Corporate Governance for Listed Companies in China
I. Ensuring the Basis for an Effective Corporate Governance Framework The corporate governance framework should promote transparent and efficient markets, be consistent with the rule of law and clearly articulate the division of responsibilities among different supervisory, regulatory and enforcement authorities.	**1. Lay solid foundations for manaagement and oversight** Recognise and publish the respective roles and responsibilties of Board and management.	**Chapter 1: Shareholders and Shareholders' Meetings** This covers issues and practices to ensure the equal treatment and the protection of legitimate rights and interests of all shareholders, and includes sections on (1) Protection of the Rights of the Shareholders, (2) Rules and procedures for Meetings, (3) Related Party Transactions.
II. The Rights of Shareholders and Key Ownership Functions The corporate governance framework should protect and facilitate the exercise of shareholders' rights.	**2. Structure the Board to add value** Have a Board of an effective composition, size and commitment to adequately discharge its responsibilities and duties. For example a majority of the board should be independent.	**Chapter 2: Listed Company and Its Controlling Shareholders** This covers issues and practices to regulate the Relationship Between Listed Company and Its Controlling Shareholders, and includes sections on (1) Behavior Rules for Controlling Shareholders and (2) Independence of Listed Company.

continued

TABLE 6.1 *continued*

Summary of OECD's 6 Principles of Corporate Governance	Summary of ASX 10 Principles of Corporate Governance	Overview of Code of Corporate Governance for Listed Companies in China
III. The Equitable Treatment of Shareholders The corporate governance framework should ensure the equitable treatment of all shareholders, including minority and foreign shareholders. All shareholders should have the opportunity to obtain effective redress for violation of their rights.	**3. Promote ethical and responsible decision making** Actively promote ethical and responsible decision-making. For example establish a code of conduct for directors and key executives to ensure someone is responsible and accountable for reporting and investigating reports of unethical behaviour.	**Chapter 3: Directors and Board of Directors** This covers issues and practices to strengthen the Directors' Duties of Good Faith and Due Diligence and includes sections on (1) Election Procedures for Directors, (2) The Duties and Responsibilities of Directors, (3) Duties and Composition of the Board of Directors, (4) Rules and Procedure of the Board of Directors, (5) Independent Director, (6) To Establish Special Committees under of the Board of Directors.
IV. The Role of Stakeholders in Corporate Governance The corporate governance framework should recognise the rights of stakeholders established by law or through mutual agreements and encourage active co-operation between corporations and stakeholders in creating wealth, jobs, and the sustainability of financially sound enterprises.	**4. Safeguard integrity in financial reporting** Have a structure to independently verify and safeguard the integrity of the company's fnancial reporting. For example the Board should establish an audit committee.	**Chapter 4: The Supervisors and the Supervisory Board** This includes sections on (1) Duties and Responsibilities of the Supervisory Board, and (2) The Composition and Steering of the Supervisory Board.

continued

TABLE 6.1 *continued*

Summary of OECD's 6 Principles of Corporate Governance	Summary of ASX 10 Principles of Corporate Governance	Overview of Code of Corporate Governance for Listed Companies in China
V. Disclosure and Transparency The corporate governance framework should ensure that timely and accurate disclosure is made on all material matters regarding the corporation, including the fnancial situation, performance, ownership, and governance of the company.	**5. Make timely and balanced disclosure** Promote timely and balanced disclosure of all material matters concerning the company.	**Chapter 5: Performance Assessments and Incentive and Disciplinary Systems** This covers issues and practices to establish and Strengthen the Performance Appraisal System Assessments and Incentive and Disciplinary Systems for the Boards and the Management and includes sections on (1) Performance Assessment for the Directors, and Supervisors and Management Personnel, (2) Selection of Management Personnel, (3) Incentive and Disciplinary Systems for Management.
VI. The Responsibilities of the Board The corporate governance framework should ensure the strategic guidance of the company, the effective monitoring of management by the board, and the board's accountability to the company and the shareholders.	**6. Respect the rights of shareholders** Respect the rights of shareholders and facilitate the effective exercise of those rights. For example design and disclose a communications strategy to promote effective comunication with shareholders and encourage effective participation at general meetings.	**Chapter 6: Stakeholders** This covers issues and practices to ensure the Legal Rights of Interested Parties and Protection of Stakeholders Rights.

continued

TABLE 6.1 *continued*

Summary of OECD's 6 Principles of Corporate Governance	Summary of ASX 10 Principles of Corporate Governance	Overview of Code of Corporate Governance for Listed Companies in China
	7. Recognise and manage risk Establish a sound system of risk oversight and management and internal control.	**Chapter 7: Information Disclosure and Transparency** This covers issues and practices to strengthen Information Disclosure and Enhance Transparency of Corporate Governance and includes sections on (1) Listed Companies' Ongoing Information Disclosure, (2) Disclosure of Information Regarding Corporate Governance, (3) Disclosure of Controlling Shareholder's Interests.
	8. Encourage enhanced performance Fairly review and actively encourage enhanced Board and management effectiveness.	
	9. Remunerate fairly and responsibly Ensure the level and composition of remuneration is sufficient and reasonable and that its relationship to corporate and individual performance is defined. For example establish a remuneration committee.	

continued

TABLE 6.1 *continued*

Summary of OECD's 6 Principles of Corporate Governance	Summary of ASX 10 Principles of Corporate Governance	Overview of Code of Corporate Governance for Listed Companies in China
	10. Recognise the legitimate interests of stakeholders Recognise legal and other obligations to all legitimate stakeholders.	
Source: Adapted from: Organisation for Economic Co-operation and Development 2004, *OECD principles of corporate governance.*	*Source:* CPA Australia 2004, *A guide to understanding corporate governance,* based on *Principles of Good Corporate Governance and Best Practice Recommendations ASX Corporate Governance Council,* ASX, March 2003.	*Source:* Adapted from: China Securities Regulatory Commission, State Economic and Trade Commission, 7 January, 2002.

Although there are differences among these summaries, you should have recognised that many of the principles are similar. As these illustrate, although there is no single model of corporate governance, three areas are common foci in corporate governance. These are interrelated. As this text examines them in more detail, you should recognise that all of these areas are concerned primarily with reducing the potential problems that may occur in corporations because of the separation of management and ownership.

Controlling and directing the directors (and senior management)

This area focuses on trying to ensure that the key managers make appropriate decisions; that they cannot and do not act in their own interests to benefit themselves against the interest of other stakeholders (in particular shareholders). Examples of possible corporate governance practices in relation to this area include:

- *Codes of conduct for directors.*
- *Minimum standards or levels of experience for directors.* This will often include a requirement that excludes directors who have certain criminal convictions and may also require professional expertise or training to ensure directors are competent to do their work.
- *Requirements that most of the board of directors be independent.* An independent director is not part of the management team that effectively runs the company. The premise behind this is that there may be a conflict of interest if members of management are part of the board of directors whose duties include evaluating the performance of management (Colley et al. 2005, p. 80).
- *Formation of a nominating committee to identify potential new directors.* This tries to ensure that potential directors are considered on merit.

- *Formation of a remuneration committee*. This aims to ensure that directors and senior management employment contracts are fair, and encourages directors to act in the interests of shareholders, avoiding the situation in which the directors are determining and approving their own remuneration.
- *Setting out the responsibilities and duties of directors and specifying the liability of directors who breach their obligations.*

You should see that these practices are aimed at, first, encouraging directors to make appropriate decisions and, second, preventing abuse of the position of directors by putting in place controls and restraints (such as committees or penalties for breaching duties).

Role of shareholders (and other stakeholders)

This area focuses on trying to ensure that shareholders have the ability to protect their interests in the corporation. This area also considers, in some cases, a broader category of stakeholders (such as employees). Examples of possible corporate governance practices in relation to this area include:

- *The requirement to provide information to shareholders (such as the annual report).*
- *Requirements to treat all shareholders equally and take into account the interests of minority shareholders*. These are particularly important if there are controlling shareholders who have the ability to dominate because of the size of their voting rights.
- *Rules relating to shareholders meetings, including notice to be given (to ensure shareholders are informed), and the right to place items on the agenda.*
- *Rules relating to shareholders' voting rights*. These include rights to vote for the appointment and removal of directors, how votes are counted and whether proxy votes are allowed, whether shareholders vote on the appointment and removal of auditors and whether shareholders can nominate directors or need to approve the appointment and remuneration of the directors.
- *Rules and rights for shareholders to call extraordinary meetings in particular circumstances, and to take action if their rights are violated.*
- *Codes of conduct in relation to other stakeholders*. These will often include the requirement to ensure the company meets the legal rights of other parties (such as creditors, employees) but may be broader.

You should see that these practices are aimed at ensuring that shareholders have the ability to participate in directing the company and can effectively exercise some control at the oversight level. Many of the rights of shareholders (such as those relating to voting rights) will be enforceable by law under specific legislation relating to corporations.

Transparency and accountability

This area focuses on trying to ensure that the stakeholders (including shareholders) are sufficiently informed about the activities of the company and its management, and to allow managers to meet their obligations to be accountable.

Examples of possible corporate governance practices in relation to this area include:

- *The requirement to prepare quarterly and annual reports, and provide them to shareholders*. In many cases, a time limit is specified in which these reports must be provided.
- *The requirement to have the annual reports audited*.
- *Rules relating to the appointment of auditors, including the requirement for them to be independent, the establishment of an audit committee, and the rotation of auditors*.
- *Details of specific information to be disclosed*. This may include the disclosure of:
  - related party relationships and transactions (e.g. loans to family members of directors)
  - amounts received by directors (including salary, shares and pension)
  - corporate governance practices.
- *Requirements that directors make a declaration that accounts are correct*. In some countries (e.g. the United States), chief financial officers (i.e. the head accountant in the company) also need to make this statement.

You should see that these practices are aimed at ensuring that the company provides enough timely and accurate information. Many of these disclosure requirements will be enforceable by law because of specific legislation on corporations, often with penalties if they are not met.

These three areas are interrelated. For example, shareholders may have rights to vote on the remuneration of directors but unless they understand how the remuneration was decided and also have adequate and accurate disclosures on it, they may not be able to assess or identify whether there are problems or concerns. Transparency and accountability are useless without the ability to participate and take action (Shailer 2004, p. 13). As stated by Witherell (2004), 'At the end of the day good corporate governance comes down to effective *and* informed owners' (emphasis added).

Approaches to corporate governance

Two broad approaches to corporate governance can be identified, although for most countries and corporations, the position taken on corporate governance will lie somewhere in between the two. These approaches can be compared with the two divergent methods of accounting standard setting: the rules-based and the principles-based approach.

The rules-based approach to corporate governance

This approach identifies precise practices that are required or recommended to ensure good corporate governance. For example, there may be a rule that an audit or remuneration committee be established. This approach is often associated with enforcement by legislation or listing rules, with imposition of penalties if the rules are not followed. The clearest example of this approach is elements of the Sarbanes–Oxley Act in the United States. It was introduced after a string of accounting abuses (including Enron and WorldCom) and gives legal backing, with associated penalties, to requirements in the corporate governance area. For example, the Sarbanes–Oxley Act:

- requires the chief financial officer to certify the correctness of the financial reports (s. 302) and imposes potential penalties of up to US$5 million and 20 years' imprisonment (s. 906).
- requires audit partner rotation at least every five years.
- bans loans to directors (s. 402).
- requires disclosure whether there is a code of ethics for senior financial officers or reasons no code of ethics is in place (s. 406).

The advantages of this approach are that it provides at least a set of *minimum* corporate governance practices that must be followed by all corporations, and that there is no uncertainty as to which practices are required. This aids enforcement and helps clarify potential liability in terms of litigation.

The disadvantages of this approach are:

- Although it provides a minimum set of practices, it is likely that good corporate governance requires more.
- It also can encourage a 'checklist' (form over substance) approach to corporate governance. This has been seen with 'rules-based' accounting standards, where although corporations may follow the letter of the standard and 'meet' the rules, financial reports may not provide an adequate understanding of the company's performance.
- The legislative backing of rules can result in the view that corporate governance is about dealing with legal liability rather than about promoting the interests of shareholders and stakeholders (Bruce 2004).

As noted, it is generally accepted that there is no 'one' model of corporate governance and this will vary depending on the specific circumstances of the entity (e.g. the size and influence of particular shareholders). Yet a rules-based approach is essentially a 'one size fits all' approach.

The principles-based approach to corporate governance

Rather than identifying specific practices or rules, this approach identifies general principles or objectives for the corporate governance system to aim to achieve. For example, the general principle may be that the corporation should ensure that there is accurate and adequate disclosure of information. Rather than identifying the exact practices that may help meet this aim (such as directing specific times for rotation of auditors, certification of financial reports), responsibility is placed on the managers to consider which practices are appropriate, given their circumstances.

The are several advantages to a principles-based approach:

- It arguably places a higher level of duty on directors to determine which corporate governance practices are required, rather than simply accepting a minimum set of practices as being adequate.
- Its flexibility means that the corporate governance practices can be adapted for the particular circumstances and environment of the entity.

The key disadvantage of this approach is that it essentially leaves it to the directors to interpret these principles and decide which corporate governance practices are needed, so it relies on their honesty, integrity and commitment to good governance. If directors are competent and act in good faith, then this would not be a problem, but many of the corporate abuses that have renewed the interest in corporate governance practices have stemmed from people not acting appropriately.

Practical considerations

In practice, in most countries, corporate governance involves various combinations of both the rules- and principles-based approaches with:

- *Specific legislation that requires certain corporate governance practices to be followed by law*. The specific practices, plus penalties and degree of enforcement varies from country to country. Common examples of legislated practices are:
  - requirements for audit committees, and that accounts be audited
  - shareholders' rights to vote to remove directors
  - requirements to appoint independent directors to the board
  - legal penalties for directors' breaches of duty.
- *Codes of corporate governance practice (based on principles) issued by government or industry groups and also by stock exchanges*. These may suggest specific examples as best practice, although corporations are not required by law to follow them. Common examples are:
  - Best practice recommends separation of the chairman of the board of directors and the CEO, although in most countries (e.g. Singapore) this is not legally required.
  - A remuneration committee is recommended best practice in the code of corporate governance but may not be required by law (as in Malaysia).

As Cowan (2004) notes, the success of 'voluntary codes depends on the willingness to implement them' (p. 165). So the actual standard of corporate governance practices will be influenced by the nature of the requirements, the environment in which the corporation operates, and the commitment of management. Allen & Roy (2001) cite the example of Hong Kong, which despite having the highest corporate governance standards in China, they claim, has few companies whose practices would be considered world class. This is partly caused by the concentration of ownership and limited shareholder activism in Hong Kong, the voluntary nature of some practices and the lack of effectiveness of enforcement (p. 31).

Role of accounting and financial reporting in corporate governance

Accounting clearly has a central role in directing and controlling a corporation. Internal accounting information (management accounting) provides a significant part of the information on which company operations will be decided. For example, estimates of costs of production, savings in costs of outsourcing or costs involved in reducing the environmental impacts of production processes will often be influential in determining how a company operates (what products it makes and how it makes them). At the other end, accounting also provides the means for outsiders to monitor the corporation and to assess how well those responsible for managing the corporation have performed. You will recall from chapter 2 that historically, the main purpose of financial statements and accounting was stewardship or accountability. This role of accounting is an integral part of any corporate governance system. Furthermore, a key feature of all corporate governance systems and requirements is the need for corporations to be transparent about what they do. It is not enough for corporations to 'do the right thing'; they need to be seen to do it, and people outside (such as shareholders) need to be able to check on what is being done. In other words, a critical part of good corporate governance is for corporations to be open and honest, and to provide sufficient accurate information for corporate activities to be monitored.

The requirements for corporations to provide financial reports, and for these to be audited, can be identified as perhaps some of the earliest corporate governance practices, even before the term 'corporate governance' was used.

> The origins of corporate governance can be found in the desire to improve the transparency and accountability of financial reporting by listed companies to their shareholder, [and although] it has since developed far beyond this, transparency and accountability remain the fundamental elements (HKSA 2004, p. 2).

Two key roles can be identified for accounting and financial reporting in encouraging good corporate governance.

Deterring, preventing and encouraging certain actions and decisions

There are two ways in which accounting is used to direct and control the managers of a corporation. One is to use accounting information to *promote* appropriate decisions. As noted in discussing agency theory, linking managers' performance to a bonus that depends on accounting profit, for example, links the interests of managers and shareholders, and so encourages managers to make decisions (such as making higher-return investments) that improve profitability. This is a direct way to use accounting information. Indirectly, that managers' performance will be based (at least in part) on the figures in the financial statements also encourages managers to make decisions that will impact positively on financial performance of the corporation, presumably in the best interest of shareholders.

The second way accounting can help corporate governance is through disclosures. Accounting standards require specific disclosures about areas or issues related to corporate governance. For example:

- *IAS 24/AASB 124 Related party disclosures* requires extensive disclosures, including the names and compensation of directors and key management personnel, and any transactions between entity and directors (e.g. loans and purchases).
- *IFRS 2/AASB 2 Share-based payment* includes requirements that share-based payments to directors or other employees be disclosed and also treated as an expense in the profit and loss.

It is natural that needing to tell people what you have done will in some ways control and constrain behaviour. That the activities (e.g. loans or remuneration) of managers will be disclosed in itself provides a disincentive for inappropriate actions by managers.

Informing shareholders and stakeholders

The key role for financial reporting in corporate governance is to provide the information needed to assess the performance of the corporation and its managers. Historically, accountability was the main purpose of financial statements and accounting, which required the managers to provide a report to the providers of resources to explain how well they have managed the resources. It is still widely considered that an 'absolute core value for corporate governance is to deliver improved accountability' (Cowan 2004, p. 167) and that accountability is essential for effective corporate governance. Think of a small sporting or social club, at which members pay fees, and leave the running of the club to a few, often dedicated individuals. Regardless how much you trust the people who are in charge, would you allow them to say 'trust us' and provide no explanation of how the money is or was to be spent? You would still want an account of where the money went! 'A strong disclosure regime that promotes real transparency is a pivotal feature of market-based monitoring of companies and is central to shareholders ability to exercise their ownership rights on an informed basis' (OECD 2004, p. 49). However, to be useful, the financial reports provided must be transparent, unbiased and complete.

There are various mechanisms in force to increase the reliability and accuracy of financial reports. These include requirements that reports be consistent with accounting standards. *IAS 1/AASB 101 Presentation of financial statements* requires that the financial report present fairly the financial position and performance of the entity, and that the entity disclose whether IFRSs have been complied with.

One impetus behind the spread of adoption of the international accounting standards is also to improve corporate governance. For example, a key recommendation of the Asian Roundtable on Corporate Governance was the priority to converge with international accounting and auditing standards on the basis that:

> full adoption of international accounting, audit and financial disclosure standards and practices will facilitate transparency, as well as comparability, of information across different jurisdictions. Such features, in

turn, strengthen market discipline as a means for improving corporate governance practices (OECD 2003, p. 6).

As noted, requirements for audit, auditors, audit committees and certification of financial statements by managers can also improve the accuracy and reliability of financial reports.

Therefore, accounting is an essential component of any corporate governance system. Furthermore, many of the corporate governance systems and practices (such as audits committees) are in place to ensure that the accounting information to be used for corporate governance (and others) is not compromised. So why are there potential problems with accounting information?

Learning tips
Do you know...

6.4 Corporate governance practices are affected by the nature of the particular company (including its ownership structure) and the legal, regulatory and social environment in which the corporation operates. There is no 'ideal' system of corporate governance.

6.5 The three key areas that are the focus of corporate governance practices are (a) controlling and directing the directors and managers, (b) the role of shareholders and other stakeholders and (c) ensuring transparency and accountability. Accounting has a key role in each of these areas.

6.6 The two broad approaches to corporate governance are (a) the rules-based approach, which specifies particular practices that must be followed and (b) the principles-based approach, which provides general principles to guide corporate behaviour. Each of these approaches has advantages and disadvantages and, in practice, a combination is often used.

Financial reporting 'problems'

Ideally, financial reports are transparent, complete and unbiased. If they are not, how can corporate governance work? However, historically and in more recent times, there have been financial reporting failures: cases such as Enron, WorldCom, HIH are just some of the most publicised. The nature of accounting itself, and the pivotal role accounting and financial reporting play, can not only improve corporate governance but can also result in pressures for accounting to be used (or abused) to its detriment.

How accounting can cause these problems

Financial reports should be transparent and accurate but agency theory explains that managers will be concerned with ensuring that they maximise their own bonuses. Often choices are allowed in accounting methods, so a manager's choice of accounting method may be influenced by the potential impact on his or her bonus. In other words, the choice of accounting policy will not be neutral or unbiased.

Furthermore, increasingly, the share price of corporations is viewed as the ultimate measure of a corporation's (and its management's) success. Indeed, a large part of managers' remuneration is often paid in the form of shares or share options. To maintain the share price, it is necessary to meet the expectations of the market. Again, this can encourage accounting choices or even distortion of accounting information to provide a favourable report to the market. It is paradoxical that the very mechanism for aligning managers' interest with that of shareholders (i.e. bonuses based on accounting profit or issuing shares or share options) has provided incentives for this manipulation. But this has been identified as a contributor to accounting 'abuses' or failures, including Enron. As the Institute of European Affairs (2003) states:

> Whereas accounting was traditionally understood as a tool for the board to assess the performance of managers, and a tool for investors to assess the value of a company compared with its peers, it has recently, according to Commissioner Bolkestein, 'become a means for managers to deliver a steady flow of information to the markets in ways that push up or prop up the share price'.

Even if managers do not directly receive shares, that their performance will at least in part be judged on the company's share price provides a powerful incentive to 'show' the market the performance it wants or expects to see. This can also affect the actions taken by companies.

The research in accounting confirms the two key incentives for profit manipulation: first, the contract or agency incentives from bonus contracts identified under agency theory and second, manipulating (or manufacturing) earnings to meet market expectations (Lambert et al. 2004).

Many accounting standards, particularly principles-based standards, allow choices (this may be a choice to capitalise or expense, or a choice of depreciation methods, for example) and require professional judgement to be exercised in determining them. The flexibility provided by accounting standards is provided to allow the methods that best reflect the economic circumstances of the entity to be selected. However, in reality, in many cases, there have been attempts by management to influence the accountants within the organisation, and the auditors, in the choices made. The following example from Pierpont (2004) provides an example:

> Anthony Wight, a former accountant with the Adelaide retailer [Harris Scarfe], told a South Australian court the company had been falsifying its accounts from 1994 until it went into voluntary administration in 2001.
> Anthony said Harris Scarfe's chief financial officer, Alan Hodgson, had directed him to falsify accounts in 1994. Hodgson has since pleaded guilty to 32 dishonesty offences and is now completing a six-year term of home detention.
> Most of the falsification concerned inflation of inventory records, with the gap between the accounts and reality growing larger every year. By the time Harris Scarfe hit the wall, about one dollar in every six of

inventory value wasn't there. And over that period, two successive audit firms missed the falsifications.

Of course, it is in the self-interest of the employees of a corporation (such as their accountants) and the auditors to, wherever possible, meet the needs of management, given that their livelihood can be affected. The ability and willingness to remain independent in the light of pressure from management depend in part of the integrity of the individuals involved, the consequences and what systems are in place to reduce such influence. Some key corporate governance practices (such as the requirement for auditor independence, audit committees and certification of accounts by financial officers) are specifically aimed at reducing the influence of managers and ensuring that the financial reports present an unbiased view.

If the flexibility is removed from accounting standards, for example, with rules-based standards, undue influence in the judgement of accounting policy choice can be avoided, but risks that financial statements will not be transparent, complete and unbiased will, by the nature of the standards, result. The problem with a specific rule (such as a requirement to apply consolidation accounting if you own more than 50 per cent of a company or to recognise a finance-leased asset and liability only if the lease term is for more than 75 per cent of its useful life) is that this allows an entity to avoid the reporting requirements by interpreting or engineering transactions so that the transactions do not meet the specific rule, and hence the accounting requirements do not need to be applied. These actions also are often associated with attempts at hiding debt and off-balance-sheet financing and have been associated with corporate reporting 'failures'. As Berkwitz & Rampell (2002) state, in relation to rules-based standards:

> The big firms have concocted all kinds of slippery methods that enable companies to comply with the exact letter of the rules while still managing to mislead investors. Case in point: Enron and its multiple 'special purpose entities,' which allowed it to omit substantial liabilities from its balance sheets while staying within the rules of the accounting game.

The problem is that, whether using rules- or principles-based standards, financial reports can meet the specific accounting requirements but still result in misleading or incomplete disclosures. Because unbiased, complete and transparent reporting is considered a critical and necessary condition for effective corporate governance, this is a problem.

These types of financial reporting problems, resulting from flexibility in accounting rules themselves or from engineering transactions to avoid the rules, are often referred to as 'creative accounting'. Essentially, the 'letter of the law' of the accounting requirements is followed, although the interpretations and actions would not be in the 'spirit of the rules'. Some of these may involve deliberate attempts to distort the financial statements, others may be caused by differences in judgements, influenced to varying degrees by self-interest. Of course, some problems in financial reporting (and corporations) are the result of dishonesty, of deliberate misstatements and lies in financial reports, in other words, of fraud. Although many corporate governance practices can minimise the opportunity for fraud, wherever people are involved it will inevitably occur. This leads to considering the role of ethics in both accounting and corporate governance.

▪ The role of ethics

Corporations are artificial, legal constructions. *People* make the decisions in corporations (whether they are directors, executives, auditors, accountants or other employees) and, ultimately, good corporate governance is about people making the 'right' decisions. Making the right decisions requires people to behave ethically.

Ethics is a discipline in its own right, which will not be considered in detail (such as alternative ethical theories) here. However, in simple terms, to behave ethically can be equated with the common concept of 'do unto others as you would have done unto you' (Cowan 2004, p. 9). In the

ethics: The standards of conduct that indicate how one should behave based on moral duties and virtues

context of corporate governance — the directing and controlling of a company — what makes certain behaviour or decisions 'right'? How does the context change whether a decision is ethical or whether ethical decisions are made? Are there different standards of ethics for a person making a decision as a 'corporate' employee rather than as an individual?

Let's take an example. Mitsubishi in Japan failed to inform customers of potential safety problems with vehicles or recall them for repair. It is claimed that part of the reason for not wanting to make the recall was the impact on the balance sheet that it would have. The failure to make the recall, it is claimed, led to accidents, including one resulting in the death of the driver (*Asahi Shimbun* 2004). Given that a key objective of the corporation is to maintain shareholder value, and that recalling vehicles would undoubtedly reduce this, was the decision to not recall the vehicles ethical? You would expect that if family members of corporate employees who knew about these defects owned these vehicles, the family members would have been told about the defects! If the principle 'do unto others as you would have done unto you' is applied, the decision not to recall the vehicles was not ethical. This is perhaps a relatively clear case. If this happens in clear cases, what happens in more ambiguous circumstances? Would it perhaps have been ethical if the defects in the vehicles had been minor, and would reduce the life of the vehicles but were not likely to cause accidents?

As discussed in the context of accounting rules, specific rules, principles or practices do not guarantee acceptable application or outcomes. *How* people interpret and implement these rules and principles, and whether they consider the intention and spirit rather than comply in form only, matters. The same considerations apply with corporate governance principles and practices. Particular principles, or the existence of particular practices or procedures (such as the auditing of accounts or existence of a remuneration committee), will not *guarantee* good corporate governance. Indeed, some commentators argue that Enron appeared to practise, and indeed exemplify in some ways, good governance practice before its downfall. People are often influenced by several factors in making the right decisions and behaving ethically. These include personal integrity, conflicts of interest, pressures and expectations of and from peers and colleagues, and the culture of the corporation itself. Of course, the difficulty with corporations is how it can be known whether the managers are ethical. As Flanagan, Little & Watts (2005) note:

> When monitoring a company from the outside, it is impossible to observe the character of the directors and their integrity in making decisions. Directors have many ways of erecting smokescreens to hide what they are doing and how they are doing it (p. 12).

The culture of the corporation — the values it develops and promotes — is considered a key factor in good corporate governance and is widely acknowledged as an essential component. For example:

- The Sarbanes–Oxley Act in the United States requires disclosure of whether or not there is a code of ethics for senior financial officers.
- Guidance by CPA Australia (2004) argues that implementation of a corporate governance structure is not sufficient and will only work if the culture of the corporation supports good governance.
- The Hong Kong Society of Accountants (2004) guidelines for public bodies places emphasis on the personal qualities of individuals as the foundation for good corporate governance and identifies the qualities of selflessness, integrity, objectivity, accountability, openness, honesty and leadership.

To be effective, the culture needs to be embedded throughout the corporation and supported. An example of part of a strategy to implement ethical conduct is provided in the In Focus vignette that follows.

 infocus *Texas Instruments provides ethical guidelines*

The following is the contents of a pamphlet that is provided, business card size, to all employees of Texas Instruments, a US company that have received awards for its leadership in business this practices. This pamphlet provides a checklist for employees facing a decision which may have an ethical implication. The checklist asks employees to consider:

- Is the action legal?
- Does it comply with our values?
- If you do it, will you feel bad?
- How will it look in the newspaper?
- If you know it is wrong, don't do it.
- If you're not sure, ask.
- Keep asking until you get an answer.

Source: This material appeared in *Accountancy Ireland.*

You cannot have good corporate governance without ethics. Corporate governance relies on people. It is about how people behave and the decisions they make. As Wallenberg (2004) states:

> More importantly, corporate governance codes, voluntary or otherwise, are worthless if they are divorced from strong, ethical business leadership. The Enron scandal has demonstrated that in the most regulated market of all, even the best-written governance documents are of little use in the absence of a management culture which embodies real, committed and responsible business ethics. A slavish focus on a rigid set of codes can have the converse effect of encouraging complacency rather than dynamic and proactive management of pressing governance issues.

International perspectives and developments

As noted, the Anglo-Saxon model placing emphasis on shareholders interest dominates in the United States, Australia, Canada and the UK. Asia is also increasingly adopting the Anglo-Saxon shareholder model (Allen 2000). However, in many areas, corporate governance codes have now extended (at least in principle) the model to include consideration of the needs of broader stakeholders. This is based on the opinion that the traditional view of corporate responsibility as being to increase profits (as espoused by Friedman) is not longer appropriate. As Hinkley states:

> [T]oday corporations are our most powerful citizens and it is no longer tenable that they be entitled to all the benefits of citizenship, but have none of the responsibilities (cited in Burmoister 2000, p. 23).

Most European countries, rather than have legislated practices, have voluntary codes of corporate governance practices, and compliance varies (*The Economist* 2004, p. 4). In Europe, there is more direct recognition of alternative stakeholders (such as employees in France and creditors in Germany). The key differences between European corporate governance practices and those in other areas results from the emphasis given to employees. Some countries give employees the right to representation on the board of directors.

In Asia, although the Anglo-Saxon model is now increasingly being adopted, particular characteristics and environmental features provide problems with ensuring good corporate governance. In particular, many corporations in the area have dominant shareholders (such as families or the state), and enforcement mechanisms vary considerably throughout the region. It is argued that this has resulted in 'many companies following more the form rather than the substance of corporate governance' (Allen 2000, p. 26).

In the future, it is likely that corporate governance will increasingly consider broader stakeholders. Although a principles-based approach appears to be prevailing at the moment, backed by legislation for particular practices, it is inevitable that future collapses and financial reporting failures will influence future directions and approaches.

Conclusion

This chapter considers the nature of corporate governance. You should recognise that corporate governance is a multidisciplinary area (involving for example law, accounting, management, organisational behaviour). The attempt here is not to provide with a working knowledge of corporate governance but an understanding of its nature and its relationship with accounting. As Sloan (2004) states:

> The study of corporate governance is concerned with understanding the mechanisms that have evolved to mitigate incentive problems created by the separation of the management and financing of business entities. Financial accounting provides the... primary source of independently verified information about the performance of managers. Thus it is clear that corporate governance and financial accounting are inexorably linked. (pp. 335–6).

Almost every corporate 'scandal' and abuse of corporate ethics or law has involved some accounting problem. Accounting and financial reporting will always require professional judgment and it is important for accountants to understand the role of accounting and its potential misuse or abuse. Good corporate governance practices both require and assist accountants in providing reliable information. Of course, this is not to say the corporate governance is the answer to all corporate woes — there will still be corporate failures despite best practice and the best of intentions.

Summary

Understand what corporate governance is and why good corporate governance systems are needed.

- Corporate governance is the system of directing and controlling the corporation, and is aimed at ensuring that despite the separation of ownership and management, managers act in the best interests of the corporation and its stakeholders. A key aim of good corporate governance is to enable markets to operate efficiently.

Outline the role of the following concepts in agency theory: agency contract; monitoring costs; bonding costs; residual loss.

- Agency theory identifies three costs associated with the agency relationship between managers and shareholders. An agency contract is undertaken when the principal delegates decision-making responsibility to an agent. Monitoring costs are involved in scrutinising the agent's actions to ensure he or she acts in the principal's best interests. Bonding costs are incurred when the agent makes a decision in the principal's best interest but not in his or her own best interest. Residual loss is sustained when the agent's decisions are less than ideal for the principal.

Explain the nature of manager–shareholder agency problems: risk aversion; dividend retention; horizon disparity, and derive the bonus plan hypothesis.

- There are three problems in the manager–shareholder relationship. Risk aversion occurs when managers undertake less risky decisions to maximise short-term value that may reduce long-term value. Dividend retention refers to the withholding of dividend payments to allow expansion or investment in the company while reducing investors' returns. Horizon disparity occurs when managers focus on performance for the relatively short-term length of their employment in the company at the expense of long-term value for shareholders. Bonus plans attempt to deal with these issues by linking managers' rewards to shareholders' interests. However, this creates incentives for managers to manipulate accounting figures to increase their bonuses.

Understand the key areas involved in corporate governance and the alternative approaches.

- Corporate governance principles and practices concentrate on directing and controlling directors and management, shareholders' interests and rights, and transparency and accountability. There are two approaches to corporate governance: rules-based and principles-based, and each has its advantages and disadvantages. In practice, corporate governance is usually a mix of both.

Understand the role and impact of accounting in and on corporate governance.

- Accounting information is an essential component of any corporate governance system and has two key roles: to control and direct actions and decisions, and to inform shareholders and other stakeholders. The accounting information and reports need to be correct, complete and unbiased. However, accounting information can be comprised or manipulated for several reasons.

Understand the role of ethics in corporate governance.

• Good corporate governance is about people 'doing the right thing'. Despite prescribed practices, it essentially can only be achieved through the ethical behaviour of managers.

Key terms

agency relationship   155
bonding costs   156
bonus plan hypothesis   160
corporate governance   153
ethics   177
monitoring costs   156
residual loss   156

Review questions

6.1. Explain what is meant by corporate governance and why it is needed.

6.2 'Corporate governance is primarily focused on protecting the interests of shareholders.' Discuss.

6.3 What are risks of poor corporate governance and the advantages of good corporate governance?

6.4 Explain what is meant by the agency relationship and explain the following costs: monitoring, bonding, residual loss.

6.5 Explain the agency problems that arise in the manager–shareholder relationship.

6.6 Explain how the bonus plan hypothesis is derived from agency theory.

6.7 Identify the key areas addressed in corporate governance and provide examples of practices related to each of these areas. Explain how any individual practices identified help ensure good corporate governance.

6.8 What is the rules-based approach to corporate governance and what are the advantages and disadvantages of this approach?

6.9 What is the principles-based approach to corporate governance and what are the advantages and disadvantages of this approach?

6.10 'Any corporate governance system is only as good as the people involved in it.' Discuss.

Application questions

6.11 Obtain the annual reports of a range of companies in the same industry and country and search for any disclosures in relation to corporate governance principles and practices. In relation to these disclosures:
(a) Identify the key areas considered by these companies.
(b) Are there any differences or similarities in corporate governance practices?

(c) Do you believe you could judge or rank the relative standard of corporate governance of these companies based on the information provided? If not, what other information would you need to do so?

(d) Which company would you identify has having the best (or worst) corporate governance from these disclosures? Explain how you have arrived at this decision.

6.12 Obtain the annual reports of a range of companies in the same industry in different countries and search for any disclosures in relation to corporate governance principles and practices. In relation to these disclosures:

(a) Identify any differences or similarities in corporate governance practices.

(b) Can you provide any reasons from the business and regulatory environments in the countries that would explain these differences?

6.13 Many small companies argue that corporate governance requirements are too costly and onerous and should be restricted to the large 'top' companies.

(a) Do you think that corporate governance principles should apply to smaller companies?

(b) Are there any particular corporate governance practices or principles that you do not think should apply to smaller companies?

(c) What would be the advantages of smaller companies complying with corporate governance principles?

(d) What might be the consequences for smaller companies of not complying with corporate governance principles?

6.14 A friend cannot understand why executives and directors of companies are often paid bonuses and not simply paid a set salary.

(a) Using principles from agency theory, explain the reasons for, and nature of, bonus plans offered to directors and executives.

(b) Because share-based payments to employees (including directors) are now required to be recognised as expenses, would this reduce the need to use shares or share options as part of a manager's remuneration package?

6.15 Obtain the annual report for a listed company and examine the remuneration packages provided for executives.

(a) Identify the key components of the remuneration packages for directors and executives. Do the principles of agency theory provide a rationale for each of these components?

(b) Would these packages provide incentives for these executives to manipulate accounting figures?

(c) How much information is provided about any bonuses paid? Is this information sufficient to allow shareholders to determine if these packages are reasonable?

6.16 In many countries in Asia it is claimed that concentration of ownership/control by families of companies causes particular difficulties with corporate governance. For example, Hong Kong billionaire Richard Li owns 75 per cent of Singapore-listed Pacific Century Regional Developments.

(a) Examine corporate governance guidelines and identify specific recommendations for practice aimed at protecting minority investors.

(b) Would these suggested practices be effective where there is a higher concentration of family control in a company?

6.17 Each year various bodies give corporate governance awards. Examples are, in Malaysia, an annual award is made by *Malaysian Business*, sponsored by the Chartered Institute of Management Accountants (CIMA), and with The Australasian Reporting Awards (Inc.), an independent not-for-profit organisation makes annual awards.

(a) Locate the criteria on which these awards are based and compare these for different awards.

(b) Are there any significant differences between the criteria?

(c) In what areas of corporate governance reporting did winning companies outperform other companies?

(d) Does the winning of an award for reporting necessarily mean that these companies have best corporate governance practices?

6.18 Australian companies listed on the ASX must report on their corporate governance practices on the basis of 'comply or explain'. That is, they are not required to comply with all of the specific corporate governance practices detailed by the ASX but if they choose not to comply, they must identify which guidelines have not been ignored and provide a reason for their lack of compliance.

(a) Examine the corporate governance disclosures of some Australian listed companies and identify any instances where best practice recommendations of the ASX have not been met.

(b) Do you believe that the noncompliance in these instances is justified?

(c) What are the advantages of having a 'comply or explain' requirement rather than requiring all companies to comply with all best practice recommendations?

6.19 In the 2005 annual report of Boral Ltd (an Australia-listed company), the corporate governance disclosures include the following note:

> The Board has considered establishing a nomination committee and decided in view of the relatively small number of Directors that such a Committee would not be a more efficient mechanism that the full Board for detailed selection and appointment decisions.

(a) Examine the ASX corporate governance principles and identify the best practice recommendations in relation to nomination committees.

(b) What potential governance problems are these recommendations designed to meet?

(c) Is Boral's deviation from these best practice recommendations justified?

6.20   In the 2005 Annual report of Biota Ltd (an Australia-listed company), the corporate governance note disclosed an audit committee composed of two directors (chaired by an independent nonexecutive director and supported by one other nonexecutive director).

(a)   Examine the ASX corporate governance principles and identify the best practice recommendations in relation to audit committees.

(b)   What potential governance problems are these recommendations designed to meet?

(c)   Does Biota's audit committee meet these guidelines and if not, is any deviation from these best practice recommendations justified?

6.21   At any time there are problems (and subsequent investigations) with corporate governance, which include deficiencies in financial reporting.

(a)   Search the website of regulatory authorities (such as the Australian Securities and Investments Commission or the Securities and Exchange Commission in the United States) and identify a case that has been investigated that involves issues of corporate governance.

(b)   Briefly discuss the corporate governance issues and what part financial reporting played in these.

case**study**   **6.1**

Ethical Cleansing: companies on trial

Despite appearing to be a model corporate citizen, Enron was anything but. Stuart Lauchlan examines the fallout.

There is in existence a videotape from 1997 of a farewell dinner for Rich Kinder, the former president of Enron. On the tape, Kinder's executive assistant performs a skit in which he pretends to be his outgoing boss holding a budget review meeting with the incoming president Jeff Skilling and a company accountant.

Skilling makes a joke about moving the company from 'market-to-market' accounting to something he calls 'hypothetical future value accounting'. This will, he says, 'add a kazillion dollars to the bottom line'. When the accountant points out that the Securities and Exchange Commission (SEC) will have problems with this, Skilling waves his hand dismissively and calls him a 'spoilsport'.

This goes down well with the audience at the dinner who laugh uproariously at what is so clearly an absurd notion. Of course back in 1997, it still was an absurd notion. Whether the attendees at that dinner would have laughed quite so loudly if they had realised that 'hypothetical future value accounting' pretty much summed up Enron's real book-keeping philosophy is another matter entirely.

Even back in 1997 Enron was a remarkable company. To the outside world, it was a perfect example of the American dream in practice, voted onto the list of the 100 best companies to work for in America three years in succession. It consistently found itself on the receiving end of accolades and plaudits, doing particularly well in 2000 when it notched up no fewer than six environmental awards.

Culturally the company also appeared to be a shining example to corporations across all business sectors. Enron CEO Kenneth Lay was a regular speaker on the conference circuit, his specialist subject being corporate ethics, while Enron note-pads carried inspirational quotes from the likes of Martin Luther King Junior. 'Our lives begin to end the day we become silent about the things that matter,' read one notable example.

The quote of course is particularly ironic as it was the silence of all too many Enron executives, and those associated with them that ensured that all the apparent good things about the organisation have been consigned to the dustbin of corporate history. Enron is now and always will be a by-word for financial mismanagement and accounting irregularities. It now stands as the leading example of the antithesis of corporate governance.

Suspended ethics

But at the time of its collapse, the decline of Enron came as an enormous shock to the whole of corporate America and beyond. 'Enron, in fact, gave every appearance of being a model corporate citizen,' notes Bob Wright, vice-chairman of the board and executive officer, General Electric Company, and CEO of the NBC TV network. 'At the same time, as we know, the appearance did not match the reality. This was the same company whose board twice voted to suspend their own ethics code.'

Wright continues: 'The tone for a company's ethical culture is set at the top. Employees, consciously or not, will follow the lead of their supervisors and managers. If they see rules being bent, they will bend the rules. And once that process starts, it is very difficult to stop.

Enron without a doubt had thousands of good, honest, hardworking employees. Unfortunately, they were working in a company infected with a fatal virus: a virus of bending the rules, looking the other way, and thinking that stock-price perform-ance was the only measure of success. They had failures of leadership, ethics, and governance, a sure recipe for catastrophe.'...

But US organisations need to maintain a desire to change if the abuses of the past are not to be repeated. As the respected US academic Michael Novak, the George Frederick Jewett scholar in religion, philosophy and public policy at the American Enterprise Institute, puts it: 'Corporate responsibility can be backed up by good law, but it cannot be completed by law alone. The law often arrives . . . after the damage has been done, in time to put up some monuments.

Between the cutting edge of change and the slow course of the law must come something else: character and conscience.'

Source: This article appeared in *MIS Australia*.

---

1. This article discusses the issue of corporate culture in corporate govern-ance. Discuss whether corporate culture is important for corporate governance.
2. What is 'market-to-market' accounting? How could this add 'false' value to a company's financial statements?

3. The article discusses the issue that the silence of executives contributed to the problems. What can be done in corporations to avoid a 'culture of silence'?
4. The article links financial mismanagement and accounting irregularities. What practices can be implemented to try to ensure that accounting irregularities do not occur?
5. The article mentions the focus on stock price being considered the only measure of success. What could contribute to this concentration on stock price?

case**study** 6.2

S&P: Study shows Hong Kong companies' disclosure standards low

The standards of disclosure among the Hong Kong companies on the Hang Seng Index (HSI) appear low, according to a study carried out by Standard & Poor's Governance Services and the Corporate Governance & Financial Reporting Centre (CGFRC) at the National University of Singapore (NUS).

'Most of the corporate governance scores appear to be clustered between 11 and 40 points, out of a maximum of 140,' said Calvin Wong, managing director of Standard & Poor's Governance Services.

The results of the study are published in a report titled 'Corporate Governance Disclosures in Hong Kong.' The latest annual reports (available as of June 30, 2004) for each company were used in the assessment of the corporate governance disclosure practices.

This is part of a series of country-specific corporate governance disclosure studies being conducted by Standard & Poor's and CGFRC. Studies on Thailand, Malaysia, Singapore, and Indonesia companies were published between April and August. In terms of mean score for the companies sampled from the five countries, Hong Kong ranks third — behind Singapore and Malaysia.

'The data from the study showed that independence of the boards of directors for most companies on the HSI is very low,' said Associate Professor Mak Yuen Teen, vice dean of the NUS Business School and co-director of CGFRC.

In the study, the top five companies, in alphabetical order, were BOC Hong Kong (Holdings) Ltd., CLP Holdings Ltd., COSCO Pacific Ltd., HSBC Holdings PLC, Li & Fung Ltd.

'The study highlighted some areas where the top five companies were significantly better in disclosure,' said Dr. Mak.

Although the top five companies have better disclosures relative to their peers, there were some key areas where disclosures were found lacking or short of global best practices. Here are some of the areas:

– All but one of the top five companies have less than one-third of the board composed of independent directors and no company has a board with majority of independent directors.
– Only one company had a nominating committee made up entirely of independent directors.
– Only three companies had totally independent audit committees.

The corporate governance disclosure scorecard developed by Standard & Poor's was used to assess the corporate governance practices of the companies. The scorecard items reflect principles and best practices embodied in international corporate governance codes. Although the disclosure items in the scorecard represent key components of corporate governance, it should be noted that the individual company scores derived from this study are not proxies for corporate governance assessments.

Thorough corporate governance assessments require a more flexible and qualitative analytical approach. For those companies that have an interest in a more thorough diagnostic, Standard & Poor's provides an interactive corporate governance scoring service that involves a much more detailed and in-depth analysis of corporate governance practices.

Standard & Poor's has been developing criteria and a methodology for assessing corporate governance practices since 1998 and has been actively assessing companies' corporate governance practices since 2000. Its proprietary methodology is based on a synthesis of governance codes and guidelines of global best practices, as well as its own experience in conducting detailed reviews of individual companies. Its internationally applicable approach is consistent with the overarching principles of the OECD governance guidelines.

Source: This article appeared in *The Asian Banker.*

1. This article discusses the use of ratings by Standard & Poor's to assess corporate governance for individual corporations. What aspects or practices do you think would or should be examined to determine the standard of corporate governance for a company?
2. Research undertaken has argued that using formulas or scorecards to rate corporate governance is not appropriate. Can you see any problems or deficiencies in using a numerical ratings system to assess corporate governance?
3. The article notes deficiencies identified in the practices of Hong Kong companies. What business, environmental or regulatory factors would influence these practices?
4. The article refers to problems with the composition of boards. What is the problem with having most board members not being independent directors?

5. The article notes that the scores should not be seen as proxies for corporate governance assessments. What is the difference between corporate governance disclosures and corporate governance assessments? How could you assess the latter?

Recommended readings and websites

Goodwin Procter 2002, 'Sarbanes–Oxley Act of 2002 enacts major new corporate governance reforms', public company advisory. An overview can be accessed by searching the publications page of Goodwin Procter: www.goodwinprocter.com.

For a comparison of corporate governance practices across Asia refer to the OECD 2003, *White paper on corporate governance in Asia*, www.oecd.org.

For a critical analysis of many aspects of corporate governance including the adoption of the American or Anglo-Saxon corporate governance model in the context of China and problems with the rules-based approach, refer to the 2005 special issue of *Advances in Public Interest Accounting*, vol. 11.

References

Allen, J 2000, *Code convergence in Asia: smoke or fire?*, Asian Corporate Governance Association, 1 CGI, www.acgaasia.org.
—— & Roy, F 2001, *Corporate governance in greater China: a comparison between China, Hong Kong and Taiwan, from structuring for success: the first 10 years of capital markets in China*, Asian Corporate Governance Association.
Asahi Shimbun 2004, 'Another denial in Mitsubishi trials', 7 October.
Berkwitz, A & Rampell, R 2002, 'The accounting debate: principles vs. rules', *Wall Street Journal Online*, 2 December.
Bruce, R 2004, 'Courtrooms concentrate the minds — corporate governance', *Financial Times*, 9 September, p. 2.
Burmeister, K 2000, 'Corporate responsibility: a matter of ethics or strategy?', *The Issues*, no. 1, Blake Dawson Waldron, www.bdw.com.cn.
Colley, JL Jr, Doyle, JL, Logan, GW, Stettinuis, W 2005, *What is corporate governance?*, McGraw-Hill, New York.
Cornford, A 2004, *Enron and internationally agreed principles for corporate governance and the financial sector*, G-24 discussion paper series, no. 30, June, United Nations.
Cowan, N 2004, *Corporate governance that works!*, Prentice Hall Pearson Education, Singapore.
CPA Australia 2004, *A guide to understanding corporate governance*.
—— 2005, *Module on corporate governance*, revised by P Leung.
The Economist 2004, 'Parma splat; what are the lessons from the scandal at Europe's largest dairy-products group?', 15 January.

Flanagan, J, Little, J & Watts, T 2005, 'Beyond law and regulation — a corporate governance model of ethical decision-making', *Advances in Public Interest Accounting*, Ed. C Lehman, vol. 11, pp. 271–302.

Godfrey, J, Hodgson, A & Holmes, S 2003, *Accounting theory*, 5th edn, John Wiley & Sons, Brisbane.

Hong Kong Society of Accountants (HKSA) 2004, *Corporate governance for public bodies: a basic framework*.

India Info Line 2005, 'What is corporate governance?', www.indiainfoline.com/nevi/what.html.

Institute of European Affairs 2003, 'EU–US Project Group EU–US relations: corporate governance', www.iiea.com.

Jensen, MC & Meckling, WH 1976, 'Theory of the firm: managerial behavior, agency costs and ownership structure', *Journal of Financial Economics*, October, pp. 305–60.

Lambert, C & Sponem, S 2004, 'Corporate governance and profit manipulation: a French field study', *Critical Perspectives on Accounting*, article in press.

Organisation for Economic Co-operation and Development 2004, *OECD principles of corporate governance*, OECD Publications Service, Paris.

Pierpont 2004, 'Perspective: Pierpont's dubious distinction awards for 2004', *Australian Financial Review*, 29 December, p. 22.

Shailer, GEP 2004, *An introduction to corporate governance in Australia*, Pearson Sprint Print, ANU.

Sloan, RG 2001, 'Financial accounting and corporate governance: a discussion', *Journal of Accounting and Economics*, vol. 32, pp. 335–47.

Wallenberg, J 2004, 'Viewpoint: Achieving 3Cs is no mean feat — conformance, competition and culture are the key to good corporate governance', *The Banker*, 1 July.

Witherell, B. 2004, 'Corporate governance, stronger principles for better market integrity', *OECD Observer*, no. 243, May.

7 ENVIRONMENTAL AND SOCIAL REPORTING AND ACCOUNTING

LEARNING OBJECTIVES

After reading this chapter, you should be able to:

- define social and environmental reporting, and discuss the measurement of social costs (or externalities)

- identify different stakeholder groups and the reasons for their interest in a firm's environmental and social performance

- explain the existing reporting practices and guidelines for social and environmental reporting

- discuss the practical applications of reporting systems to social and environmental disclosure

- identify the role of the accounting profession in social and environmental reporting

- discuss the influence of the share market and financial performance on social and environmental reporting.

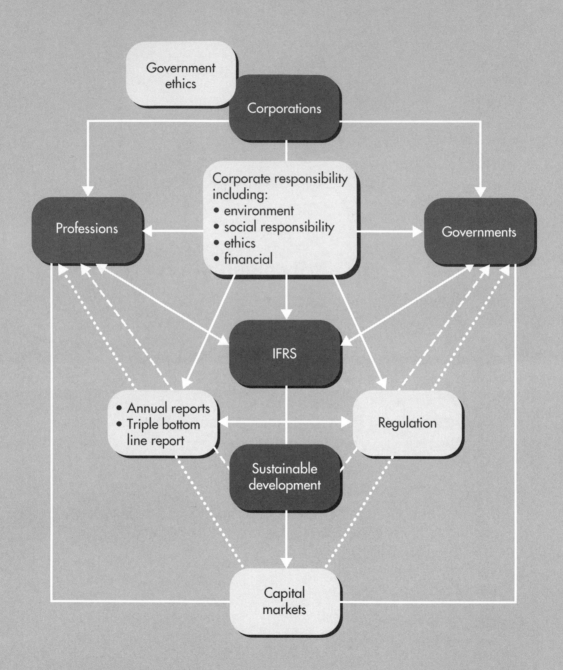

Introduction

The complex relationship between economic returns and corporate values for environmental and social issues has continually been challenged by academics and interest groups. In their focus on capital markets and financial returns, corporate executives have not traditionally considered the social and environmental issues associated with their business activities. Even a proliferation of regulations over recent decades to prompt this consideration could not insure against corporate failure, global warming and social injustice in the workplace. Consequently, firms have been pressured to be more accountable and responsible and to provide stakeholders with more transparent and relevant information to help them make decisions about the firm.

The purpose of this chapter is to discuss accountability and reporting issues from the perspective of the individual firm. Although the major focus of this discussion is voluntary corporate disclosure, the scope of the chapter also includes issues related to measuring social costs and externalities, social and environmental reporting practices, the role of the accounting profession and the influence of the share market.

What social and environmental reporting is

Over the past few decades, community values have been undergoing incremental changes to reflect a growing concern for social and environmental issues, highlighted by the comments of the United Nations Conference in Stockholm (Declaration, 1972):

> A point has been reached in history where we must shape our actions throughout the word with a more prudent care for their environmental consequences. Through ignorance or indifference we can do massive and irreversible harm to the earthly environment on which our life and well-being depend ... To achieve this environmental goal will demand the acceptance of responsibility by citizens and communities and by enterprises and institutions at every level, all sharing equitably in common efforts. Individuals in all walks of life as well as organisations in many fields, by their values and the sum of their actions, will shape the world environment of the future (paras 6 and 7).

Since the United Nations statement in 1972, legal requirements for corporations to integrate social and environmental responsibility into normal business activities have been wide-ranging. In many cases, not only is a corporation now liable for its environmental and social activities and impacts, but various regulatory requirements may also incorporate the personal liability of managers.

Stakeholders have applied increasing pressure for continued accountability and transparency in relation to a firm's activities and its decisions involving environmental and social issues. This pressure initiated a growth in voluntary corporate reporting. At the firm level, a voluntary corporate report can provide accountability and transparency to external parties on (a) the firm's compliance with mandatory requirements and (b) management's responses to environmental and social issues.

In 1987, Gray, Owen & Maunders defined **social and environmental reporting** as 'the process of communicating the social and environmental effects of organisations' actions within society and to society at large' (p. 76).

Many firms use the term corporate responsibility, or corporate citizenship, instead of sustainability. **Sustainability**, as discussed later in the chapter, has implications for intergenerational equity, and is often deemed more theoretical than practical for business firms, whereas corporate responsibility embraces governance issues (ICAEW 2004). The former relates to social equality, whereas the latter is more concerned with transparency and ethics.

Unfortunate commercial accidents have awakened international stakeholder attention to the stewardship of our natural resources. These incidents include:

- the disastrous 1984 explosion at the Union Carbide pesticide plant in the densely populated city of Bhopal, India, which resulted in the death of about 3000 and injured more than 300 000 people
- the nuclear meltdown at Chernobyl in the Ukraine in 1986
- the devastating man-made Exxon Valdez oil taker in 1989 when oil infiltrated pristine ecological regions of Prince William Sound, Alaska
- the Esmeralda cyanide spill in 2000, which contaminated a large area of central Europe along the Danube River catchment, including Romania, Hungary and Serbia
- the wreck of the Prestige oil tanker in 2002, when oil infiltrated pristine ecological regions of Galicia, Spain
- the Jilin chemical plant explosions in China in 2005, which created a benzene slick on the Songhua River, which poisoned the drinking water for 80km downstream into Russia.

More specifically, these incidents drew attention to the inability of policies and systems to:

- measure environmental impacts from the perspective of society
- include environmental and social costs in the price of the firm's goods and services (Shrivastava 1987).

Social costs, or externalities

The priority of economic and financial outcomes over social and environmental values highlights the problem of **social costs**, or **externalities**. The American Accounting Association (1973) defined externalities in the following way:

It can be argued convincingly that a contributing factor to pollution is the failure of the material decision making process to consider all the cost of producing and distributing a product. These costs not considered are called social costs, or the external diseconomies. Such costs have been external to the economic entity and its decision making unit. Ideally, they should be identified and allocated to the individual firms whose actions caused them. Internalization of these costs would force managers to consider them along with other internal costs when making decisions about matters with environmental implication (p. 76).

These social costs or externalities were historically 'free' to the business unit. For example, the logging of a forest or mining of a deposit may have resulted in loss of habitat, species extinction or a complete cultural change for the local population (Hawken 1994). Because there was no direct impact on the profit of individual firms, management was not concerned or legally required to take responsibility for these aspects of its business operations. The general community (usually taxpayers) was paying for the environmental and social mishaps of business decisions, and it became increasingly agitated.

Stakeholder pressure

In 1987, the United Nations World Commission on Environmental Development (the Brundtland Commission) produced a report *Our common future* (termed the Brundtland Report), which outlined and defined a practical solution to internalise social costs. It was based on the term **sustainable development**, which was defined as 'development that meets the needs of the present without compromising the ability of future generations to meet their own needs' (p. 8), highlighting the trade-offs between the use of renewable and nonrenewable resources.

sustainable development: Development that meets the needs of the present without compromising the ability of future generations to meet their own needs

The problem with satisfying the inclusion of social costs is measurement, particularly in monetary terms. With no monetary value placed on social and environmental issues, the communal view of the business sector was that social and environmental issues were very much subordinate to profit concerns (Hawken 1994). However, the profitability of the business sector cannot be isolated from social and environmental issues.

The business community, the natural community and the social community are interconnected. Firms operate as part of society, and with its permission. **Legitimacy theory** suggests that society will penalise firms that fail to conform to community expectations and values (Lindblom 1994). Commercial transactions infiltrate the daily lives of employees, lenders, shareholders and others. Their inputs are drawn from natural resources, and the output of their activities may adversely affect our ecology and, indirectly, society. Based on the premise of **accountability** or **stewardship**, stakeholders require information on the social costs and the economic, social and environmental performance associated with corporate activities.

legitimacy theory: The theory that suggests society will penalise firms that fail to conform to community expectations and values

accountability (stewardship): The responsibility of providing information to enable users to make informed judgements about the performance, financial position, financing and investing and compliance of the reporting entity

The relationships among stakeholder expectations, corporate business decisions — the environmental and social values upon which the firm conducts its normal oper-

stakeholder theory: The theory that incorporates the interests of a broader range of stakeholders in an entity, not just the shareholders

ations — and corporate reporting strategies have been discussed in the academic literature for decades under **stakeholder theory** (see for example Ullman 1985; Roberts 1992, Gray, Kouhy & Lavers 1995). Stakeholder dialogue is recognised as an important issue and is, at an international level, systematically incorporated into the formation of the GRI Reporting Guidelines (2002–06), which are discussed in more detail in following sections.

Naturally, different stakeholders have different requirements and require different information on economic performance, social costs and environmental performance (Elkington 1998).

A list of examples of individual stakeholders and associated social costs or benefits is provided in table 7.1. See Gray, Owen & Maunders (1987) and Richardson (2004) for further discussion on the reporting and measurement of externalities.

TABLE 7.1 A stakeholder perspective: accounting for externalities

| Stakeholders | Examples of external costs and benefits | | |
	Environmental	Social	Economic
Customers	Environmental costs or benefits in the use and disposal of products	Ethical, social and health costs or benefits associated with the product	Consumer surplus over and above the market place
Suppliers	Environmental impacts associated with the production of purchased goods and services	Ethical, social and health costs or benefits associated with the production of purchased goods and services	Stimulation of economic growth through the supply chain
Employees	Environmental benefits or risks associated with the workplace	Workplace social costs (unpaid overtime) and benefits	Employment creation through economic multiplier effect
Community	Emissions, effluents and waste to land, air and water (local, regional, national and international)	Community health impacts; wider social impacts of redundancy and plant closure; nuisance and disturbance	Urban and rural regeneration; infrastructure (e.g. transport links and congestion)
Investors	Risks to investors from poor corporate environmental reputation	Risk to investors from poor corporate social and ethical reputation	Risks to investors from poor corporate economic reputation

continued

TABLE 7.1 *continued*

	Examples of external costs and benefits		
Stakeholders	**Environmental**	**Social**	**Economic**
Public sector	Environmental benefits from public-sector investment of corporate taxes in environmental protection	Social benefits from public-sector investment of corporate taxes in health, education and social programmes	Public-sector economic multiplier effects

Source: Richardson, J 2004, 'Accounting for sustainability: measuring quantities or enhancing qualities', in Henriques, A & Richardson, J (eds), *The triple bottom line: does it all add up?* Earthscan, London, p. 38.

Increasingly, regulations have increased compliance, cleanup, restoration, compensation costs and so on, and also potential liabilities. Regulatory interference adopted a 'polluter pays' approach. The basis of this approach is that firms are forced to pay compliance costs, regulatory impositions or both for carelessly polluting the environment. These costs do not provide any economic benefits to the firm. The regulatory increase in costs for waste and disposal has provided incentives for firms to reassess their processes and production systems for cleaner, more efficient operations. The integration of environmental and social concerns with economic decisions has supported efficiency increases, in terms of resource consumption, waste reduction and also productivity, sufficient to provide greater cost savings and benefits to the firm (Hawken 1994, based on Pigou 1920).

Management issues

Reactive management strategies simply pay the compliance costs without any associated benefit to the firm. Alternatively, **proactive management strategies**, which act in favour of social and environmental issues, consider that benefits in terms of stakeholder relationship can offset the costs of compliance. For example, the replacement of equipment, processes and raw material resources with those that are more environmentally friendly can reduce the risk of noncompliance with regulations, and more efficient processes may save costs. Sound environmental management practices may reduce financial risk, as may supply chain management, in which large firms require suppliers and contractors to conform to their environmental policies and procedures (see for example the International Standards Organisation, Environmental Management Standard: ISO 14000 series). For this reason, information related to environmental issues associated with management decisions is important to external parties. However, the

reactive management strategies: Compliance with legislative requirements after the event; for example, clean-up, compensation or the payment of penalties for breaches of legislation

proactive management strategies: Preventative measures involving risk management to predict and avoid breaches of legislation; for example, pollution prevention, recycling and cleaner processes

results of an early survey undertaken in 1994 of firms operating in the chemical industry in the United States, the UK and Australia indicated that, at that time, compliance issues were the predominant factor prompting expenditure on environmental issues (Raar 1998).

To link environmental and financial issues, the uncertainty surrounding the dollar values attached to, for example, the cleaning up of a contaminated site may require cost estimates. But overlooking the associated financial implications may jeopardise the long-term financial position of the firm. Estimates are made even more difficult because the specific time and scope boundaries for the individual firm's liability have not been resolved. Henriques (2004) suggests that the measurement of environmental or social impacts in monetary terms only uses financial units to measure environmental performance. It does not, in itself, measure financial performance, nor does it accurately reflect the impact of environmental performance (good or bad) on the bottom line of the company. The damage caused to a firm's reputation by an environmental disaster can far outweigh the initial cost of a cleanup. Similarly, the benefits to a company's employment record derived from socially conscious recruitment policies are extremely difficult to quantify. (The reader is referred to Kaplan & Norton 2004 for further information on strategic planning.) Therefore, voluntary reporting is an important element for a firm in the process of communicating to stakeholders its environmental and social performance.

Learning tips

Do you know...

7.1   *Social and environmental reporting is designed to generate business value through measurement and management of environmental risks and opportunities, and to respond to the growing expectations of customers, business partners, investors and the wider community.*

7.2   *Social costs traditionally impose no financial cost on the entity themselves — society usually pays, either financially or through social or environmental degradation.*

7.3   *A variety of stakeholders, including shareholders, suppliers and consumers, financial lending institutions and creditors, industry associations, employees, government and regulatory bodies, community groups and management themselves, have an interest in a firm's environmental and social performance.*

7.4   *Reactive and proactive management strategies have associated costs and benefits related to regulatory compliance and risk management, and can affect the firm's financial health.*

■ Reporting practices

General purpose financial statements contain information to satisfy differing stakeholders, each with its own individual economic decision-making needs. In general, accounting conceptual frameworks provide guidelines for preparers and users of general purpose financial statements.

Appropriately, and as mentioned earlier in the chapter, the disclosure of environmental and social performance is also required by a range of stakeholders with different needs for different purposes.

In 1994, John Elkington created the term **triple bottom line** (Elkington 1997, 1998, 2004). Triple bottom line reporting is the provision of information that allows stakeholders to determine not only the economic value added by the firm, but also the environmental and social value (Elkington 2004, p. 3). The popularity of this term and reporting approach has underpinned a transition to the voluntary provision of separate reports for economic, social and environmental bottom lines.

triple bottom line: A practice that reports on the economic, social and environmental management and performance of a firm

Some advantages of voluntary environmental and social reporting (triple bottom line reporting) are:

- authentication of the firm's activities as part of community values
- demonstration of the firm's internal values
- improved access to information by stakeholders, by channelling information to target stakeholders and increasing corporate visibility
- identification of potential areas of risk (for management)
- reduction in risk profile (for stakeholders)
- alignment of the information needs of individual stakeholder groups with management focus
- provision of a basis for stakeholder dialogue
- improving public image, which attracts investors and helps build reputation over the longer term
- benefits for management from eco-efficiency in terms of reduced waste, disposal and associated costs
- encouragement and facilitated management particularly in information systems that determine, manage and monitor risk and performance benchmarks.

Essentially, firms have had to develop their own formats and disclosure criteria. Consequently, as the impetus for voluntarily reporting environmental and social issues has increased, so has the diversity and range of content the reports contain. Social and environmental issues are predominantly expressed in nonmonetary or descriptive terms. This use of different indicators and the variable quality and quantity of information have hampered users understanding and comparing reports among and within firms. Furthermore, managers are viewed as *rational utility maximisers*, which may lead them to choose to disclose information based only on public relations concerns, rather than on accountability, stewardship and the decision-making needs of stakeholders. Consequently, attestation of these reports has become important to support the reliability and credibility of social and environmental information. This has prompted a concerted push for national and international guidelines.

Importantly, the problem of measuring environmental and social performance, including the full impact of a firm's normal business activities on the environment, has obstructed the formation of a one-size-fits-all best practice set of methods and guidelines. However, nonfinancial reporting guidelines and frameworks have evolved and continue to evolve, allowing stakeholders to understand corporate citizenship performances better. The Global Reporting Initiative (GRI) G3 guidelines, released in October 2006, aim to provide more user-friendly guidance on determining the issues to deal with and the material indicators to select, and to increase the comparability of voluntary reports among companies (www.globalreporting.org). These guidelines and the GRI are discussed in further detail in the next section. The In Focus vignette that follows outlines some of the guidelines and strategies followed by Novo Nordisk, one the leaders in the disclosure of social and environmental information.

 infocus *Novo Nordisk: a global leader in environmental reporting*

The Danish healthcare firm, Novo Nordisk, recognised in the 1990s the relationship between sustainability in the longer term and business issues in the shorter term. Its 1999 social and environmental case study of a section of its business adopted a stakeholder perspective to social and environmental reporting. Novo Nordisk is now one of the global leaders in environmental reporting. Before 2004, it reported its social and environmental information in three separate publications. In 2004, it integrated a collection of inform-ation on social, environmental and financial issues into an annual report using the GRI guidelines as a framework. Its reports now include both financial and nonfinancial performance measures.

An extract from Novo Nordisk's 2005 annual report, which incorporates both the firm's attitude towards the triple bottom line approach, and the inclusion of financial and nonfinancial measures within an annual report, is provided later (www.annualreport.novonordisk.com).

The Novo Nordisk report follows international standards in terms of both mandatory and voluntary reporting: IFRS, Sarbanes–Oxley, securities laws and corporate governance codes in Denmark, the UK and the United States, AA1000 Framework, GRI and the Global Compact. The report is audited by PricewaterhouseCoopers, which also assured the printed report and assessed the information presented online (Ethical performance mailing list 2006).

Business Cases: Building Relationships

Novo Nordisk employees take pride in the company's Triple Bottom Line approach and its commitment to financial, environmental and social responsibility. This is one of the most frequently cited aspects that make Novo Nordisk a 'great place to work', according to people who work with Novo Nordisk.

The *Triple Bottom Line* as a business principle is a way to make sustainability thinking part of everyday business practice. Such an approach offers new opportunities, but indeed also challenges. For how can it be proven that this is the way to achieve better business results? How can we measure the benefits, for the business as well as for society? And how can we ensure that decisions are always made in a way that balances considerations for the Triple Bottom Line?

The answer is simple: We cannot! That is to say — with current methods of measuring, quantitatively or qualitatively, conclusive evidence of the 'business case' for this approach has yet to be presented.

What we can do, though, is to identify potential business benefits and potential financial impact, and here we can indeed suggest a range of *building blocks* of a robust business case.

We aspire to become a model of sustainable business, to be a preferred business partner, to be a trusted company, and to come across as a pharmaceutical company with a heart. Building the business case for the Triple Bottom Line approach is a key factor in earning stakeholder trust and retaining our reputation as a sustainability-driven business leader. The financial impact of our sustainability strategy is not our main motivator. On the other hand it is clear that without a business rationale, sustainability-thinking would run the risk of being merely a nice add-on. Two examples underscore how we mean business when talking sustainability: *Changing diabetes* is an expression of our aspiration to defeat diabetes. *TakeAction!* is the employee programme that encourages everyone to make the Triple Bottom Line their business.

Source: This article appeared at http://annualreport.novonordisk.com.

Guidelines for voluntary disclosure

A few of the more common and well-known best practice guidance publications for voluntary reporting at the national and international level are listed in table 7.2. Note that some of these focus primarily on social issues, others mainly on environmental, while some also incorporate ethical and governance issues.

TABLE 7.2 Best practice voluntary reporting guidelines: international and national

Source	Location	Objective	Website
Global Reporting Initiatives (GRI) G3 guidelines (2006)	International	An international framework to provide guidance on social, economic and environmental reporting	www.globalreporting.org
Institute of Social and Ethical Accountability: AA1000 standards series	International	Guidance on stakeholder engagement and linkages with key performance indicators (KPI) and reporting. An assurance standard	www.accountability.org.uk

continued

TABLE 7.2 *continued*

Source	Location	Objective	Website
Social Accountability International: SA8000 standard	International	A standard for social accountability that incorporates verification	www.sa-intl.org
Ecological Footprint standards 1.0 (end of 2006)	International and some individual nations	Guidelines on implementing the Ecological Footprint indicator of sustainable resource use. Includes a measurement and management tool	www. footprintnetwork.org
Department of Environment and Heritage, Australia	National	Process for preparation of public reporting including environmental indicators	www.deh.gov.au
International Organisation for Standardisation ISO14000 family of environmental management standards	International	Generic management system standards for environmental management including communication and performance evaluation	www.iso.org
United Nations Global Impact	International	Human rights, the environment and labour	
OECD principles of corporate governance (1999–2004)	International	The corporate governance framework to promote transparency and accountability, consistent with 'rule of law'	www.oecd.org

Source: Adapted from Group 100 2003, *Sustainability: a guide to triple bottom line reporting*, Group of 100 Incorporated, Melbourne.

International disclosure and reporting

One of the most widely recognised sets of international guidelines is the GRI. Established in 1997, it 'is a multi-stakeholder process and independent institution whose mission is to develop and disseminate globally applicable Sustainability Reporting Guidelines' (www.gri.org). GRI has adopted a formal policy that considers the information needs of as many organisations as are willing to commit to the mission of the initiative. The structure of the institution allows for an unlimited number of organisational stakeholders to participate in the governance, strategy and policy decisions made by the board.

The GRI 2006 (G3) guidelines require that the content of a voluntary environmental and social report include a statement detailing the scope of the report and the profile of the organisation, followed by the approaches used by management to provide a context to the firm's performance and then a selection of various performance indicators. This structure is outlined in figure 7.1.

STRATEGY AND PROFILE

Disclosures that set the overall context for understanding organisational performance such as its strategy, profile and governance. For example:
- Strategy and analysis
- Organisational profile
- Report parameters
- Governance, commitments and engagement.

MANAGEMENT APPROACH AND PERFORMANCE INDICATORS

This section includes stakeholder engagement, policies, structure and performance indicators from economic, environmental and social categories. For example:

ECONOMIC
- performance
- indirect economic impacts.

ENVIRONMENTAL
- energy
- water
- biodiversity
- emissions
- effluents
- waste
- compliance.

SOCIAL PERFORMANCE INDICATORS
- labour practices and decent work
- human rights
- society
- product responsibility.

FIGURE 7.1 Structure and content of an environmental and social report

Source: Adapted from Global Reporting Initiative 2006, *Sustainability reporting guidelines version 3.0*, Global Reporting Initiative, Amsterdam. www.globalreporting.org.

The previous set of GRI guidelines, GRI 2002, was replaced by the G3 version, but had similar requirements and expectations. Westpac Bank and BHP Billiton have previously prepared reports in accordance with the GRI 2002 reporting guidelines. The following is an extract from BHP Billiton's 2006 sustainability report (http://sustainability.bhpbilliton.com):

> Our Full Report on our website has again been prepared in accordance with the Global Reporting Initiative 2002 Sustainability Reporting Guidelines, and we believe it represents a balanced and reasonable representation of our organisation's economic, environmental and social performance. We remain committed to the UN Global Compact, and this year we have expanded our reporting on UN initiatives in our Full Report to show how we are contributing to the achievement of the UN Millennium Development Goals.

In this report BHP Billiton consider their stakeholders as follows:

> Our vision for sustainable development is to be the company of choice — creating sustainable value for shareholders, employees, contractors, suppliers, customers, business partners and host communities. Central to our vision is our aspirational goal of Zero Harm to people, our host communities and the environment.

The environmental and social activities of a firm can result in financial penalties, outlays, and add to their monetary costs. BHP Billiton is an example of a firm adopting a triple bottom line approach to reporting, by providing a separate sustainability report. Financial performance is contained within their annual report. However, some firms also include social and environmental information within the scope of their annual report.

The release of the third GRI guidelines, G3, is a critical step in the current reporting process, with the evolution of a facility-level report. Currently being pilot tested is a facility reporting project launched by CERES and Tellus Institute and developed in conjunction with the GRI. It focuses on the individual facilities of a firm, and its direct and indirect impacts to the environment.

This facility aspect of reporting is particularly relevant for organisations with diversity in social and environmental activities, with different processes and performance criteria. Facilities may be conducted in different global jurisdictions or under different management. The success of this reporting strategy is expected to provide both management and external stakeholders with more information on the understanding each facility's environmental and social activities, allowing a greater comparison both within and among facilities (www.ceres.org/sustreporting).

Australian disclosure and reporting

Social and environmental reporting has historically been a voluntary exercise. The Australian Deparment of Environment and Heritage website (Table 7.2) provides firms with guidelines for reporting their social and environmental performance voluntarily. In Australia, the only mandatory requirements for environmental and social reporting are covered under the following legislation.

- s. 299(1)(f) of the *Corporations Act 2001*, which requires companies to include details of breaches of environmental laws and licences in their annual reports. This section of the act, requiring directors to report on compliance with environmental legislation, was due for repeal in the first draft of the draft amendment bill to the Corporations Act. However, the *Corporations Amendment Bill (No. 2) 2005* allows s. 299(1) (f) to remain.
- s. 1013 (A) to (F) of the *Corporations Act 2001*, which requires providers of financial products with an investment component to disclose how much labour standards or environmental, social or ethical considerations are taken into account in investment decision making.
- the National Pollutant Inventory, which requires firms to report on toxic industry pollutant emissions (www.npi.gov.au).

In June 2005, the department of the prime minister and cabinet issued a statement of the requirements for annual reports for public service departments. The primary purpose of this statement is accountability. This relates to the effectiveness and efficiency with which resources have been managed. Importantly for social and environmental issues, the statement also required, for 'departments whose outputs may impact on social justice and equity outcomes in the community, reference to the social justice impacts' (p. 7): an **eco-justice** approach.

eco-justice: Intergenerational and intragenerational equity and social equality

It is easier to measure and disclose **eco-efficiency** activities and outcomes than eco-justice. They are short term and more reliable. However, to tackle the longer-term issues of eco-justice (termed **intergenerational equity** by the Brundtland Report) requires disclosure of the firm's input and output to the environment; that is, its contribution to sustainability (Howes 2001).

eco-efficiency: A focus on the efficiency of activities to minimise their effect on the environment, which is short term

intergenerational equity: A concept that, consistent with the definition of sustainable development, recognises that the Earth is a finite planet and all humans require its natural resources. It has a longer-term focus; that is, on future generations.

A short-term focus on the financial markets and a longer-term focus on environmental and social issues may bring management and reporting paradoxes. For example, a firm may make donations or use environmentally friendly practices in the short term, but the longer-term impact of its product on human health or the environment may be the real cause for concern. Management may or may not be aware of long-term issues associated with its activities at the time decisions are made and reports formulated. Long-term impacts may not be evident or indeed measurable in the shorter term.

The tobacco industry and the potential impact of cigarette smoking on the health of smokers provide a topical example of this issue, as do the building firm James Hardie and the health implications connected to its former production of asbestos. Similarly, a firm may recycle, and reuse product materials, and as result be placed on a 'good citizen' list. However, the same firm may also pay its employees poor wages or emit toxic fumes to the atmosphere. Critics suggest that voluntary reporting in practice means that disclosure is restricted merely to the 'good deeds', while the 'bad deeds' are either hidden in the fine print or ignored completely (Adams 2004).

To counter this impression, the Australian government (2005) announced its intention to consider enacting legislation to include social and community obligations within the realm of directors' duties. The announcement led to a variety of responses relating to the responsibility of corporations for their social and environmental relationships. These suggestions included:

- making social responsibility as a replacement for profit objectives
- including a risk management undertaking to reduce opportunities for financial penalties or litigation resulting from environmental or workplace legislation infringement (Grossman 2006).

Reporting excellence

To promote the prospective benefits of social and environmental reporting, firms are judged for both national and international sustainability reporting awards each year. The Association of Certified Chartered Accountants (ACCA) gives awards to:

> around the world reward companies for excellence in environmental, social and sustainability reporting. The aim of our Awards is to identify and reward innovative attempts to communicate corporate performance, although we do not comment on performance itself. Our aim is to reward transparency' (www.accaglobal.com).

In the Australian and New Zealand region, environmental reporting awards were won by the companies listed in table 7.3.

TABLE 7.3 ACCA Australian and New Zealand Awards for Sustainability Reporting (2005)

Award	Recipient
Best Sustainability Report	Mecu Limited 2005 sustainability report www.mecu.com.au
Award for continued high-quality sustainable reporting	Watercare Services Watershed — an integrated approach (Annual report 2005) www.watercare.co.nz
Award for continued high-quality SME sustainability reporting	Australian Ethical Investment Australian Ethical Investment Sustainability Report 2005 www.austethical.com.au
Award for sustainability communication using the internet	BHP Billiton A sustainable perspective — BHP Billiton Sustainability Report http://sustainability.bhpbilliton.com

continued

TABLE 7.3 *continued*

Award	Recipient
Commendation for achievements in sustainability reporting	Vodafone New Zealand What in the world have we done? Vodafone New Zealand corporate responsibility report 2004–05 www.vodafone.co.nz
	IAG New Zealand Sustainability Report 2005 www.iag.co.nz/Sustainability
	URS New Zealand The things we value — 2004 report on our economic, environmental and social performance www.urscorp.co.nz

Source: ACCA Australia 2006, www.accaglobal.com.

Another recognition system, the Global 100 Most Sustainable Corporations in the World project, analyses 'non traditional drivers of risk and shareholder value including companies' performance on social, environmental and strategic governance issues' (www.global100.org). In 2006, only two Australian firms were listed, namely, Westpac Bank and Insurance Australia Group (www.global100.org/2006).

Learning tips
Do you know...

7.5 *Reporting practices are traditionally voluntary and may form part of the general purpose financial statements or a separate report for the entity.*

7.6 *Triple bottom line reporting refers to the provision of information relating to the economic, social and environmental value of the firm.*

7.7 *Guidelines for voluntary disclosure have been developed, including the international GRI's G3 guidelines.*

Practical applications

If a firm spends money, it affects its financial performance and position. The impact can be minimal or quite substantial in either the short or longer term. It is important, therefore, for firms to anticipate the outlay of expenditure on social and environmental initiatives or compliance as part of their risk management strategies. In an attempt to gauge the scope and coverage of this issue in current reporting practices, an international review of corporate sustainability reports by the United Nations Environment Program, the UNEP Financial Institutions Initiative on the Environment, was launched in 1991. The purpose was to include a wide range of financial institutions in the environmental and social agenda.

Surprisingly, UNEP, SustainAbility and Standard & Poor's, *Risk and opportunity: best practice in non-financial reporting* (2004) found only three firms that had identified the balance-sheet implications of key environmental and social risks. Risk management is important to a firm's:

- short-term liquidity
- long-term solvency
- creditors, which undertake liability for these issues in lending contracts
- insurers
- market capitalisation.

In the longer term, financial risk resulting from irresponsible management decisions will be reflected in the price of the firm's shares. The trend towards **ethical investment funds** aligns individual investor decisions with sound financial, environmental and social performance. To understand the firm and its attitude to risk, ethical fund managers and their investors require relevant information.

ethical investment funds: Investment funds that screen potential investments for not only economic performance, but also social and environmental attributes; for example, whether the company conducts experiments on animals or is involved in armaments

The annual report has historically been the tool to communicate financial information with which to gauge associated risk. The triple bottom line approach attempts to help the communication of social and environmental issues, including risks. For example, the global resources group BHP's *Sustainability report 2005* covers BHP's business approach, environmental record and role in society. In this report, BHP included areas include:

- detail on BHP's approach to risk management
- a description of the processes and outcomes of dialogue and engagement with external parties (http://sustainability.bhpbilliton.com).

More recently, corporate reporting has tended towards the inclusion of sustainability issues and biodiversity risk: a longer-term focus. This is particularly so in the nonprivate sector of the business community. It can be expected that this will flow through to the industry level, particularly in terms of biodiversity risk. This is exemplified by The British Land Company, as discussed in the following In Focus vignette.

 in focus *The British Land Company PLC: at the forefront of biodiversity and risk reporting*

One firm at the forefront of biodiversity and risk reporting is The British Land Company PLC. Two extracts from *The British Land Company corporate responsibility report 2005*, which includes risk and biodiversity, are provided in the following.

Managing risks and realising opportunities

Over the last two years, British Land has undertaken a process of external consultation and internal assessment to identify and manage the corporate responsibility risks and realise the opportunities that face the business.

As part of the risk management process, British Land has identified a property lifecycle consisting of five stages: site acquisition; design and planning; construction; asset management; and sale of assets. At each of these stages, the potential risks and opportunities are prioritised based on the level of potential negative or positive impact, the likelihood of occurrence and British Land's level of influence over them. The process of review used to identify the risks and opportunities and assign the key focus areas for the Company's corporate responsibility management activities is illustrated below.

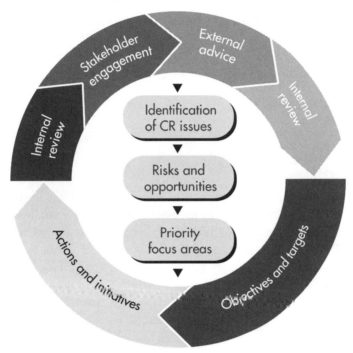

FIGURE 7.2 Risk and opportunity review process

The Company consults with external stakeholders and specialists in relevant areas of expertise, including: Arup on environmental issues; Corporate Culture on social issues; Hewitt Bacon & Woodrow on employee issues and the SMART Company on local community partnerships.

British Land commissioned independent stakeholder research in 2004 and 2005, on both occasions agreeing the scope of the research with external advisors. The findings of this formal research highlighted the issues of most importance to the Company's stakeholders.

British Land also draws on regular informal stakeholder dialogue e.g. analyst sessions with socially responsible investors, meetings with Government officials and local councils, discussions with local community groups, and employee workshops.

In 2004, an internal review by British Land management, including the Corporate Responsibility Committee, the Strategy Working Group and other project working groups, identified the Company's main areas of potential corporate responsibility risk and opportunity. These were approved by the Audit Committee and are reflected in the Corporate Responsibility section of the Company's 2005 Annual Report.

Based on the 2005 stakeholder research and consultation programmes and the Company's knowledge of the property investment, development and management sectors, British Land senior management and external consultants have further developed and refined the risks and opportunities identified in the 2005 Annual Report to become seven focus areas of corporate responsibility risk and opportunity.

These seven areas, reflected in the structure of this 2005 Corporate Responsibility Report, are: British Land people; supply chain; regeneration; community; resource use; waste management; and biodiversity. Each section is headed by the principal risks and key opportunities that faced the business in 2005.

Source: The British Land Company 2005, 'Managing risks & realising opportunities', *The British Land Company corporate responsibility report 2005*, www.britishland.com.

Reputation

Reputation from an accounting perspective is an *intangible item*, because it does not have a physical identity. Significantly for external reporting, reputation is classified as an internally generated asset, which is not separately identified, and according to AASB 138, cannot be reliably measured. Therefore, it is not reported on the balance sheet as an intangible asset. However, the firm's reputation may form part of a combination of items termed goodwill, which can be purchased by another organisation. Then reputation can be included in the asset *purchased goodwill* and recorded on the balance sheet of the purchaser.

Natural capital

According to Gray, Bebbington & Walters (1993, p. 290) natural environmental assets fall into three categories:

- *critical natural capital:* those elements of the biosphere that are essential for life and, for sustainability, must remain inviolate (examples include the ozone layer and a critical mass of trees)
- *other (sustainable, substitutable or renewable) natural capital:* those elements of the biosphere that are renewable (e.g. nonextinct species, woodlands) or for which reasonable (however defined) substitutes can be found (perhaps, for example, energy from fossil fuels versus energy from renewable sources, given the right capital investment)
- *artificial capital:* those elements created from the biosphere, which are no longer part of the harmony of the natural ecology, including such things as machines, buildings, roads, products, wastes).

Gray Bebbington & Walters (1993) draw attention to the *artificial capital* category, which is already covered by conventional accounting. Many of these items will fall under the Australian Accounting Standards Board (AASB) conceptual framework and can be listed on the balance sheet as assets.

However, as Gray, Bebbington & Walters (1993) point out, *critical natural capital* will decline unless there is a way to maintain it similarly to how individuals need to ensure that financial capital is not diminished before determining income. A sustainability report on the firm's relationship with the environment can be implemented based on an input and output approach, using nonfinancial measures. For example, the biosphere is affected by pollution, and if it is unable to renew itself, ecological problems arise (Corriher 1976). In an effort to minimise the influence of pollution, capital markets can exchange permits for emission. If, for example, one firm implements more efficient processes and reduces the amount of pollution it produces, it may trade the difference in emissions credits in the capital markets.

Therefore, from an accounting perspective, this aspect of the biosphere can be included in the financial reports and measured in monetary terms. Other ecological issues include the conservation of flora and fauna. The business activities of each individual firm would need to be considered carefully before measurement in monetary terms within the jurisdiction of the present accounting standards. Two examples are discussed in more detail in the following:

- Greenhouse gas emissions can be traded in an active market, for example the Chicago Board of Trade, which conducts auctions on the Environmental Protection Agency's sulphur dioxide permits (Annala & Howe 2004; Gibson 2002). Emission permits that are tradable in the market can be classified as an asset under the definition and recognition criteria for an asset outlined previously. The following questions are raised:

    whether the emission permits should be included in accounting records at market price or cost

    – the difference between instruments traded

    – the relationship between the pollution reduction and the asset value

    – whether if pollution is reduced as a result of increased technology and more effective and efficient production processes, this can form part of the value of the marketable emissions instrument (Annala & Howe 2004).

    While a more detailed discussion on tradable permits is outside the scope of this chapter, the interested reader is referred to Gibson (1999, 2002). In addition, emission permits could be reported according to the relevant accounting standard (Financial Accounting Standards Board or AASB) for *derivative* and *hedging instruments*.

- In terms of conservation firms, Jones (2001) undertook a study of the Elan Valley Estate, a water catchment, which also provided a haven for conservation of wildlife animals. The study undertook a habitat survey of woodland, scrub and so on, and also listed critical wildlife species. A natural inventory model was used to place a monetary valuation on habitats, and to include their critical fauna and flora species. For example, ferns, grasses, birds, butterflies, moths, mammals were included in the annual reporting information, in terms suitable for auditing. However, Jones did not attach a monetary value to the fauna.

In Australia, a similar effort was undertaken by a former public listed conservation company, Earth Sanctuaries Ltd (ESL), which did attach a monetary value to native fauna. ESL used the former Australian Accounting Standard AASB 1037 (replaced with *AASB 141 Agriculture* which does not allow this option) to report on *self-generating and regenerating assets* (SGARAs), which included native flora and fauna. AASB 1037 allowed for an increase (or decrease) in the volume of SGARAs to be measured at a monetary value deemed the *best indicator* of net market value. Because these fauna were not legally marketable, the best indicator was a dollar value attached to individual animals. The figure used was based on expert judgement as to the 'recovery of sanctuary costs in re-establishing species populations and associated translocation expenses, which include the capture of the native fauna in the wild'. For example, *rare* species of native fauna were valued at $2500 per animal. When multiplied by the volume of population increase, this was included as unrealised revenue in the financial statements (Raar, Purnell & Hone 2002; Purnell, Raar & Hone 2003).

AASB 141 in Australia has focused on the development of agricultural assets into a product that is eventually harvested and sold in the marketplace. At some point, the agricultural asset must be exchangeable. This is a longer-term perspective than that of other accounting standards.

The role of the accounting profession

Over the years, conceptual reporting models have been formulated at a macro and micro level, each prepared as a practical tool to report socioeconomic impacts and relationships. Traditionally, the accounting profession has been concerned with the practical complexities of attaching a monetary measurement to socioeconomic impacts for external reporting purposes. However, in the 1970s, the accounting profession began to consider the relationship of accounting to social and environmental issues.

The past

Accounting professional guidelines were prepared to help measure social costs, account for social performance and even measure the effectiveness of social programs (AAA 1972, 1973, 1974, 1975). Some of these earlier discussions, for example Ramanathan (1976), proposed that at the firm level, internal accounting systems should be designed and operated so that corporate social performance measures were routinely made available (p. 518). In 2006, this viewpoint that internal accounting systems should be linked to social performance measures still underpins the reporting of sustainability performance. It forms the basis of the UK's professional accounting standard Reporting Standard (RS) 1, which is discussed in more detail in the next section. The profound difference between earlier research efforts and the current standard is the apparent acceptance by the accounting profession, financial institutions and external parties, that nonfinancial performance measures can form part of an external accounting report.

The future

In the UK, the Companies Act Regulations 2005 for the first time required directors of British based companies, listed on the London or New York stock exchanges, to commence producing operating and financial reviews (OFRs) for social and environmental performance from April 2005.

Subsequently, the accounting regulatory body in the UK, the Accounting Standards Board (ASB), issued the RS 1 *The operating and financial review (OFR)*, which made the report mandatory in the UK for all companies listed on the stock exchange. In response to pressure from the business sector, this aspect of the regulations has been repealed, and is no longer mandatory. However, it is still recommended best practice for all listed firms.

> The OFR shall provide information to assist members to assess the strategies adopted by the entity and the potential for those strategic to succeed. The key elements of the disclosure framework necessary to achieve this are:
>
> a. the nature of the business, including a description of the market, competitive and regulatory environment in which the entity operates, and the entity's objectives and strategies;
> b. the development and performance of the business, both in the financial year under review and in the future;
> c. the resources, principal risks and uncertainties and relationships that may affect the entity's long-term value;
> d. the position of the business including a description of the capital structure, treasury policies and objectives and liquidity of the entity, both in the financial year under review and the future. (para. 28, pp. 11–12).

To meet these requirements, the OFR should include information about:

a. environmental matters (including the impact of the business of the entity on the environment);
b. the entity's employees;
c. social and community issues (para. 29, p. 12).*

Environmental risk and uncertainty are also included. It is suggested in the OFR standard that firms prone to significant environmental footprints and risks adopt certain risk assessment strategies with associated monitoring. Other areas of management are expected to have KPIs, particularly in relation to:

• water use
• energy use
• waste
• climate change impacts, including global warming and emissions management
• ozone depleting substances (para. IG 22, p. 64).

With the impetus from accounting requirements for firms to supply future-oriented information, the focus on short-term profit margins has shifted to include longer-term and other issues — environment and social — that form part of the firm's strategic stance. Firms have also been prompted to install systematic and robust internal information systems to allow verification of the information they supply to external parties.

The influence of financial performance and the share market

Community pressure for firms to internalise social costs, either through regulation or voluntarily, will have implications for financial performance. Firms may have social and environmental goals that conflict with their financial goals and objectives. For example:

- Outsourcing work to an Asian firm, with cheaper labour, may boost profit. However, the social goals of a responsible firm may be to ensure that staff in Australia are helped financially when retrenched, which has a direct financial impact.
- A road transport firm may have to choose between a fleet that meets financial criteria but emits a lot of pollution and one that is more 'environmentally friendly' but also more expensive.

A conceptual link between social and environmental issues and financial performance is provided in figure 7.3.

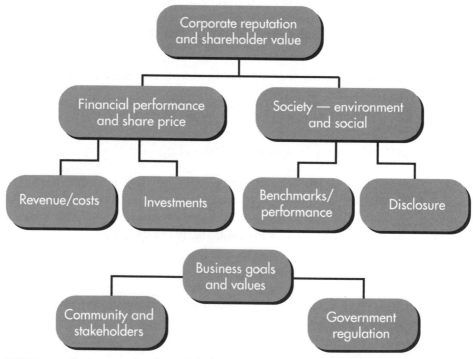

FIGURE 7.3 Environmental and social disclosure and financial performance

The relationship between social and environmental disclosure and performance and economic performance has been the subject of considerable academic and professional research. A comprehensive literature review of social and environmental performance and its relationship to financial performance can be found in Orlitzky, Schmidt & Rynes (2003) and Al-Tuwaijri, Christensen and Hughes (2004).

The relationship is discussed further in the following sections.

The influence of the share market

Based on the efficient market hypothesis, firms communicate to stakeholders their potential to generate future cash flows and returns. Social responsibility and ethical behaviour can also add value to the corporate image, and ultimately the value of the firm (Bauer & Fenn 1972).

The capital markets have added a level of sophistication to this view of corporate social and environmental reputation. In 1999, Sustainable Asset Management linked with Dow Jones & Company and developed the Dow Jones Index Sustainability World Indexes, which track the financial performance of sustainable firms worldwide. In Australia, the third Annual Corporate Responsibility Index was published in May 2006, with Westpac at the top of the list. Although they identify a gap between rhetoric and practice, these indices nevertheless provide investors with confidence (Holliday, Jr, Schmidheiny & Watts 2002). Consequently, internationally and nationally, there has been a growth in mutual funds whose criteria for entry are sustainability goals and performance: **socially responsible investment** (SRI) funds. This exerts even more pressure for reporting transparency.

Different investment fund managers may have different values and preferences. Some fund managers use the **exclusion approach** to decide which firms are to be listed in their socially responsible investment fund is. That is, the fund managers exclude firms from the list on certain criteria, such as:

* operating within particular industry groups; for example, gambling
* manufacturing certain products; for example, cigarettes.

Active fund managers are now using more sophisticated methods, such as sustainability ratings or indices to choose and assess firms for inclusion in socially responsible investment funds. These methods require relevant data, mostly provided by the increase in voluntary reporting by firms (Koellner et al. 2005).

In addition, in April 2006, the United Nations launched Principles for Responsible Investment, which was signed by:

> the heads of 18 major institutional investors from nine countries, representing more than $2 trillion in assets...They join a group of 32 institutional asset owners representing the original $2 trillion which backed the Principles during the international launch in New York (www.unpri.org).

socially responsible investment: Investment concerned with socially and environmental criteria or benchmarks, together with financial performance of a firm. Groups of firms meeting the specified criteria of research analysts combine to form an SRI fund.

exclusion approach: The process by which firms are excluded from an SRI fund on certain criteria

The principles 'are underpinned by a set of 35 possible actions that institutional investors can take to integrate environmental, social and corporate governance (ESG) considerations into their investment activities' and also reference the GRI reporting guidelines as a mechanism to assist with reporting transparency (GRI April News Update, 28 April 2006). In Australia, some religious-based superannuation funds have agreed to adopt the principles.

Link to financial performance

Hasseldine, Salama & Toms (2005) researched the quality of the information signalled to stakeholders. The results of the empirical study indicated that the quality of disclosure, rather than the quantity of information provided, influenced environmental reputation.

In 2005, CPA Australia undertook a survey of shareholders, financial advisors, directors and auditors to determine their *confidence in corporate reporting*. The results indicate that employees (or potential employees) and investors were discouraged from either working for, or investing in, a firm with a bad social reputation. To a lesser extent, the sample also indicated that social reputation may influence consumers when making decisions about purchasing a firm's goods or services.

More traditional financial parameters were examined in the CPA Australia project *Sustainability reporting practices, performance and potential* (2005). The report found:

- an association between lower financial distress ratings and firms that disclosed a higher level of sustainability
- a positive relationship between sustainability disclosure and firm financial performance (p. 85).

Summary

Define social and environmental reporting, and discuss the measurement of social costs (or externalities).

- Social and environmental reporting is defined as the disclosure of information on social and environmental-related issues and performance; the process of communicating the social and environmental effects of an organisation's actions within society and to society at large. Its purpose is to generate business value through measurement and management of environmental risks and opportunities, and reporting this information in a fashion that responds to the growing expectations of customers, business partners, investors and the wider community. A social cost is one that is free to the business unit incurring it. Society pays.

Identify different stakeholder groups and the reasons for their interest in a firm's environmental and social performance.

- Stakeholders include shareholders, suppliers and consumers, financial lending institutions and creditors, industry associations, employees, government and regulatory bodies, community groups and management. Associated social costs and benefits relating to environmental and social issues can include environmental, social or health implications associated with the product, supply lines, the workplace, the physical environment and perception and reputation. Reactive and proactive management strategies have associated costs and benefits related to regulatory compliance and risk management.

Explain the existing reporting practices and guidelines for social and environmental reporting.

- Reporting practices are traditionally voluntary and may form part of the general purpose financial statements, or a separate report for the entity. Triple bottom line reporting refers to the provision of information relating to the economic, social and environmental value of the firm. Guidelines for voluntary disclosure have been developed, including the international GRI's G3 guidelines. In Australia, guidelines are provided by several sections of the *Corporations Act 2001*, and by various federal government departments. ACCA awards international and regional firms for reporting excellence.

Discuss the practical applications of reporting systems to social and environmental disclosure.

- With the increase in reporting, the financial impacts of social and environmental initiatives by a firm have become more important. The trend towards ethical investment funds has prompted the extension of value assessment by the accounting profession to include social and environmental factors. The concept of a firm's intangible asset, reputation, is subject to the accounting profession's definition and recognition criteria for its potential inclusion in the annual report as an asset on the balance sheet. The measurement and assessment of critical natural capital, including biodiversity, is still a problematic issue.

Identify the role of the accounting profession in social and environmental reporting.
- The accounting profession has been charged with the task of developing professional guidelines for the inclusion of social and environmental factors in the reporting systems of firms and making performance measures routinely available. In practice, this has resulted in a shift to mandatory reporting of environmental and social issues within a firm, particularly in the UK, with the revision of the OFR regulations.

Discuss the influence of the share market and financial performance on social and environmental reporting.
- Increasing stakeholder concern and community awareness of ethical, social and environmental awareness have underpinned an evolution of share market investment mechanisms to include ethical investments, and a demand for more transparency in the corporate reporting process. Capital markets and SRI funds exert enormous influence on the communication of a firm's corporate responsibility and internal management systems, and the influence of a firm's reputation on investor perception of sound management cannot be underestimated.

Key terms

accountability (stewardship)   195
eco-efficiency   205
eco-justice   205
ethical investment funds   208
exclusion approach   215
intergenerational equity   205
legitimacy theory   195
proactive management strategies   197
reactive management strategies   197
social and environmental reporting   194
social costs (externalities)   194
socially responsible investment   215
stakeholder theory   196
sustainability   194
sustainable development   195
triple bottom line   199

Review questions

7.1   Explain the term social and environmental reporting.
7.2   Explain the term social costs or externalities.
7.3   Explain the term sustainability in relation to environmental and social issues.
7.4   Why is it important to include social costs in the in accounting system?
7.5   The following is a list of items that are related to environmental and social activities. Under the Australian Accounting Standards (AIFRS), which of these can be classified as an (a) intangible asset or (b) asset?

- cost of developing a patent for an item of capital machinery that reduces pollution
- savings from reduction in waste disposal costs
- fine for illegal waste disposal into a river
- firm's inclusion in the capital markets as an SRI
- hire of consultant to develop a new environmentally friendly product
- costs of promoting a corporate citizenship image
- costs of preparing the information for a triple bottom line sustainability report

7.6   List some of the criteria that fund managers in the share market would consider necessary to list a firm as 'socially responsible'.

7.7   Some would argue that there is no linkage between environmental and social management and reporting and the financial aspects of the individual firm. Do you agree or disagree? Explain your reasons.

7.8   Explain the difference between eco-efficiency and eco-justice. In which section (if any) of the financial reports would each of these be more likely found?

7.9   Gray, Bebbington & Walters (1993) uses the terms critical natural capital and other sustainable, substitutable or renewable natural capital. Explain the difference between these terms.

7.10   Define the term triple bottom line reporting.

7.11   Consider and list the reasons firms should realise the need for cleaner more efficient work processes.

7.12   Why are social costs hard to measure for the individual firm?

7.13   List three stakeholders and explain how they can prompt firms to conduct their activities with concern for the environment and society.

7.14   Explain the purpose of the GRI.

7.15   Is the GRI consistent with the international (now adopted in AIFRS) accounting conceptual framework or standards?

7.16   Explain the relationship between:
- the motivation for management to provide a triple bottom line report and communicate transparent information on their social and environmental performance to investors and potential investors
- the firm's share price.

7.17   You have just gained a new job with your qualifications, as an accountant, and also as a financial investment advisor. A client has $100 000, which he or she requests you invest in a soundly managed firm that has a reputation for responsible management. Explain to your client the meaning of an SRI fund.

Application questions

7.18   The CEO of Revmotor Company has requested that you redesign the motor sold by the company. The fuel the motor currently uses is damaging to the environment. He wishes to manufacture a motor that uses a cleaner fuel.

The CEO considers it is in the best financial interests of the firm to make this change. Comment on this statement.

7.19 Refer to the information provided in question 16. Revmotor Company proceeds to spend $500 000 dollars on research in 2006, and also in 2007. The firm also spends $5 million dollars on developing this new engine over five years to 2011. The probability of obtaining revenue from the new engine is high, although company will not commence sales until 2012.

Explain the associated accounting entries for 2006 and onwards.

7.20 You are the accountant of a global corporation, with operations on two continents: Australia and North America.

(a) Explain how facility reporting, a continuing focus of GRI communication tools, would help you communicate your social and environmental activities.

(b) The accounting standards in Australia still differ from those in the United States. Would this affect your answer to part (a)?

7.21 The accounting profession in Australia has not issued a formal accounting standard for the reporting of social and environmental activities. Explain the problems for the accounting profession in including social and environmental information in:

(a) the annual report

(b) the balance sheet.

7.22 The management of ABC Ltd in the past was not concerned with environmental responsibility, and was polluting the land upon which its factory operated. The firm now needs to expand its manufacturing facilities, and wishes to sell the land and the factory building.

Potential buyers have shown interest in purchasing the property. However, it seems that lenders are not prepared to provide funds for a buyer. Explain why this might be the case.

7.23 Dumpit Ltd is a household name in technological equipment, including digital equipment to download music and movies. Increased competition has prompted management to shift its manufacturing operations from Australia to an underdeveloped country, where the wages for employees are cheaper. It has recently been announced in the media that Dumpit Ltd has been paying children to work in its assembly plants at $5 per week. The retail price of its product in Australia is $200.

(a) From the information given, what is the primary objective of Dumpit Ltd's management?

(b) List some of the social impacts of Dumpit Ltd moving from Australia to another country.

(c) You have decided to purchase new equipment to download music. The product offered by Dumpit Ltd is $50 cheaper than that of the nearest competitor. Would you be prepared to purchase its product? State your reasons.

Twenty years on: lest we forget the lessons from Chernobyl

Nuclear power has never made any social, financial or environmental sense, writes Anthony Albanese.

The meltdown of the Chernobyl nuclear reactor 20 years ago was one of the most significant disasters of the 20th century, and the effects of it are still being felt. To get a sense of the scale of the disaster, authorities are still trying to prevent more radiation from leaking and there is still a 30-kilometre security radius around the site.

As Mikhail Gorbachev declared this month: 'Chernobyl opened my eyes like nothing else. It showed the horrible consequences of nuclear power, even when used for non-military purposes.'

The International Atomic Energy Agency concluded that radiation exposure from the Chernobyl disaster will lead to the deaths of up to 4000 people, and there have been 4000 cases of thyroid cancer, mostly in children. The agency found that 350 000 people were displaced, with relocation a 'deeply traumatic experience'.

Chernobyl showed the world that nuclear power was not safe, but just 20 years later our Prime Minister is ready to bring nuclear power to Australia.

On April 7 John Howard told Southern Cross Radio: 'My philosophy is that if it became economically attractive, I would not oppose [nuclear power] any more than I oppose the export of uranium.'

The Treasurer, the Defence Minister, the Industry Minister and the Environment Minister have all said Australia should consider establishing a nuclear power industry.

The ALP has opposed nuclear power in Australia for decades. Its platform states that 'Labor will prohibit the establishment in Australia of nuclear power plants and all other stages of the nuclear fuel cycle'.

Nuclear energy doesn't add up economically, environmentally or socially, and after more than 50 years of debate, we still do not have an answer to nuclear proliferation or nuclear waste.

Nuclear power is the most capital intensive to establish, decommissioning is extremely expensive and the financial burden continues long after the plant is closed. On March 30 Britain estimated it will cost $170 billion to clean up its 20 nuclear sites.

In the US, direct subsidies to nuclear energy totalled $115 billion between 1947 and 1999, with a further $145 billion in indirect subsidies. In contrast, subsidies to wind and solar energy combined during the same period totalled only $5.5 billion. Those costs don't include the black hole of nuclear waste — because there is no solution.

The Defence Minister, Brendan Nelson, said on November 27: 'In terms of high-level waste, if it were ever to be produced from an Australian nuclear industry, well that will be a matter for the governments of the day'.

What an abrogation of responsibility.

The issue of nuclear proliferation is another critical concern that cannot be left to a future government.

According to the Oxford Research Group, a nuclear weapons designer could construct a nuclear weapon from three or four kilograms of reactor-grade plutonium. About 250 000 kilograms of civil plutonium has been reprocessed world-wide — enough to generate 60 000 nuclear weapons.

It has also been suggested that two or three people with appropriate skills could design and fabricate a crude nuclear weapon, using a cricket ball-sized sphere of reactor-grade plutonium.

Last year's Nobel Peace Prize winner, Mohamed ElBaradei, the head of the International Atomic Energy Agency, warned about the dangers of nuclear pro-liferation: 'Our fears of a deadly nuclear detonation…have been reawakened… driven by new realities. The rise in terrorism. The discovery of clandestine nuclear programs. The emergence of a nuclear black market.'

This is the reality that must shape the nuclear debate. Australia should lead the world in the adoption of clean energy. We should seize the economic benefits of the push to cleaner energy and renewable energy.

There is a $1 trillion industry emerging globally in carbon-friendly technologies. During this month's visit by the Chinese Premier, Wen Jiabao, a $300 million deal was signed by the Tasmanian renewable energy company Roaring 40s to provide three wind farms in China.

China's renewable energy target of 15 per cent by 2020 puts the Howard Government's 2 per cent target in perspective.

With investments in solar and wind power, clean coal and gas technology, and with the right price signals in place, Australia can transform today's energy industry into tomorrow's energy economy without investing in nuclear power.

Now is the time to reflect on the lessons from the Chernobyl disaster. We should ask ourselves if we want a clean energy future or a toxic waste future.

Source: This article appeared in *The Sydney Morning Herald*.

---

1. List some of the social costs and issues associated with
   (a) oil and coal-based energy and
   (b) nuclear power.
   Adopting an accounting perspective, what is the entity?
   • The individual oil corporation?
   • The industry group?
   • The planet Earth?
   Explain your answer.
2. Explain the issues relating to the suggested social costs at the industry and firm level if a government decided to adopt nuclear power.
3. Assume the government decided to place a carbon tax on coal, as an alternative to changing to nuclear power. As a manager of a manufacturing firm with average pollution levels, would it change your fuel resource?
4. Would it be necessary to integrate the longer term health issues associated with nuclear waste storage into the costs of the individual energy firm?

Banks set to go green and caring

The heads of two of Australia's big four banks have unveiled their vision for caring, sharing companies that would measure their success in community respect as well as profits.

In a reversal of the profit-obsessed 'bastard bank' philosophy of the 1990s, the heads of Westpac and ANZ said banks needed to focus on sustainability, environmental issues and caring for their staff and customers.

Of course, the added benefit is that the new approach could mean even bigger bank profits.

In a speech to stock analysts in Sydney yesterday, Westpac boss David Morgan said the bank had focused on lowering electricity use, reducing greenhouse gas emissions, developing 'switched-on' employees, lowering staff turnover and fostering a healthy engagement with the community.

He said Westpac cut electricity consumption by 5 per cent last year with measures such as reducing lighting for signage at its branches. The company had cut greenhouse gas emissions by 35 per cent since 1996, he said.

Paper use fell dramatically after the bank's fleet of photocopiers was switched over to double-page imaging.

But one of the biggest savings — about $50 million a year that would otherwise have been spent on recruitment and staff training — was from reduced employee turnover as the Westpac workforce became more committed to their jobs, Mr Morgan said.

For example, productivity rose when the bank introduced the option of taking a day off a year on full pay for community work.

Mr Morgan told the stock-market analysts that corporations were only as strong as the 'weakest link' between employees, customers, shareholders and the community.

He noted that a recent global survey of investment funds managing more than $US30 trillion ($41 trillion) found most of the funds expected social and environmental performance to become mainstream issues for investment management within 10 years.

Leading bank analyst Brian Johnson of JP Morgan, who attended the Westpac briefing, said he weighs up the sustainability of a financial result when he values a company.

'But I'd also say that doing the right thing is sometimes more important than a financial outcome,' he said.

Mr Morgan's counterpart at ANZ Bank, John McFarlane, echoed the sustainability message in Wellington on Tuesday, when he told the trans-Tasman Business Circle that people were searching for new meaning in their lives.

'I believe we are now firmly in a new age where spirituality, humanity and community will mean much more,' the bank chief said.

Mr McFarlane said the 'people agenda' was the key factor that would reshape the ANZ and become the 'bedrock of its sustainability'.

The truth was that few corporations survived as thriving entities, with only five of Australia's top 20 companies in 1980 still on the list, he said.

Mr Morgan gave an indication last week of his determination to push a sustainability agenda when he broke ranks with the mainstream big-business community on the issue of greenhouse gas emissions.

He joined five other CEOs in calling on the Howard Government to take faster action to force companies to limit their greenhouse emissions.

Source: This article appeared in *The Australian*.

---

1. Identify the major stakeholder groups concerned with the environmental and social performance of large banks, and the associated reasons for their interest.
2. Why did Westpac and ANZ initiate the changes outlined?
3. Categorise the type of information you consider necessary for Westpac and ANZ to include in their social and environmental reports.
4. Explain the role of staff in the banks' focus on sustainability.
5. Compare an eco-justice approach with sustainability with the comment in the case study 'But I'd also say that doing the right thing is sometimes more important than a financial outcome' from bank analyst Brian Johnson of JP Morgan.

Recommended readings and websites

Adams, R 1992, 'Why is the environmental debate of interest to accountants and accountancy bodies?' in D Owen (ed) *Accountancy and the Challenge of the nineties*, Chapman & Hall, London.

Association of Certified Chartered Accountants (ACCA), Sustainability Awards, www.accaglobal.com.

Bloom, GF and Morton, MSS 1991, 'The concept of social accountability in accounting literature', *Journal of Accounting Literature*, vol. 5, pp. 167–82.

Clikeman, P 2004, 'Socially conscious corporation', *Strategic Finance*, April, pp. 23–7.

Corporations and Markets Advisory Committee 2005, *Corporate social responsibility: discussion paper*, Corporations and Markets Advisory Committee, Sydney.

Department of the Environment and Heritage, 'Corporate sustainability', www.deh.gov.au.

Gibson, K 1999, 'National emissions trading: what are the boundaries', *News Journal of the Asia Pacific Centre for Environmental Accountability*, vol. 5, no. 2, pp. 12–16.

—— 2002, 'Accounting for greenhouse gas emissions', *Australian CPA*, vol. 72, iss. 7, pp. 70–3.

Global 100: Most sustainable corporations in the world, www.global100.org.

Global Reporting Initiative, G3 Guidelines, www.globalreporting.org.

Inside Green Business 2006, 'Inside Washington publishers', http://insidegreenbusiness.com.

International Organization for Standardization, ISO14000 family series of international environmental management standards, www.iso.org.

Mathews, MR 1993, *Socially responsible accounting*, Chapman & Hall, London.

Mobus, JL 2005, 'Mandatory environmental disclosures in a legitimacy theory context', *Accounting, Auditing & Accountability Journal*, vol. 18, no. 4, pp. 492–517.

Organisation for Economic Co-operation and Development, 'Principles of corporate governance', www.oecd.org.

Riahi-Belkaoui, A & Pavlik, EL 1992, *Accounting for corporate reputation*, Quorum Books, Westport, Connecticut.

Schaltegger, S & Wagner, M (eds) 2006, *Managing and measuring the business case for sustainability: capturing the relationship between sustainability performance, business competitiveness and economic performance*, Greenleaf, San Francisco.

United Nations Environment Program (UNEP), SustainAbility and Standard & Poor's 2004, *The global reporters 2004 survey of corporate sustainability reporting: risk and opportunity: best practice in non-financial reporting*. SustainAbility Ltd, London www.sustainability.com.

Yale Centre for Environmental Law and Policy and Centre for International Earth Science Information Network 2005, 2005 *environmental sustainability index*, Yale University and Columbia University.

References

Accounting Standards Board 2005, *Reporting standard 1: Operating and financial review*, ASB Publications, Surrey.

Adams, CA 2004, 'The ethical, social and environmental reporting-performance portrayal gap,' *Accounting, Auditing & Accountability Journal*, vol. 17, no. 5, pp. 731–57.

Al-Tuwaijri, SA, Christensen, TE & Hughes II, KE 2004, 'The relations among environmental disclosure, environmental performance, and economic performance; a simultaneous equations approach' *Accounting, Organizations and Society*, vol. 29, pp. 447–71.

American Accounting Association (AAA) 1972, 'Report of the committee on measures of effectiveness for social programs', *The Accounting Review*, no. 47 (supplement).

American Accounting Association 1973, 'Report on the committee of environmental effects of organisational behaviour', *The Accounting Review*, vol. 48 (supplement).

—— 1974, 'Report on the committee on the measurement of social costs', *The Accounting Review*, no. 49 (supplement).

American Accounting Association (AAA) 1975, 'Report of the committee on accounting for social performance', *The Accounting Review*, no. 50 (supplement).

Annala, C & Howe, H 2004, 'Trading solutions for lowering air pollution', *Strategic Finance*, September, pp. 41–4.

Association of Certified Chartered Accountants (ACCA) 2006, ACCA Australia and New Zealand Awards for Sustainability Reporting, www.accaglobal.com.

Bauer, RA & Fenn DH 1972, *The corporate social audit*, Russell Sage Foundation, New York.

Corriher, JJD 1976, *A study of the impact of pollution control upon accounting*, University of Alabama, p. 298.

CPA Australia 2005a, *Confidence in corporate reporting*, CPA Australia, Melbourne.

—— 2005b, *Sustainability reporting practices, performance and potential*, CPA Australia, Melbourne.

Elkington, J 1997, *Cannibals with forks — the triple bottom line of 21st century business*, Capstone Publishing, Oxford.

—— 1998, 'The triple bottom line, seven business revolutions for the 21st century', *Proceedings of world best practice in corporate environmental management conference*, 29th April, Melbourne.

—— 2004, 'Enter the triple bottom line', in Henriques, A & Richardson, J (eds), *The triple bottom line: does it all add up?*, Earthscan, London.

Global Reporting Initiative 2006, 'Declaring use of the guidelines: two new systems proposed', news update, 31 March, Global Reporting Initiative, Amsterdam, www.globalreporting.org.

Gray, R, Bebbington, J & Walters, D 1993, *Accounting for the environment: the greening of accountancy, part II*, Association of Chartered Certified Accountants, Paul Chapman Publishing, London.

Gray, R, Kouhy, R & Lavers, S 1995, 'Corporate social and environmental reporting: a review of the literature and a longitudinal study of UK disclosure', *Accounting, Auditing and Accountability Journal*, vol. 8, no. 2, pp. 47–77.

Gray, R, Owen, D & Maunders, K 1987, *Corporate social reporting: accounting and accountability*, Prentice Hall International, Englewood Cliffs, New Jersey.

Grossman. HA 2006, 'More than "social welfare" in disguise', *The Age*, 16 February, p. B8.

Hasseldine, J, Salama, AI & Toms, JS 2005, 'Quantity versus quality: the impact of environmental disclosures on the reputations of UK plcs', *The British Accounting Review*, vol. 37, pp. 231–48.

Hawken, P 1994, *The ecology of commerce*, HarperCollins, New York.

Henriques, A 2004, 'SCR: sustainability and the triple bottom line', in Henriques, A & Richardson, J (eds), *The triple bottom line: does it all add up?*, Earthscan, London.

Holliday Jr, CO, Schmidheiny, S & Watts, P 2002, *Walking the talk: the business case for sustainable development*, Greenleaf, San Francisco.

Howes, R 2001, *Taking nature into account and the evolution of a sustainability accounting framework: advances in environmental accounting and management*, Association of Chartered Certified Accountants, London, pp. 28–38.

Institute of Chartered Accountants in England and Wales (ICAEW) 2004, *Sustainability: the role of accountants*, Institute of Chartered Accountants in England and Wales, London.

International Organisation for Standardisation 2002, *ISO 14000 family series of international environmental management standards*, International Organisation for Standardisation, www.iso.org.

Jones, MJ 2003, 'Accounting for biodiversity: operationalising environmental accounting', *Accounting, Auditing and Accountability Journal*, vol. 15, no. 5, pp. 762–89.

Kaplan RS & Norton, DP 2004, *Strategy maps: converting intangible assets into tangible outcomes*, Harvard Business School Press, Boston, Massachusetts.

Koellner, T, Weber, O, Fenchel, M & Scholz, R 2005, 'Principles for sustainability rating of investment funds', *Business Strategy and the Environment*, vol. 14, pp. 54–70.

Lindblom, CK 1994, 'The implications or organisation legitimacy for corporate social performance and disclosure', *Critical Perspectives in Accounting Conference*, New York.

Orlitzky, M, Schmidt, FL & Rynes SL 2003, 'Corporate social and financial performance: A meta-analysis', *Organization Studies*, vol. 24, no. 3, pp. 403–41.

Pigou, AC 1920, *The economics of welfare*, McMillan & Co., London.

Purnell, A, Raar, J & Hone P 2003, 'Valuation and reporting of native fauna in monetary terms: compatibility between a market based system and natural resources?', in Featherstone, T & Batten, J (eds), *Research in International Business and Finance*, vol. 17.

Raar, J 1998, 'Exploring environmental costs and information for purposes of reporting and decision-making: an industry perspective', unpublished PhD thesis, RMIT University.

Raar, J, Purnell, A & Hone P 2002, 'Earth bound?', *CPA Australia*, April, pp. 66–7.

Ramanathan, K 1976, 'Towards a theory of corporate social accounting', *Accounting Review*, vol. 51, no. 3, pp. 516–28.

Richardson, J 2004, 'Accounting for sustainability: measuring quantities or enhancing qualities', in Henriques, A & Richardson, J (eds), *The triple bottom line: does it all add up?*, Earthscan, London.

Roberts, R 1992, 'Determinants of corporate social responsibility disclosure: an application of stakeholder theory', *Accounting, Organizations and Society*, vol. 17, no. 6, pp. 595–612.

Shrivastava, P 1987, *Bhopal: Anatomy of a Crisis*, Ballinger, Cambridge.

Ullman, A 1985, 'Data in search of a theory; a critical examination of the relationships among social performance, social disclosure, and economic performance of US firms', *Academy of Management Review*, vol. 10, no. 3, pp. 540–57.

United Nations 1972, 'Stockholm declaration of the United Nations Conference on the Human Environment, adopted by the UN Conference on the Human Environment at Stockholm, 16 June, 1972', *Report of the UN Conference on the Human Environment, Stockholm 5–16 June 1972*.

United Nation World Commission on Environment and Development 1987, *Our common future (the Brundtland report)*, OUP, Oxford.

8 INTERNATIONAL ACCOUNTING

LEARNING OBJECTIVES

After reading this chapter, you should be able to:

- identify the principal reasons for the development of a single set of accounting standards

- describe the process of development of international accounting standards

- explain the structure of the international standard-setting process, and outline the organisation and purpose of each component

- explain the history and development of Australia's adoption of international standards, and discuss its role in the continuing work of the international standard setter.

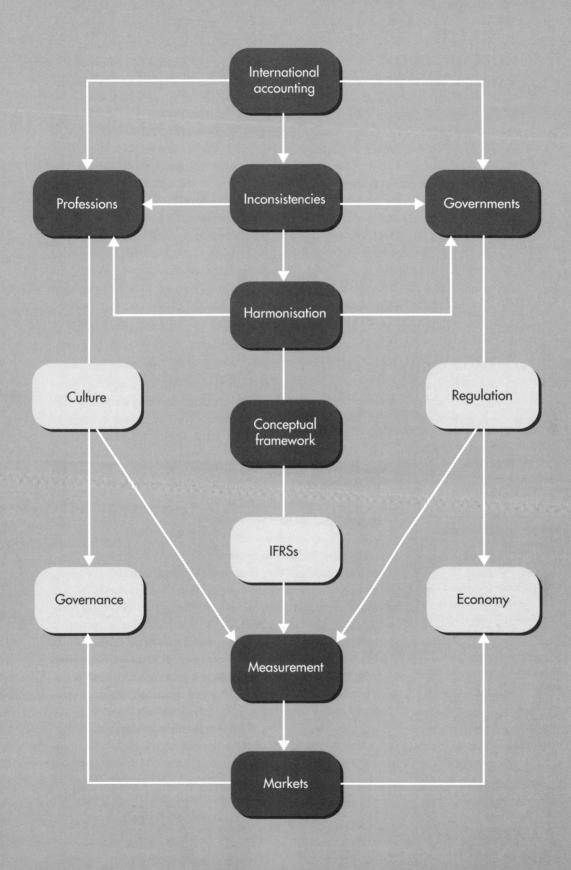

Introduction

Australia is one of a range of countries that have sought to adopt and implement accounting standards issued by the International Accounting Standards Board (IASB) and its predecessor board, the International Accounting Standards Committee (IASC) over the past decade. Each jurisdiction has had its own reasons for choosing to implement accounting standards issued by these bodies, ranging from the need to ensure that listed company accounts are understood by analysts and users of accounts irrespective of where they are in the world, to third-world governments being required to adopt them to receive funding from organisations such as the Asian Development Bank and the International Monetary Fund. This has made the role of the IASB and its various committees more important.

This chapter explores the role of the IASB and the various forces that seek to influence its decision making. These forces include the various international and global lobby groups, as well as professional accounting firms and securities regulators operating in different countries. Each party is seeking to have a high level of political influence on the product being developed for financial reporting globally.

An inevitable journey

The **IASB** was created in 2000 and started operations in 2001. It is a group of 14 individuals, which is attempting to create a single set of accounting standards that are recognised as being suitable for use across a range of jurisdictions that have different legal regimes, different cultures, different political systems and also different reasons for moving towards the adoption of a single accounting framework. The members of the IASB are faced with pressures from various jurisdictions — most notably the United States and the European Union (EU) — to deliver a framework those regions will find easier to implement in their own corner of the world.

International Accounting Standards Board (IASB): The London-based standard setter developing accounting standards for worldwide use

Securities and Exchange Commission: The securities regulator in the United States, which has the power to set listing requirements for entities seeking to source debt or share capital from American companies or individuals

Financial Accounting Standards Board: The accounting standard setter in the United States first created in 1973

Countries on the European continent have generally come from conservative accounting backgrounds with a heavy suspicion directed at anything that emerged from the US standard-setting regime, which has a structure dominated by the **Securities and Exchange Commission** (SEC) and the **Financial Accounting Standards Board** (FASB). This has led to tensions related to the project to converge the conceptual frameworks, accounting standards and interpretations of the IASB and FASB over the next decade. The aim of convergence is to deliver a framework for accounting that will lead to the removal by the SEC of the requirement for companies that seek to raise equity or debt in the United States to provide a reconciliation with FASB accounting standards. Critics claim, however, that the IASB spends too much time dealing with the US convergence issue, and not enough time working with countries that have already adopted the new standards.

Other countries such as China and Japan have also, over time, indicated a willingness to cooperate with the IASB to achieve a single set of accounting standards. Some countries, such as Malaysia, have been working with international accounting standards even before the creation of the current IASB standards. The challenge for countries such as New Zealand and Australia will now be how to maintain a high level of enthusiasm and involvement in the international process, given that larger and more powerful economies are now engaged in strong lobbying of the international board.

Impetus for change

Historically, international standards were developed by the **IASC**. It was established in 1973 and over almost two decades issued a suite of accounting standards that were mostly regarded as a source of accounting standards for those jurisdictions without standard-setting structures of their own. Countries such as Australia, the UK, the United States, New Zealand and Canada, with well-established standard-setting regimes, participated at an international level through membership of the **International Federation of Accountants** (IFAC). IFAC is a forum at which, even today, professional accounting bodies from all over the world participate in the development of auditing standards and ethical pronouncements.

Although Western regulators made significant financial investments in the IASC and its parent body, IFAC, they tended to have limited regard for the IASC's work, preferring the products of more established standard setters, such as the **Accounting Standards Board** (ASB) in the UK and the FASB in the United States, which were perceived as being more thorough and backed by invaluable experience. The IASC standards, on the other hand, were seen as being heavily compromised by lack of independence, resulting in a tendency to incorporate more than one accounting method for a specific transaction to encompass several jurisdictions' preferences.

The push to establish an authority to develop high-quality international accounting standards, was prompted by a series of factors. An association of global regulators known as the **International Organisation of Securities Commissions** (IOSCO) established a working party to review the standards issued by the IASC. Its task was to determine whether regional standards were sufficiently robust and suitable for use by companies entering into cross-border transactions. IOSCO was interested in ensuring that there was a set of standards of reasonable quality that would reassure the regulators that were members of IOSCO. The release of that report in May 2000 in Sydney was the culmination of several years of work conducted by the IOSCO working party. The report made a series of recommendations dealing with specific amendments to individual accounting standards.

International Accounting Standards Committee (IASC): An accounting standard setter overseen by the International Federation of Accountants that existed between 1973 and 2000

International Federation of Accountants: The representative body for professional accounting organisations worldwide

Accounting Standards Board: The accounting standard setter in the UK

International Organisation of Securities Commissions: The umbrella body for securities regulators across the world

The work of IOSCO was not the only impetus for improvement into the new century. The Asian financial meltdown of the late 1990s created a crisis in confidence in the quality of financial reporting in the region. Pressure began to mount on governments within the Asian region to build reporting controls that could be trusted by international lending bodies such as the International Monetary Fund, World Bank and the Asia Development Bank. Each of these bodies developed their own projects designed to increase the credibility of the reporting and governance structures of underdeveloped nations, and a unified, truly international system became even more desirable.

Further momentum was gained following a series of accounting scandals that besieged the United States. A succession of prosecutions against accounting firm Arthur Andersen, as well as the high-profile collapses of Enron and WorldCom, provided much needed ammunition for advocates of international accounting standards to argue for the largest capital market in the world to begin replacing its complex regime of financial reporting with the work that was being done by the IASC.

This series of developments resulted in an increasing number of calls for a transparent, high-quality and comparable set of international standards that would simplify the task of extracting usable information from company reports. However, while the notion of a single set of accounting standards appealed to many, there were grave concerns about the structure of the IASC at that time.

■ The development of international standard setting

Initially, the IASC was formed as a subsidiary body under the auspices of IFAC, which represents most of the key professional accounting bodies in the world. The standard-setting body was funded by the members of IFAC, and the membership was subject to nominations put forward by IFAC members in each country. There was no independent mechanism for evaluation of the technical competency or professional development of those selected, nor was there a guarantee that the individuals would be serving or former standard setters in their own jurisdiction. Some countries, such as Australia, made the decision that it was to the advantage of both domestic and international accounting standard setters that their members had some input into the domestic standard-setting structure. For example, Ken

Australian Accounting Standards Board: The body responsible for setting accounting standards in Australia

Spencer, a former chairman of the **Australian Accounting Standards Board** (AASB), was a member of the Australian delegation to the IASC during the latter part of the 1990s. This ensured that the international board's activities and those of the domestic board were monitored by individuals engaged in both jurisdictions.

Stakeholders generally agreed that the structure of the oversight body would need a great deal of refinement to achieve transparency and accountability. There was concern from regulators, particularly in the United States, that the structure under IFAC could not meet independence benchmarks set by the creation of the

FASB in 1973. The FASB's constitution prescribes strict conditions for the selection of the seven members of the board. Members of the FASB must be full-time standard setters, and when appointed they are required to sever all links with their previous employers.

All technical discussions of the board are held in the public domain, and members are prohibited from meeting in secret sessions. There are limits on the number of members that can meet together outside of the formal meetings. This means that members of the FASB cannot meet as a complete group during education sessions to avoid the appearance that they are deliberating on technical issues away from the public eye. In the same way, all submissions to the FASB are published on the FASB website for public scrutiny. Members of the FASB are responsible only for the technical side of decision making. They are not involved in the solicitation or allocation of funds. Matters related to resourcing and funding are administered by the Financial Accounting Foundation, the oversight body responsible for the financial management of the board.

In contrast, the structure of the IASC lacked independence and transparency. The activities of the board were funded by the IFAC, through the membership fees of professional organisations. Members of the IASC were also part time, holding other positions within the public and private sectors. Members were exposed to accusations of conflict of interest and private agenda setting because of their day-to-day work. Overcoming the lack of transparency and absence of an oversight mechanism independent of funding considerations was key to gaining the support of key players within the United States, such as the SEC, the powerful securities regulator in America.

An additional factor that became apparent during the development of accounting standards internationally was the difference in accounting standard setting between the nations on the European continent and the countries known as the **Group of Four plus One** (G4+1). The G4+1 was a group of national standard setters that had formed a network for sharing ideas. It consisted of the United States, Canada, the UK, Australia, New Zealand and the

Group of Four plus One: A group of national standard setters from Australia, Canada, New Zealand, the UK and the United States that met along with the IASC to develop joint views on accounting matters

IASC. Standard setters from each of the countries participated in technical meetings held in various locations around the world as a way of promoting consistent accounting in each jurisdiction. They published detailed technical papers that dealt with various topics such as business combinations, share-based payment and lease accounting. Each of these papers was exposed by the members for public comment as a part of the due process.

The G4+1 shared similar objectives that focused on improving the use of accounting numbers to reflect economic phenomena such as the impact of hedging and derivatives. They believed this would allow external users to better understand the financial position and financial performance of an entity. European standard setters, however, were reluctant to accept a greater focus on accounting for such transactions. Again, this disparity prompted the call for a more unified approach.

8.1   _The push for a single set of international accounting standards developed from the need for comparability in cross-border transactions, and for high-quality regulation and governance in less-developed countries dealing with international organisations._

8.2   _Concerns about the transparency and accountability of the original international standard setter involved a perceived possibility of conflicts of interest, the absence of a standard-setting mechanism independent of funding considerations and the lack of a comprehensive and independent due process._

▪ The structure of international standard setting

In response to the growing demand for both a set of stable, high-quality standards and an accountable and transparent decision-making structure, IFAC instigated a complete reform of the standard setter's constitution and procedural design. From April 2001, the board has operated within a support structure designed to ensure technical expertise, independence and diversity of opinion. The organisation consists of an oversight body (the International Accounting Standards Committee Foundation; IASCF), the standard setter (the IASB), an interpretive body (the International Financial Reporting Interpretations Committee; IFRIC) and an advisory body (the Standards Advisory Council; SAC). The organisational relationships among these entities are outlined in figure 8.1 on page 236.

The governing body

The structure of the **IASCF** is designed to ensure that operational and financial issues remain separate from the technical aspects of standard setting. The board

---

International Accounting Standards Committee Foundation (IASCF): The organisation that houses the board of trustees of the IASB, the standard setter and associated committees and operational and technical staff

---

consists of 22 trustees, and vacant positions are appointed by the remaining trustees after an extensive process of consul-tation. Trustees are bound by the constitution of the foundation to maintain a mix of trustees that 'broadly reflect[s] the world's capital markets and a diversity of geographical and professional backgrounds...[involving] individuals that as a group provide an appropriate balance of professional backgrounds, including auditors, preparers, users, academics, and other officials serving the public interest' (IASCF constitution 2005).

The range of critical tasks the board of trustees performs is set down in the foundation's constitution (IASB 2006). These tasks can be broken up into two types: administrative tasks that may affect the operations of the standard setter, and other duties that have a greater and more direct impact on the composition and agenda

of the IASB. Those tasks that are broadly administrative in nature are listed in paragraph 13. These duties are the:
- assumption of responsibility for seeking and maintaining a suitable level of funding for the IASCF
- creation of operating rules for the trustees
- determination of what type of legal entity should house the IASCF with a specific condition that the structure must confer limited liability on its members and that any documents establishing that structure contain the same types of conditions for running the IASCF as are detailed in the constitution
- review of the location of the IASCF, which includes a review of both the location of the legal entity and the physical operating headquarters of the IASCF
- exploration of the various legal rules existing for charities or similar organisations to determine whether the IASCF could qualify as a charity or association. This status may, for example, attract tax deductions for donations and derive more funding to the IASCF as a result
- holding meetings of the trustees in public, although the trustees can hold discussions related to personnel issues and funding in private
- annual publication of a report detailing the activities of the IASCF, which contains audited financial statements and priorities for the future.

A quorum for a meeting of trustees is 60 per cent of the 22 members. They can attend either in person or by phone. Decisions are made by a simple majority of the trustees but in some circumstances, the vote must be 75 per cent, including, but not limited to, the termination of a trustee's appointment or amendments to the constitution.

Each of the responsibilities mentioned above ensures that the trustees focus on the governance of the foundation and its subsidiary entities. The second level of responsibilities relate to the oversight of the standard setter and its various related committees. These responsibilities include but are not limited to:
- appointing the members of the IASB, the IFRIC and the SAC
- setting down service contracts for the members of the IASB. Such a requirement does not exist for either IFRIC or the SAC because most members of those bodies are not employees of the IASCF.
- reviewing the IASCF's strategy and the IASB's strategy and performance. This includes the need for the trustees to consider the work program set down by the standard setter.
- reviewing and approving the funding arrangements and the budget for the IASCF
- considering the various matters affecting the development and content of accounting standards, which includes within it a responsibility to promote the adoption and implementation of the international standards
- creating, reviewing, assessing compliance with and amending when necessary, the operating rules, consultation processes and the due processes of the IASB, IFRIC and SAC
- making amendments to the IASCF constitution following a due process involving the IASCF's constituents and the SAC

- encouraging and overseeing the development of educational materials and courses that match the IASCF's objectives.

The trustees are required to review the structure and constitution of the foundation every five years to ensure its effectiveness, with 'such review to include consideration of changing the geographical distribution of Trustees in response to changing global economic conditions, and publishing the proposals of that review for public comment' (IASCF constitution 2005).

The foundation is also required to review 'broad strategic issues' affecting the agenda of the IASB, but the constitution expressly prohibits the trustees from involvement in any of the technical deliberations of the standard setter, to maintain the integrity and independence of the decision-making process. The following In Focus vignette illustrates some of the due process involved in the 2004 constitutional review.

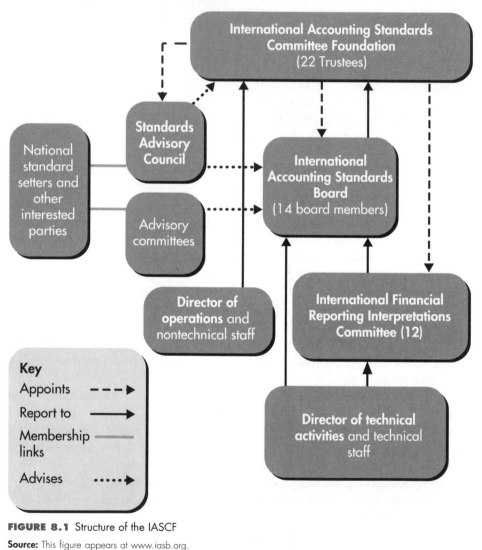

FIGURE 8.1 Structure of the IASCF

Source: This figure appears at www.iasb.org.

infocus *Independence and accounting standards*

The trustees overseeing the IASB held a series of public hearings in 2004 when the review of the constitution was taking place. Among those giving evidence during a public hearing held in New York in June of that year was Lynn Turner, a former chief accountant of the SEC. Turner expressed his concerns regarding attempts to change the way in which the IASB's work program was determined as a result of concerns some commentators had with answers that were being produced by the accounting standards issued by the IASB.

Turner rejected any notion of amending the IASB's voting regime from being a simple majority to a supermajority — a point he ultimately lost because of the change to the IASB's voting numbers — because of how a supermajority made it more difficult for the FASB to pass a standard.

A further point contested by Turner in his prepared remarks delivered at the New York hearings on the IASCF's constitutional review is the view some commentators have had regarding trustees having greater control over the technical agenda of the IASB. Turner's prepared remarks state:

> Some have questioned whether the Trustees should have greater input or control over the agenda of the IASB. Such questions were also raised with respect to the FASB in the United States by members of the business community, including the Business Roundtable. However, with the support of investors, such proposals were soundly rejected as having a detrimental impact on the independence of the Board and ultimately its product.
>
> I believe that if the Trustees were composed of a majority of investors, such requests would not be made. I also believe that any movement towards greater control over the agenda of the IASB by the Trustees, Standards Advisory Council or other organization, including any governmental organization, will result in undermining investors' confidence in the process and product.

Source: Turner, L 2004, *International accounting standards constitution committee public hearings*, 3 June, New York.

IASB

The international standard setter is responsible for the publication of the **International Financial Reporting Standards** (IFRSs). The IASB consists of a board of 12 full-time and two part-time members (see table 8.1). Full-time members must commit all their paid-employment time to the board, while part-time members may remain employed by another entity, subject to rigorous diligence and independence requirements established by the IASCF trustees. The inaugural chairman of the IASB, effective from 1 January 2001, was Sir David Tweedie, who had previously served as chairman of the ASB and as a

International Financial Reporting Standards: A single set of enforceable global accounting standards that require transparent and comparable information in general purpose financial statements, produced by the IASB

technical partner with KPMG in the UK, and has a distinguished academic record. His lengthy experience with the G4+1 meant that his appointment was seen as crucial to fostering an effective bridge across the political divides that existed between the North American standard-setting culture and the standard-setting environment in Europe. Table 8.1 lists the members of the board in November 2006. The current board members are listed on the IASB website (www.iasb.org) along with short biographies outlining each member's qualifications for appointment.

TABLE 8.1 Membership of the IASB as at 30 May 2006

IASB members (Board members are full time unless otherwise stated)	Country
Professor Sir David Tweedie (chairman)	UK
Thomas E Jones (deputy chairman)	United States
Professor Mary E Barth (part time)	United States
Hans-Georg Burns	Germany
Anthony T Cope	United States
Jan Engström	Sweden
Robert P Garnett	South Africa
Gilbert Gélard	France
James J Leisenring	United States
Warren J McGregor	Australia
Patricia L O'Malley	Canada
John T Smith (part time)	United States
Tatsumi Yamada	Japan
Philippe Danjou	France

Source: This table appears at www.iasb.org.

Most decisions of the board require the approval of a simple majority at the vote, provided at least nine members of the board are in attendance. However, subsequent to the 2005 constitutional review, the release of an exposure draft, final standard or interpretation document now requires approval by a supermajority of nine of the 14 board members. Lobbying from representatives of the EU, after protracted debates on financial instruments and standards such as share-based payment, led to this change in the IASB's voting arrangements to increase the credibility of the standards approved.

Appointment criteria

The appointments of all of the board members are subject to a series of criteria set down in the constitution. A primary criterion is the need for the individuals around the board to be technically competent, although other considerations are also factored into the selection of board members. Regarding technical competence as the sole criterion for selection could result in a situation where members are selected from one location with the same current work profile and similar perspectives on technical matters. As for the IASCF, the constitution requires that the IASB consist of individuals with a broad range of experience, not only in accounting but also a variety of business backgrounds. Although IASB members are not appointed according to geographical criteria (as are trustees of the IASCF), paragraph 20 of the constitution emphasises the need for the trustees to ensure that the standard setter is not dominated by any single jurisdiction. The rules for appointment also state that the board should be composed of individuals of varying professional backgrounds, such as academics, users, preparers and analysts.

The selection criteria, which are determined by the trustees of the IASCF and appear in the appendix to the constitution, are:

- demonstrated technical competency and knowledge of financial accounting and reporting
- ability to analyse
- communication skills
- judicious decision making
- awareness of the financial reporting environment
- ability to work in a collegial atmosphere
- integrity, objectivity and discipline
- commitment to the IASCF's mission and public interest (adapted from IASB website).

These criteria are used to evaluate individuals coming before the board of trustees as potential appointments to the international board. Other considerations the trustees need to factor into the appointment process include ensuring that all board members do not retire at the same time; to this end, appointments to the IASB are staggered. Board members can be appointed for a maximum of five years during their first term, which can be renewed once. This practice mirrors the process in the United States, where board members can only serve a maximum of two consecutive terms on the FASB.

How the IASB works

Standard setters are like any form of rule-making organisation. A series of procedures are imposed on the standard setters by the trustees of the IASCF, as well as by the IASB itself, to ensure potential affected parties are afforded every opportunity to contribute to the discussion preceding any pronouncement on the way entities prepare financial statements. The IASB is no exception in this regard. It does, however, face several challenges in relation to its **due process** — a term used to describe the consultation and decision-making process — because of the broad constituency with which it must consult to achieve its global objectives. These include language barriers in communicating with accountants from a range of countries, dealing with different political and legal systems and a wider range of preparer lobby groups arguing their case on proposed accounting standards.

due process: The consultation and decision-making process of a standard setter

The due process of the IASB would generally unfold through the following stages:

- IASB staff receive a request from board members to examine a particular topic. They must identify all of the critical issues and apply the Framework to the set of issues identified for analysis.
- Relevant accounting standards from other jurisdictions are examined to determine whether a suitable solution already exists. This process would usually involve discussions with national standard setters such as the Australian AASB, Accounting Standards Board of Japan or the Malaysian Accounting Standards Board.
- The SAC, made up of representatives of professional organisations and other interested parties, is consulted to determine whether the topic of discussion should be added to the agenda.
- An advisory group may be formed to help the IASB on the project.
- A **discussion paper** or an **invitation to comment** may be issued to canvass public opinion.
- An **exposure draft**, accepted by a supermajority (nine of the 14 members) of the board, is issued for public comment. Exposure drafts are typically issued in three parts: main body of the standard; **basis for conclusions**, detailing the IASB's reasons for coming to a particular view, including any dissenting opinions, and implementation guidance where relevant.
- Comments are collated and analysed for IASB members' consideration.
- Public hearings, round tables or field visits may be considered as a part of the consulting process, particularly to assess any application issues.
- The IASB will, at the conclusion of this process, provided at least nine members vote in favour of the proposal, issue an accounting standard. A published standard must include a basis for conclusions and the text of any dissenting views expressed by board members.

discussion paper (invitation to comment): The first phase in the development of an international standard, in which the IASB engages its constituents in considering a range of issues on a topic

exposure draft: A proposed accounting standard issued for public comment

basis for conclusions: A part of a standard that outlines the reasons the standard setter chose particular accounting treatments of one kind over others

Publication of dissenting views has been a feature of the standard-setting system in the United States for many decades. It is one way in which the standard-setting system recognises the existence of alternative points of view. Dissenting opinions are published in the applicable standard, so that users are able to understand the rationale provided by the standard setter for decisions made by a board but also the reason some board members chose to vote against a particular pronouncement. These dissents are important because they contribute to the development of future accounting standards. A future board may decide that a previous accounting standard was inappropriate and use a dissenting view from a previous era as a source of alternative views.

Dissents to accounting standards at an international level have been recorded by several IASB members in the standard on financial instruments known as IAS 39.

Seven IASB members, including Australian Warren McGregor, dissented from various parts of the financial instruments standard, which deals with the recognition and measurement of financial liabilities (IASB 2006). McGregor particularly disagreed with the recognition of changes in value of financial assets classified as available for sale in equity. 'Mr McGregor believes that all changes in the fair value of assets classified as available for sale should be recognised in profit or loss. However, such a major change to the Standard would need to be subject to the Board's full due process,' the basis for conclusions to IAS 39 states (IASB 2006, p. 1881). Although there were six other members dissenting to aspects of IAS 39 all 14 members of the IASB voted to allow the standard to pass.

IASB and interpretations: IFRIC

One of the most important issues in international accounting is how the standards are interpreted by those that deal with accounting problems in practice. Some of these people share cultural backgrounds and a common training in accounting; others work within diverse legal systems or less developed financial reporting regimes. The difference in the interpretation of standards in practice can lead to different reporting outcomes. The IFRIC was established to help in the process of publishing authoritative interpretations in circumstances where conflict has been identified.

The committee deals with topics that are nominated by an agenda committee, consisting of the chairman (also an IASB member) and IFRIC members from the Big Four accounting firms. The agenda committee will reject issues it believes do not require an interpretation from IFRIC and these rejections are published on the IASB website and in IFRIC updates so that constituents understand why a formal ruling from IFRIC was deemed unnecessary.

Once a topic is admitted to the agenda, several steps must be followed. These steps require IFRIC staff to:
- examine all potential issues related to the topic and apply the financial reporting framework to the problem at hand
- consult the various sets of national accounting standards to determine whether the issue or part of the issue had been dealt with previously in a jurisdiction
- publish a draft interpretation for the purposes of public comment. An exposure draft can be published only if no more than three IFRIC members vote against a proposal.
- analyse comment letters received during the comment period
- present the **draft interpretation** to the IFRIC for approval. This requires no more than three IFRIC members to vote against the proposed standard.
- approval of the interpretation by nine members of the 14-member IASB.

draft interpretation: A document proposing an interpretation of an accounting standard or accounting standards that is released for public comment

IFRIC has also been asked to fill gaps in accounting standards from time to time by the IASB where the main board is unable or unwilling to take an issue up itself. An example of this type of issue is one related to service concessions. This topic involves IFRIC determining the appropriate accounting for entities involved in public–private partnerships, considering issues of what assets the 'private entities', which in Australia can often be listed property trusts or stapled securities, have from that arrangement. Although the private sector/for-profit entity's accounting is covered by pronouncements from the IASB, the accounting by governments for assets in this kind of agreement is outside the jurisdiction of both the IASB and IFRIC. Public sector accounting is typically dealt with by boards such as the Government Accounting Standards Board (GASB) in the United States or the International Public Sector Accounting Standards Board (IPSASB), which is a board that is administered by IFAC. In some cases, such as the FRSB in New Zealand and the AASB in Australia, the accounting for the for-profit and not-for-profit sectors is determined by one standard setter.

The IASB and the United States

The move to a single European market, with the need for a completed body of standards available for 1 January 2005, spurred on a burst of activity at the IASB between 2001 and 2004. The European adoption date drove much of the IASB's activity to facilitate a smooth transition to the new standards. Harmonisation with IASB pronouncements in the largest capital market, the United States, however, proceeded at a much more cautious pace.

The United States has historically had by far the most comprehensive set of accounting standards. Regulators in the United States, particularly the SEC, also play a strong role in developing and enforcing listing rules. These are perceived by various commentators to be onerous and complex but worth complying with if an entity wants to seek investment in the American marketplace. When combined, the two regulatory authorities, the FASB and the SEC, impose a formidable set of compliance conditions for listed entities. Of particular concern for foreign registrants operating in the United States is the requirement for reconciliation to the accounting standards set by the FASB. Some commentators have argued that these reconciliation requirements are unnecessarily onerous, and recommend removing them as soon as possible.

Once the IASB was accepted by the European continent as the appropriate body to generate financial reporting pronouncements for use by entities in cross-border listing, the FASB and IASB began developing a strategy that would allow a single set of standards and a revised conceptual framework acceptable to both the IASB's global constituency and the more insular American business community to be produced. The result of these high-level discussions was a document known as the *Norwalk agreement* jointly issued in October 2002 by the FASB and the IASB.

The agreement, struck at Norwalk, Connecticut, the location of the FASB headquarters, set down several principles for cooperation between the two standard setters as they move to fulfil an ambitious objective: to deliver a stable platform of accounting standards delivering reporting guidance, irrespective of the location of the entity. The IASB's work since its creation in 2001 has been an attempt to develop a pathway for acceptance in the US market of its accounting standards, but has generally accepted that such a situation was unlikely to be achieved without the close cooperation of the FASB.

The terms of the *Norwalk agreement* outline four key objectives for the standard setters to meet. These objectives were to:

- remove a range of differences between US generally accepted accounting principles and pronouncements of the IASB as a part of a short-term convergence program
- remove other differences through aligning work programs, which would have both boards dealing with the issues in sync
- continue progress on joint projects in existence at the time of the agreement
- encourage coordination of activities by their respective interpretative boards.

The *Norwalk agreement* was the beginning of the process of getting the two standard-setting operations working more closely with each other. As time went on, the notion of having one project team comprising people from both standard-setting teams caught on, eliminating the need for the duplication of papers for the two boards and also the waste of resources.

The proposed joint project team had some critics, however, highlighted by PricewaterhouseCoopers in a letter on the 2005 review of the constitution of the IASB. 'We are aware of the intention to have joint project teams of the IASB and FASB going forward. This is a welcome development — convergence needs to be the ultimate goal — but the Trustees and the IASB need to be conscious of external perceptions,' the PricewaterhouseCoopers letter dated 23 February 2005 states. 'Although we understand that it is not intended to have decision-making on new standards by means of a "merged" Board, we believe that the relationship with FASB will change the perceived geographical balance' (PricewaterhouseCoopers 2005). Joint work between standard setters may create a closer relationship between the two technical teams, but without a commitment from a regulator, such as the SEC, to accept the international framework, it becomes a mere knowledge-sharing exercise. The agreement reached in Norwalk in October 2002 needed to lead to more than just a friendly exchange of ideas in the interest of reaching a common set of standards. It had to lead to some change in heart from the US regulator. This was evidenced in the *Roadmap for convergence* issued by the IASB early in 2006.

The Roadmap for convergence

On 27 February 2006, the IASB and FASB released a memorandum of understanding (MoU). This MoU details the list of projects that must either be completed or started to create the conditions for the SEC to remove the reconciliation requirement. The four-page memorandum sets down an agreed plan of action for the two standard setters over three years concluding in 2008, which includes a short-term convergence project list consisting of ten topics such as joint ventures, borrowing costs, income tax, investments properties and government grants. These topics are among a group that must be completed in the form of an accounting standard by 2008. There is another list of topics for which the IASB and FASB have set themselves targets, such as publishing an exposure draft or discussion paper, to ensure they are on their way to dealing with issues such as accounting for intangible assets and accounting for the effect of income taxes that have been identified during various debates between the standard setters and also their constituents as being areas needing attention.

The priority being set for convergence with the United States has caused some concern on the European continent because the focus on the United States is perceived to be drawing attention from the jurisdictions that are applying the IASB product. Representatives of the **European Commission** have made calls for the international standard setter to focus more on those countries that may have a need for clarification because they are already using IASB standards, rather than forging stronger relationships with other parts of the world that are yet to commit. The European commissioner for internal markets and services, Charlie McCreevy, told the economic and monetary affairs committee of the European parliament on 1 February 2005 that there should be greater representation of countries that directly apply the standard-setting product among the ranks of the IASB and IASCF (McCreevy 2005). McCreevy also argued that the IASCF should have the power to approve the work program of the standard setter, rather than have that responsibility remain a part of the standard setter's agenda.

> **European Commission:** The authority in Europe that deals with regulatory issues affecting the single European market

> The work program should take due account of our priorities. If the oversight is effective — management of the organization will improve and confidence will grow. We also need a more welcome approach from the IASB and more effort to find common ground. We all want decision-making that is free from undue political interference but the standards it draws up must meet the needs of users and be in touch with business reality.
>
> Broadening the geographical base of its members would help in this regard. We need to encourage top quality people to put themselves forward in this regard. We also need to strengthen then the **European Financial Reporting Advisory Group** and define the limits between EFRAG and the IASB (McCreevy 2005, p. 4).

> **European Financial Reporting Advisory Group:** A body based in Europe consisting of accounting experts that drafts responses on technical issues to the IASB

The IASB has also established MoUs with the standard setters in China and Japan as part of the continuing convergence efforts. Other jurisdictions, such as Australia, have taken a different route in how they deal with the integration of the international accounting framework with their own regulations. Australia chose to pledge full adoption for financial years beginning on or after 1 January 2005.

● Australia's adoption of international standards

The AASB has spent the past decade bringing the Australian accounting standards into line with the pronouncements produced by the IASB and its predecessor, the IASC. Historically, this has been achieved through two separate approaches to harmonisation. The first emerged during the period between 1996 and 1999. This approach aimed to ensure that companies complying with Australian standards could state they were also in compliance with international pronouncements. This did not mean outright adoption of the international standards in Australia but that Australian standards would undergo an improvement process, during which they would be brought closer in line with international requirements. There was a general commitment to ensure options available in international standards were removed to maintain comparability and consistency within financial reporting in the country.

This approach to changing accounting standards was gradually replaced by a general demand for the full adoption of international standards in Australia. Constituents arguing for the adoption of the standards included the Australian Securities Exchange (ASX), large corporations with multinational operations and opinion leaders within the accounting profession. This ultimately led to the Financial Reporting Council directive of June 2002 stating that Australia would adopt international accounting standards in time for 1 January 2005.

Key arguments presented by adoption advocates included the potentially lower cost of capital for companies on foreign markets because of greater comparability, and adoption filling long-standing gaps in financial reporting in Australia such as financial instruments, accounting for defined benefit superannuation plans and detailed principles on accounting for intangible assets.

Critics of adoption argued that Australia would be moving to poorer accounting in several areas, most notably government grants and intangible assets, because they believed existing practice in Australia was superior to the accounting required by the accounting standards generated by the IASB's predecessor body on those topics. For example, a newsletter produced by accounting firm Ernst & Young in 1998 (the year the IASC accounting standard on intangible assets was finalised) stated that the balance sheets of Australian companies would lose $40 billion that had been capitalised to reflect what companies felt was the value of various intangible assets.

Arguments against the adoption objective also included that the United States, the largest capital market, had not yet recognised the international accounting standards as being of equal quality to its own standards. It was further argued that adoption would lessen the bargaining power of a country such as Australia at the international table. The concern was that once a nation was committed to adoption, the IASB may not prioritise problems or issues raised by that jurisdiction, focusing instead on encouraging convergence in other nations.

Adoption and decision making

The **FRC** in Australia was the body responsible for issuing the adoption directive in June 2002. Unlike the IASB, the FRC has the power to establish a strategic direction that can directly impact on the content of the accounting

Financial Reporting Council (FRC): The oversight body that has among its various responsibilities the task of reviewing the operations and performance and strategies of the AASB and the AUASB standards produced by the standard setter in Australia. Financial reporting in the for-profit area is only one part of the remit of the FRC, however, because it also has the responsibility to provide strategic directions for not-for-profit accounting, as well as the government sector, auditing standard setting and auditor independence. The FRC has specific oversight responsibility for the **Auditing and Assurance Standards Board** (AUASB), as well as the AASB. These areas create further issues in regard to international comparability because the IASB only deals explicitly with for-profit entity reporting. The FRC and the standard setters under its jurisdiction also must monitor the work of the **International Public Sector Accounting Standards Board** (IPSASB) and the **International Auditing and Assurance Standards Board** (IAASB) — both committees under the jurisdiction of IFAC — to benchmark the work being done in accounting and audit regulation in Australia. The organisational structure of the Australian standard setting process can be found in figure 3.1. These institutional arrangements are also on the AASB website, www.aasb.com.au.

Auditing and Assurance Standards Board: The body that has the responsibility to set auditing standards in Australia

International Public Sector Accounting Standards Board: Body overseen by IFAC that sets accounting standards for the government sector

International Auditing and Assurance Standards Board: A committee overseen by the IFAC that sets standards for auditors

Among the core oversight powers of the FRC is its responsibility to appoint the members of the AASB and the AUASB. Members of the FRC have the power to choose and appoint members of the standard-setting board with the exception of two people: the chairs of the AASB and AUASB. The appointment to those two posts is made by the federal treasurer. When retired Andersen audit partner Keith Alfredson was appointed to be the first AASB chair to operate under the new structure, the FRC had already appointed the remaining nine members of the ten-member board. Federal Treasurer Peter Costello appointed Alfredson to the post having regard to recommendations in favour of his appointment. The initial AUASB chair went to professional director Merran Kelsall, a former partner with a second-tier firm, BDO, in August 2004 after the legislation transferring the audit standard-setting function was passed by the federal parliament.

The FRC has the task of monitoring and approving the work program, priorities, business plan and staffing arrangements of the AASB, with the assistance of a secretariat that is part of the federal treasury. The responsibility to seek out funding for the standard-setting regime, either from parliamentary appropriation out of the federal budget or external funding sources, is also a significant part of its mandate. The professional accounting bodies — CPA Australia, Institute of Chartered Accountants in Australia and the National Institute of Accountants — provide funding by lump sum to the process each year, as do the state and territory departments of treasury.

Support from the corporate sector has been disappointingly sparse, resulting in the need for the FRC to consider alternative funding models, such as a levy on listed companies through the ASX or even a contribution from the fees collected by the Australian Securities and Investments Commission (ASIC) for annual lodgements of company details.

Among the most controversial of its responsibilities is the power the FRC has to set the strategic direction of the two standard setters. In June and December 2002, the FRC moved to set strategic directions for the AASB for both the for-profit and not-for profit sectors. The first directive required the AASB to adopt IFRSs for all Australian companies beginning on or after 1 January 2005. This directive to adopt international accounting standards was decided by the FRC in June 2002 without consulting New Zealand, Australia's nextdoor neighbour and the country with which Australia has an agreement to pursue closer economic relations. The result of this failure to consult with New Zealand meant that Australia's neighbour chose to move towards adoption of international accounting standards by 1 January 2007, instead of the 2005 date.

The strategic direction to adopt international accounting standards was reconfirmed at the March and April 2004 meetings of the FRC, despite a growing chorus of complaint from some parts of the corporate sector that the Australian board was moving to adopt the entire body of standards too early, particularly since the European Commission had not yet endorsed some standards still regarded as contentious. The FRC was lobbied by organisations such as the Group of 100 seriously to consider delaying the adoption of international accounting standards for at least a year, particularly after the corporate sector failed to win concessions from the IASB for the grandfathering of accounting for intangible assets. Companies such as Coca-Cola Amatil (CCA) were at the forefront of this attempt.

The second directive was for the AASB to harmonise accounting principles with a statistical basis, known as government finance statistics. This strategic direction led to a fairly public rift between former AASB chairman Keith Alfredson and former FRC chairman Jeff Lucy, as a result of the FRC's failure to provide members of the council with timely information, and a general lack of consultation with constituents on the proposed changes . The FRC altered the wording of the directive following objections expressed by the standard setter and opposition senators during a senate estimates committee hearing early in 2003. The hearing dealt with the council's role in setting a directive that was argued by Senator Stephen Conroy to have breached the guidelines of the *Australian Securities and Investments Commission Act 2001*. The FRC must appear before the federal parliament and answer questions about how it conducts its role, but a general prohibition against recommending or specifying the content of an accounting standard — the province of the AASB — exists in the enabling legislation.

Learning tips
Do you know...

8.3   *The international standard-setting system consists of an independent oversight body, the IASCF, the standard setter, the IASB, an interpretations committee, the IFRIC, and an advisory council, the SAC.*

8.4　Each component participates in an independent and transparent due process designed to consult with interested parties and different viewpoints from stakeholders around the world.

8.5　In Australia, the standard-setting board, the AASB, comes under the jurisdiction of the FRC, which is also responsible for not-for-profit entities, government accounting, and auditing and compliance.

8.6　The FRC has the power to set directives for the AASB that prescribe a direction the board must follow but it does not have the power to veto individual accounting standards.

The AASB

The AASB, which has 12 part-time members (see figure 8.2) and a full-time chairman, has the task of developing and issuing accounting standards for use in the Australian marketplace. This involves consideration of the effects potential standards will have on how companies account for transactions, and also how published information will be used by individuals reading a company's financial report. Traditionally, standards are revised when deficiencies in the reporting framework are observed by the board or the technical staff. The standards regulating an area of accounting are examined and compared with other ideas that may have emerged over time. Technical staff engage the board in debate over the merits of various approaches, resulting in a draft standard that is released for public comment.

At the conclusion of the comment period, all submissions received by the deadline are collated and the views discussed by technical staff and the board members during a meeting. This process is a two-way street, however, because there are times when individuals or organisations write to the standard setter to point out problems that exist with accounting standards of their own accord and suggest improvements the standard setter can make.

PricewaterhouseCoopers, for example, submitted comments to the AASB before the release of the Australian equivalents of IFRSs in July 2005. The firm was concerned about variations in the wording between IASB standards and the intended Australian standards, and on July 16 it forwarded a rough analysis of the impact of these differences to warn of the potential impact on the preparation of financial statements. Some of the comments made resulted in changes to the standards before they were formally endorsed and published.

By law, the AASB must consider several issues before supporting a standard that is, in its view, suitable for Australian conditions. These include whether the information produced from the provisions of an accounting standard is relevant and reliable, facilitates comparability and is readily understandable. These qualitative characteristics emerge from the *conceptual framework* for accounting standard setting and are entrenched in law. The law also directs the standard setters to ensure that the standards produce information that allows users to make and evaluate decisions about allocating scarce resources, and directors to fulfil their corporate governance responsibilities in communicating the financial performance and position of an entity.

Mr David Boymal Chairman Melbourne VIC	**Mr Bruce Porter** Deputy Chairman Deloitte Touche Tohmatsu Melbourne VIC
Mr Glenn Appleyard Economic Consultant Hobart TAS	**Ms Sue Highland** Director Financial Management Branch Queensland Treasury Brisbane QLD
Ms Jan McCahey Partner PricewaterhouseCoopers Melbourne VIC	**Mr Brett Kaufmann** Assistant Secretary Australian Government Financial Reporting Department of Finance and Administration Canberra ACT
Mr Frank Palmer Director Corporate Reporting Group Macquarie Bank Sydney NSW	**Mr John O'Grady** Partner Ernst & Young Melbourne VIC
Ms Kris Peach Partner KPMG Melbourne VIC	**Mr Colin Parker** Director GAAP Consulting Melbourne VIC
Ms Joanna Perry Chair Financial Reporting Standards Board New Zealand	**Mr Des Pearson** Auditor-General Victoria Melbourne VIC
Mr Brett Rix Manager Group Accounting Policy – Policy and Governance BHP Limited Melbourne VIC	
Observers	
Mr Peter Batten IPSASB Observer Department of Treasury and Finance Victorian Govermemnt Melbourne VIC	**Ms Judith Downes** SAC Member Chief Operating Officer Institutional Division ANZ Banking Group Melbourne VIC
Mr Warren McGregor IASB Member	

FIGURE 8.2 Membership of the AASB as at 8 March 2007

Source: This table appears at www.aasb.com.au.

Interpretations of standards in Australia

As discussed in chapter 3, before June 2006, the AASB was served by an interpretations subcommittee, the Urgent Issues Group (UIG). The group's role was to provide a ruling on accounting issues that emerged when the application of standards resulted in divergent or unacceptable accounting treatment.

With the rapid harmonisation of Australian and IASB standards, it became important for UIG abstracts to ensure consistency with interpretations published by IFRIC. Initially, the UIG and its technical support staff consulted regularly with the international interpretative body to avoid divergence from the accounting requirements. Then, in 2005, the AASB sought feedback from constituents on the arrangements, with an objective to change the way Australian interpretations were developed. Given the adoption of IASB standards, the standard setter considered IFRIC interpretations in most cases sufficient, without the need for unique Australian adaptations except in 'rare and exceptional circumstances' (AASB 2006, p.3). In an effort to reduce perceived inefficiencies, therefore, the UIG was disbanded in June 2006, and replaced by a three-person Interpretations Agenda Committee (IAC), consisting of the chairman and two other members of the AASB, which reports directly to the AASB. Specialist advisory panels are formed on the recommendation of the IAC, once the board has decided a matter requires expert deliberation. This panel system replaces the need for monthly committee meetings, and reduces the duplication of decisions made through the IFRIC process. In this way, the analysis of proposals emerging from the London-based IFRIC is incorporated by the AASB's input into IASB exposure drafts.

The implementation of the new structure was not unanimous, with board member Colin Parker expressing concerns about changes to the existing interpretations model. Parker questioned the need for change, given the continued viability and efficacy of the UIG process, and cautioned against any perceived disenfranchisement of the smaller, less influential parts of its constituency that were still vitally important (AASB 2006, p. 5).

Corporate disclosure and transitional issues

Australia moved to full adoption of IFRS from 1 January 2005, with a period of transition between 30 June 2004 and 30 June 2005. Australian companies were obliged to document the various changes to accounts that arose during the period of transition. A unique accounting standard, AASB 1047, dictated disclosure requirements for companies during the move. ASIC and the FRC jointly wrote to listed companies in October 2003 to warn them to prepare properly for the introduction of the new accounting standards, and to reinforce the legal status of AASB 1047 (see the following In Focus vignette for a discussion of the warning). Companies with a June balance date were expected to have some indicative disclosures in their financial statements for the year ended 30 June 2004 that provided shareholders and other stakeholders with a taste of what impact the new standard would have. The accounting standard provided several indications of where the key changes to the accounting framework were located so that preparers and other people using the standard were given some idea of what they should be aiming to disclose.

By the 30 June 2005 financial year, companies should have prepared their opening balance sheets and income statements under the new accounting standards for the purpose of collecting comparative information, which was required under the standard on first-time adoption. The IASB's accounting standards required companies to have complied with all of the accounting standards (except in the case of financial instruments because of its delayed implementation date) for the comparative and the current-year figures before they were able to claim that they complied with the new accounting standards. Entities were also obliged to comply with the standards for both the comparative and current-year figures so that they could take advantage of some of the exemptions allowed for standards such as business combinations.

 infocus *Companies and disclosure obligations related to standards*

The joint letter sent by the ASIC and the FRC in 2003 to all listed entities set down a range of issues related to communication to stakeholders, which served as a warning for entities that were required to report in accordance with the new set of accounting standards. Although both organisations acknowledged that survey results demonstrated a high level of knowledge about the existence of the new suite of standards and the imminent deadline for transition to the new requirements, they also warned of dire consequences for those entities that failed to observe the demand for appropriate disclosure.

We are aware of recent surveys undertaken in Australia about the level of awareness of the forthcoming changes. While encouraged by the high level of awareness by chief financial officers, financial controllers and accountants, the surveys indicate varying degrees of preparedness in terms of detailed knowledge of the requirements, resourcing, systems process and information gathering implications and analysis of the financial impact.

It is acknowledged that dealing with some aspects of preparing a starting statement of financial position, for example at 1 January 2004, may be delayed by the fact that not all of the proposed converged accounting standards have been approved and may not be until April 2004. Nevertheless, this does not prevent the development and implementation of business strategies to manage what is in effect a business and regulatory risk. Up until this time, the AASB will issue 'proposed standards' so that the text of the standard is available to interested parties. The extent of company preparedness is critical to a smooth transition and represents the key risk in 2005 adoption.

As the standards will be law, failure to plan for the transition and implement an effective business strategy to meet the 2005 deadline may result in your company being at risk of breaching the financial reporting requirements of the *Act*.

The letter from the FRC and ASIC places significant emphasis on the needs of users to understand how a corporation's stated financial position and reported financial performance will change with the application of some of the new standards.

A proactive approach to the implementation of the standards and analysing their impact will also help in keeping investors and users fully informed of the outcomes. It is important that companies disclose to shareholders any material difference from current Australian accounting standards that may arise from applying the new standards. In this context, consideration should also be given to if and when any impact on the reported financial position of the company is of such significance that a continuous disclosure obligation may arise.

Source: The letter appears at www.frc.gov.au.

One of the areas where several entities felt the need to explain their situation in a lot of detail related to the new requirements for intangible assets because of how the new accounting standards forced companies to reconsider balance sheet items. For example, soft drink giant CCA advised the financial markets in August 2004 that it was facing a $1.9 billion write-down on its investments in bottling agreements when the new accounting standards were implemented in Australia (CCA 2004, pp. 14, 29).

A half-year announcement lodged with the ASX at that time advised that the investments in bottling agreements were permitted by the accounting standard to remain on CCA's balance sheet. These agreements can be recognised as assets on its balance sheet because they were acquired. The accounting issue centred on the need to pare back the balance-sheet figure related to these bottling agreements (amounting to $3.3 billion) because the assets do not have an active secondary market.

The approach taken under AASB 138 prohibits companies revaluing certain intangible assets because there is no liquid or active market for those assets. An active market is defined in AASB 138 as being one in which the items traded are homogenous, willing buyers and willing sellers can be found at any time and prices for the assets are available to the public (Institute of Chartered Accountants in Australia 2006, pp. 1011–39). The rule affects companies when they adopt the Australian equivalents of IFRSs for the first time because adoption rules in AASB 1 require that all items that appear on balance sheet and in the income statement must comply with the new accounting standards.

CCA advised the market the change in accounting would reduce retained earnings, changing the net asset position of the company. CCA also notified the market of its lobbying of the federal government in an attempt to gain some concessions to rules requiring the write-off of the value of assets.

The soft-drink behemoth joined the three commercial, free-to-air television networks — channels Seven, Nine and Ten — in a joint effort to seek political intervention that would enable them to avoid significant asset write-downs. All four entities have assets on their balance sheets that are unable to be revalued following transition to the new body of standards.

In the case of the television stations, television licences and the revaluations associated with those licences were the focus of concern. Channel Seven, owned by the Seven Network Ltd, had to drop $480 million from the value of its $1 billion television licence, based on a 1998 independent valuation. 'The requirement is retrospective which means there is no option to use the current carrying value under Australian [accounting standards] as the deemed cost on first time adoption of IFRS, as was permitted on first time adoption of AASB 1041,' the Channel Seven financial statements for the 2003–04 financial year state (Seven Network Ltd 2004, p. 76). (AASB 1041 was the previous Australian accounting standard dealing with accounting for the revaluation of assets.) The $1.3 billion television licence on the balance sheet of Publishing and Broadcasting Ltd, the owner of Channel Nine, was reduced by $423 million on adoption of the new standards (Publishing and Broadcasting Ltd 2004, p. 71).

The Ten Network had a slightly different accounting dilemma. An adjustment to the accounting done by the Ten Group Pty Ltd, controlled by Ten Network Holdings Ltd, needed to change, but the holding company had the licences in its books at cost so there was no impact upon adoption of the new body of standards.

> The impact to The Ten Group Pty Limited, a controlled entity, will be that television licenses will be reduced by the revaluation increment of $751m resulting from the 2002 independent valuation. This reduction will also result in the reversal of a deferred tax charge on the revaluation of $225m. The net of these adjustments, $526m, will be made to the opening balance of reserves and retained earnings on the first time adoption of IFRS, assuming there is no impairment under Australian **GAAP** prior to IFRS. There will be no impact on television licenses in the Ten Network Holdings Limited consolidated entity as these are carried at cost. Deferred tax balances will be debited by $225m with the corresponding credit being adjusted to retained earnings (Ten Network Holdings Ltd 2004, p. 47).

Generally Accepted Accounting Principles (GAAP): Accounting principles that are in most cases embedded in a conceptual framework and accounting standards. Sometimes, GAAP are represented by evolving practice.

This means that because of a company structure difference, Network Ten's numbers at the holding company level did not change, avoiding the write-down situation faced by the other two networks.

Australian companies will continue to tell shareholders about the implications of new accounting standards as a result of the work being done by the IASB, FASB and other standard setters around the globe to bring about a single set of accounting standards. They are required under accounting standards to forewarn the market of the expected impact of a new standard once it has been issued even if it is not effective for a current reporting period. This requirement will see detailed disclosures published in accounts even though an accounting standard will not apply for some time.

Australian regulators, standard setters and companies have spent the past few years preparing the marketplace for changes in reporting. In particular, the corporate regulator, the ASIC, and the FRC, the domestic oversight body, encouraged entities to prepare clear disclosure on the move to the new body of accounting standards. To try to provide a period of stability, and the chance for increased consultation and implementation discussions, the IASB has placed an embargo on the application of any new standards before 1 January 2009. This will hopefully allow the Australian standard-setting process a period of consolidation and reflection, as well as an opportunity to analyse and share the Australian experience with other nations considering adoption. This should result in a more robust procedure.

Summary

Identify the principal reasons for the development of a single set of accounting standards.

- The push to establish a single set of accounting standards can be traced initially to the work of IOSCO, which was interested in establishing the quality of regional standards in various jurisdictions, to aid regulators dealing with cross-border transactions.
- The Asian meltdown also highlighted the need for high-quality reporting standards in countries relying on grants from international lending bodies. Further momentum came from a series of spectacular corporate collapses in the United States, where accounting deficiencies and complexities were implicated.

Describe the process of development of international accounting standards.

- Although the implementation of international accounting standards is an objective for countries in Asia and Europe, the various jurisdictions have differing legal environments. This means accounting standards need to fit within a pre-existing legal structure.
- Concerns about the transparency and accountability of the existing international standard setter involved a perceived possibility of conflicts of interest, the absence of an oversight mechanism independent of funding considerations and the lack of a comprehensive and independent due process.

Explain the structure of the international standard-setting process, and outline the organisation and purpose of each component.

- Since 2001, the international standard setting process has operated within a support structure designed to ensure technical expertise, independence and diversity of opinion.
- The organisation consists of an oversight body (the IASCF), the standard setter (the IASB), an interpretive body (the IFRIC), and an advisory body (the SAC).

Explain the history and development of Australia's adoption of international standards, and discuss its role in the continuing work of the international standard setter.

- Australia's standard-setting process is governed by an independent board, the AASB, with oversight from the FRC. Unlike the IASB, the FRC and AASB in Australia are also responsible for the standards regulation of government and non-profit sectors.
- Full adoption of international standards came into effect in Australia after 1 January 2005, and the Australian experience, particularly during the transition period, continues to provide a wealth of insight into the process of adoption. Australian companies have nonetheless adjusted well, and a period of respite from the application of new standards until 1 January 2009 will allow further analysis of the adoption experience, and continue to strengthen the convergence program around the world.

Key terms

Review questions

8.1   The IASCF has a board of trustees. What role does the board of trustees play in the international standard-setting structure?

8.2   What role does the IASB play in the regulation of global financial reporting?

8.3   Describe the remit of the IFRIC. Identify and describe at least two bodies with a similar type of function operating in a particular jurisdiction.

8.4   Many countries have chosen to adopt in whole or in part the standards of the IASB. Give at least three reasons stated by jurisdictions for the adoption of IASB standards.

8.5   What is the significance of the *Norwalk agreement* between the IASB and the US FASB?

8.6   The SEC in the United States is the key securities regulator in that jurisdiction. The SEC demands entities listing in its market comply with a series of stringent disclosure and lodgement requirements. Describe the role of the SEC and FASB in the process of convergence with IASB standards.

8.7   Different jurisdictions set accounting standards using different authorities. Describe at least two types of organisation that have the responsibility for the setting of accounting standards.

8.8 What institutions — local or international — have the responsibility for enforcing compliance with standards issued by the IASB?

Application questions

8.9 Assume you are the chairman of the board of Company X, which is listed on the ASX. You are presiding over the Company X's annual general meeting, which goes extremely smoothly except for the questions of one shareholder related to accounting standards. That shareholder states that the new annual report looks more confusing than last year's report and asks you to explain why the company has had to adopt a new suite of accounting standards. You respond to the question verbally but also promise to provide a continuous disclosure notice offering the same explanation to all of the investors in writing. Explain to the users of Company X's annual report why the reporting changes have occurred. Remember that your audience is an unsophisticated user of financial statements.

8.10 Visit the website of the IASB and IFRIC and read the due process the international body undertakes in developing an accounting standard or an accounting interpretation. Discuss whether you believe the IASB process is sufficiently robust.

8.11 Choose one national accounting standard setter and identify the present constituents of that particular standard setter. Analyse the background of the various individuals involved in the national standard setter and discuss whether the composition of the standard setter provides the decision-making process with an adequate blend of backgrounds.

8.12 You are involved in a corporate lobby group and your fellow lobbyists are critical of the federal government of Australia for moving to a different body accounting standards. They have charged you with the task of drafting a letter to the federal treasurer to complain about the changes in financial reporting. Identify and describe any shortcomings or disadvantages of adopting a set of accounting standards that are set by a foreign organisation in the form of a draft letter.

8.13 Accounting standards are law in various jurisdictions around the globe including Australia. Outline the complications of processes that make accounting standards law. Consider the difficulties of keeping in step with the IASB in an environment where accounting standards have legal backing under a company code.

8.14 Discuss whether you believe a corporate regulator such as the ASIC is entitled to develop and articulate a view on the appropriate application of accounting standards.

8.15 Visit the website of the ASX at www.asx.com.au and select three entities from the same industry. Download the most recent set of financial statements for those entities and evaluate the disclosures describing the impacts of the new body of accounting standards. Discuss your view on the standard of disclosure provided by the three entities and provide specific examples from the annual financial statements to substantiate your assertions.

8.16 'Domestic regulators have a role in interpreting international accounting standards'. Identify and discuss the various reasons for and against a domestic regulator involving itself in the interpretation of international accounting standards.

8.17 Use the Internet to identify pressure groups interested in international financial reporting issues. Choose one group and describe how that organisation seeks to influence developments in accounting standards. Search the Internet to see whether any claims made by that organisation about their interest in financial reporting matters are substantiated by any submissions lodged with the IASB.

8.18 'Smaller entities around the world deserve a specific accounting standard on their own.' Explore and discuss the implications of the preceding statement to the reporting frameworks of counties that adopt IFRSs.

8.19 IFRSs are criticised from time to time for having options within them. Discuss whether you believe having options in international accounting standards provides any benefits to users of financial statements seeking to understand a company's financial state.

8.20 Form a research team from within your tutorial group and identify an industry that is particularly affected by accounting issues. Explore and discuss those accounting challenges and explain to your tutorial group what accounting standard setters are doing to resolve those accounting dilemmas.

8.21 Choose an accounting standard from the IFRSs. Identify disclosures made by at least ten companies regarding the impact of that particular standard. Evaluate the quality of disclosures and discuss whether you believe the disclosures sufficiently clear to be understood by an unsophisticated user. Discuss your conclusions with colleagues in your tutorial group.

8.22 Review a current exposure draft issues by the IASB and — individually or with colleagues — draft a response to the proposed standard in the form of a submission to the IASB. Submit the letter to the international standard setter as a contribution to the international debate.

8.23 Assume you are an officer in a corporate regulator with the responsibility for taking enforcement action in circumstances where companies have breached accounting standards and other reporting obligations. You have discovered a set of accounts in which a company has amortised goodwill in equal amounts over a 20-year period, which is known as the straight line method. Write a letter to the company's management explaining why this accounting treatment for goodwill is inappropriate under new accounting standards. In your draft correspondence you should make reference to the accounting standards dealing with business combinations, impairment and intangible assets. The intended audience for this letter is a board of directors lacking a detailed understanding of financial reporting.

8.24 Use the Internet find a copy of the 'Statements of membership obligations', which set down the key obligations for accounting bodies that are the members of the IFAC. Explain the relevance of these obligations, and identify the statement or statements that relate to financial reporting and audit.

8.25 Identify at least five different groups that have sent submissions to the IASB on an exposure draft of your choosing by visiting the IASB website. Describe their constituencies and their views on the exposure draft you have chosen.

8.26 Visit the website of the SEC and explain the role of the Office of the Chief Accountant at the SEC. Also, briefly explain why the role of the Office of the Chief Accountant differs from that of the body known as the Public Company Accounting Oversight Board.

case**study**   **8.1**

Political power and international accounting standards

The fate of any regulation, ordinance or accounting standard can be decided by a politician, in either house of Federal Parliament, who can gather together enough like-minded colleagues to vote against a measure. This means that work done by statutory boards such as the Australian Accounting Standards Board (AASB) and public sector bureaucrats, on sometimes complex technical, legal or accounting matters, may be struck out because of a simple exercise in arithmetic (a vote count), irrespective of the merits of what is laid on the parliamentary table.

Action of this nature could derail or delay aspects of the push by the Financial Reporting Council (FRC), the AASB and the Federal Government to have companies reporting in accordance with international accounting standards (IASs) from January 1, 2005.

Senator Stephen Conroy, the Opposition spokesman on corporate-governance issues, has already flagged that he has at least one accounting standard — on foreign currency — in his sights because he believes Australian shareholders should receive annual reports presented in Australian dollars rather than in a foreign currency.

He warned the AASB chairman, David Boymal, to expect the matter of companies reporting in the Australian market in currencies other than the Australian dollar to be the subject of parliamentary debate.

Conroy said during a Senate estimates committee hearing on February 18: 'I have not met an Australian shareholder yet who has asked to have reporting in anything other than Australian dollars.

'While I appreciate that you may receive many requests or [the Australian Securities & Investments Commission (ASIC)] may have met a few managements of companies, this opens up an approach of essentially self-regulation, which the Opposition is not excited about at all.

'I would probably foreshadow that this may be debated on the floor of the parliament. It is possible that Labor will move to disallow that portion that allows the option to report in other than the home currency.'

And the senator has warned in other speeches that the foreign currency matter may not be the only one about which he is concerned.

Disallowance motions can be put by any politician in either house and — unlike the legislative process that results in the creation of an act of parliament — such a motion requires only one house to disapprove of a particular piece of delegated legislation.

Disallowance in the House of Representatives is unlikely, largely because the ruling Coalition has a majority there. The Senate — where the Government does not command a majority — is more fertile ground for action against a particular regulation, ordinance or accounting standard.

The process for striking out any piece of legislation produced by a statutory board or similar delegated authority is fairly straightforward: a politician has 15 parliamentary sitting days in which to propose disallowance and for that vote to occur. The 15 sitting days can sometimes be spread over several months because of the parliamentary meeting pattern.

For a motion to have any chance of success, it must have the support of more than one of the parties or individuals represented in the Senate.

For example, in March, the votes of the senators from the Australian Democrats, the ALP, the Australian Greens' Bob Brown and Kerry Nettle, Senator Meg Lees (the sole member of the Australian Progressive Alliance) and the independent senators, Brian Harradine and Shayne Murphy, were required to disallow disclosure regulations relating to fee disclosures required under the new financial services regulatory regime.

The motion — moved by Conroy — related to whether a regulation would have required advisers working with the main superannuation or financial services houses to disclose how much consumers were paying for the services of a particular financial planner.

A central objection to the regulations as proposed in parliament, said Conroy, was the generally vague nature of the paragraph setting down the conditions under which companies, particularly banks, should be disclosing what their customers were paying in charges in one simple number.

Conroy and Democrats Senator Andrew Murray painted a picture during the debate of an industry that appeared to them and others to have significant difficulties with the concept of disclosing, and breaking down, the cost of services for which customers pay.

Conroy said: 'Let us make it clear, what we have is an industry that has concentrated from a vast array of companies down to ... if you want to be generous, six, the big four banks and AMP, and you can toss Axa in as well. Something like 80% of financial plans written nowadays are controlled by those five or six companies. This is an extraordinary concentration. It is putting enormous power in the hands of the banks and a few other financial services companies.' The financial services regulation was disallowed in the Senate by 36 votes to 30.

Source: This article appeared in *CFO*.

1. What powers does the parliament of the Commonwealth of Australia have regarding delegated legislation?
2. What benefits are conferred on the process of law making by having a system of delegation of legislative power?
3. Describe any risks you can identify in the process of delegation where accounting standards are concerned, particularly in the context of adopting international pronouncements.
4. There has been only one instance of disallowance of an accounting standard in Australia. Using the Internet, identify the standard that was disallowed and the reason for its disallowance. *Hint:* The disallowance occurred in the Australian Senate in February 2000.
5. List one argument for and against the review of accounting standards by elected representatives.

case**study** 8.2

The *Norwalk agreement*

The Financial Accounting Standards Board (FASB) and International Accounting Standards Board (IASB) have issued a memorandum of understanding, marking a significant step toward formalizing their commitment to the convergence of U.S. and international accounting standards. The FASB and IASB presented the agreement to the chairs of leading national standard setters at a two-day meeting being held in London. The agreement between the FASB and IASB represents their latest commitment, following their September joint meeting, to adopt compatible, high-quality solutions to existing and future accounting issues.

The agreement follows the decisions recently reached by both Boards to add a joint short-term convergence project to their active agendas. The joint short-term convergence project will require both Boards to use their best efforts to propose changes to U.S. and international accounting standards that reflect common solutions to certain specifically identified differences.

Working within each Board's due process procedures, the FASB and IASB expect to issue an Exposure Draft to address some, and perhaps all, of those identified differences by the latter part of 2003. The elimination of those differences, together with the commitment by both Boards to eliminate or reduce remaining differences through continued progress on joint projects and coordination of future work programs, will improve comparability of financial statements across national jurisdictions.

Robert H. Herz, Chairman of the FASB, commented, 'The FASB is committed to working toward the goal of producing high-quality reporting standards worldwide to support healthy global capital markets. By working with the IASB on the short-term convergence project — as well as on longer-term issues — the chances of success are greatly improved. Our agreement provides a clear path forward for working together to achieve our common goal.'

Hailing the agreement, Sir David Tweedie, Chairman of the IASB, remarked, 'This underscores another significant step in our partnership with national standard setters to reach a truly global set of accounting standards. While we recognize that there are many challenges ahead, I am extremely confident now that we can eliminate major differences between national and international standards, and by drawing on the best of U.S. GAAP, IFRSs and other national standards, the world's capital markets will have a set of global accounting standards that investors can trust.'

Source: 'FASB and IASB agree to work together toward convergence of global accounting standards', FASB News Release, 29/10/02.

1. Outline some of the reasons the IASB and the FASB would work together on developing accounting standards.
2. What, if any, negative aspects to the convergence agreement can you identify? Explain why the point you have chosen to highlight is relevant.
3. The *Norwalk agreement* dates back to October 2002. Visit the IASB website and list the convergence projects that are on the current work program of the IASB, along with a brief summary of the reason the projects have been chosen by the two boards.
4. What other countries have established formal convergence agreements with the IASB?
5. What is the name of the US authority that the IASB is hoping will drop the requirement for foreign registrants to reconcile their domestic accounts with those standards issued by the FASB? What is it expecting the IASB to deliver in exchange for dropping the reconciliation requirement?

Recommended readings

Committee on Concepts and Standards for External Financial Reports 1977, *Statement on accounting theory and theory acceptance*, American Accounting Association, Sarasota, Florida.

International Accounting Standards Board 2006, *International financial reporting standards (IFRSs) 2006*, International Accounting Standards Board, London.

Moonitz, M 1974, *Obtaining agreement on standards in the accounting profession*, American Accounting Association, Sarasota, Florida.

Ravlic, T 2005, *Readings in financial reporting*, John Wiley & Sons, Brisbane.

Spacek, L 1969, *A search for fairness in financial reporting to the public: volume I*, Arthur Andersen & Co, Chicago.

—— 1973, *A search for fairness in financial reporting to the public: volume II*, Arthur Andersen & Co, Chicago

Zeff, SA 1972, *Forging accounting principles in five countries: a history and analysis of trends*, Stipes Publishing Company, Champaign, Illinois.

—— & Keller, TF 1985, *Financial accounting theory*, 3rd edn, McGraw-Hill, New York.

References

Australian Accounting Standards Board (AASB) 2006, 'Approved minutes for the 65th meeting of the Australian Accounting Standards Board', www.aasb.com.au/workprog/aasb_index.htm.

Coca-Cola Amatil (CCA) 2004, *Australian Stock Exchange listing rules disclosure half year report for the period ending 2 July 2004*, Coca-Cola Amatil, Sydney, www.ccamatil.com.

Financial Accounting Standards Board (FASB) 2000, *Financial accounting research system*, CD ROM, Financial Accounting Standards Board, Norwalk, Connecticut.

Institute of Chartered Accountants in Australia 2006, *Financial reporting handbook 2006: volume 1*, John Wiley & Sons, Brisbane.

International Accounting Standards Board (IASB) 2006, *International financial reporting standards (IFRS) 2006*, International Accounting Standards Board, London.

McCreevy, C 2005, 'Governance and accountability in financial services', speech delivered to the economic and monetary affairs committee of the European parliament in Brussels, 1 February 2005 , European Commission, Brussels.

PricewaterhouseCoopers 2005, 'IASC Foundation — review of the constitution — proposals for change', submission Cl43, 23 February, www.iasb.org.

Publishing and Broadcasting Ltd 2004, financial report for the year ended 30 June 2004, www.pbl.com.au.

Seven Network Ltd 2004, *Annual report 2004*, www.sevencorporate.com.au.

Ten Network Holdings Ltd 2004, 'Ten Network Holdings Limited for the year ended 31 August 2004', www.tencorporate.com.au.

9 CAPITAL-MARKET RESEARCH AND ACCOUNTING

LEARNING OBJECTIVES

After reading this chapter, you should be able to:

- explain the role of capital-market research for accounting

- outline the relationship between accounting measures of financial performance and share prices

- distinguish an event study from an association study

- identify findings of capital-market research relevant to accounting

- understand the role of information and information intermediaries in capital markets

- distinguish between behavioural finance findings and mainstream finance findings

- comprehend how behavioural research contributes to an understanding of decision making.

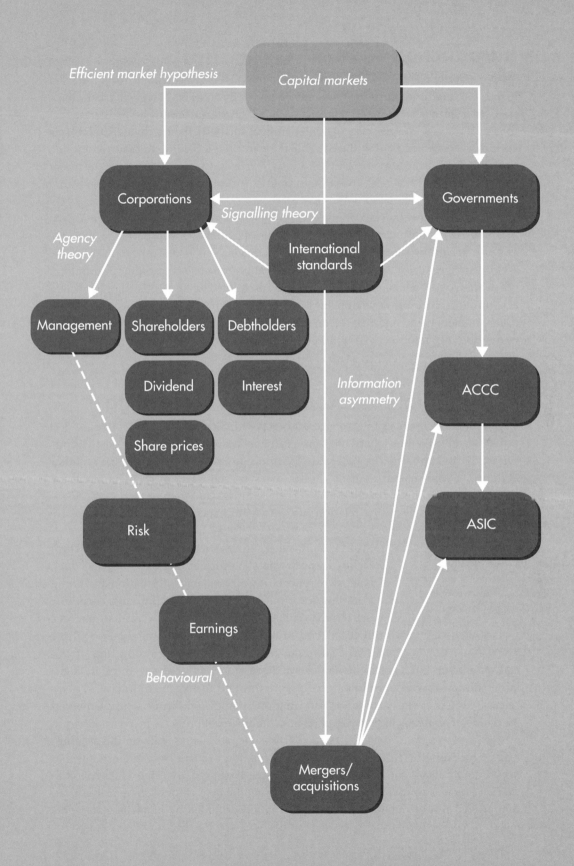

Introduction

Share markets have been popularised over the past two decades. This is reflected in regular media reports on the state of the daily markets. Share markets have particular importance to accounting because of the generally held assumption that accounting informs capital- or share-market participants. In Australia, this assumption is embedded in the *conceptual framework*. According to that framework, accounting aims at providing investors with relevant information for investment decision making, enabling investors to predict future cash flows and assess future risk and returns associated with particular shares.

The assumption that accounting provides information useful to participants in share or capital markets raises the issue of whether those participants actually use accounting information in their decisions. This is an important issue for accounting because if capital-market participants *do not* use accounting information when making decisions relating to share transactions, what then is the purpose of accounting? Since the development of a conceptual framework for accounting, its policy makers have concentrated on improving this kind of information, so finding that it does not inform capital markets would be devastating for accounting and its policy makers.

Capital-market research and accounting

Capital markets have been extensively researched. Since the seminal study by Ball & Brown (1968), more than 1000 papers have been published covering various aspects of the capital markets. Because the important issue for accounting is whether accounting information informs capital markets, the focus in this chapter is on research investigating the relationship between the two. Much of this research has focused particularly on the relationship between financial performance and share prices.

efficient market hypothesis: A market in which all share prices reflect fully all the available information, so that investors cannot make excessive returns by exploiting information

Much capital-market research relies on the **efficient market hypothesis**. An efficient market is one in which share prices reflect fully all available information, including accounting information. Under this hypothesis, corporate disclosure is critical to the functioning of capital markets. But not all corporate disclosure is accounting based. Firms disclose through annual reports, including the financial statements and notes, management discussion and analysis, through regulatory filings as well as voluntary disclosure through management forecasts, press releases, Internet sites and so on. Information arising from firms is supplemented by financial analysts, industry experts and the financial press.

Accounting's policy makers, particularly standards setters, rely on the assumption of market efficiency because decisions relating to matters such as changes in accounting policies should not affect share price. An alternative view is that capital-market efficiency provides justification for using the behaviour of share prices as an operational test of the usefulness of information provided by financial statements

(Ball & Brown 1968). But market efficiency is being challenged. Some findings of capital market research suggest that markets are not efficient. Behavioural finance research also contradicts the assumption that capital markets are efficient.

Research methods: event studies and association studies

If capital markets are efficient, share prices must reflect fully and quickly any new information, including accounting information. New information causes market participants to revise their expectations of future cash flows. Their revisions cause them to act so that share prices change.

There are two main methods that are used to examine whether share prices react to accounting information.

An **event study** examines the changes in the level or variability of share prices or trading volume over a short time around the release of accounting or other information. Information is assumed to be 'new' if the release revises the market's expectation, as evidenced by changes in level of prices or in the variability of prices around the disclosure date.

event study: Research methods that examine the changes in level or variability of share prices or trading volume around the time new information is released

An **association study** does not assume a causal connection between an accounting performance measure and share price movements. Rather, this type of study aims to see how quickly accounting measures capture changes in the information that is reflected in share prices over a

association study: Research method that looks for correlation between an accounting performance measure and share returns

given period. So an association study looks for correlation between an accounting performance measure (such as earnings or income) and stock returns where both are measured over relatively long, contemporaneous time periods.

What market response studies tell us

Most event studies focus on earnings announcements. The general assumption underlying the research is that an earnings announcement with good news should cause a share price to increase; one with bad news should cause a share price to decrease. Observing the volatility of returns on announcement days can indicate whether earnings convey information to investors. Releases of earnings numbers should also result in significant increases in trades if they are a source of information for investors.

Research shows that disclosures of earnings lead to significant share price changes or trading volume increases, thus providing evidence that there is information content in announcements of accounting earnings. These results are consistent across all countries studied. The assumption of some studies that the greater the surprise in disclosures, the larger will be the investor reaction has also been confirmed, with trading volumes, volatility of returns or mean abnormal returns all positively related to the size of unexpected earnings (Dumontier & Raffournier 2002).

Association studies also show that accounting earnings capture part of the information set that is reflected in share prices. Although this is good news for accounting, there is some bad news. The evidence suggests that much of the information is captured from nonaccounting sources that compete with the earnings number. This means that annual financial statements are not a timely source of information for the capital market.

Interim disclosures of accounting information may help investors predict the annual earnings number. Share price reactions to half-year releases are statistically significant but their information content appears to be less than that of the annual report.

Certain factors such as firm size and the ability of investors to use accounting information seem to modify results. The larger the market value of the firm, the smaller its abnormal returns at announcement dates. For large firms, information disclosed at typical announcement dates is usually pre-empted by the attention given to large firms by investment analysts and fund managers. Sophistication of investors also accounts for the positive association between price changes and unexpected earnings. Unsophisticated investors are defined as those who react mechanically to reported earnings. A positive investor sophistication effect has been observed. Less sophisticated investors react to good news but under-react to negative unexpected earnings in comparison with their sophisticated counterparts (Dumontier & Raffournier 2002).

Prices lead earnings

As mentioned above, not all of the information captured in share prices is accounting information. Beaver, Lambert & Morse (1980) put forward the idea that the information reflected in prices is richer than the information in accounting earnings. This idea is called '**prices lead earnings**', which means that the information set reflected in prices contains information about future earnings.

> **prices lead earnings:** The finding that earnings lag prices because prices contain information about future earnings

So why do earnings numbers lag prices? The fundamental principles in the calculation of earnings relate to revenue realisation and expense matching. These principles are conservative. According to Kothari (2001), accounting 'garbles' an otherwise 'true' earnings signal about firm value.

The divide between accounting measures of earnings and share prices is referred to as the *deficient-GAAP argument*. This argument suggests that financial statements are slow to incorporate all of the information that investors use to value shares. There is information asymmetry between managers and outsider investors. This information asymmetry, together with the threat of litigation against managers by outsiders, produces a demand for and supply of conservative accounting numbers. The Generally Agreed Accounting Principles (GAAP) have responded by having different timings for good and bad news: bad news is disclosed more timely than good news. In other words, accounting recognition criteria are less stringent for losses than for gains. This may be a response to the lobbying of standard setters as demonstrated in the following In Focus vignette.

The Financial Accounting Standards Board (FASB) and the capital markets

Some people who prepare financial statements apparently do not buy into the paradigm that uncertainty results in a higher cost of capital. This is apparent from the resistance we get at the FASB almost every time we propose to issue a new standard directed toward improving the understanding of a company's financial position and results of operations. Consider disclosures about derivatives, for example. I voted for Statement 119, *Disclosure about Derivative Financial Instruments and Fair Value of Financial Instruments*, even though its disclosure requirements were limited only to the effects of the derivatives themselves, largely because I thought that, given the bad connotation that any use of derivatives had at that time, issuers of financial statements would want to tell the whole story. I thought concerns about how users of financial statements would react to an entity's use of derivatives, especially if the derivative positions had resulted in losses for the period, would compel people to provide an in-depth explanation of their risk-management policies and how the derivatives held or used related to or offset the underlying exposures that they were trying to hedge. I was wrong. Except for financial institutions, which do a pretty good job of explaining their risks, most entities have simply complied with the minimum disclosure requirements that are now embodied in Statement 133, *Accounting for Derivative Instruments and Hedging Activities*. Companies generally do not relate their derivative transactions to the risks that they are hedging or explain how gains and losses on the derivatives are offset by losses and gains on other transactions. The result is that investors and potential investors still do not understand many companies' risk-management activities.

Source: 'FASB and IASB agree to work together toward convergence of global accounting standards', FASB News Release, 29/10/02.

Because of the differences in accounting's recognition criteria, accruals and cash flows are the two most commonly examined components of earnings (Kothari 2001). Accruals are the means by which accountants attempt to transform operating cash flows into an earnings figure that is more informative about firm performance. From positive accounting theory, it is known that managers might use accounting information opportunistically, and so manipulate accruals for their own ends, distorting the earnings figure as a measure of firm performance.

Post-earnings announcement drift

Much evidence (Kothari 2001) indicates that the stock market underreacts to earnings information. This means that the market does not recognise accounting earnings information as soon as the figure is released. Instead, the market recognises its full impact gradually. This evidence is inconsistent with the assumption of capital-market efficiency. An efficient market should react instantaneously and completely to value-relevant information.

This gradual adjustment in prices makes it seem that investors underreact to the information. This phenomenon is termed **post-earnings announcement drift**.

post-earnings announcement drift: The finding that prices adjust gradually to new information

The drift seems to be related to the extent of good news in an announcement. Unexpected good news causes the market to react as predicted by the efficient market hypothesis, but drift follows bad news announcements. Contrary evidence has been found; for example, in Finland, post-announcement drift is higher following positive earnings surprises (Booth, Kallunki & Martikainen, 1996). Johnson & Schwartz (2000, cited in Dumontier & Raffournier 2002) show that the drift persists in the United States among small firms and among firms with little analyst coverage.

Not all studies concentrate on the association between share prices and earnings. Some studies have used inflation-adjusted earnings, residual earnings and operating cash flows as measures. Recently, performance measures such as comprehensive income compared with earnings per share, economic value added against earnings or measures specific to particular industries have been used. Evidence from these studies is important to accounting because it suggests that performance measures that have evolved in an unregulated environment are more informative than those mandated by regulation (Kothari 2001).

Learning tips

Do you know...

9.1   *Investors are assumed to be rational decision makers.*

9.2   *Efficient markets fully reflect new information.*

9.3   *Announcements of accounting earnings have information content.*

9.4   *Accounting has less stringent recognition criteria for losses than for gains.*

Association studies

Recall that association studies regress accounting numbers on capital-market data to test for significant relationships to assess the **value relevance** of information.

value relevance: An item of accounting information that makes a difference to the decisions made by users of financial statements

An item of accounting information is considered relevant if it has the ability to make a difference to the decisions of financial statement users. An accounting number is value relevant if it conveys information that results in the modification of investors' expectations about future payoffs or associated risk (Barth, Beaver & Landsman 2001).

Studies have focused on accounting information by examining four different associations:

• earnings and security returns
• the value relevance of nonearnings data
• the value relevance of different accounting practices
• the value relevance of different GAAP.

Studies examining these associations use three different research methods (Holthausen & Watts 2001) as follows.

- *Relative association studies* compare the association between stock market values or changes in those values and alternative bottom-line accounting measures. The accounting number with the greater R^2 is described as being more value relevant.
- *Incremental association studies* investigate whether the accounting number of interest is helpful in explaining value or returns over a long period. The accounting number is said to be value relevant if its estimated regression coefficient is significantly different from zero.
- *Marginal information content studies* investigate whether a particular accounting number adds to the information set available to investors. Typically, these are event studies examining whether the release of an accounting number is associated with value changes. Price changes are considered evidence of value relevance. These studies represent less than 10 per cent of the value relevance studies.

Note that these studies explore an **association**. An association signifies that when two or more sets of numbers are regressed and give an R^2 that suggests a relationship between the numbers, they may be related. However, the use of the term *association* signifies the lack of theory to explain why the sets of numbers are related.

association: A suggestion of a relationship between two or more sets of numbers when regressed

Holthausen & Watts (2001) find two implicit but different theories in this literature. The first assumes that accounting earnings tend to be highly associated with equity market value changes. In the second theory, accounting's role is to provide information on inputs to valuation models that investors use in valuing firms' equity. Most researchers assume that the main role of financial reporting is to provide measures associated with value or measures of value or information relevant for equity valuation, an assumption criticised by Holthausen & Watts. As noted in previous chapters, accounting information is an important input into other contexts, not just capital markets, and is used by many noninvestor user groups.

Holthausen & Watts (2001) identify three assumptions underlying the value relevance literature:

- Equity investors are assumed to be the main or dominant users of financial reports. They are assumed to use those reports mainly for the valuation of equity.
- Share prices adequately represent investors' use of information in valuing equity securities.
- Share-priced-based tests of relevance and reliability measure relevance and reliability as defined by FASB statements (reflecting the heavy dominance of American researchers in stock market research).

What value relevance studies tell us

Studies of the relationship between accounting earnings and share returns have analysed data from most of the world's major stock exchanges. Results show that any relationship evident is at best weak.

Reported earnings are not good measures of the value-relevant events that are built into share prices in the periods studied. The relatively low association between reported earnings and share prices suggests that earnings do not capture all the information incorporated into share prices.

One reason for this may be that investors focus on all events that affect future cash flows, while earnings only capture those events that meet the criteria for accounting recognition. Other reasons refer to managers' risk preferences and negative earnings. Risk-averse managers are likely to report more conservative earnings figures than less risk-averse ones, and are likely to report bad news earlier. Both of these actions have been confirmed. Another explanation may be that negative earnings are not value relevant because investors do not expect losses to persist, but firms with losses are included in test samples, lowering the association. Additionally, losses do not provide information about a firm's ability to generate future cash flows.

Relevance and reliability

Value relevance research examines the association between accounting amounts and equity market values (Barth, Beaver & Landsman 2001). An accounting amount is considered value relevant if it has an association with equity market values. As mentioned, value relevance research focuses on the relevance and reliability criteria that are used in conceptual frameworks to choose among accounting methods. *The assumption is that an accounting amount will be value relevant only if the amount reflects information relevant to investors in valuing the firm, and if the amount is measured reliably enough to be reflected in share prices.*

Some studies have tried to decompose earnings and test the association of decomposed items with share prices. The evidence conflicts. Some studies show that partitioning earnings into pre-exceptional, exceptional and extraordinary improves the association, while others contradict these findings, especially in relation to extraordinary earnings. Earnings are more correlated with share returns than cash flows for short periods, but with increased time intervals, both tend to have the same level of correlation with returns. Inclusion of nonearnings variables increases the correlation between returns and accounting data (Dumontier & Raffournier 2002).

Fair value accounting is a focus of value relevance research. For example, pension assets and liabilities are perceived by investors as assets and liabilities of the firm, although they are less reliably measured than other recognised assets and liabilities (Barth, Beaver & Landsman 2001). The fair value of pension assets measures the pension asset implicit in share prices more reliably than the book value of those pension assets. Other findings are that disaggregated costs are potentially more informative to investors than aggregated costs. Investors perceive the fair value estimates of debt and equity securities and bank loans as more value relevant than historical cost amounts. As well, investors perceive fair values of derivatives as reflecting more precision than their notional amounts in relation to the underlying economic value.

The costs of intangible assets are relevant to investors, and are reflected in share prices with some reliability. Investors perceive expenditures on research and development and advertising as capital acquisitions. In contrast, fair value estimates of tangible long-lived assets are not value relevant, although this may because these values are not always reliably estimated. Consolidated earnings were found to have an incremental information content beyond that of the parent company, so that consolidation improves the value relevance of earnings. However, no value relevance was found for the minority interest portion of earnings and equity.

For Finnish investors at least, restating local GAAP earnings to conform to international accounting standards has helped meet foreign investor needs but appears to have been of limited use for domestic investors. Asset revaluations under Australian GAAP, on the other hand, are relevant and estimated with some reliability but are not considered timely (Barth, Beaver & Landsman 2001). The degree of association for value relevance of earnings differs internationally. The degree of association is lower in countries with bank-oriented rather than market-oriented economies, in countries in which private-sector bodies are not involved in the standard-setting process and in continental Europe. Differences, especially between the UK and the United States, seem to be sensitive to the earnings measure analysed (Dumontier & Raffournier 2002).

Whether auditors or intermediaries add value to accounting information

Capital providers require firms to employ an independent auditor as a condition of financing, even when it is not required by regulations. Although little or no research has examined the reasons capital providers require independent audits, that they do *implies* that capital providers consider that auditors increase credibility. Audited financial statements are generally accepted as giving credibility to the annual report in which they are found. Intuitively, qualified audit reports should be more valued by market participants. However, they do not provide timely signals to capital markets, basically because the qualification has been expected (Healy & Palepu 2001).

In contrast, the work of financial **intermediaries** adds value in the capital market. Analysts' earnings forecasts are more accurate than time-series models of earnings. Their accuracy is affected by innate ability, company assignments, brokerage affiliation and industry specialisation.

intermediaries: Financial analysts, auditors, managers and others who examine primary data and send a message about that data to investors

Their earnings forecasts and recommendations affect share prices. However, their forecasts have been found to be biased in an overly optimistic direction, especially when their brokerage house has been hired to underwrite particular security issues (Healy & Palepu 2001).

 Is there no drop to Google stock?

Google's shares have been on a tear since the company's August 2004 initial public stock offering. The stock glided past three milestones last year — $200 in April, $300 in September and $400 in November... One Wall Street analyst

predicted that Google's shares would hit $600 by the end of the year. Another predicted that Google's shares will hit a whopping $2000, eventually.

...

Not surprisingly, these lofty predictions about Google's stock price often become self-fulfilling prophecies. Investors read about an analyst's strong confidence in a company and pour money into the stock, hoping to catch whatever upside remains. Google's shares marched steadily upward in the days after Rashtchy and others released their lofty price targets.

Professor Werner De Bondt of DePaul University's Graduate School of Business is an expert on investor psychology. He says most investors do not understand how to evaluate a company's financial condition, so they seek out 'anchors' to help them judge a stock's worth.

Analyst price targets serve as anchors for many investors. And as they rise, so does investor confidence.

...

But there are Google skeptics emerging from the shadows.

Henry Blodget, the bubble-era analyst famous for touting Internet stocks, recently offered one of the few notes of caution about Google's fortunes. Blodget, who once predicted that Amazon.com's shares would hit $400 (they did), laid out a scenario in which Google's advertising revenue — its chief revenue stream — plummets through a combination 'market saturation and price pressure' and other issues.

Blodget said Google's shares could plummet to $100, if the right — or wrong — pieces fell into place.

'Is such a scenario likely?' Blodget wrote on his blog. 'Probably not. But it's certainly within the realm of possibility. (How do we know this? Because the same thing just happened to Yahoo, AOL, and every other advertising-driven dot-com on the planet — except that in those cases, the fallout was worse).'

Hennessy is even more bearish. He evaluates a company's stock price against its sales numbers. He looks at Google and sees a company far too overvalued by the market. In fact, he said, even if Google were to double its sales next year, he would find it hard to justify buying the stock.

'Is it worth that much money? I would say no. I'm not sure that emotion isn't getting the best of people,' he said.

Source: This article appeared in *Knight Ridder Tribune Business News.*

Voluntary disclosure theory

According to Core (2001), the voluntary disclosure literature offers the best opportunity for increasing understanding of the role of accounting information in firm valuation and corporate finance. The most important questions relate to which firms voluntarily disclose, how stakeholders use this information in allocating capital to firms and how the various people who produce or use this information verify, regulate and interpret it. Although the literature has theorised about voluntary disclosure, empirical evidence from reputable studies is scant.

Voluntary disclosure theory predicts that shareholders optimise disclosure policy, corporate governance and management incentives to maximise firm value (Core 2001). Increased disclosure lowers information asymmetry, thus lowering the cost of capital. However, this has to be weighed against the costs associated with incentives, litigation and proprietorship. Increased disclosure does not mean credible or unbiased disclosure because it is too costly to eliminate all the ways that managers can use to add some bias. The theory predicts that even though disclosure is somewhat biased, on average it will be credible. Although manipulation of disclosures is possible, corporate governance is designed to constrain managers to follow the optimal policy. Firms will differ in their disclosures according to their disclosure policy and the ability of the individual firm's governance to enforce the policy.

The evidence shows that managers with shares or share options may take actions to manipulate the prices of their share or option holdings. They delay disclosing good news and speed up the release of bad news before their stock option award periods to maximise their stock-based compensation because managers may find it more profitable to buy shares before their stock options are awarded. Management forecasts are associated with trading by insiders in the firm's shares, and with share option compensation that is at risk because of firm performance. Firms with greater information asymmetry use more share and option incentives. Greater information asymmetry is associated with more voluntary disclosure, because managers do not want to bear any risk associated with any misvaluation of shares. Firms that warn investors that bad news is imminent have significantly more negative returns per unit of unexpected earnings than firms that do not warn, suggesting that firms are penalised for disclosing bad news early (Healy & Palepu 2001; Core 2001).

Cosmetic accounting choices

Because accounting allows management to make some choices about accruals and methods, management is likely to have incentives to convey self-serving information when preparing financial statements. When accounting choices are used to achieve a particular goal, the choice is described as *earnings management*.

Earnings management occurs when managers use judgement in financial reporting and in structuring transactions to alter financial reports to either mislead some stakeholders about the underlying economic performance of the company or to influence contractual outcomes that depend on reported numbers (Healy & Wahlen 1999). In an earlier definition, Schipper (1989) emphasised the purposefulness of the process order to obtain some private gain to managers and perhaps shareholders. The discretion they use may not be necessarily opportunistic. Healy & Palepu (1993), for instance, view earnings management as the means by which management conveys either its private information about the firm's prospects or a more accurate picture of the firm's performance. For example, informed management imparts information to less informed users about the timing, magnitude and risk of future cash flows. For earnings management to be successful, users of the financial statements must be either unable or unwilling to unravel the effects of earnings management (Fields, Lys & Vincent 2001).

Recent research has focused on whether management compensation contracts provide incentives for managers to achieve desired financial reporting objectives. Managers are hypothesised to select accounting methods to increase their compensation or to reduce the likelihood of violating debt covenants. The debt covenant hypothesis predicts that when a firm is close to violating an accounting-based debt covenant restriction, its managers are expected to make income-increasing accounting choices to relax the debt covenant restriction and lower the expected costs of technical default, such as renegotiation costs or bankruptcy costs.

Managers seem to take advantage of discretion in methods to manage reported earnings to increase their compensation (Fields, Lys & Vincent 2001). Some contradictory evidence suggests that an income-smoothing hypothesis better explains the evidence. Other evidence suggests that management may engage in 'big bath' accounting. When earnings for a period are below expectations, managers may write off as many costs as possible in that period to allow improved performances in subsequent periods. Similar actions have been observed with changes in executives or CEOs. The evidence suggests that investors react positively to such actions (Fields, Lys & Vincent 2001). Additionally, managers seem to manipulate discretionary accruals in the period before announcing a management buyout, presumably to reduce the share price.

Capital markets and their participants' reaction to accounting disclosures

In an efficient market, firm value is defined as the present value of expected discounted future net cash flows (Kothari 2001). An important input into the market's assessment of value is a firm's current performance, reflecting the conceptual framework's focus on financial statements providing information useful in assessing the amounts, timing and certainty of future cash flows.

Disclosures of accounting earnings numbers lead to share price changes or increases in the volume of trading, providing evidence that capital-market participants do use accounting information, reacting more quickly to bad news than good. However, the conservative principles that govern the calculation of accounting earnings 'garble' the signal sent to the capital market.

The good news for accounting is that participants use accounting information; the bad news is that accounting earnings numbers are poor measures of the relevant events that are incorporated into share prices. Forecasts of future revenues, expenses, earnings and cash flows are the core of valuation. Financial statements, with their backward focus, are poor indicators of value. Accounting's reliability and recognition principles are blamed for financial statements not providing forward-looking information.

Managers' behaviour suggests that they believe accounting information is used by capital market participants. The reaction of investors to voluntary disclosures by managements and to some earnings management strategies confirms that accounting information is used by them.

Do you know...

9.5   Accounting numbers that modify investors' expectations are relevant.

9.6   Investors are assumed to be the main users of financial statements.

9.7   Accounting earnings numbers do not capture all the information used to value shares.

The efficiency of capital markets

Capital markets are assumed to be efficient. The hypothesis suggests that if accounting choices and changes do not affect cash flows, investors will not alter their assessment of share prices. Therefore, market efficiency is important to accounting because the assumption means that investors would see through alternative or opportunistic accounting choices. If markets are not efficient, then discretionary accruals (or earnings management) can fool investors.

Researchers have had little success in resolving the question of whether markets are efficient in relation to discretionary or cosmetic accounting choices. Tests for earnings management generate results with little explanatory power for earnings management (Kothari 2001). Dechow & Skinner (2000) argued that it is sufficient in well-functioning markets for information to be disclosed, because rational investors will process the information appropriately. Not all empirical evidence is consistent with this opinion (Fields, Lys & Vincent 2001).

Testing whether capital markets are efficient

Market efficiency is important to accounting because this assumption means that investors would see through alternative or opportunistic accounting choices. If markets are not efficient, then discretionary accruals can fool investors. Tests of market efficiency in the late 1970s and 1980s began to undermine the efficient hypothesis, although the research methods employed were unable to determine whether investors could see through cosmetic changes or mandated accounting changes (Fields, Lys & Vincent 2001).

Most short-window event studies are generally consistent with market efficiency although sometimes the market does not react quickly to information, so that there is a 'drift', which contradicts market efficiency. Longer-period tests assume that the market can over or under react to new information because of human judgement and behavioural biases. Recent evidence such as large abnormal returns spread over several years after well-publicised events such as initial public offerings also contradict market efficiency. According to Kothari (2001), collectively this research poses a formidable challenge to the efficient market hypothesis.

Evidence in studies examining manipulation of discretionary accruals immediately before initial public offerings and other equity offerings also challenges market efficiency. These studies suggest that the market fails to recognise the optimistic bias in earnings forecasts, even though owners, managers and analysts have incentives to issue overly optimistic forecasts (Kothari 2001; Fields, Lys & Vincent 2001).

Statistical anomalies continue to appear in studies using the capital asset pricing model (CAPM). Investors were shown not to react 'logically' to new information (Olsen 1998). In 1992, Eugene Fama, a key figure in the development of the CAPM model, withdrew his support from it. Defenders of the efficient market hypothesis began to argue that noisy data, measurement errors and selection bias could explain anomalies. Fields, Lys & Vincent (2001) conclude that the evidence about market efficiency is not conclusive that markets are inefficient or not. Researchers finding evidence of market inefficiency are likely to draw on the behavioural literature for support, arguing that investors are not necessarily rational.

Prices in an efficient market reflect all that there is to know about capital assets. This ideology endorsed markets as a perfect allocative device. However, as discussed, anomalies (information that conflicts with the efficient market hypothesis) have begun to appear. The main anomalies are:

- The *small firm effect:* CAPM understates cross-sectional returns of listed firms with low market values of equity and overstates those of firms with high market values of equity.
- The *neglect effect:* returns of firms not followed by analysts are inferior to those of firms followed by many analysts.
- The *exchange effect:* investor interest and publicly available information vary according to the market in which a firm's shares are traded.
- The *exotic effect:* there are end-of-month, end-of-year, weekend, Yom Kippur and January effects. For example, many of the abnormal returns for smaller firms occur during the first half of January; and stock returns are predictably negative over weekends. These results cannot be explained by the efficient market hypothesis and CAPM combination.

■ Behavioural finance

With increasing uncertainty over whether markets are efficient, behavioural finance has become a topic of considerable interest (Fuller 1996). Although the origins of behavioural finance date to 1951, about the same time as modern finance was being born, interest in it did not gain momentum until the late 1980s. This renewed interest seems to have been engendered by two developments:

- mounting empirical evidence suggesting that existing finance theories appear to be deficient in fundamental ways
- the development of **prospect theory** by Kahneman and Tversky. This theory is based on the simple idea that the pain associated with a given amount of loss (say $100) is greater than the pleasure derived from an equivalent gain,

prospect theory: The theory that suggests that the pain associated with a given amount of loss is greater than the pleasure associated with an equivalent gain

so that investors attach more importance to avoiding the loss (Fuller 1996). The underlying assumptions of this alternative model of decision making are more realistic than those of existing finance theories (Olsen 1998). This model of investor behaviour is reviewed in the following In Focus vignette.

Road to wealth may lie in marching out of step

If the price of a share you owned fell below what you'd paid for it, would that make you more likely or less likely to want to sell it?

One company's profits have been buoyant in recent times, whereas another company hasn't been doing at all well. Which company's shares would you be more inclined to buy?

If in answer to the first question you said you'd be less likely to want to sell a share that had fallen below what you paid for it, congratulations — you're normal.

Unfortunately, you're also sadly misguided. That fact should have no bearing on your decisions about whether to sell the share.

Why not? Because what you paid for a share is in the past. There's nothing you can do to change it, so you should ignore it. It's what economists call a 'sunk cost' and what accountants call 'irrelevant information'.

The point is that the only thing you can hope to influence is the future, so that's what you should focus on. And the question you should ask yourself is this: do I know of any other share (or other investment) that offers a better prospect of gain than the share I've got my money in now?

If so, sell the old one and buy the new one. If not, stick with the old one. If there isn't a lot in it, sit tight — because you pay brokerage fees every time you change horses.

But why do so many investors find it so hard to live by that simple rule? Why do we find it so hard to ignore what we paid for our T2 Telstra shares, for instance?

Well, as we're reminded in an interesting little booklet from JP Morgan Asset Management, *A Primer in Behavioural Finance Theory*, these are the sort of questions that specialists in 'behavioural finance' seek to answer.

The two American psychologists who pioneered this school of thought, Daniel Kahneman and Amos Tversky, discovered almost 30 years ago that losses create much more distress among investors (and ordinary consumers) than the happiness created by equivalent gains.

Whereas conventional economists believe people are 'risk averse', it's more accurate to say most people are 'loss averse'. They're highly reluctant to crystallise a paper loss by selling up and, in fact, often are willing to take more risks to avoid losses than to realise gains.

The behavioural finance specialist Professor Terrance Odean examined data on the whole of the Taiwanese share market and found that, similar to previous studies, people were four times more likely to sell a winner than a loser.

He also looked at investors who repurchased shares they'd previously owned and found they were much more likely to repurchase a stock they sold for a gain than for a loss.

Our obsession with the price we paid for shares is a specific instance of a wider behavioural bias psychologists call 'anchoring' — we make decisions based on a single fact or figure that should have little bearing on the decision.

Salespeople often exploit our tendency to focus on figures of limited relevance. Car salespeople, for example, may anchor their prospective buyers to a vehicle's sticker price.

Bargaining with the buyer and slowly lowering that price makes the buyer think they're getting a good deal. But the sticker price may have been deliberately set too high.

The JP Morgan booklet says even experienced investment analysts can be guilty of anchoring. When faced with new information that contradicts their forecast, they tend to dismiss it as a short-term phenomenon.

This in direct contradiction to conventional finance theory — the 'efficient market hypothesis' — which holds that all new information is almost instantly incorporated into the market and reflected in share prices.

OK, let's turn to the second question: more inclined to buy the share of a buoyantly profitable company or one that hasn't been doing so well?

Of course you'd buy the one that had been doing well. And, simply because so many other people act that way, it's a pretty good bet you'd be rewarded by seeing the price of the share keep rising after you'd bought it.

The efficient market hypothesis holds that, because all new information is immediately incorporated into a share's price, and because we don't know whether the next bit of information to come along will be good or bad, it's impossible to predict whether the next move in a share's price will be up or down.

But the behavioural finance people had disproved that contention, demonstrating that if a share price has been rising, it's more likely to rise further than to fall back. Similarly, if it's been falling, it's more likely to keep falling.

In other words, share prices tend to develop momentum. And the market contains a lot of 'momentum traders' who follow a policy of buying shares whose price is rising and selling shares whose price is falling.

But going along for the ride will benefit you only in the short term. Longer term, it's quite likely that a share whose price has risen a long way because everyone's been piling into it may by now be overvalued.

Similarly, a share whose price has fallen a long way may by now be undervalued — and so represents good buying.

Studies show that shares with a low P/E (ratio of price to earnings) tend to outperform those with a high P/E. (They get a low P/E by being undervalued and a high P/E by being overvalued.)

And then you have that familiar statutory warning — 'past performance is no guarantee of future performance' — we all keep forgetting to heed.

Just because a company's had a good run of profits lately doesn't mean the good run's likely to continue.

And just because another company's had a bad run lately doesn't mean the bad run's likely to continue.

Indeed, there's a statistical phenomenon called 'reversion to the mean' which says an exceptionally good run is more likely to be followed by a weak performance, while an exceptionally bad run is more likely to be followed by a strong performance.

Why? Because, in the end, most things tend to average out.

JP Morgan's point about behavioural finance is that, because so many investors act irrationally, but in systematic and hence predictable ways, there ought to be ways for the better-informed investor to make a quid out of second-guessing them.

Source: This article appeared in *The Sydney Morning Herald.*

In their work, Kahneman and Tversky integrated psychology and economics, so providing the intellectual foundations of behavioural finance. Their focus was decision making under uncertainty, a characteristic of capital markets. They demonstrated that decision making involves the use of **heuristics**, and systematically departs from the laws of probability. Modern finance involves little

> **heuristics:** Rules of thumb derived from past experience that are used in decision making

or no examination of individual decision making. Deduction is prominent, so that decision making is a 'black box'. Because finance is concerned with prediction rather than description or explanation, finance theorists constructed abstractions of the decision process (Olsen 1998).

Investment decisions are characterised by high exogenous uncertainty because future performance must be estimated from a set of noisy and vague variables. Investors who make decisions have an intuitive, less quantitative, emotionally driven perception of risk than that implied by finance models. Decision makers' preferences tend to be multifaceted, easily changed and often only formed during the decision-making process. They seek satisfactory rather than optimal solutions. The typical investor can be termed *homo heuristics*, not *homo economics*, a completely rational decision maker focused on utility or wealth maximisation (Olsen 1998).

Cornerstones of behavioural finance

There are two cornerstones of behavioural finance: cognitive psychology and the limits to arbitrage (Ritter 2003). The *limits to arbitrage* are that:

- Not all arbitrage agents are rational.
- High-frequency evidence supports market efficiency but low-frequency evidence does not.

Cognitive psychology suggests the following:

- People make systematic errors in the way they think. They use heuristics or rules of thumb to make decision making easier, which can lead to biases and sub-optimal investment decisions.
- People are overconfident about their abilities. Men are more overconfident than women. Entrepreneurs are especially likely to be overconfident.

- People put too much weight on recent experience so that they underweigh long-term averages.
- Mental accounting separates decisions that should be combined.
- *Framing* says that how a concept is presented to people matters. This refers to the old adage about whether a glass is half full or half empty and how each gives us a different perception about the quantity in the glass.
- People avoid realising paper losses but seek to realise paper gains. This behaviour is called the *disposition effect*.
- *Anchoring:* people tend to rely on a numerical anchor value that is explicitly or implicitly presented to them and use it as an initial starting point. When things change, people tend to be slow to pick up on the changes as well as to underreact because of their conservatism. Any evaluation of returns is distorted by size of the anchor.
- *Representativeness:* people tend to rely on stereotypes; for example, past performances are extrapolated without considering the exogenous uncertainty and randomness of financial markets. Good brand image and high brand awareness result in a lower perception of investment risk.
- *Affect heuristic:* emotions affect risk–return perceptions and investment behaviour. Positive emotional associations result in lower perceived investment risk.

Whether expertise moderates these outcomes is uncertain. Some findings show that investor expertise has no influence on the use of heuristics. Other evidence suggests that individual knowledge has a moderating effect.

These observations contradict the core theories of modern finance, which assume that:

- Investors are perfectly rational (or markets act as if they were).
- Markets are efficient.
- Transaction costs are so small that informed traders quickly notice and take advantage of mispricing, driving prices back to 'proper' levels (Gilson & Kraakman 2003).

Behavioural finance argues that investors, based on these observations, are not rational, so that there are observable biases. The list of biases is growing, and includes:

- *overconfidence:* the tendency of investors to overestimate their skills
- *endowment effect:* the tendency of individuals to insist on a higher price for something they wish to sell than to buy the same item if they do not already own it
- *loss aversion:* the tendency for people to be risk averse in relation to profit opportunities but to be willing to gamble to avoid a loss
- *anchoring:* the tendency for people to make decisions based on an initial estimate that is later adjusted, but not sufficiently adjusted to eliminate the influence of the initial estimate
- *framing:* the tendency to make different choices based on how the decision is framed, especially if it is framed in terms of a likelihood of a good outcome or the reciprocal bad outcome
- *hindsight:* the tendency to read the present into assessments of the past.

Learning tips

Do you know...

9.8   Increasingly, capital market research challenges market efficiency.

9.9   Investors attach more importance to avoiding a loss than making a gain.

9.10 Investors are not rational but biased in their decision making.

Those who study capital markets are becoming increasingly disillusioned with the assumptions that underlie the notion that markets are efficient. So what are the implications of markets not being efficient and of behavioural finance for accounting? Accounting policy makers have relied on market efficiency to make choices between accounting methods. How will the tenets of behavioural finance affect accounting policy choice? This is one issue that relies on a 'wait and see' answer.

Summary

Explain the role of capital-market research for accounting.
- Capital-market research suggests that the main role of financial reporting is to provide information relevant for equity valuation.
- Capital-market research indicates which disclosures have information content for investors.

Outline the relationship between accounting measures of financial performance and share prices.
- Accounting information provides investors with information relevant for investment decision making.
- Disclosures of earnings lead to significant share price changes or increases in trading volumes.
- Financial performance numbers are slow to incorporate all of the information investors use to value shares.

Distinguish an event study from an association study.
- The main difference is time: an event study is conducted over a short period; an association study over relatively long periods.
- Event studies examine changes in the level or variability of share prices or trading volumes.
- Association studies examine the correlation between accounting performance measures and share returns.

Identify findings of capital-market research relevant to accounting.
- Annual financial statements are not a timely source of information for capital markets.
- Interim disclosures of accounting information have less information content than annual reports.
- The relation between security returns and contemporaneous earnings is low.
- Capital-market research validates the relevance of accrual accounting.
- Consolidated accounting data is more value relevant than unconsolidated data.
- No relation has been observed between inflation accounting and share prices and returns.
- The information content of accounting varies with firm and country characteristics.

Understand the role of information and information intermediaries in capital markets.
- Information informs capital markets.
- Share prices reflect available information.
- Capital markets react to new information.
- Auditors appear to add credibility to financial information.
- Financial analysts' forecasts affect share prices.
- Managers, as intermediaries, voluntarily disclose information.

Distinguish between behavioural finance findings and mainstream finance findings.

- Mainstream finance assumes that investors are rational; behavioural finance shows that investors are not rational.
- Mainstream finance assumes decision making is a 'black box'; behavioural finance studies decision making.

Comprehend how behavioural research contributes to an understanding of decision making.

- Behavioural finance argues that investors are not rational.
- There are observable biases such as overconfidence, endowment effects, loss aversion, anchoring, framing and hindsight.
- Investors tend to use heuristics in their decision making.

Key terms

association   271
association study   267
efficient market hypothesis   266
event study   267
heuristics   281
intermediaries   273
post-earnings announcement drift   270
prices lead earnings   268
prospect theory   278
value relevance   270

Review questions

9.1 Explain what is meant by an 'efficient market'.

9.2 Distinguish an event study from an association study.

9.3 Explain why accounting earnings do not capture all the information contained in share prices.

9.4 Explain how accounting's recognition and realisation principles affect the relationship between earnings and share prices.

9.5 What is meant by the term 'post-earnings announcement drift'? What implications does this phenomenon have for the efficient market hypothesis?

9.6 In what ways are the finance definition of 'relevance' and the conceptual framework definition provided in chapter 2 similar?

9.7 When is an accounting number said to be 'value relevant'?

9.8 Explain why earnings are not good measures of value relevance.

9.9 International accounting standards are conservative in their treatment of intangibles. Will this conservative treatment conflict with investors' perceptions of the value of intangibles to a firm?

9.10 Summarise the main findings of the value relevance literature in relation to accounting.

9.11 What principles are blamed for financial statements being poor indicators of value? How do these principles inhibit valuation?

9.12 Read the section on earnings management in chapter 5. How does that view of earnings management differ from the view held in the finance literature? Why would investors react positively to earnings management?

9.13 What is prospect theory? What are the implications of prospect theory for finance?

9.14 In the literature on which this chapter is based, the notions of the efficient market hypothesis and the CAPM are referred to as a 'paradigm'. Findings that conflict with these hypotheses are called 'anomalies'. Find definitions of these terms. How do they explain the progress of knowledge in the finance discipline?

9.15 Behavioural finance, in contrast to mainstream finance, focuses on what aspects of capital markets?

9.16 What does cognitive psychology tell us about investors?

9.17 Does cognitive psychology supply explanations of why investors have flocked to subscribe in high-profile companies such as Woolworths or Telstra?

9.18 Evaluate whether behavioural finance is able to explain the main anomalies of efficient markets.

9.19 What are heuristics? How can they lead to poor decision making?

9.20 How would you evaluate large amounts of research findings that are based on associations, without much theoretical underpinning?

Application questions

9.21 The year 2004 was an interesting one for capital markets. On 12 August 2004, Telstra announced its highest ever full-year net profit of $4.12 billion. But Telstra's share price fell after the announcement. How would you explain this market reaction? What would you intuitively expect to be the market reaction?

9.22 At the same time that Telstra announced record profits, Coles Myer, Australia's largest retailer, also announced strong results but added that sales of its food and liquor unit would slow. Shares fell 20 cents to $8.80. How do you explain the market's reaction?

9.23 News Corporation also reported a record profit, together with strong sales of film and TV titles in the home entertainment market. Higher advertising rates resulted in increased TV earnings. Forecasts for the year ahead were optimistic. News Corporation ordinary shares fell 5 per cent after the announcement. How do you explain the market's reaction? Intuitively, how would you have expected the market to react?

9.24 Examine critically the following statements by analysts about Motorola Inc., the world's second largest mobile-phone maker. (The statements were published by *Knight Ridder Tribune Business News*, 20 October 2004.)

(a) 'People were expecting a lot from a stock that gained 25 per cent in recent months. That set a backdrop where Motorola had to deliver tremendous results.'

(b) 'Wall Street estimates have finally caught up with the company's performance.'

(c) 'It's been a blockbuster year so far for Motorola.'

Based on these statements, how would you expect the market to react to the earnings announcement?

9.25 Read the accounting standard on earnings per share. How is it calculated? What are some of the allocations, predictions and wild guesses that go into the calculation of net income? In light of the allocations, predictions and guesses, how reliable do you think the earnings per share are as a summary of a firm's activities for a period?

9.26 For the 2004 financial year, Tower had:
- an annual profit of $54.6 million (boosted by a $12 million revaluation)
- operating earnings of $27.9 million (compared with a loss of $9.7 million for the previous year)
- investment return on shareholder funds of $23.2 million ($10.7 million the previous year)
- assets under management of $22.6 billion ($20.8 billion the previous year)
- negative cash flow at –$37.3 million (–$125.3 million the previous year)
- $200 million of debt repaid.

Tower also announced that it would spin off its Australian wealth management business as well as undertaking a $130 million capital raising.

How do you think the market reacted to the results and announcement? Explain your reasoning.

9.27 Geoffrey Hill, a private share consultant, made the following statements in an article in *The Courier-Mail* on 27 November 2004. Comment on each statement, noting that some might require some research on your part.

> (a) 'The trouble with all of this overseas money flowing into our market and pushing it to new levels is that overseas investors have different views on what "value" means. The sheer weight of money obviously increases share prices but the institutions investing for overseas investors have scant regard to the level of risk that they are adding to everyone's portfolios.'

(i) What do you understand by 'value' in the context of this statement?
(ii) What is a portfolio? What role does risk play in the composition of a portfolio?

> (b) 'We have become accustomed to low oil prices, over the past 20 years. This has created a disincentive not to develop alternative energy supplies due to economics. But it is a different story now with the oil price near $US50 a barrel. Pacific Hydro operates hydro and wind farms in Australia, Chile, Fiji and the Philippines. As new projects come on line, the economics and profit become stronger. It is trading on a P/E of 16 and dividend yield of 1.4 per cent. There is no value here for the Chartist's Portfolio so we will not be investing.'

(i) What is a 'Chartist'?
(ii) What makes his or her share purchasing decisions distinctive?

Rupert's shareholders lose out

No shareholder in their right mind would vote in favour of the News Corp move to the US as it now stands.

The bovver boys in News Corp's papers are aggressively spruiking the deal, as you'd expect, with statements like: 'News Corp has to shift to the US. No half sane, half-intelligent person believes otherwise.'

In fact, looked at objectively, the reverse is true: the possession of half a set of marbles and half a brain would prompt anyone to vote against it.

That's because for shareholders other than the Murdochs it is a proposal with only vague and illusory benefits but very concrete problems.

The heart of the deal — and possibly its main purpose — is that shareholders are being asked to hand greater control of the company to Rupert Murdoch and his heirs and give up their protection against him, selling control without a full takeover.

In return they get the possibility of a re-rating of the share price in America. As we shall see, that re-rating is smoke.

Once it becomes a Delaware corporation, News Corp will no longer be subject to the Australian takeover threshold, which says that once someone buys more than 20 per cent of a company they have to make a bid for the rest at the same price. That is one of the pillars of Australian corporate law and is designed to ensure all shareholders participate when a premium is paid for control.

It means Murdoch, with just under 30 per cent, could sell out without triggering a full takeover, or he could buy more to cement his control, or he could combine with 9 per cent shareholder John Malone — also without triggering the takeover threshold.

By the way, the otherwise loose Delaware company law prohibits 'business combinations' between a company and an 'interested stockholder' (someone who owns more than 15 per cent) for a period of three years.

However, the information memorandum reveals that News Corp US 'has elected not to be governed by this Delaware statute'. Just like that. Apparently they have optional laws in Delaware — amazing. News Corp would not have put that in for nothing.

Another important change is that News Corp US will be free to issue shares with differential voting rights. In 1993 Murdoch proposed an issue of what were called 'super voting shares' — that is, shares that would have more than one vote per share until they were sold, enhancing Murdoch's control.

To Murdoch's fury, the ASX knocked the idea back and News Corp issued non-voting preference shares instead. News Corp US would be able to revive the super voting shares idea and, if the ASX cut up rough, it could become a 'foreign exempt listed company' in Australia, which means it would not be bound by local listing rules while remaining listed here.

The third important change is that directors can only be removed for 'cause', which is defined as moral turpitude, misuse of assets, fraud, embezzlement and so on. Not incompetence or because control of the company has changed hands. Nor can shareholders call an extraordinary general meeting to remove directors.

This means that if someone got control of the company or shareholders became unhappy with directors, none could be removed until they had to stand for re-election after three years. No company would make a hostile takeover offer for News Corp under those circumstances.

The net effect of all this is that takeovers are blocked; Murdoch can sell for a premium without triggering a bid or he can buy more without bidding himself; and he has a blank cheque to issue whatever differential voting shares he wants in order to enhance his control.

In return, shareholders' stock is apparently going to be worth more, although the independent expert, Grant Samuel, is not exactly sure: 'The evidence is ambiguous but, on balance, it is Grant Samuel's view that, in time, there should be some positive effect on value from the change of domicile.'

Rubbish. As of yesterday, US media stocks were trading, on average at 10.1 times 2004 EBITDA (roughly, cash flow). The average in Australia is 11.8 times. In other words, the average media company stockmarket rating in the US is 20 per cent lower than Australia.

Moreover, its profit will fall under US accounting rules. The information memorandum officially shows that earnings per share will fall from 59c to 55c, or 7 per cent, under US rules. But that's after non-recurring items. Normal profit, according to News Corp's own figures, will fall from 59c to 48c — a drop of nearly 20 per cent.

So that's a 20 per cent lower multiple on 20 per cent lower earnings. Investors probably won't take too much notice of all this: they have been valuing News Corp according to American multiples and accounting standards for years already, so it's unlikely that the share price will drop 40 per cent.

But what absolutely won't happen is an increase in News Corp's share price.

It's one thing to get screwed. Rape is a different matter altogether.

Source: This article appeared in *The Sydney Morning Herald*.

1. What do you perceive to be the main motivation for the move of News Corporation to the United States?
2. Why was registration in Delaware, rather than another US state, so important to Rupert Murdoch?
3. Research the differences between ordinary shares and preference shares, including the various kinds of preference shares. What rights and obligations attach to the different shares?
4. Why does Murdoch favour the issue of nonvoting shares?
5. What is 'corporate governance'? Why is corporate governance so important when ownership of a corporation is separated from control of that corporation?

6. What are the implications of the move to Delaware for the corporate governance of News Corporation?
7. Why are takeovers regulated? How do the Murdoch proposals for News Corporation effectively prevent takeover offers?
8. Why do you think Grant Samuel believed that the move would have positive effects on the value of News Corporation?
9. Debate whether you would buy News Corporation shares after the move. What strategy would you employ if you bought them?
10. Why are News Corporation's financial statements less favourable under US accounting rules, compared with those reported under Australian rules? *Hint:* Read Norton, JE 1997, 'The News Corporation', *The Journal of Accounting Case Research*, vol. 4, no. 1, pp. 132–43.

case**study** 9.2

Women take more risks when investing: survey

Women are greater risk takers than men when investing, new research revealed this week. Women are also more exposed to growth assets than men, especially as they head towards retirement.

The research appears to debunk previous findings showing women are more conservative investors than men because they tend to have fewer overall assets.

Conducted by BT Financial Group and the University of Western Australia (UWA), the research, which spans more than three decades and draws on BT funds data for 850 000 investors, also confirmed that men trade more frequently than women.

The study, presented at a University of NSW superannuation conference this week, collected demographic details, including age, gender, postcode; whether the investor is a direct investor or is advised; 6.8 million daily transactions data; and more than 1.8 billion investor-fund-days (that is, the number of days investors were invested).

Supporting the so-called life-cycle theory of investing, the research shows those in their 20s are exposed to growth assets 60 per cent of the time. But by the time they hit their 60s, this had fallen to 46 per cent.

Being wealthy does affect the riskiness of assets invested in, with 'growth assets' (stocks and listed property style investments) accounting for 61 per cent of investor fund days of the wealthiest investors, but only 50 per cent of those in the lowest tax quartile.

'The research also found that conservative, wealthy, older and male investors were more likely to sell their winning investments and hold their losers than other types of investors,' says Tracey McNaughton, an economist at BT and a co-author of the survey. 'As expected, the research did confirm that men trade more frequently than women, wealthier investors have a greater proportion of their portfolio in riskier assets and, supporting the "life-cycle theory of investing", older investors are more likely to move from risky to safe assets as they age.'

This research also appears to demonstrate that managed fund investors act more rationally than their direct equity (those investing in shares) counterparts when choosing to sell investments, she says.

'Previous research on the same subject shows that direct share investors found gains are realised 50 per cent more often than losses. That is, investors tend to sell winners and hold on to their losers.'

And yes, this does affect investment performance. The same research found unsold losers returned 5 per cent in the next year while sold winners returned a further 11.6 per cent.

McNaughton says a well-documented finding in behavioural finance is the tendency for investors to hold on to losing investments while selling winners. The BT/UWA research found this bias was not displayed by Australian managed fund investors.

'And, in stark contrast to one of the most robust findings in behavioural finance, the research found that overall female investors have a greater appetite for risk than men,' McNaughton says.

A need to catch up later in life might be one reason, she says.

Source: This article appeared in *The Weekend Australian*.

---

1. What do you understand by a 'life cycle theory of investing'? Does the research by BT and UWA support this theory?
2. How does being wealthy affect investment choices?
3. What other factors seem to affect investment activity?
4. How do the findings by BT and UWA differ from the findings and predictions of behavioural finance?
5. In what ways do the BT and UWA findings confirm or deny the predictions and findings of behavioural finance?

Recommended readings

Dechow, P & Skinner, D 2000, 'Earnings management: reconciling the views of accounting academics, practitioners and regulators', *Accounting Horizons*, vol. 14, no. 2, pp. 235–50.

Healy, PM & Wahlen, JM 1999, 'A review of the earnings management literature and its implications for standard setting', *Accounting Horizons*, vol. 13, pp. 365–84.

Schipper, K 1989, 'Commentary on earnings management', *Accounting Horizons*, vol. 3, pp. 91–102.

References

Ball, R & Brown, P 1968, 'An empirical evaluation of accounting income numbers', *Journal of Accounting Research*, vol. 16, no. 2, pp. 159–78.

Barth, ME, Beaver & Landsman, WR 2001, 'The relevance of the value relevance literature for financial accounting standard setting: another view', *Journal of Accounting and Economics*, vol. 31, nos 1–3, pp. 77–104.

Beaver, W, Lambert, R & Morse, D 1980, 'The information content of security prices', *Journal of Accounting and Economics*, vol. 3, no. 1, pp. 3–8.

Booth, G, Kallunki, J & Martikainen, T 1996, 'Post announcement drift and income smoothing: Finnish evidence', *Journal of Business Finance and Accounting*, vol. 23, no. 8, pp. 1197–211.

Core, JE 2001, 'A review of the empirical disclosure literature: discussion', *Journal of Accounting and Economics*, vol. 31, nos 1–3, pp. 441–56.

Dechow, P & Skinner, D 2000, 'Earnings management: reconciling the views of accounting academics, practitioners and regulators', *Accounting Horizons*, vol. 14, no. 2, pp. 235–50.

Dumontier, P & Raffournier, B 2002, 'Accounting and capital markets: a survey of the European evidence', *The European Accounting Review*, vol. 11, no. 1, pp. 119–51.

Fields, TD, Lys, TZ & Vincent, L 2001, 'Empirical research on accounting choice', *Journal of Accounting and Economics*, vol. 31, nos 1–3, pp. 255–307.

Fuller, RJ 1996, 'Amos Tversky, behavioral finance, and nobel prizes', *Financial Analysts Journal*, vol. 52, no. 4, pp. 7–8.

Gilson, RJ & Kraakman, R 2003, 'The mechanisms of market efficiency twenty years later: the hindsight bias', *Journal of Corporation Law*, vol. 28, no. 4, pp. 715–42.

Healy, PM & Palepu, KG 2001, 'Information asymmetry, corporate disclosure, and the capital markets: a review of the empirical disclosure literature', *Journal of Accounting and Economics*, vol. 31, no. 4, pp. 405–40.

Healy, PM & Wahlen, JM 1999, 'A review of the earnings management literature and its implications for standard setting', *Accounting Horizons*, vol. 13, no. 4, pp. 365–84.

Holthausen, RW & Watts, RL 2001, 'The relevance of the value-relevance literature for financial accounting standard setting', *Journal of Accounting and Economics*, vol. 31, nos 1–3, pp. 3–75.

Kothari, SP 2001, 'Capital markets research in accounting', *Journal of Accounting and Economics*, vol. 31, nos 1–3, pp. 105–231.

Olsen, RA 1998, 'Behavioral finance and its implications for stock-price volatility', *Financial Analysts Journal*, vol. 54, no. 2, pp. 10–18.

Ritter, JR 2003, 'Behavioral finance', *Pacific-Basin Finance Journal*, vol. 11, no. 4, pp. 429–37.

Schipper, K 1989, 'Commentary on earnings management', *Accounting Horizons*, vol. 3, no. 4, pp. 91–102.

10 SMALL AND MEDIUM-SIZED ENTITIES

After reading this chapter, you should be able to:

- outline the variety of definitions of a small and medium-sized entity (SME)

- understand characteristics of the SME sector

- outline the Australian perspective on financial reporting for SMEs

- describe the development of international accounting standards for SMEs

- evaluate some of the specific differences in standards for SMEs.

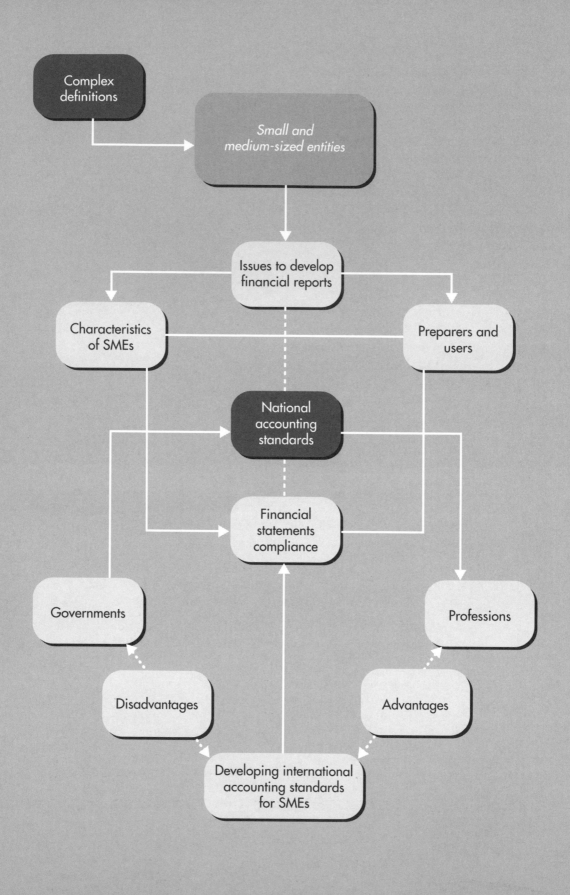

Introduction

SMEs have considerable economic significance both nationally and internationally, and governments around the world have recognised the importance of their success. However, the nature of these enterprises, their financial position and their organisational structure require creative strategies on behalf of regulatory bodies. In most countries, this means that SMEs are subject to reporting regimes with differing degrees of exemptions.

In terms of size, legal structure, financial position and function, the SME sector is extremely diverse, and one of the first hurdles facing regulatory bodies is practically characterising and defining the sector. This involves understanding what is meant by the term 'SME', a task complicated by the existence of broad regional and national jurisdictions. This chapter explores these differences, and further describes the sector by analysing information on SMEs' economic contribution, considering regional and industry variations that impacts on the sector, and exploring the lack of suitable government policies for Australian SMEs.

The development of financial reporting requirements for SMEs is explored from a global perspective. The objectives of the International Accounting Standards Board (IASB) in developing global reporting standards are covered. Arguments for and against international convergence for SMEs are discussed, and some International Financial Reporting Standards (IFRSs) for SMEs are explained.

Defining an SME

SMEs are both the most common and diverse types of business across the world. To develop effective management, support and supervision frameworks, regulatory bodies need to recognise and understand their defining characteristics. However, the continuing lack of consensus on this task demonstrates the difficulties involved in defining SMEs and separating them from larger businesses (Casson 1999).

small and medium-sized entities (SMEs): Entities that do not have public accountability and do not publish general purpose financial statements for external users

In the past, many have agreed that size alone is an inadequate definition of an SME. Consequently, there is a variety of different measures used to define a small business, including the number of employees, sales revenues or turnover, total assets and net worth (Bolton Committee 1971; Department of Employment, Workplace Relations and Small Business 1999).

Despite this diversity, researchers generally acknowledge that an effective definition of small business should possess three basic features (Osteryoung, Constand & Nast 1992):
- It must be measurable and observable.
- It must be congruent with the perceptions of financial markets.
- It must be meaningful.

Many jurisdictions around the world have developed their own definitions of the term SME for a board range of purposes, including prescribing financial reporting obligations. The content of these definitions can be either qualitative or quantitative, although a combination of the two is used in most cases.

Qualitative definitions

Researchers' definitions fall into two broad groups. The first of these, outlined by the Bolton Committee (1971, p. 1), is a definition based on economic or qualitative characteristics. These generally relate to organisational structure, market influence and management features, such as:

- A small firm is one that has a relatively small share of its market. Because of this, SMEs generally do not have the capacity to influence market prices or product quantities.
- An SME is managed by its owners or part-owners in a personalised way, and not through the medium of a formalised management structure. This generally means that SMEs lack a formal segregation of duties or decision making, which can manifest as a lack of objectivity.
- An SME is also independent, in the sense that it does not form part of a larger enterprise and the owner–managers should be free from outside control in taking their principal decisions. This ultimate authority, however, can also be a potential source of subjective decision making.

Qualitative definitions can help us to understand the nature of SMEs, and the roles of the owner and other interested parties in the running of the business. However, they are based on subjective and incomparable observations, which are extremely difficult to measure and analyse. As an alternative, then, researchers have developed empirical dimensions that are easily measured and compared.

Quantitative definitions

Quantitative or 'statistical' definitions are based on definable and measurable variables that can be used to characterise the SME sector. Some common measures include:

- number of employees
- total assets
- sales turnover.

Quantitative definitions have several advantages over qualitative evaluations, in that they allow broad descriptions to be made of and comparisons to be made among measures (Bolton 1971). These may include:

- quantification of the small firm sector as a whole, and its contribution to economic aggregates such as gross domestic product (GDP), employment, exports and innovation
- assessment of changes to this economic contribution over time
- comparisons between the contributions of small firms in one country with those of other nations.

Quantitative measures are by no means infallible, however, and have their own inherent definition difficulties. For example, using the total number assets of an entity to differentiate between small and large is no longer effective when one business purchases its assets while the other elects to lease.

Similarly, while the *Corporations Act 2001* specifies the differentiating criteria of revenue, assets and employees to define small entities but these are not conceptually based but arbitrary (Faux & Wise 2005). Other measures may well determine the difference between small and large entities just as effectively. The measures used by in the Corporations Act also have little correlation with other measures used by the Australian Bureau of Statistics (ABS), the Australian Taxation Office (ATO) and other business councils. The multiplicity of measures serves only to confuse matters.

Size

Research studies commonly use three measures for enterprise size: sales revenues, total employment and total assets. These measures are not perfect; for example, total employment can include full-time staff, part-time staff or part-time and casuals. Agriculture numbers are generally not included in SME data because temporary labour is often used and hard to quantify. Table 10.1 shows the importance of the agriculture sector for small-business statistics and highlights the difficulties in using size measures in a definition.

TABLE 10.1 Share of self-employed in total employment by sector in European countries (%)

	Agriculture	Industry	Services
EU15	68.7	11.9	15.2
Belgium	83.4	10.2	17.2
Denmark	51.3	6.8	8.2
Germany	47.0	6.6	11.6
Greece	96.0	31.2	33.2
Spain	64.1	16.7	22.1
France	71.5	9.9	10.1
Ireland	80.5	11.8	14.1
Italy	64.5	18.2	30.1
Luxembourg	71.0	5.0	8.3
Netherlands	62.2	7.3	10.6
Austria	86.9	4.8	10.2
Portugal	85.6	17.0	21.0
Finland	75.3	9.7	10.7
Sweden	68.3	10.2	9.6
United Kingdom	55.5	14.4	11.4

Source: EUROSTAT 1998, cited in Rosti, L & Chelli, F 2005, 'Gender discrimination, entrepreneurial talent and self-employment', *Small Business Economics*, vol. 24, no. 2.

Size measures are often used to compare the SME sector with other business sectors across the globe. For example, a survey in the UK in 2003 estimated 4.0 million private sector business enterprises, excluding government and non-profit organisations, across the country. Almost all of these enterprises (99.2 per cent) were small (0 to 49 employees). Only 26 000 (0.6 per cent) were medium-sized (50 to 249 employees) and 6000 (0.2 per cent) were large (250 or more employees) (SBS 2004).

Legal structure

Definitions of SMEs sometimes contain divisions related to legal structure. Empirical studies have generally categorised businesses according to the legal structure that is, rather than that when the business began. Choice of legal structure has implications for the business, ranging from how it is taxed to the legal liability of its owner–manager and meeting financial reporting requirements. In Australia, the legal structure of an SME can take any of the following forms:

- sole trader
- partnership
- proprietary company.

Forty-five per cent of all small businesses in Australia are companies, with the balance operating as sole traders and partnerships. Larger businesses that employ more than 100 are mainly (83 per cent) companies (Small Business Research Program 1997, p. 8).

In the UK, businesses with no employees (sole proprietorships) number more than 2.52 million. This legal structure comprises only the self-employed owner–manager, and companies comprising only an employee–director.

International definitions

Given the lack of consensus on measurement, it is not surprising to find a similar diversity in the definitions used by different nations to categorise an SME.

The European Commission (EU 2005) adopted a new definition of micro, small and medium-sized enterprises. The new definition was shaped by two rounds of extensive public consultation and includes both a staff threshold and either a balance-sheet total or turnover total threshold. Medium-sized enterprises are defined between 50 and 249 employees, with a turnover threshold of €50 million or a balance-sheet total of €43 million or more. Small enterprises have between ten and 49 employees, and the turnover and balance-sheet thresholds are both €10 million. Micro-enterprises have fewer than ten staff, with a threshold of €2 million for both the turnover and the balance-sheet total (EU 2005).

In the United States, fewer than 20 employees is considered very small, between 20 and 99 employees small, and fewer than 500 medium. Definitions in the United States often vary depending on the industry being considered, with small retailers defined as having fewer than 100 employees, while car manufacturing enterprises may have as many as 500 employees and still be considered small, relative to the average for that industry.

In Australia, the ABS states that a small business is defined as a business employing fewer than 20 people. Categories of small businesses include the following (ABS 2000).

- *nonemploying businesses:* sole proprietorships and partnerships without employees
- *micro-businesses:* businesses employing fewer than five people, including non-employing businesses
- *other small businesses:* businesses employing five or more but fewer than 20 people.

Australia, as do most other nations, excludes agricultural businesses from these quantitative criteria because many agricultural enterprises can run large-scale operations with relatively few permanent workers, relying on seasonal and itinerant workers to satisfy short-term labour needs. Small businesses are also described as having the following management or organisational characteristics:

- independent ownership and operations
- close control by owners–managers who also contribute most of if not all the operating capital
- principal decision making by the owners–managers.

Statistics are also presented for the following categories:

- *medium businesses:* businesses employing 20 or more but fewer than 200 people
- *large businesses:* businesses employing 200 or more people.

The International Accounting Standards Committee Foundation (IASCF 2006, p. 6) states that a clear definition of the class of entity for which the IFRS for SMEs is applicable is essential so that:

- the board can decide on the standards that are appropriate for that class of entity
- national regulatory authorities, standard setters and reporting entities and their auditors can be informed of the intended scope of applicability of IFRSs for SMEs.

The In Focus vignette that follows highlights the importance of consistent definitions in the tax industry.

 ## Regulatory burden on small business

The Institute [of Chartered Accountants in Australia] is vigorously continuing its efforts to reduce the regulatory burden on small business. Most recently, a submission was made to the board of taxation in response to its scoping study of small business tax compliance costs.

[I]ncluded in the package sent to the board was an Institute-commissioned report, released publicly in February, focusing on ways to improve access to the various tax concessions currently available to small businesses in the income tax, FBT and GST legislation.

At the moment, various definitions for a small business are scattered through the tax legislation, having emerged over time with the introduction of an array of provisions applying specifically to small business. This has increased complexity and the cost of compliance for small business.

Key recommendations of the report, prepared by professor Neil Warren and colleagues from Atax, University of New South Wales, are that simplification of the definition of a small business could be achieved by consolidating all the relevant access definitions in a single area, with turnover being the main criterion for access to small business concessions. Policy may dictate deviations from this, but the starting point should be the basic definition used to the maximum extent possible.

The report can be downloaded from the Institute's website at www.icaa. org.au.

Source: This article appeared in *Charter*.

National jurisdictions

In developing a definition for SMEs for the *International financial reporting standards for small and medium-sized entities* (IFRSs for SMEs), the IASCF (2006) acknowledges that many jurisdictions around the world have developed their own definition for the term SME for many purposes, including financial reporting obligations. These definitions can include quantified criteria based on revenue, assets, employees or other factors, and are often directed at financial statements produced for the owner-manager or tax reporting or for some other nonsecurities regulatory filing purposes. Furthermore, each jurisdiction has its own tax laws and because the objectives of general purpose financial reports are different from the objectives of reporting taxable income, the standards developed in the IFRSs for SMEs are unlikely to result in statements that comply with all the measurements required for tax laws and regulations. The standard recommends jurisdictions consider this added 'dual reporting burden' on SMEs and structure their tax reporting requirements accordingly.

■ Characteristics of the SME sector

The last three decades has seen a growing realisation of the importance of the SME sector. Despite variations in industry basis and political governance, the SME sector makes a significant contribution to most world economies. SMEs provide a substantial employment base, greater competition, stimulus for innovation and a wider distribution of economic wealth and opportunities. Furthermore, SMEs can provide a range of specialised products and services that larger corporations do not. Certain characteristics of small businesses, including their organisational and financial structure, put them in an ideal position to perform functions not feasible in larger businesses, the government or the not-for-profit sector.

Economic significance

SMEs make an important contribution to most national economies by providing employment opportunities, a vehicle for innovation and entrepreneurial activity, export possibilities and an outlet for highly specialised products and services. In addition, small businesses connect with larger firms in many ways, providing competition and decentralisation but also support services, component parts, retail distribution and specialist consultancy resources. Some of these small firms will go on to provide the next generation of larger firms — as successful SMEs expand they grow into large enterprises, eventually replacing older firms that have ceased to exist for whatever reason. Given these possibilities, it is not surprising that their contribution is assessed regularly. Because they provide considerable employment opportunities, relative employment is often used as an indicator of economic contribution, but contribution to GDP, wage expenditure and total profit can also provide insight into the involvement of SMEs in the greater economy.

For example, Asia–Pacific Economic Cooperation (APEC) forum studies suggest that SMEs represent more than 95 per cent of all businesses across the 21 Pacific-Rim nations under the APEC banner. These businesses account for more than 60 per cent of employment in the region, and contribute between 30 per cent and 60 per cent of GDP and up to 35 per cent of exports in APEC economies (www. apecsec.org.sg). World Bank data, however, shows that the importance of the SME sector can vary widely between regional economies. In parts of central Europe and the Caucasus, such as Ukraine and Azerbaijan, SMEs employ less than 5 per cent of the formal workforce, while in Chile and Greece, this figure can reach more than 80 per cent. Similarly, in Luxembourg, SMEs contribute more than 75 per cent of total GDP, whereas in Belarus, this figure is less than 10 per cent (Ayyagari, Beck & Demirguc-Kunt 2003).

Even within countries, these figures can vary across different industries. In the UK, SMEs account for 58 per cent of employment and 51 per cent of national turnover. These figures fluctuate across industries, however, with SMEs accounting for 93 per cent of employment in the agriculture, fishing and forestry sectors but only 14 per cent in the financial intermediation industry (www.sbs.gov.uk/smes).

SMEs play an important role even in the largest national economy in the world: the United States, with a GDP for 2005 of US$12.41 trillion. Businesses with fewer than 250 employees account for 99 per cent of all businesses in the United States, and are responsible for 48 per cent of private sector employment. Small firms generate between 60 per cent and 80 per cent of new jobs annually, and make up 97 per cent of exporting entities, accounting for more than 28 per cent of export value (www.sba.gov).

In Australia, small business also accounts for a disproportionate share of new jobs (53 per cent of new jobs, out of an employee share of 47 per cent) and in 2001 employed almost 3.6 million people (ABS 2002a). Figure 10.1 illustrates the position of all businesses in Australia in 2000–01.

FIGURE 10.1 Structure of Australian business 2000–01

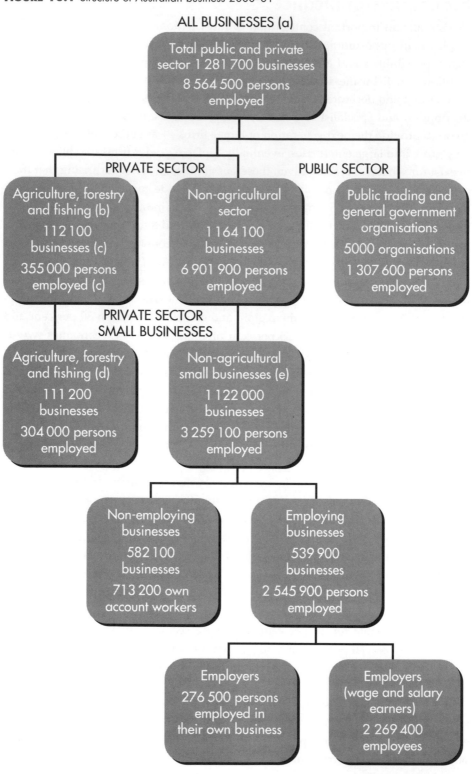

ALL BUSINESSES (a)

Total public and private sector 1 281 700 businesses
8 564 500 persons employed

PRIVATE SECTOR

Agriculture, forestry and fishing (b)
112 100 businesses (c)
355 000 persons employed (c)

Non-agricultural sector
1 164 100 businesses
6 901 900 persons employed

PUBLIC SECTOR

Public trading and general government organisations
5000 organisations
1 307 600 persons employed

PRIVATE SECTOR SMALL BUSINESSES

Agriculture, forestry and fishing (d)
111 200 businesses
304 000 persons employed

Non-agricultural small businesses (e)
1 122 000 businesses
3 259 100 persons employed

Non-employing businesses
582 100 businesses
713 200 own account workers

Employing businesses
539 900 businesses
2 545 900 persons employed

Employers
276 500 persons employed in their own business

Employers (wage and salary earners)
2 269 400 employees

FIGURE 10.1 *continued*

(a) Generally, the number of businesses (management units) and persons employed have been obtained by averaging the estimates for the middle months of each quarter for the 2000–2001 financial year.

(b) Includes ANZSIC Subdivisions 01 – Agriculture, 02 – Services to Agriculture; Hunting and Trapping, 03 – Forestry and Logging and 04 – Commercial fishing.

(c) Estimates are based on data from two different sources; ANZSIC Subdivision 01 data are drawn from the 1999–2000 Agricultural Finance survey, while ANZSIC Subdivisions 02, 03 and 04 estimates are drawn from the 1999–2000 Economic Activity Survey. Exclude management units in ANZSIC Subdivision with an estimated annual value of agricultural operations (EVAO) of less than $22 500. Employment estimates exclude unpaid family helpers.

(d) Agricultural small businesses include those management units coded to ANZSIC Subdivision 01 with an EVAO of more than $22 500 but less than $400 000, and those management units coded to ANZSIC Subdivisions 02, 03 and 04 which employ less than 20 persons.

(e) Small business (except in agriculture) are defined as those management units which employ less than 20 persons.

Source: Australian Bureau of Statistics 2002b, 'Small business in Australia 2001'.

In 2004, it was estimated that there were 3.010 million enterprises with fewer than 200 employees in Australia, with more than 70 per cent (just more than two million) self-employed (ABS 2004a).

Importantly, small businesses contribute to the economic prosperity of Australia by:

- providing jobs growth, generating more than half the jobs growth in the past decade (ABS 2000, 2002b)
- operating in regional areas, with nearly 40 per cent of small businesses based outside major urban centres (ABS 2004b)
- creating opportunities for women, who operate about one-third of small enterprises (www.abs.gov.au).

As in other economies around the world, the number of small businesses varies across industries, with particularly high numbers in property and business services, construction and retail, as shown in figure 10.2.

Industry characteristics

SMEs generally fall into two broad categories: those in traditional or established industries, and those in new industries. The traditional SMEs could be viewed as micro-enterprises: family enterprises, income substitution entities and self-employed operators. In most cases, these businesses start small and stay small. The past decade, however, has seen a growth in new industries, including in the technology and finance areas. These new industries have initiated a new generation of SMEs that have tended to grow more rapidly in size than traditional ones, fuelled by innovation and entrepreneurship.

Recent Australian examples of this shift include businesses such as Boost Juice Bars and Wotif.com Holdings. They both started as very small businesses and have become leaders in their respective fields. The first Boost juice bar opened in Adelaide in 2000, and since then the company has expanded through a successful franchise operation into major shopping centres and retail precincts across Australia and New Zealand. Wotif.com has taken advantage of the opportunities offered by the Internet to create a live online database and booking service for last-minute accommodation bookings. From a single office in Brisbane, the company now operates in more than 20 countries, covering Australia, New Zealand, Asia, America and Europe. In both cases, these small businesses began with an innovative idea to fill a gap in the existing market, allowing accelerated growth and unprecedented visibility for an SME.

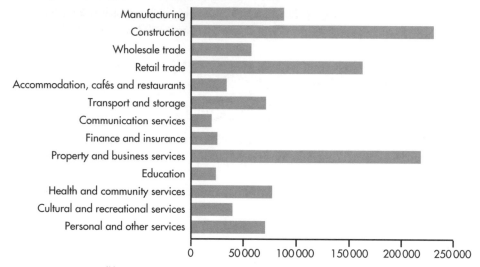

FIGURE 10.2 Small-business representation by industry

Learning tips
Do you know...

10.1 *Definitions of an SME can vary from country to country. Definitions can give qualitative or quantitative measurements, or a combination of both.*

10.2 *In Australia a small business can be five or more employees, whereas in the UK and United States, small would be regarded as 20 employees.*

10.3 *In most jurisdictions, SMEs make up a significant sector of the economic community and contribute to employment opportunities, regional business growth, entrepreneurial and innovation activity and support for women and the underprivileged.*

10.4 *SMEs are usually between 1 and 200 employees, and are usually unlisted on a stock market. The vast majority are sole traders and small partnerships, including family businesses.*

An Australian perspective

The nature of the SME sector means that the owner–manager often takes responsibility for personally preparing all the financial information for the company. In a larger enterprise, this may be undertaken by a dedicated department of highly trained professionals. The SME business owner, however, may not have the expertise needed to prepare complicated financial reports, and even if this work is outsourced (e.g. to a professional accountant or bookkeeper), the owner still needs an understanding of the process to make informed decisions.

Similarly, because of the legal structure of most SMEs, which operate under a sole trader or partnership structure, the business owner–managers carry more personal responsibility and risk for the financial health of the business. Often, much of the capital invested in the business is derived from their own personal finances, including home equity, and owners are personally responsible for the debts and liabilities of the firm.

Financial control is therefore very important to small-business owner–managers, and regulations and accounting standards need to reflect the less than expert knowledge most of them have. Accounting reporting requirements and statutory regulations need to be simplified and easily completed, without being a complicated and time-consuming process.

In Australia, the legal requirements for financial reporting by SMEs have come principally from two federal government sources. The first was the ATO, empowered by legislation to collect income, capital gains and other forms of taxation information. The second was the Australian Securities and Investments Commission (ASIC), through company, investment and financial securities regulations. Historically, therefore, the financial reporting demands on SMEs in Australia were administered through the regular record keeping and business operations reporting required by these two bodies.

For SMEs that were not incorporated, these requirements included an annual income taxation return, from which income tax payable was calculated. A statistical summary relating to the business operations and the financial report position was also included as an appendix to the annual return. Sole traders and partnerships lodged individual returns, which were merely a record for the business.

If the business were incorporated, however, ASIC requirements demanded an annual return be lodged with it, which then became a public record of the operations of the business.

In 2000, with the introduction of the goods and service tax (GST) requirements, financial reporting for SMEs became more regulated. Once again, the diversity and characteristic independence of SMEs has made the search for a suitable reporting standard difficult. The type and size of small business revenues and expenses can vary as significantly as the businesses themselves. The current reporting requirements, and their subsequent role in SMEs, determine the use of financial information and possible improvements within current reporting requirements. The following In Focus vignette discusses these issues.

The critical start date for Australia's adoption of international accounting standards, 1 January 2005, has come and gone and, for some time now, reporting entities have been grappling with the major issues involved. They have been preparing their transition balance sheets, reviewing their accounting policies and preparing firstly to disclose and then quantify the effects of the changeover to the Australian equivalents to International Financial Reporting Standards (AIFRS) in their 30 June 2005 balance sheets in accordance with the requirements of Australian Accounting Standards Board (AASB) 1047.

However many 'non-reporting' entities are only now starting to consider the impact of AIFRS as they move into their 30 June 2006 financial year — their first annual reporting period starting after 1 January 2005 and therefore their first year of reporting under the new standards.

This article summarises the main issues for non-reporting entities in relation to the applicability of the new standards through a series of frequently asked questions received by our technical enquiry service.

My client is a non-corporate non-reporting entity and we produce special purpose financial reports to satisfy its financial reporting obligations. Please explain the effect of the new 2005 international accounting standards on this type of entity.

The new 2005 standards come into force for annual reporting periods beginning on or after 1 January 2005. This means that they first apply to financial reports prepared for years ending 31 December 2005 if entities balance on 31 December or 30 June 2006 for entities that balance on 30 June. While most of the old AAS and AASB standards have been replaced with the revised AASBs1 being the Australian version of the international accounting standards, these new standards remain mandatorily applicable only to Corporations Act entities, non-corporate reporting entities and other entities producing general purpose financial statements.

The transition to AIFRS has not changed the reporting entity concept that underlies the Australian financial reporting framework. SAC 1 'Definition of the Reporting Entity' has not been replaced.

While the AIFRS definition of reporting entity (contained in AASB 3 Business Combinations) is not identical to that contained in SAC 1, its meaning is essentially the same. In addition paragraph 8 of the MSB's new Framework document (which replaces SAC's 3 and 4) also refers to SAC 1 for the definition of a reporting entity.

Therefore the applicability of the new 2005 accounting standards to non-corporate non-reporting entities producing special purpose financial reports remains unchanged.

Of course, the obligation remains firmly on members to ensure that the financial reports they are producing or auditing are in fact for 'non-reporting entities' (as defined in SAC 1) and clearly state to what extent accounting standards have or have not been applied (refer APS 1 paragraph 20).

The changeover to AIFRS is an ideal opportunity to review the nature of the financial reports being produced and to formally document why particular accounting policies and presentations best meet the needs of users, especially since what constitutes Australian Generally Accepted Accounting Practice (GAAP) is undergoing fundamental change.

Interestingly, such a review process is mandated for all Corporations Act entities through paragraphs 10 and 11 of AASB 108 (see below), which require them to 'consider' the effect of new accounting standards in their selection of accounting policies.

While compliance with AASB 108 is not mandated for non-corporate non-reporting entities, failure by the management of such entities, their accountants and their auditors to consider the impact of changes to our GMP introduced by AIFRS could result in their 2006 special purpose financial reports not meeting the needs of their users.

In 2003, the ICAA released a Business Practice Guide for Non Reporting Entities which is available on the ICAA website under technical resources: www.icaa.org.au.

It is currently being updated for the effect of the new international accounting standards and provides helpful guidance in the preparation of best practice financial reports for non-reporting entities.

... How do I handle initial adoption in a non-reporting entity?

The transition to the new standards requires the resolution of a range of issues that are applicable in the first annual report of a company adopting the new AIFRS standards. To assist in this process the AASB released AASB 1 'First time adoption of Australian equivalents of AIFRS'.

This standard requires entities to adopt AIFRS at the beginning of the first reporting period contained in its AIFRS compliant financial statements (i.e. 1 July 2004 for a 30 June 2006 year end). It requires entities to adjust comparatives and opening balances as necessary to ensure the financial statements presented are consistent and comparable. Reconciliations to their previously published financial statements are also required.

However, most importantly it contains various transitional exceptions and exemptions to assist in the transition process and ensure the costs of producing the new information do not outweigh the benefits.

AASB 1, however, only applies to reporting entities and is applicable only in their first annual report where they make an explicit and unreserved statement of compliance with AIFRS.

ASIC has recognised that this presents a problem for non-reporting entities preparing financial reports under Chapter 2M of the Corporations Act and has issued Class Order 05/639.

This class order allows non-reporting entities to take advantage of the same concessions to the measurement requirements of accounting standards granted to reporting entities by AASB 1 in the preparation of their reports using the new AIFRS standards, provided the non-reporting entity complies with all recognition and measurement requirements of the standards.

What effect is the IASB's SME reporting project likely to have on the Australian financial reporting environment?

The International Accounting Standards Board (IASB) is currently undertaking a project which is reviewing the applicability of international accounting standards to small and medium enterprises (SMEs) as there is no concept of 'reporting entity' internationally. The IASB has flagged the prospect of measurement and recognition modifications in its SME standard, and the ICAA is part of the wide constituency base that is working with the IASB on this project.

In the light of this project, the AASB discussed, at its July and September meetings, the application of accounting standards to non-reporting entities that are required to lodge accounts with ASIC.

The board agreed to address the issue and consider how best to deal with SMEs in the Australian context. Such a review will involve reconsideration of the concepts of reporting entity and general purpose financial reports.

Source: This article appeared in *Charter.*

Users of SME financial statements

Generally, the purpose of financial statement reporting for SMEs is different from that for larger corporations. SMEs often produce financial statements only for the use of the owner–manager, or for tax reporting or other nonsecurities regulatory filing purposes. In this instance, the statements produced take the form of special purpose, rather than general purpose financial statements. The rationale behind this difference involves the needs of end-users — those interested in the financial performance of an SME are likely to be less interested in the contents of a general purpose statement, and more interested in specific information, such as short-term cash flows, liquidity, balance-sheet strength and interest coverage, and in the historical trends of earnings and interest coverage.

You should see that if it is important to consider the skills of the preparers (often owners) of small-business financial information, it is equally important to consider the requirements of the final users of such information. The kind of information required by users of SME financial statements is likely to be very different from those of large corporations.

Even within the sector, there are significant differences between user groups of the smallest versus the larger SMEs. Some SMEs are unlikely to comply fully with all the measurements required for tax laws and regulations. Jurisdictions may be able to lessen the 'dual reporting' burden on SMEs by structuring tax reports as reconciliations from IFRSs for SMEs, or similar dual-purpose disclosures.

Statutory requirements

In Australia, different classes of enterprise operate under different reporting requirements. The Corporations Act imposes accounting and financial reporting requirements on an unlisted company according to size criteria. An unlisted company is classified as small if it satisfies at least two of the following tests:

- gross operating revenue of less than $10 million for the year
- gross assets of less than $5 million at the end of the year
- fewer than 50 employees at the end of the year.

The Corporations Act (s. 10.1) states that an unlisted company that does not satisfy at least two of these tests is classified as large. A large unlisted company must prepare annual financial reports and a directors' report, have the financial report audited and send both reports to shareholders (s. 10.3). For the remaining majority of unlisted companies in Australia, which are therefore classified as small under these tests, the act requires an annual financial report only under one of two further conditions:

- Shareholders controlling at least five per cent of the votes give the company the direction to do so.
- It is controlled by a foreign company (s. 10.3).

If obliged to report, the small company annual financial report must include a profit and loss statement, a balance sheet, a statement of cash flows and a directors' report (outlining the company's operations, dividends paid or recommended, options issued and so on) in accordance with applicable accounting standards.

◼ Developing international accounting standards for SMEs

The adoption of the new IFRSs by many countries, including Australia, New Zealand and particularly the members of the EU, has brought the question of suitable accounting standards for SMEs to the discussion table. In most cases, the purpose of these discussions has been to assess the need for exemptions from onerous reporting standards for SMEs, with a view to reducing the burden on nonexpert owner–managers and employees. Of particular concern are the dangers of a one-size-fits-all approach, considering the diversity of SMEs around the world. These issues include the potential differences in requirements for different industries, including manufacturing, services, agriculture and others such as traditional and cottage industries.

International convergence

Some of the dilemmas of nondifferential reporting include undue burdens and disproportionate costs, as well as a perceived lack of relevance of financial reports to the main user groups.

Differential reporting is the notion that there should be different forms of generally accepted accounting principles (GAAP) within the same regulatory framework. It aims to

> **differential reporting:** The notion that different categories of entities should be subject to different accounting and reporting rules

achieve comparability, reliability and the perception that statutory financial statements satisfy some information needs and provide some protection to stakeholders without access to inside information. To date, the costs and benefits of reporting by SMEs have been inconsistent even within the same regulatory framework.

SME reporting objectives, strategies and accountability relationships differ from those for larger entities, which operate with more public accountability. It may well be that the objectives and concepts underlying IFRSs may not be suitable for SMEs, and a different conceptual framework may be required.

Mandatory fallback versus management judgement

The IASCF recognises that the diversity of SMEs around the world creates problems for any set of international standards designed specifically for SMEs. In the cases, therefore, in which IASB Standards for SMEs did not deal with a particular problem, particularly related to accounting recognition or measurement, the IASCF proposes a consistent strategy for SMEs to follow. It is important that SMEs recognise that these approaches are designed to work in single instances only, and that IASB Standards for SMEs would be used for the remaining financial reporting disclosures made by the entity. To this end, the board has considered two different approaches. First, the mandatory fallback to IFRSs (the differential reporting approach), which would require the entity to look to the full IFRSs to address the particular issue only, with the remainder of the report structured according to the IASB Standards for SMEs. This is the approach currently advocated in Canada, where if an entity does not choose a particular option, the relevant SME accounting standard applies.

The second alternative would allow the entity to use its judgement to develop an appropriate policy to deal with that particular instance, using the full IFRSs and interpretations as a source of guidance. This strategy would involve stringent requirements for the quality of the policy developed and the information produced by its use. These requirements would be similar to those in IAS 8, in that the policy should result in information that is:

(i) consistent with the IASB *Framework*;
(ii) consistent with other IASB Standards for SMEs;
(iii) relevant to the economic decision-making needs of users; and
(iv) reliable, in that the financial statements:
  (a) represent faithfully the financial position, financial performance and cash flows of the entity;
  (b) reflect the economic substance of transactions, other events and conditions, and not merely the legal form;
  (c) are neutral, i.e. free from bias;
  (d) are prudent; and
  (e) are complete in all material respects (IASB 2004, p. 27).

This second approach is similar to that advocated in the UK, where SMEs are enjoined to prepare statements according to accepted practice, and to develop policies with regard for other accounting standards and interpretations as 'a means of establishing current practice' (IASB 2004, p. 28).

Supporters of the differential reporting approach advocate its consistency, arguing that SMEs are more likely to approach similar problems in the same way, allowing for greater comparability. It is also easier to ensure SME accounting policies are consistent the IASB *Framework*. For these reasons, the IASCF currently favours this 'mandatory feedback/differential reporting' approach. Advocates of the second 'management judgement' approach argue that mandatory fallback requires SMEs to be familiar with both the SME reporting standards, and the full IFRSs, and that this increases, rather than decreases the burden of regulatory requirements on SMEs. In effect, they argue, SMEs would be subjected to compliance with two sets of standards.

Australian position on differential reporting

In Australia, the Government's Financial Reporting Council (FRC) considered a paper on differential reporting in December 2006. Prepared by the Commonwealth treasury in consultation with the AASB, it examined a range of issues for future consideration. FRC members noted that relieving the compliance burden on SMEs was a high priority and the FRC is expected to issue further opinions on the policies of the IASCF when the IASB Standards for SMEs are more firmly established. It acknowledges that tackling this issue should increase support for IFRS implementation in Australia.

Generally, the arguments for **international convergence** of accounting and financial reporting standards include:

- increased comprehensiveness and comparability of cross-national financial reports
- increased international capital flows
- cost savings accruing to multinational corporations
- raised level of accounting
- provision of low cost financial accounting standards to countries with limited resources (Saudagaran & Diga 1997).

> **international convergence:** The adaptation of national accounting standards to align with the international accounting standards administered by the IASB

The relevance of these points to SMEs and any associated regulatory regime is still debatable, and arguments both for and against have legitimate concerns. These are examined further in the following sections.

Arguments for international convergence

The purpose of international convergence is that financial reporting practices among countries become the same, eliminating national differences in accounting methods for transactions and events. This allows the results of published financial information for SMEs operating in different countries to be comparable. This becomes important as the number of multinational corporations increase and investors take a more global approach to investing (Fisher 2003). It is also assumed that the development of an international standard for SMEs would facilitate the wider adoption of IFRSs, reducing the costs of implementation and further improving international comparability.

Arguments for convergence are particularly focused on the benefits of a standardised approach across jurisdictions, particularly within the EU, where common accounting standards are fundamental to the continued development of global securities markets (Fearnley & Hines 2006). It is also argued that the quality of international standards would represent a significant improvement on existing regulations in some jurisdictions, as well as reducing the cost of developing their own set of standards from scratch (Nobes & Parker 2002). Furthermore, SMEs have considerable significance in most national economies, and it makes good economic sense to support their growth and performance.

Arguments against international convergence

Arguments against international convergence for SMEs focus on the problems with a 'one size fits all' approach, particularly given the incredible diversity of SMEs around the world. In developing nations, particularly, international standards may be unnecessarily complex for the types of business and the industries in which SMEs operate. A lack of sufficiently qualified accounting professionals may also be a factor in these nations (Saudagaran & Diga 1997).

Supporters of this view also argue that industrialised countries have developed their own set of national financial reporting standards in response to local needs and priorities, and that every country has different business environments, legal systems, cultures, language and political environments, and accounting standards should cater for this individuality.

The costs of adoption or transition to international standards is also touted as an argument against their implementation, particularly for SMEs that operate on small margins. The first-time adoption of IFRSs for SMEs can be of huge cost and disruption, particularly if existing national standards are significantly different from the international approach.

Other views focus on more fundamental conceptual issues, particularly given the stated purpose of IFRSs to serve participants in capital markets. Consequently, IFRSs are primarily designed for companies that have securities traded on the capital markets (listed companies). Companies that do not have securities traded on capital markets (unlisted companies) and the needs of their stakeholders are therefore fundamentally divergent (Faux & Wise 2005). Very little is known about the needs of these stakeholders, and it cannot be assumed that their requirements would be the same as those using the statements of large, public-interest enterprises.

While the IASB Framework's objectives and concepts of financial reporting are focused on large entities with public accountability, in the SME environment, objectives, strategies and accountability relationships can change constantly, both within an entity and between entities. Therefore, the objectives and concepts underlying IFRSs may not be suitable for SMEs. A different conceptual framework may be required. The complexity of the IFRS accounting model would impose significant burdens on preparers of SME financial reports (Fearnley & Hines 2006). Differential reporting can involve disproportionate costs as well as a perceived lack of relevance of statutory accounts to the main user groups. Research shows the costs and benefits of reporting by SMEs is inconsistent even within the same regulatory framework (Evans & di Pietra 2006).

Finally, some countries object to a perceived lack of independence of the IASB, particularly given the program of convergence with US standards, and are critical of the inability of other countries to influence the international standard-setting process. This has developed into a debate about the governance and accountability of the IASB, which, it is argued, can make it quite difficult for SMEs from small countries to have a notable representative (Fearnley & Hines 2006).

IASB developments

Recognising the need for formal consideration of the topic, the IASB issued a discussion paper in June 2004 entitled *International accounting standards for small and medium-sized enterprises (SMEs)*. This contained the IASB's preliminary views on the issue of suitable accounting standards for SMEs, and called for comments from any interested parties.

The board's position was that full IFRSs were regarded as suitable for all entities because the objectives of general purpose financial statements are fundamentally the same for all entities. Paragraph 12 of the IASB Framework states:

> The objective of financial statements is to provide information about the financial position, performance and changes in financial position of an entity that is useful to a wide range of users in making economic decisions.

Given this definition, complete IFRSs should fulfil the needs of all users of financial statements, regardless of the size of the entity. However, the board acknowledged the number of complaints from SMEs citing onerous paperwork and information-gathering processes, and excessive costs in applying IFRSs to SMEs.

In developed countries in which IFRSs are used either by regulation or at the option of the entity, the primary adopters are entities whose securities are publicly traded. In many cases, standards are applied without rigorous enforcement or quality control, particularly since IFRSs are most often only legally required for listed or larger corporations.

In acknowledging these difficulties, the IASB called for public comment on two alternative options for tackling the SME issue. These were:
- The board should not develop special financial reporting standards for SMEs. Full IFRSs should be regarded as suitable for all entities including SMEs.
- The board should develop special financial reporting standards for SMEs ('IASB standards for SMEs'). The IASB should indicate the types of entities for which it believes those standards are suitable. National jurisdictions should determine whether all such entities as defined by the board, or only some, should be required or permitted to use the IASB standards for SMEs.

The IASB received 120 comment letters from professional bodies, governmental departments, auditing and accounting practitioners, academics and other entities from all over the world. From this discussion, different opinions on global accounting standards for SMEs emerged.

Disclosure

The public discussion surrounding this issue identified areas in which national financial reporting systems currently provide reduced and simplified presentations and disclosures for SMEs:

- Presentation differences may include condensation of financial statements, omission of one or more financial statements (e.g. the statement of comprehensive income), exemption from preparing consolidated financial statements and exemption from providing some supplemental reconciliations or schedules.
- Areas in which disclosure exemptions and simplifications may be necessary include management remuneration, fair values of assets and liabilities, provisions and contingencies, impairments, income taxes, depreciation, discontinued operations, inventory and cost of sales, asset disposals, business combinations and pensions and other employee benefits.

UK experience suggests that disclosure and presentation modifications alone do not necessarily result in lower levels of disclosure and cost savings. Therefore, the general opinion implies that the scope of standards for SMEs should extend beyond disclosure and presentation requirements, and should cover different measurement and recognition rules solely to suit SME needs. Presentation and disclosure exemptions are unlikely to achieve genuine cost savings. There may well be additional disclosures uniquely appropriate for SMEs to justify the recognition and measurement differences.

Learning tips
Do you know...

10.5 *One difficulty experienced in Australia concerns the definition of a 'non-reporting entity' used in the Australian standards but not differentiated in the IFRSs.*

10.6 *Statutory requirements in Australia are stated in the Corporations Act 2001, which contains a size test, along with conditions under which qualifying entities must produce financial reports.*

10.7 *In response to concerns expressed by many interested lobby groups, the IASB initiated a discussion and research project into the development of a specific set of international accounting standards for SMEs, which would aim to reduce the cost burden of financial reporting on small enterprises.*

Current position

In July 2006, an IASB update referred to a draft of an exposure draft of an IFRS for SMEs. The particular issue raised in the update centred on financial instruments and their classification, derecognition, hedge accounting and income taxes. The draft section would simplify the provisions of *IAS 39 Financial instruments: recognition and measurement for SMEs*. The proposals for these sections of the standard are discussed further in the next sections.

Classification of financial instruments

Financial instruments that meet specified criteria would be measured at cost or amortised cost, and all others at fair value through profit and loss. The available-for-sale and held-to-maturity classifications in IAS 39 would not be available. Financial instruments measured at cost or amortised cost would be:

> **financial instruments:** Contracts that give rise to a financial asset of one entity and a financial liability or equity instrument of another entity

- normal receivables, payables and similar debt instruments
- commitments to make or receive loans that cannot be settled in cash and, when settled, will result in delivery of a financial instrument that qualifies for recognition at cost or amortised cost
- equity instruments that are not publicly traded and whose fair value cannot otherwise be measured reliably, and options on these instruments.

The entity could choose to measure the first two types of instruments at fair value through profit or loss or at amortised cost.

Derecognition

The draft proposed a simple principle for derecognition, specifically that an entity would derecognise a financial asset only when:

- the contractual rights to the cash flows from the financial asset expire or are settled
- the entity transfers to another party all of the significant risks and rewards relating to the financial asset or
- the entity transfers physical control of the asset to another party and the transferee
  - has the practical ability to sell the asset in its entirety to an unrelated third party and
  - is able to exercise that ability unilaterally and without needing to impose additional restrictions on the transfer.

Hedge accounting

The draft focused on the types of hedging that an SME was likely to do, specifically hedges of:

- interest rate risk of a debt instrument measured at amortised cost
- the foreign currency exposure in a commitment or highly probable forecast transaction
- the foreign currency risk exposure in a net investment in a foreign operation.

The board will explore two approaches to hedge accounting simplification. One would impose strict conditions on the designation of a hedging relationship, with subsequent hedge effectiveness assumed without the need to measure ineffective-ness. The other would require periodic measurement of effectiveness but under less strict conditions than those in IAS 39.

Tentatively, the board has decided that an SME should have a choice of following either the requirements for financial instruments in the IFRS for SMEs or the require-ments of IAS 39 in accounting for all of its financial instruments.

Income taxes

An explanation of the timing differences approach to accounting for income taxes in IFRS for SMEs will consider:

- An SME would recognise current tax as a liability to the extent unpaid or as a receivable to the extent overpaid and recoverable.
- An SME would recognise deferred tax on all differences between income and expenses recognised in measuring taxable income and income and expenses recognised for accounting purposes either in measuring accounting profit and loss or directly in equity. Timing differences are differences that originate in one period and reverse in one or more subsequent periods (*IASB Update* 2006).

The proposals contained in the exposure draft are expected to attract a lot of attention from interested parties all over the world. Although the board expects changes will be made to the draft in response to the comments received by various segments of the community, it is hoped that a more robust standard will be avail-able for SMEs by the time the IASB embargo on new standards is lifted on 1 January 2009. The In Focus vignette that follows identifies some concerns expressed by the European Commissioner for Internal Market and Services Charlie McCreevy.

 infocus *IFRSs for SMEs in Europe*

In his address to the Business Leader Forum for the Association of Chartered Certified Accountants (ACCA) in Ireland, European Commissioner for Internal Market and Services Charlie McCreevy said any new accounting system for SMEs will have to be simple and practical to be adopted by the EU. His opinion mirrors that of other jurisdictions around the world.

SMEs Accounting

Let's turn to SMEs. Today, 99% of all EU enterprises are SMEs. There are 23 million SMEs in the EU, which employ 75 million workers. SMEs account for more than 80% of employment in some industrial sectors such as textiles. SMEs play a crucial role in our economy.

As the Commissioner responsible for Internal Market and Services, I want to make sure that SMEs can fully reap the benefits of the internal market — and of the global chances beyond it.

This is why I will start discussing what the future accounting requirements for these companies should be. At present, the accounting requirements for unlisted companies are contained in the Fourth and Seventh Company Law

Directives. The Directives already contain exemptions from some of the accounting requirements for SMEs. But we will need to review the existing rules to assess whether or not they are all relevant for SMEs' business needs today. These Directives have been in force for over 20 years, now they need modernisation.

Improving the quality of unlisted company financial statements should also help them to obtain finance. Unlisted companies generally use their local bank and not the capital markets. High quality financial statements won't of course guarantee a successful outcome of a loan application to a bank but can certainly aid a better informed decision on the part of the bank and help underpin confidence in the decision-making process.

I have repeatedly stated that accounting for SMEs must be simplified and that the level of accounting complexity should be aligned with the nature of the activities of these companies. We have to identify SME's real needs and those of their financiers and use them as the basis for deciding on their future accounting requirements.

I am aware that this is a politically sensitive issue — so there will be extensive consultation with all stakeholders. We will listen very carefully to the concerns of SMEs before taking any decision.

As you know, the IASB intends to publish an exposure draft on accounting standards for SMEs. There will be a period of consultation afterwards. I have made it clear already that only simple, easy-to-apply standards will be acceptable to us. Nobody should assume that the standards will be automatically transposed into European law.

Source: This material is extracted from a speech available at http://ec.europa.eu.

▪ Differences in standards for SMEs

Small companies have fewer resources available to deal with financial reporting compliance for securities than do large companies, so it seems that concerns regarding the financial reporting burden on SME are justified. The next sections discuss in detail several differences in standards for entities for which securities are not publicly traded.

IAS 14 Segment reporting

Some disclosures in IFRSs are intended primarily to meet the needs of users of financial statements of entities with public accountability. This is the basis for restricting the applicability of *IAS 14 Segment reporting*, which is considered to have a minor impact on reporting.

So an entity using IFRS for SMEs is not required to present **segment information**. However, one that elects to disclose segment information in accordance with *IAS 14 Segment reporting* must comply fully with its requirements.

segment information: Financial information related to the different types of products and services an entity produces and the different geographical areas in which it operates

IAS 27 Consolidated and separate financial statements

IAS 27 Consolidated and separate financial statements deals with **consolidated financial statements** and is considered to have a moderate impact on reporting.

---
consolidated financial statements:
The financial statements of a group of entities consisting of a parent and one or more subsidiaries

---

Those financial statements include all subsidiaries of the parent (IAS 27.12). In other words, financial statements present financial information about the group as a single economic entity (IAS 27.4, 27.22).

IAS 27 also deals with separate financial statements, which are those presented by:

- a parent, an investor in an associate or
- a venturer in a jointly controlled entity.

IAS 28 Investments in associates

IAS 28 Investments in associates defines an **associate** as an entity, including an unincorporated entity such as a partnership, over which the investor has significant influence and that is neither a subsidiary nor an interest in

---
associate: An entity, including an unincorporated entity such as a partnership, over which the investor has significant influence, which is neither a subsidiary nor an interest in a joint venture

---

joint venture. It also refers to the significant influence but not control or joint control (IAS 28.2). In other words, the investor holds between 20 per cent and 50 per cent of the voting power under normal circumstances. A venturer is a party to a joint venture who has joint control over the joint venture (50 per cent of the voting power).

The standard looks at the measurement after initial recognition: choosing an accounting of cost, equity or fair value. Disclosures for investments in associates should disclose separately the associates' share of profit or loss, the carrying amount of the investment and the entity's share in any discontinued operations of the associates (IAS 28.38). IAS 28.38 also states that an investor should classify investments in associates as noncurrent assets.

IAS 33 Earnings per share

IAS 33 Earnings per share requires presentation of earnings per share data only for entities whose ordinary shares or potential ordinary shares are publicly traded, and is regarded as having a moderate impact on reporting.

IAS 40 Investment property

IAS 40 Investment property states that an asset will be recognised as investment property only when:

a) it is probable that the future economic benefits that are associated with the investment property will flow to the entity; and
b) the cost of the investment property can be measured reliably (IAS 40.16).

Measurement at transaction cost will be included in the initial measurement (IAS 40.20). Measurement after recognition uses the fair value or cost model, and with disclosure treated differently under each method.

IAS 41 Specialised industries

IAS 41 Specialised industries covers the agriculture, extractive and insurance industries.

The key feature for the agriculture industry is that an entity using IFRS for SMEs should determine, for each of its biological assets, whether the fair value of the biological asset is readily determinable.

Entities in the extractive industries that use IFRS for SMEs and are engaged in exploration for, evaluation of or extraction of mineral resources should recognise exploration expenditure as an expense in the period in which it is incurred. In accounting for expenditure on the acquisition or development of tangible or intangible assets for use in extractive activities, the entity should apply the appropriate sections.

Insurance has a different requirement because an insurer holds assets in a fiduciary capacity for a broad group of outsiders, it has public accountability and, therefore, is not an SME as defined. The IFRS for SMEs is not intended for, and should not be used by, insurers.

Summary

Outline the variety of definitions for an SME.

- Definitions of an SME can vary from country to country. They can give qualitative or quantitative measurements, or a combination of both. In Australia, a small business can have five or more employees, whereas in the UK and United States, small would be regarded as 20 employees or more.

Understand characteristics of the SME sector.

- The SME sector is usually characterised by its economic significance, size, legal structure and, often, industry. In most jurisdictions, SMEs make up a significant sector of the economic community and contribute to employment opportunities, regional business growth, entrepreneurial and innovation activity and support for women and the underprivileged.
- SMEs usually have between 1 and 200 employees, and are usually unlisted on a stock market. The vast majority are sole traders and small partnerships, including family businesses.

Outline the Australian perspective on financial reporting for SMEs.

- Reporting requirements for SME in Australia in the past were administered by ASIC and the ATO. The introduction of the GST meant an increase in reporting regulations.
- One difficulty experienced concerns the definition of a 'non-reporting entity' used in the Australian standards but not differentiated in the IFRSs.
- Statutory requirements in Australia are stated in the *Corporations Act 2001*, which contains a size test, along with conditions under which qualifying entities must produce financial reports.

Describe the development of international accounting standards for SMEs.

- The transition to international convergence by jurisdictions in Australia and the EU raised arguments about the applicability of full IFRSs for SMEs.
- In response to concerns expressed by a large number of interested lobby groups, the IASB initiated a discussion and research project into the development of a specific set of international accounting standards for SMEs, which would aim to reduce the cost burden of financial reporting on small enterprises.
- Particular areas of difficulties specific to SMEs that are currently under discussion at the IASB include the classification of financial instruments, derecognition, hedge accounting and income tax.

Evaluate some of the specific differences in standards for SMEs.

- Specific standards in which requirements for SMEs differ from full IFRSs include segment reporting, consolidated financial statements, investment in associates, earnings per share, investment property and specialised industries.

Key terms

Review questions

10.1   What is the Australian SME definition?

10.2   Explain the economic differences between small businesses in Australia and those in the UK and United States.

10.3   Does the small-business sector make an economic contribution?

10.4   What are the differences between traditional and new industries?

10.5   How are SMEs defined?

10.6   What qualitative measures are used to define SMEs?

10.7   What quantitative measures are used to define SMEs?

10.8   Does the size of an SME matter in financial reporting?

10.9   How does the legal structure of an entity affect SME financial reporting?

10.10   Explain the global development of SME financial reporting.

10.11   What is the current status of SME financial reporting?

10.12   List the arguments for international convergence for SMEs.

10.13   What effect will the growth of an entity from a small to a large business have on its financial reporting requirements?

10.14   List the arguments against international convergence for SMEs.

10.15   Explain the structure of private sector small business in Australia, and outline its contribution to the Australian economy.

Application questions

10.16   Obtain definitions of 'small business' from the Internet.
   (a) Identify some of the key measurements used.
   (b) Are there any differences or similarities between definitions?
   (c) Do you believe you could judge the differences between small and medium-sized entities using these definitions?
   (d) How do these small-business definitions compare with those for large entities?

10.17   Obtain information from the Internet about SMEs within three different industries.
   (a) Identify any differences or similarities among industries.
   (b) Can you provide any reasons different industries might require specific regulations?

10.18   Many small businesses argue that financial reporting is too costly and onerous and should be restricted to the large 'top' companies.
   (a) Do you think that financial reporting should apply to smaller companies?

(b) Are there any particular financial reporting standards that can be used by both small and large enterprises?

(c) What would be the advantages of smaller companies complying with financial reporting standards?

(d) What might be the consequences for smaller companies of not complying with financial reporting standards?

10.19 A small-business operator asks you for some information on the measurement of investment properties. What information can you give that is relevant?

10.20 A friend wants to know what is meant by SME. Explain, with reference to several different countries.

10.21 What are some of the differences between international standards for small and large enterprises?

10.22 Where would you locate information on economic statistics pertaining to SMEs?

10.23 Give some statistics outlining the numbers of small businesses in Australia, the UK and the United States. How do different definitions affect the statistics? Are the statistics comparable?

10.24 (a) What reports must an owner–manager in Australia prepare?

(b) Does it depend on size?

(c) Does it depend on legal structure?

10.25 What measurement methods can be used for investors in associates?

10.26 How can investment properties be recorded?

10.27 What are the rules for first-time adoption of small-business financial reporting?

10.28 Identify the benefits for SMEs adopting small-business financial reporting.

10.29 Identify the costs for SMEs adopting small-businesses financial reporting.

10.30 Explore the position of small-business financial reporting in other Asian countries.

case**study**   **10.1**

Spotlight on AASB 140

AASB 140 is Australia's new standard on investment properties, applicable for financial years beginning on or after 1 January 2005. What makes it of particular interest is that Australia has never had a standard on investment properties before, although the international one is now several years old.

In the past, Australian GAAP on this subject was determined using AASB 1015, which applied to the initial recognition of investment property, and AASBs 1010 and 1041, which regulated the carrying value of non-current investment property.

In general this meant that investment property was initially recognised at its cost of acquisition and subsequently carried at either cost (subject to recoverable amount testing) or fair value in accordance with AASB 1041 and AASB 1010. Where investment properties were revalued in accordance with AASB 1041, revaluation increments were taken to a reserve. Depreciation was not required as investment properties were outside the scope of AASB 1021.

The IASB issued IAS 40 'Investment properties' in April 2000 and it has remained largely unchanged since that date. Its Australian equivalent AASB 140 was issued in July 2004 as part of the AASB's stable platform for adoption in 2005.

The new standard is applicable to all reporting entities for financial years beginning on or after 1 January 2005.

Definition

AASB 140 defines investment property as:

- property (land, buildings — or part of a building — or both) that is held by the owner or by the lessee under a finance lease to earn rentals or for capital appreciation or both.

It is contrasted with 'owner-occupied property', which is held for use in the production or supply of goods or services or for administrative purposes and with development sites held for sale in the ordinary course of business.

The holding of investment property for rental and/or capital appreciation means that it is generating cash flows that are largely independent of the other assets of the entity. This is unlike owner-occupied property, the cash flows of which are attributable not only to the property but to the other assets used in the process of production and supply. AASB 116 applies to owner-occupied property, AASB 140 to investment property.

Items that would generally be classified as investment property are:

- land held for capital appreciation (meaning land currently unused with no determined future);
- buildings owned and leased under operating leases (including vacant ones held to be leased);
- existing investment property that is being redeveloped for use as investment property.

Items that would not be generally classified as investment property are:

- property intended for sale in the ordinary course of business or in the process of construction or development for such sale (see AASB 102 Inventories);
- property being constructed or developed on behalf of third parties (see AASB 111 Construction Contracts);
- owner-occupied property (AASB 116)
- property that is being constructed or developed for future use as investment property. AASB 116 applies to such property until construction or development is complete and at that time the property becomes investment property and AASB 140 applies;
- property that is leased to another entity under a finance lease.

A property can be part investment and part owner-occupied, but only if the portions could be sold separately. Paragraph 14 notes that 'judgement is needed to determine whether a property qualifies as investment property'. The entity should develop criteria to govern the exercise of this judgement and these criteria must be disclosed where classification is difficult. Properties can be reclassified, for example as inventory or owner-occupied properties, if there is a change in use. This may involve recognising a gain or loss between accumulated costs and fair value in the P&L. Classification may also change within a consolidated group on consolidation if a subsidiary lets property to its parent. The property may be investment property in the books of the subsidiary but becomes owner-occupied on consolidation.

The standard excludes from its scope biological assets related to agriculture — covered by AASB 141 Agriculture — and mineral rights and reserves covered by AASB 6 Exploration for and Evaluation of Mineral Resources.

Recognition and measurement

Initial recognition and measurement

AASB 140 requires investment property to be initially recognised at the cost of acquisition using the standard asset recognition criteria of probable benefits and reliable measurement. Transaction costs should also be included. Recognition of additional costs for the property is based on the same recognition criteria and the standard provides guidance on distinguishing between what expenditure can be classified as part of the asset and what is repairs and maintenance.

Where leased property is classified as investment property its value at initial recognition must be calculated in accordance with AASB 117 — Leases.

Ongoing measurement

Subsequent to initial recognition, the standard allows a choice between two models of accounting in order to determine the ongoing carrying amount of the asset.

These choices are

* the 'fair value' model — where investment property is measured at fair value and changes in fair value are recognised in the profit and loss (P&L), not in reserves like AASB 1041;
* the 'cost' model — where investment property is carried at cost less depreciation and impairment charges as specified in AASB 116: Property Plant and Equipment. (AASB 140 does not exclude investment properties from the need to be depreciated like AASB 1021.)

The standard requires an entity to choose the method that is most appropriate and this method must be applied to all its investment property (unlike AASB 1041 which is based on class of assets). The only exception to this is if part of the investment property comprises a pool-backed scheme. In this case a choice may be made for this investment and also for the rest of the entity's investment property. The standard states that there is a rebuttable presumption that an individual investment property can be reliably measured at fair value and that it should only be measured at cost when there is clear evidence that reliable measurement is not possible on an ongoing basis. Where leased property is classified as investment property the standard specifies that fair value must be chosen.

The standard contains extensive commentary on assessing fair value issues relating to property.

De-recognition

De-recognition occurs when the property is disposed of, or when no further use can be made of it. When this happens, a gain or loss is recognised in the P&L, being the difference between the carrying value and any disposal proceeds. Where items are transferred between inventory or property plant and equipment and investment property as a result of changing usage, the standard specifies the values at which the transfer should be made — mostly fair value.

Disclosures

There are extensive disclosure requirements, including, inter alia:

- the choice of accounting model;
- criteria used to distinguish investment property when classification is difficult;
- methods and assumptions used in determining fair value, including reliance on an independent valuer;
- the treatment of leases classified as investment property;
- details of amounts in the P&L;
- a reconciliation of movements in investment property;
- additional details where an entity has had to apply AASB 116 instead of fair value;
- where the cost basis has been chosen, a similar asset reconciliation and information about depreciation rates;
- rental revenue;
- a reconciliation of movements in fair value of assets from year to year including net increments and decrements from fair value changes;
- direct operating expenses relating to investment property classified by whether they did or did not generate rental revenue.

In accordance with AASB 1, comparative information for these disclosures will also be required as if the standard had always been applied.

Special issues for not-for-profits (NFPs)

AASB 140 has an additional paragraph which, if used, will not allow NFPs to claim IFRS compliance. This paragraph (Aus 20.1) requires investment property given to an NFP, or acquired by it at no cost, to be valued at fair value at the date of acquisition.

The standard also states that property held by NFPs to meet service delivery objectives, rather than to earn rental or for capital appreciation, does not meet the definition of investment property and should be accounted for under AASB 116.

Special issues for public sector

AASB 140 is not consistent with its international public sector equivalent IPSAS 16. The main areas of difference are that IPSAS 16 does not permit a property interest held by a lessee under an operating lease to be classified as investment property; it requires the measurement model chosen to be used for all investment property; and only excludes forests and similar regenerative assets from its scope (AASB 140 excludes all biological assets covered by AASB 141 Agriculture).

Conclusion

The new standard on investment properties will be a welcome addition to Australian GAAP providing a more complete set of guidance on these types of transactions.

Source: This article appeared in *Charter*.

1. What is the standard about?
2. Explain the recognition and measurement of the standard.
3. What are the issues for not-for-profit entities?
4. How will this standard affect SMEs?
5. What are the disclosure requirements for investment properties?

casestudy   10.2

Smaller businesses rev up for IFRS

Before the implementation of IFRSs in Australia, *Australian CPA* magazine produced a case study designed to outline some of the possible issues growing SMEs would need to be aware of during the transition, highlighting particular reporting requirements that might affect SMEs looking for accelerated growth through acquisition. The case study, involving a company called Growing Pains Pty Ltd, is summarised in the following.

For SMEs, the owner's ability to fund the enterprise is often a limiting factor in the growth of a successful business. Eventually, external funding, either debt or private equity, is necessary to provide the increased cash flow and finance to achieve further growth. Companies in this position can choose to grow organically, from internal resources, or to grow through the acquisition of other proven and compatible businesses. Acquisition can provide a measure of certainty for banks, private equity firms and other potential investors, which may shy away from otherwise unproven business plans.

SMEs looking to external investors to fund this growth need to consider how they communicate their expected requirements and forecasts to their potential funding providers. The implementation of IFRSs in Australia means that SMEs may need to consider changes to the way they report their own financial status. Although IFRSs are not legally required for SMEs, businesses should be aware of the requirements of larger fund providers, and the information they are likely to judge as important in their decision to participate in growth funding of the business.

Growing Pains

Growing Pains Pty Ltd (GP) is an import, manufacture and distribution business looking to accelerate its growth interstate and internationally. The company has identified a possible acquisition target with established success in the markets, which will provide the required revenue growth. Management has also identified this as an opportunity to streamline and consolidate existing processes, and expects to restructure sales and administration structures. This will involve significant upfront costs, but impressive ongoing profit growth is expected. The company approaches two firms requesting funding: VC Ltd for private equity funding and Big Bank Ltd for traditional debt funding. Both funding firms request standards of annually audited financial reports, but they differ in the information required for their analysis of the financial status of GP. Their funding strategies reflect their interests:

> VC is simply interested in revenue and profit growth. Part of its funding is convertible redeemable preferred shares with a noncumulative 8 per cent dividend, whereas the rest is ordinary shares. The preference shares have no fixed term and are redeemable only at GP's option. They convert at VC's option after three years based on the value of the company's shares determined in accordance with an independent valuation (if unlisted) or the listed share price…

> Big Bank is simply interested in liquidity. Profit is important, but annual cash flows and balance sheet strength are key. Consequently, the terms of the borrowing include debt covenants focused on EBITDA (earnings before interest, taxes, depreciation and amortisation), debt to asset and equity ratios, and working capital ratios.

The company will be required to produce general purpose financial reports. Although GP's management has submitted budgets and forecasts to both funding providers, the company will need to know how these numbers will be affected by the transition to IFRSs. Some potential issues may be encountered under the following standards:

- **AASB 1 First-time adoption and AASB 3 Business Combinations.** GP made the acquisition in April 2004. Although the basis for the restructuring plan was in place, it was not formalised until July 2004. Because the acquisition was made before the implementation of IFRSs in January 2005, GP will have to decide whether to apply the business combinations exemption under AASB1, or retrospectively restate the acquisition under AASB 3. Retrospective application would require the identification and valuation of intangible assets (customer relationships, brand names and so on), which would decrease the value of the company's goodwill (which is not amortised under AASB3). If GP, as the acquirer, recognised any restructuring provision, it would have to be expensed. This would not be the case under pre-IFRS standards, in which acquiree provisions increase the value of goodwill; therefore applying the exemption under AASB1, and maintaining the current, pre-IFRS acquisition accounting, would be advantageous.
- **AASB 132 Presentation and disclosure of financial instruments.** Management made an initial judgement to classify the redeemable preference shares as equity in the budgeted balance sheet. However, under AASB 132, this instrument would be classified as debt because potentially GP has a responsibility to provide an

unpredictable number of its own shares to reconcile the instrument if necessary. This could significantly affect liquidity and debt to equity ratios covered by the debt covenants.

- **AASB 101 Presentation of financial statements.** Supposing in several years time GP approaches the bank (and auditors) to waive a breach of the debt covenant before accounts sign-off, and allow it to remain classified as non-current. Under pre-IFRS standards this was possible as long as the breach was waived before completion of the financial report. Under AASB 101, however, this breach needs to be rectified pre-balance date; otherwise the relevant liability will require full current classification. The resulting serious working capital deficiency published in the accounts may cause concern to current and potential clients and suppliers.
- **AASB 120 Accounting for government grants.** GP is eligible for government grants as a start-up (early-stage) company. Previously, these grants were recorded as income despite relating to expenditures over a two-year period. Under AASB 120, however, grants awarded to 'for-profit' entities need to be recognised over the periods corresponding to the related costs. Any grants relating to future periods will be reclassified as deferred revenue, which will directly affect the balance sheet.

Source: Information from an article that appeared in *Australian CPA*.

---

1. Explain why first-time adoption allows GP several options of accounting procedures during the acquisition.
2. What provision of AASB 132 means that financial instruments may be classified differently from pre-IFRS requirements?
3. What requirement under AASB 101 can affect the way breaches of the debt covenant are classified?
4. Investigate the requirements for the reporting of government grants for not-for-profit entities.
5. Investigate what state and federal government grants might be available for a company like GP.

Recommended readings

International Accounting Standards Committee Foundation (IASCF) 2006, *International financial reporting standard for small and medium-sized entities (staff draft of proposed exposure draft*, August, pp. 1–236.

Jeffrey, SZ & Dale, LF 2006, 'GAAP requirements for nonpublic companies', *The CPA Journal*, vol. 76, no. 5, p. 40.

John, WG 2006, 'Section 404 for small caps', *Journal of Accountancy*, vol. 201, no. 3, p. 67.

Kathic, C & Hemant, D 2005, 'Recurring cycle of Australian corporate reforms: "a never ending story"', *Journal of American Academy of Business*, vol. 7, no. 2, p. 156.

Matthew, AC 2005, 'Top 5 SOX best practices for small companies', *Strategic Finance*, vol. 87, no. 4, p. 42.

References

Australian Bureau of Statistics (ABS) 2000, 'Small business in Australia, 1999', www.abs.gov.au.

—— 2002a, 'Australia business operations and industry performance, 2000–2001', www.abs.gov.au.

—— 2002b, 'Small business in Australia, 2001', www.abs.gov.au.

—— 2004a, 'Business register: counts of businesses', www.abs.gov.au.

—— 2004b, 'Experimental estimates, regional business statistics, Australia, 1995/96 – 2000/01', www.abs.gov.au.

Ayyagari, M, Beck, T & Demirguc-Kunt, A 2003, 'Small and medium enterprises across the globe: a new database', World Bank Policy Research Paper 3127, www.econ.worldbank.org.

Bolton Committee 1971, *Report of the committee of inquiry on small firms*, Her Majesty's Stationery Office, London.

Casson, M 1999, 'Entrepreneurship and the theory of the firm', in Acs, ZJ, Carlsson, B & Karlsson, C (eds), *Entrepreneurship, small and medium-sized enterprises and the macroeconomy*, pp. 45–78, Cambridge University Press, Cambridge, UK.

Department of Employment Workplace Relations and Small Business 1999, *Annual review of small business*, AGPS, Canberra.

European Union (EU) 2005, small business definition at http://europa.eu.

Evans, L & di Pietra, R 2006, 'Preliminary views on accounting standards for small and medium-sized entities', EAA financial reporting standards committee discussion paper.

Faux, J & Wise, V 2005, 'Financial reporting policy in a dynamic environment', *International Review of Business Research Papers*, vol. 1, no. 2, pp. 1–9.

Fearnley, S & Hines, T 2006 'Rules are a big problem for small companies', *Financial Times*, 19 January, p. 12.

Fisher, C 2003, 'A guide to international standard setting', *Chartered Accountants Journal of New Zealand*, vol. 82, no. 6, pp. 26–9.

International Accounting Standards Board (IASB) 2004, *Preliminary views on accounting standards for small and medium-sized entities*, June, pp. 1–44.

IASB Update 2006, 'Accounting standards for small and medium-sized entities: board decisions on International Financial Reporting Standards'.

International Accounting Standards Committee Foundation (IASCF) 2006, 'International Financial Reporting Standard for small and medium-sized entities staff draft of proposed exposure draft', August, pp. 1–236.

Nobes, C & Parker, R 2002, *Comparative international accounting*, 7th edn, Pearson Education.

Osteryoung, JS, Constand, RL & Nast, D 1992, 'Financial ratios in large public and small private firms', *Journal of Small Business Management*, vol. 30, no. 3, p. 35.

Small Business Research Program 1997, *A portrait of Australian business: results of the 1995 business longitudinal survey*, AGPS, Canberra.

Small Business Service, UK Department of Trade and Industry (SBS) 2004, www.sbs.gov.uk.

Saudagaran, SM & Diga, JG 1997, 'Financial reporting in emerging capital markets: characteristics and policy issues', *Accounting Horizons*, vol. 11, no. 2, pp. 41–64.

Wise, V & Faux, J 2005, 'Small enterprises and convergence with international financial reporting standards', *Small Enterprise Research*, vol. 13, iss. 1, pp. 81–91.

11 PROFESSIONAL RESPONSIBILITY

LEARNING OBJECTIVES

After reading this chapter, you should be able to:

- describe an accountant's professional responsibility and the rules of professional and ethical conduct
- evaluate taxation standards and aspects of professional conduct for tax agents
- evaluate quality control in the public practice
- evaluate quality control for financial reporting and compilation
- evaluate quality control requirements for special purpose financial reports
- identify new areas of professional responsibility.

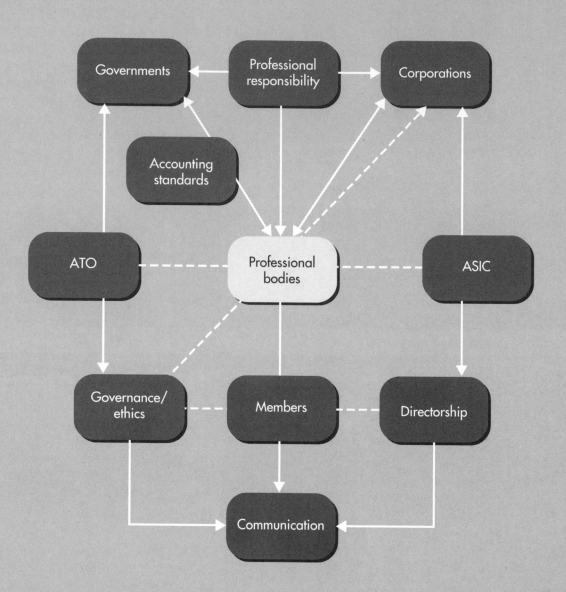

Introduction

The community expects the accountant to follow an ideal code of professionalism. In practice, this requires compliance with a variety of professional standards and laws. These include the Australian accounting standards and, in particular, *APES 110 Code of ethics for professional accountants*. An accountant must also have a working knowledge of the International Financial Reporting Standards, the Australian Securities and Investments Commission requirements, which enforce and regulate company and financial services laws, plus the rules and regulations of the Australian Securities Exchange (ASX), contract law and other relevant legislation. Furthermore, an accountant must have a thorough understanding of all Australian taxation laws, including those on the goods and services tax and superannuation, and state laws such as payroll tax and land tax, and should also comply with the *Financial Services Reform Act 2001* (FSRA). Finally, as a professional, the accountant should comply with the *Privacy Amendment (Private Sector) Act 2000* and the existing statutory, common law and industry code requirements.

Compliance with these regulations is necessary to ensure that a true, fair and objective view is provided by the accountant. In addition, an accountant is required to exercise reasonable professional care in the performance of his or her work and ensure, at all times, that the information that he or she provides is presented in a way that best supports their client's interests. The accountant must further ensure that his or her conduct does not conflict with the duties and loyalties he or she owes to the community because, along with the aforementioned professional responsibilities, the accountant also has particular obligations to the public (including clients) and others who rely on accountants to help the systematic and proficient functioning of commerce.

This chapter discusses accounting as a profession and identifies its major characteristics, and the code of ethics for professional accountants. It analyses aspects of professional responsibility for accountants acting as tax agents, and also looks at quality control requirements and procedures. Characteristics of quality control in public practice, including the provision of both general and special purpose financial reports, and new areas such as social responsibility reporting, acting as a financial adviser and new antimoney-laundering legislation are also examined.

The profession and the accountant's professional responsibility

Community perception can have high expectations of a **profession** and professionals are both obliged and legally required to follow an ideal code of behaviour. The skills and expertise of a professional are perceived to be supported by a body of knowledge based on theory and education. This body of knowledge provides a solid base

profession: A disciplined group of individuals who are accepted by the public as possessing special knowledge and skills in a widely recognised body of learning derived from research, education and training from which clients may require professionals to define and solve their problems (Leung, Dellaportas & Cooper 2005).

It follows that this advice should be based on both formal training and experience, so the maintenance and continuation of professional skills is of great concern. Accountants have a basic professional duty to remain continually informed of all changes in their particular area of expertise, and to be aware of significant changes in related areas. As a professional, they must ensure that their knowledge is up to date, keeping abreast of all new developments. The culture of this profession and others generally requires the investment of time into continuing professional education. This is considered necessary in most professional groups and the behaviour of new associates is often both formally and unofficially guided in this direction (Leung, Dellaportas & Cooper 2005).

Accounting as a profession

Accountants are able to provide information to their clients by drawing on a body of knowledge and practice that develops over time. Accountants' training and experience equip them with the skills to provide professional advice, in the form of an unbiased opinion made in accordance with current knowledge (Brown 2002). All types of clients rely on them, as professionals, to solve their financial problems.

The service ideal of accountants is to ensure the efficient and organised operation of business and government entities so that resources are successfully distributed to key projects. Accountants aspire to provide relevant and reliable information to guide decision making, and should consider and analyse issues that might arise in practice. Finally, the expectations of society are reflected in their social status as perceived by some sectors of the community.

The accountant's professional responsibility

An accountant has the **professional responsibility** to balance the various duties owed to the different users of accounting information, such as the public, clients

professional responsibility: Ability to balance the various duties owed by accountants to the users of accounting information, such as the public, clients and the profession

and the profession itself. It is the obligation of accountants to be able clearly to communicate and protect the central virtues of professionalism. Professional liability is relevant when any of those duties are neglected, and this may result in official complaints leading to disciplinary or legal action by a client or another user of information such as the Australian Securities and Investments Commission.

'The problem in trying too hard to look after the client's interest is that many complaints and actions against practitioners arise because the opposite has occurred' (Shirvington 2001).

CPA Australia, the Institute of Chartered Accountants and other accounting bodies demand high standards of professional conduct. These bodies have previously supervised the code of conduct of professional accountants, and applied disciplinary penalties when they perceived a breach of acceptable behaviour. However, from 1 July 2006, accountants must comply with the requirements of *APES 110 Code of ethics for professional accountants*. This compliance is mandatory.

To appreciate the meaning of professional responsibility and its applicability to accountants truly, the next section examines the current mandatory code of ethical and professional conduct in detail.

Professional conduct and ethics

Each day, accountants must fulfil many varied roles and maintain many different relationships. On any given occasion, they are required to interact with supervisors, other employees and their individual clients to perform their duties.

Accountants are individuals whose behaviour is greatly influenced by aspects of their personality and family background (Warnock 2006). These characteristics, in combination with various other attributes, greatly increase accountants' ability to fulfil their role as professionals. Other qualities include knowledge, experience, professional education, ethical evaluations, personal judgement and cultural background.

It is important to understand the ethical role of accountants in society. Accountants must conduct themselves in a manner consistent with the good reputation of their profession and avoid any conduct that may damage its reputation. However, for accountants to be considered ethical and professional, they are not only required to comply with the written rules of conduct. **Ethics** are also a matter of attitude and origins. Consequently, ethical behaviour is difficult to define: what may be ethical for one person may not be ethical for another, having regard to differences in their background, culture and philosophy.

> **ethics:** Compliance with the written rules of conduct of a profession, together with adherence to individual attitudes and origins, taking into account differences in background, culture and philosophy

In general, all professions prefer that their members behave ethically. To ensure the maintenance of ethics in practice, accountants must be objective. They should offer their advice free from the influence of others and without consideration of possible financial gain. Ethical behaviour is key to the professional judgement involved in each and every decision accountants make.

Accountants have an essential duty to work within the parameters set by professional norms and standards. *APES 110 Code of ethics for professional accountants*, issued by the Accounting Professional and Ethics Standards Board (APESB), clearly articulates the high standards of ethical conduct and professional practice that must be followed by accountants, practice entities and affiliates. However, accountants are expected to comply not only with the letter of this code but also with its spirit or underlying intention. Compliance with the APES 110, as previously stated, is mandatory; under section 100.8, any violation of the provisions of APES is corrected promptly and the necessary safeguards applied.

Accountants must observe the five fundamental principles of the accounting profession as set out in section 100.4. Accountants' professional responsibility is to ensure strict compliance with these principles and any departure from them can have severe consequences. The five principles are analysed as follows:

- *Integrity* refers to the accountant's obligation to be frank and honest. The principle of integrity also 'implies fair dealing and truthfulness' (APESB 2006a, s. 110.1).
- *Objectivity* imposes an 'obligation to accountants not to compromise their professional or business judgement because of bias, conflict of interest or the undue influence of others' (s. 120.1).
- *Professional competence and due care* impose the obligation 'to maintain professional knowledge and skill' and 'to act diligently in accordance to the applicable technical and professional standards' (s. 130.1).
- *Confidentiality* imposes restrictions on the disclosure of confidential information without client authority and the use of this information for the accountant's personal advantage or the advantage of third parties (s. 140.1).
- *Professional behaviour* 'imposes an obligation to comply with relevant laws and avoid any action or omission that may have a negative effect on the profession' (s. 150.1).

Compliance with these principles may be jeopardised by certain circumstances, which consequently may threaten independence (s. 100.10). 'The concept of independence is fundamental to compliance with the principles of integrity and objectivity' (s. 290). Accountants must be independent at all times because the characteristics of objectivity and integrity are essential to their role as advisers. To maintain this ideal state, accountants must ensure that they are not influenced by any financial considerations or placed in a position of conflict. Clearly, the advice provided by an accountant will only have value when the professional is free (actual independence) and appears to be free (perceived independence) from any interest that is contrary to integrity and objectivity.

Professional independence may be preserved when particular measures are taken to avoid the influence of third parties on accountants, and when external support from legislation and from professional bodies is provided. Professional bodies play an important role in the preservation of independence in that they can provide education and practical advice on ethics to accountants. The existence of professional sanctions can also help the professional (Brown 2002).

The following are some situations in which the independence of the accountant may be compromised:

- self-interest threats or familiarity, which arises because of financial or other interests with a close relationship or a family member
- intimidation threats, in which the accountant is pressured into acting subjectively
- self-review threats, which may take place when a previous judgement requires re-evaluation.

Safeguards available to the accounting professional may include education, training and continuing professional development and experience requirements for entry into the accounting practice, corporate governance regulations, professional standards, professional or regulatory monitoring and disciplinary procedures and external reviews by third parties (APESB 2006a, s. 100.12).

Rules of ethical conduct

'A distinguishing mark of the accountancy profession is the responsibility to act in the public interest' (APESB 2006a, s100.1). This may include, but is not limited, to 'clients, credit providers, governments, employers, employees, investors, the business and financial community, and others who rely on the objectivity and integrity of [accountants] to assist in maintaining the orderly functioning of commerce' (s. 100.1.1). It is important to remember, therefore, that accountants, while required to address the needs of individual clients or employers, also owe a duty to the community at large and must ensure compliance with the law. This responsibility identifies an inherent conflict of interest that may be encountered by accountants in their daily work.

The fundamental principles of ethical compliance that are defined in the code of ethics for professional accountants are discussed further in the following.

Integrity (s. 110)

In their professional and business relationships, accountants must be frank, honest and sincere. The meaning of the terms 'frank, honest and sincere' may be influenced directly by the accountant's professional judgement with further reference to individual interpretation according to culture and ethos.

Objectivity (s. 120)

Accountants must be fair and should not compromise their independence by allowing prejudice, conflict of interest, bias or undue influence from others to factor into their decisions.

Objectivity and disinterestedness are fundamental characteristics of the accounting profession. Accountants must perform their duties and roles with these essential qualities in mind. To serve the interests of their clients, the public and the profession, accountants must remain, at all times, unbiased and impartial. Neutrality is of vital importance. True independence requires high standards of honesty and objectivity, as well as the strength of character needed to maintain those standards regardless of the pressures that may be brought to bear on them by third parties (Brown 2002).

Professional competence and due care (s. 130)

Accountants must perform professional services with due care, competence and diligence. Accountants have a continuing duty to maintain their professional body of knowledge and their requisite level of skill. This ensures that they are able to offer their clients or employers a competent professional service that incorporates current developments in practice, legislation and techniques.

The competence and proficiency of accountants are integral to maintaining the esteem of the profession. The level of competence is defined by the accounting societies, which indicate to practitioners the level of education and professional development required. This may serve to protect accountants from litigation by establishing what is necessary to be competent and perform their function with due care.

Confidentiality (s. 140)

Accountants must not disclose any information or details about a client to a third party without having received specific authority to do so or without there being a legal or professional duty to disclose them. Confidential information must not be used to personal advantage or to the advantage of third parties. Confidentiality should also be kept in a social gathering and when there is an extensive friendship with a business associate or close family member.

Professional behaviour (s. 150)

This principle requires accountants to conform to applicable laws and regulations and avoid any action or omission that may bring discredit to their profession. Accountants should not overstate their ability to provide certain services and should inform clients of their precise qualifications and experience. Accountants should not make unfavourable reference or unsupported comparisons with the work of others.

Learning tips
Do you know...

11.1 *Accountants abide by an ideal code of behaviour, detailed in APES 110 Code of ethics for professional accountants. Aspects covered in the code include integrity, objectivity, professional competence and due care, confidentiality and professional behaviour.*

11.2 *Accountants have a responsibility to the broader public interest, not only to individual clients or employers.*

11.3 *Failure to comply with professional conduct regulations may result in disciplinary action.*

■ Taxation standards and aspects of professional conduct

To provide a thorough analysis of professional responsibility, it is useful to identify particular areas accountants should be aware of in which specific issues may arise with unique responsibility pressures.

One of the more common areas in which an accountant's professional responsibility may be tested is with respect to taxation standards. Clients commonly request that accountants minimise their taxation liability, which may lead to involvement in tax minimisation schemes. Accountants should be wary of these requests and should ensure they do not facilitate this behaviour by adhering to the letter of taxation law. Taxation standards are fundamental principles governing the professional responsibilities that accountants must implement in their tax practice. The overriding objective of a professional tax adviser is to ensure that the client is made aware of the relevant legislation and how it affects client's affairs so that the client can make informed decisions with respect to the client's current and future tax planning (Tax Agent's Board n.d.).

Taxation engagements

When planning to accept a taxation engagement, the accountant should discuss and agree on certain procedures with prospective clients before and during the engagement, such as:

- Correspondence is to be directed to the tax agent, as the adviser, so any issues may be dealt with promptly and efficiently.
- The client must undertake a detailed review of the return to understand and appreciate the work completed by the preparer.
- The client must agree to the deduction of accounting fees from the refund cheque, which will be deposited into the accountant's trust account.

The tax agent should carefully review and assess the previous years' tax return details to ensure they fully understand the client and their relationship with the Australian Taxation Office (ATO). These details may be retrieved from the ATO tax agent portal. Therefore, to appreciate the taxation position of the client, satisfactorily the accountant may wish to make enquiries relating to outstanding taxation commitments and lodgement disputes, taxation arrangements, prior year losses, audit activities with ATO and any franking credits, revenue or capital losses. These investigations allow the accountant to provide a more comprehensive and accurate assessment and service (CPA & ICAA 1997).

Furthermore, accountants and their associates should follow a technical approach to taxation engagements, to minimise the risk of noncompliance and subsequent litigation. All work completed should be documented, dated and, if necessary, signed by the client. For this reason, checklists should be prepared as a control function. They may include an itemised list of work completed and the details of any client query with response information and documentation. The accountant might also include on the file the details of any objections, ruling requests, amendment requests and other similar work, and any advice on taxation and other legislation such as land taxes, fringe benefits tax or stamp duties. It is imperative to invest in comprehensive computer software that will allow the accountant to keep these necessary records.

The review copy should include file notes, indicative marks of cross referencing, schedules, summary calculations, financial reports, reconciliations of income taxes and a summary of any contentious issues. The review should be executed by an experienced supervisor.

The preparation of notices of objection, ruling requests and amendment requests is another area in which caution should be exercised by the accountant. This is a specialised and technical area, in which most general practitioners lack an adequate level of expertise. Therefore, to avoid the misinterpretation of certain ATO rulings and amendment requirements, the following four steps should be taken.

1. consultation with a specialist adviser: specialist accountant or solicitor

2. maintenance of a register to include disputed or amended assessments and the relevant dates of issue
3. reviewing the notices regularly to ensure compliance with statutory time limits. All important dates should be detailed in the office calendar to minimise the risk of failing to meet the deadlines.
4. the compilation of all relevant and necessary documentation necessary.

Insofar as written advice on taxation legislation is concerned, due care and professional vigilance are particularly important. If a dispute arises with a client or if the ATO wishes to perform a financial audit, the accountant may take certain measures or precautions, such as sending letters to notify all parties, documenting the existence of any private or public rulings, the commissioner's interpretations and the reliance on an accountant's network of peers or the relevant professional body (CPA & ICAA 1997).

Verbal advice should generally be avoided; however, should it be necessary, it is reasonable for the accountant to keep a record of the advice and the facts upon which that advice was based. This file should be dated and contain the signature of all parties. This record keeping is essential because clients may misinterpret or forget the advice given or may simply hear what they wish to rather than what has been advised. If an expert opinion is required, such as the opinion of a barrister, valuer or foreign specialist, this must also be documented and specifically identified as expert advice (CPA & ICAA 1997).

Incorrect or misleading information

An accountant should ensure that returns do not contain any incorrect or misleading information or omit material information. An accountant who is responsible for preparing a taxpayer's returns cannot rely solely on the accuracy of the information provided by the taxpayer. Depending on the circumstances and where there are grounds for doing so, the accountant may be required to enquire into and check the information provided. Failure to do this may render the accountant liable for damage to the taxpayer resulting from the lodgement of incorrect returns.

If a return is suspected to contain a mistake, misstatement or omission, the accountant should immediately seek further instructions on the accuracy of the information. If it is confirmed that the return is incorrect, it should be rectified to minimise any penalties. If the client refuses to consent to the necessary correction or corrections, the accountant must decline to act in any capacity with respect to the return.

If the client has filed returns or submissions in previous years that contain incorrect or misleading information, or omit material information, the accountant must recommend to the client that he or she makes appropriate disclosures to the ATO. Alternatively, the accountant must obtain authority from the client to make disclosure on his or her behalf (CPA & ICAA 1997).

Estimates

In most circumstances, an accountant or tax agent should avoid the use of estimates when preparing returns or submissions, unless the exact data is inaccessible. When estimates are necessary, the accountant is responsible for making sure the estimates used are reasonable in the particular situation (CPA & ICAA 1997).

Tax transactions

An accountant has a duty to use professional knowledge to achieve the most favourable tax position consistent with the desires of the client, the requirements of full disclosure and the law generally. The decision to enter into any tax arrangement must always be that of the client. The client must be fully informed of the details of the arrangement and its current and future ramifications including the risks and uncertainties, particularly in relation to possible changes in the law.

The accountant undertakes not to deal with any documents or accounting entries that are intended to misrepresent the true nature of a transaction. The accountant should avoid promoting, or assisting in the promotion of, any schemes or arrangements that have no commercial justification, nor should he or she have any financial interest in any business organisation (whether incorporated or otherwise), which promotes these tax schemes or arrangements. That an accountant advises a taxpayer to enter into a tax scheme, which the commissioner later rejects as a sham, does not prove that the accountant has been negligent. The commissioner's view of the scheme cannot be assumed to be correct until tested (CPA & ICAA 1997).

'Fit and proper' person

A tax agent has the professional responsibility to be, and remain, a 'fit and proper' person. This is defined as a person of good reputation, possessing proper knowledge of taxation laws, who is able to prepare income tax returns competently and can deal expertly with any queries that may be raised by ATO officers.

Subsection 251BC (1) of the *Income Tax Assessment Act 1936* (ITAA 1936) states that a 'fit and proper' person must, among other things:

a) be of good fame, integrity and character;
b) not have been convicted of a serious taxation offence during the previous five years;
c) not be under a sentence of imprisonment for a serious taxation offence; and
d) not be an undischarged bankrupt.

Insofar as the supervision and control of employees and others is concerned, under section 251M of ITAA 1936, it is an offence if a registered tax agent (or an exempt agent) allows any person, other than an employee or a partner, to prepare tax returns or objections or conduct any tax business on the tax agent's behalf.

Other relevant considerations

The following points also need to be considered by both tax agent and client:

- Professional fees are not charged on a percentage or contingency, but according to time spent. Furthermore, section 251L of ITAA 1936 provides that it is an offence for any person other than a registered tax agent or a person exempted from registration to charge any fee for the preparation of an income tax return or for transacting any business for a taxpayer in any income tax matter.

- An accountant must comply with the requirements of sections 210.10–210.18 of *APES 110 Code of ethics for professional accountants* ('Changes in a professional appointment') when taking over the taxation work of a client. There may be a threat to professional competence and due care if a prospective accountant consents to the engagement before he has been acquainted with all the relevant facts (APESB 2006a, s. 210.10).

- All records from the accountant can be accessed by the commissioner, except for documents covered under legal professional privilege.

Legal liability and negligence of tax agents (ITAA 1936, s. 251M)

That a tax agent has been negligent does not relieve the client of tax liability. The taxpayer must pay the fine or penalty. However, they have a statutory right to recover fines, penalties or additional tax from their tax agent if it was incurred because of the tax agent's negligence (ITAA 1936, s. 251M). Clients may also sue their tax agents for other losses caused by negligence or breach of contract as a result of the implied agreement between the tax agent and the client. This implied agreement requires the tax agent 'to act in good faith in the client's interest' and to exercise the skill, diligence and care that a reasonable tax agent would employ in looking after the client's affairs.

As a further penalty, the tax agent may face suspension or cancellation of his/her registration under section 251K if he or she is found guilty of neglecting the client's business affairs.

Income Tax Ruling 2246 contains the commissioner's policy with regard to prosecutions when:

- The tax agent, on his or her own initiative, has omitted income or invented or inflated claims.
- The agent procures a signed blank return from a taxpayer and completes the return without obtaining proper instructions.
- The agent completes a certificate relating to sources of information that is false or misleading.
- The agent includes false information in an objection or in a reply to a questionnaire.
- The agent provides false information in an interview with a taxation officer in circumstances in which it is clear that the statement is being relied on by the officer as a specific statement of fact, not merely as an expression of opinion.

The following In Focus vignette looks at how to deal with legal issues surrounding taxation.

Best advice: 'fess up' and stay out of jail

Taxing times; Robert Richards CPA says a healthy dash of realism will keep your clients out of the clink, plus why the tax office prefers convoluted questions in the case of private rulings.

When I commenced practice it seemed to me that one of the advantages of tax and corporate law was that it did not involve the messier side of the legal system (that is criminal law).

It used to be the case that the worst that could happen to a tax evader was public shame. However, as the Tax Office constantly reminds us by way of media releases, this is no longer the case. Over the past year it has issued media releases that point to a:

- Four-year jail conviction for a goods and services tax fraud of $51 046;
- A two-year jail conviction for a $50 000 income tax refund fraud;
- A 12-month jail conviction for a failure to declare over $160,000 of income;
- A seven-year conviction of a tax agent (Hart) for marketing a fictitious tax-planning arrangement.

When dealing with the Tax Office, practitioners are often faced with an ethical quandary: how to cause a recalcitrant client to make full disclosure to the Tax Office without at the same time causing that client to be penalised (perhaps even sent to jail).

The Tax Office regularly says it does not decide whether a taxpayer should be prosecuted. As a consequence it will not include terms within a settlement agreement that precludes it from taking prosecution action against a taxpayer. The Tax Office says it is only the director of public prosecutions that is entitled to give immunity from prosecution.

Practically speaking, it is the Tax Office and not the DPP that decides whether a taxpayer should be prosecuted. The DPP will only prosecute a taxpayer if the Tax Office seeks to prosecute — via a brief prepared and forwarded to the DPP. This brief might include witness statements as well as other evidence.

If the Tax Office believes a prosecution would be unsuccessful (or if it does not wish to prosecute a taxpayer) it is hard to imagine that a brief would be referred to the DPP.

Although the Tax Office has prepared a detailed prosecution policy, you do not really need to spend much time studying that sizeable document. It really is quite simple: if a taxpayer has been blatant, has not taken the initiative in disclosing evasion and the tax evaded is large, you can expect that there will be little sympathy for that taxpayer.

If, however, the evasion is an aberration, the taxpayer has taken the initiative in disclosure, and restitution is made as quickly as possible, you would normally find the Tax Office will not seek to prosecute the taxpayer (and indeed would be very helpful in aiding the taxpayer in getting his or her affairs in order).

In May the Tax Office entered into a memorandum of understanding with the DPP, such that it would have responsibility for: identifying potential cases for persecution, investigating these cases, and referring them to the DPP. Strangely, the DPP seems to have little responsibility (other than having the final say on what is put to it by the Tax Office).

So, practitioners face a quandary as to how to fulfil their obligations both to the Tax Office and their clients.

Often the best approach is to assist a client in 'fessing up' and then paying any outstanding tax. The client will then be in a position (if the prosecution goes ahead) to plead this as a mitigating circumstance.

The problem practitioners face here is that while a robust defence of the client's rights is what would be expected for tax law purposes, that defence might also be misconstrued and taken as evidence of non-contrition.

Practitioners might also ask whether it would assist their client were the client to enter into a settlement agreement with the Tax Office.

The key to dealing with a tax offence is realism. Be realistic as to the consequences of the offence. Rather than trying to do a special deal, realise the odds are against your client and the best that you can do is to make sure your client shows proper contrition and that the tax offence is an aberration.

This might convince the Tax Office not to refer the matter to the DPP. If it does, at least the client can argue this cooperation in mitigation.

Source: This article appeared in *INTHEBLACK*.

■ Quality control in a public practice

One of the important issues in a public practice is the creation of a system of **quality control**. It is defined as a system of policies and procedures to address leadership responsibilities for quality within the firm, its ethical requirements, acceptance and continuance of client relationships and specific engagements, engagement performance and monitoring. This designing, developing, implementing and monitoring quality control system must be tailored to the circumstances of each individual accounting practice (CPA & ICAA 1997). Each business is unique and, therefore, one set of quality control measures will not be suitable for all practices. The APESB publishes *APES 320 Quality control for firms*, which applies to all firms.

quality control: A system of policies and procedures to deal with leadership responsibilities for quality within the firm, its ethical requirements, acceptance and continuance of client relationships and specific engagements, engagement performance and monitoring

The Firm shall establish a system of quality control designed to provide it with Reasonable Assurance that the Firm and its Personnel comply with Professional Standards and regulatory requirements and that reports issued by the Firm or Engagement Partners are appropriate in the circumstances (APESB 2006b, s320.3).

A quality control system requires thorough and detailed documentation that describes its procedures. Some of the items that should be documented include a description of the objectives of the practice, its practice's philosophy on its service and clients, and its contribution to the community and the profession.

The following issues are specified in the APES 320 (s. 320.7):

(a) leadership responsibilities for quality within the firm;
(b) ethical requirement;
(c) acceptance and continuance of client relationships and specific engagements;
(d) human resources;
(e) engagement performance;
(f) monitoring.

Accountants should provide reasonable assurance that the elements of quality control are applied.

Leadership responsibilities for quality within the firm

A member of staff such as the principal, senior staff accountant or external consultant of the accounting practice should be responsible for the quality control system. The duties of this person are to plan and supervise the implementation and maintenance of the system, as well as answering any questions when they arise. The person responsible for quality control should also alert the practice about events and technical pronouncements that may affect the practice. The partners of the firm should assume ultimate responsibility for the firm's system of quality control (APESB 2006b, s. 320.9).

When designing a system of quality control, the quality control officer must consider that as a result of the different philosophies between partners and the nature of professional judgement, accounting practices can adopt different approaches to decision making for similar issues.

Ethical requirements

The firm 'should establish policies and procedures designed to provide it with reasonable assurance that the firm and its personnel comply with relevant ethical requirements' (APESB 2006b, s. 320.14). These include 'integrity, objectivity, professional competence and due care', as well as 'confidentiality and professional behaviour'. This means that those at all organisational levels should maintain these ethical requirements, and in particular professional independence as stated in section 290. When situations and relationships impose a threat to independence, then the firm should take action to minimise those threats or to withdraw from the engagement.

An engagement may continue when it can be established that the client does not lack integrity, and that there is sufficient expertise within the firm to complete it.

Human resources

The firm should include an organisational chart showing the various functions and work relationships within the practice, and the flow of work through the practice, including correspondence, engagement completions and the names of personnel responsible for the quality control system.

The firm must have 'sufficient personnel with capabilities, competence, and commitment to ethical principles' (APESB 2006b, s. 320.36) to complete the tasks required of the firm. The persons responsible for quality must have sufficient and appropriate experience and ability, as well as the necessary authority to assume responsibility of control and supervision. Work should be performed by members of the firm with the required degree of technical training and proficiency. Personnel should seek timely and requisite guidance and assistance, from other employees with more appropriate levels of knowledge, competence, judgement and authority if necessary.

Accountants should provide reasonable assurance that the work performed meets distinct standards of quality. The extent of supervision required and the appropriate level of review will depend on:
- the complexity of the subject matter
- the qualifications and experience of the persons performing the work
- the extent of guidance and assistance available and used.

The responsibility of a practice to establish procedures for supervision is distinct from the responsibility of the person in charge to plan and supervise the work on a particular engagement adequately. The quality of a practice's professional services ultimately depends on the integrity, competence and motivation of the personnel who perform and supervise the work (CPA & ICAA 1997). Engagement must be performed in accordance with professional standards and regulatory and legal requirements (APESB 2006b, s. 320.46). Clients should be assessed to avoid the risks of association with a client whose management lacks integrity.

Monitoring

Policies and procedures should be designed to provide reasonable assurance that the system of quality control is 'relevant, adequate, operating effectively and complied with in practice' (APESB 2006b, s. 320.74). Monitoring includes timely and periodic evaluation of a practice's quality control policies and procedures including inspection and review.

Quality control monitoring requires ongoing consideration and evaluation (s. 320.77). The following is a useful checklist detailing the steps required when developing and implementing quality control.
- Analyse any new developments in professional standards and how they are reflected in the firm's quality control policies and procedures.
- Determine and document the corrective actions to implement these quality control improvements.
- Prepare or update standard forms and formats, files and related manuals.

- Communicate to all personnel the quality control policies and procedures, including any weakness identified in the system and monitor the effectiveness of the quality control system.
- Establish a definite timetable for accomplishing the various steps in the quality control program and follow-up by appropriate personnel.
- Continue professional development.

Learning tips
Do you know...

11.4 *The accountant acting as a tax agent should take measures to minimise the risk for noncompliance and subsequent litigation. Keeping necessary document-ation and adhering to the requirements of a professional will protect the tax agent.*

11.5 *Accountants are responsible for designing, developing, implementing and monitoring mechanisms for quality control, which must be tailored to the circumstances of each individual accounting practice.*

11.6 *When designing quality control, accountants should consider, among other things, the philosophy of the practice, organisational structure and the types of clients the practice deals with.*

Quality control for specific practice areas: financial reporting and compilation

Financial reporting and compilation reporting are specific accounting areas in which quality control may suffer because of specific risks that can affect the completeness and accuracy of financial statements.

Planning

Before undertaking to provide financial or compilation reporting services, it is important for accountant to understand clients thoroughly. They should document background information about the clients, such as their business structure, business activities and overall reporting requirements. A client information form may be used to make this process easier. This is a standard form that contains information about a client and is now available in electronic form with some accounting packages. It should be reviewed and updated regularly.

Furthermore, they must be aware of any significant account balances and any risks that may affect the completeness and accuracy of financial statements. These may include the risk of material misstatement or error for individual account balances, and any other information used in preparing financial statements and returns. Factors that may affect risk include:
- the nature of the industry in which the client operates
- the internal control structure

- the level of knowledge and experience of staff
- the tax practices adopted
- the client's history and background (CPA & ICAA 1997).

Accountants must also develop a working knowledge of the relevant legislation, such as the *Corporations Act 2001* and the *Associations Incorporation Act 1981*.

Differentiating compilation, audit and review engagements

The differences among compilation, audit and review engagements can be subtle and the responsibilities overlap in many ways. However, it is important to maintain the transparency and independence of each aspect. The following administration techniques can be helpful in differentiating between the different roles.

Engagement letter

An engagement letter should document and confirm the services to be provided (such as assurance, nonassurance and compilation of financial reports) as well as an estimate of the applicable fees. Auditing standard *ASA 210 Terms of audit engagements* lays the foundation of how the engagement letter should be written, time budgets kept, staff allocated and the work program for each client organised. The client should acknowledge, in writing, the contents of the engagement letter and a copy of the engagement letter should be filed in the working paper file. This will help differentiate the type of work to be performed and will minimise future misunderstandings and errors that could lead in litigation.

Work program and staff planning

The accountant must determine what information is required from the client and how much. This includes the provision of data on the client's recording of transactions, controls and systems and specific financial information such as sales, journals, aged debtors listing, accounts payable listings and valued stock counts.

When planning the program, consideration must be given to the areas of risk. If these exist, then an accountant should record additional procedures, such as detailed checks, and should also check that the client has carried out the work.

Furthermore, staff planning is essential upon the engagement of any client, and should include considering who will carry out the work and who will review it (having regard to the complexity of the assignment, the nature of the services and the risks). If no staff can perform the required work, then a specialist's assistance must be sought to carry out or review some or all of the work.

At the planning stage, the program should be approved by the principal and placed in the working paper file (CPA & ICAA 1997).

Control and review procedures

Control and review procedures must be followed and documented because of the increasing risk of litigation. Accountants should provide evidence of control and review procedures. A summary record of all discussions in meetings should be kept. For example, the following discussions should be documented:

- tax, business, financial management or other advice given
- information provided, particularly in response to questions from the client
- problems encountered during an assignment (e.g. lack of information or potential errors)
- matters raised that may require further attention but the client does not wish to pursue
- verbal opinions provided by a consultant (CPA & ICAA 1997).

It is desirable to confirm in writing any conversations with clients during meetings or over the telephone.

A review ensures that the terms of the engagement have been carried out completely and accurately, and that due care and skill have been exercised. Staff responsible for the assignment must prepare a completion memorandum that includes the following:

- the scope of the engagement (e.g. compilation or agreed-upon procedures)
- any outstanding or unresolved matters
- significant decisions made by staff in completing the assignment, particularly if they affect the financial reports or tax returns
- matters requiring the attention of the principal arising from work carried out
- a conclusion.

However, the principal of the practice is ultimately responsible for the completion memorandum (CPA & ICAA 1997).

Special purpose financial reports

Preparation of special purpose financial reports is another area with specific and unique issues of responsibility. This is because accountants prepare these reports with a specific reader in mind, for example, for the preparation of taxation returns or for the obtaining of a business loan from the bank. However, these reports may be used by other users (i.e. creditors), who can rely on these reports to provide the firm with funds that they may never be able to recover in the future. These issues are discussed in more detail below.

The **compilation report** must make specific reference to the purpose of the financial report, including clarification of whether it is a **general purpose financial report** or **special purpose financial report**.

A disclaimer of liability must appear in a compilation report, which is attached to an unaudited financial report, and is referred to on each page of the financial report. Any liability disclaimer should be carefully worded. The following In Focus vignette provides an example of a compilation report disclaimer.

compilation report: A report that makes specific reference to the purpose of the financial report, including clarification of whether it is a general purpose or special purpose financial report

general purpose financial report: A report that complies with the Australian conceptual framework (see chapter 2) and accounting standards and meets the common information needs of users who are unable to request the preparation of a report to satisfy their needs

special purpose financial report: A report that is prepared for a specific user, for example, the ATO

Compilation report to Green Investments Pty Ltd

On the basis of information provided by the directors of Green Investments Pty Ltd, we have compiled the special purpose financial report of Green Investments Pty Ltd for the period ended 30 June 200X as set out on the following pages. This report is in accordance with *APS 9 Statement on compilation of financial reports.*

The specific purpose for which the special purpose financial report has been prepared is set out in note 1. How far accounting standards and other mandatory professional reporting requirements have been adopted in the preparation of the special purpose financial report is set out in note 1.

The directors are solely responsible for the information contained in the special purpose financial report and have determined that the accounting policies used are consistent with the financial reporting requirements of Green Investments Pty Ltd's constitution. These policies meet the needs of the directors and members of the company.

Our procedures use accounting expertise to collect, classify and summarise the financial information provided by the directors, into a financial report. Our procedures do not include verification or validation procedures. No audit or review has been performed and accordingly no assurance is expressed.

To the extent permitted by law, we do not accept liability for any loss or damage that any person, other than the company, may suffer arising from any negligence on our part. No person should rely on the special purpose financial report without having an audit or review conducted.

The special purpose financial report was prepared exclusively for the benefit of the directors and members of Green Investments Pty Ltd and the purpose identified above. We do not accept responsibility to any person for the contents of the special purpose financial report.

J Accountant, Director

Dated: 14 August 200X

New areas of professional responsibility

Accountants can find themselves unexpectedly involved in litigation involving new areas of practice that may not have been expressly provided for in the firm's documentation. A letter setting out the rules of engagement, together with professional indemnity insurance cover, can protect them if they have acted in good faith. Where there is an issue as to the extent of the professional's representation, the engagement letter can become critical evidence. It will clearly state that an accountant's work papers are being prepared in case there is litigation.

The professional indemnity insurance is essential to protect both accountants and their clients and to minimise the financial damage from non-compliance. There are several reasons to insure against litigation for claims, including:

- the readiness of people to engage in litigation
- the incidence of frivolous and vexatious claims
- the scarcity of qualified and experienced staff
- the increasing complexity and diversity of the public accountant's work.

Professional indemnity insurance provides not only the funds to meet claims but also the legal expertise to deal with and minimise the effects of a claim against a practice. Furthermore, it ensures protection from claims in respect of any civil liability incurred by the accountant or the firm in connection with public practice. If for any reason the professional indemnity insurance applied for by an accountant is refused, or the policy is cancelled or lapses, the accountant is required to advise his or her professional society in writing within seven days (CPA & ICAA 1997).

Although the letter of engagement and professional liability insurance are designed to protect the accountant and firm from unexpected litigation, accountants should be aware of the following newer areas of practice.

Social responsibility reporting

It may be the accountant's responsibility to review the effectiveness of initiatives taken to achieve the firm's social objectives and improve its community position against polluters. Social and environmental reporting is a rapidly growing area of expertise, and accountants should familiarise themselves with the various guidelines when preparing reports. This topic is discussed further in chapter 7. At the very least, the economic goals of firms should be consistent with socially responsible behaviour (Henderson et al. 2006).

Financial advice

Accountants must be aware of their professional responsibilities under the FSRA. In general, accountants can provide typical professional advice that is not required to be provided by a financial services licence holder. An example of this would be advice on effective ways to acquire business assets such as motor vehicles by hire purchase or leasing (CPA Australia 2005).

Antimoney-laundering legislation

Under the new antimoney-laundering legislation, accountants need to keep records of both the identity of their direct clients and their activities. Accountants must observe any multifaceted and extraordinary transactions and report these in good faith. They must report to the Australian Transaction Reports and Analysis Centre (AUSTRAC) if they have reasonable grounds to believe a business deal is related to tax evasion, a criminal offence, proceeds of crime or a terrorist-financing offence. The duty to report a suspicious business deal is inconsistent with the duty of confidentiality owed to their clients but the *Financial Transaction Reports Act 1988* overrides client confidentiality. AUSTRAC can take court action for injunctive remedies to secure conformity with the requirements of the Act. Criminal penalties also apply for noncompliance.

Summary

Describe an accountant's professional responsibility and the rules of professional and ethical conduct.

- Accounting, as a profession, draws on a body of knowledge and practice to assure the efficient and organised operation of business and government entities by providing relevant and reliable information to guide decision making.
- Accountants abide by an ideal code of behaviour, detailed in *APES 110 Code of ethics for professional accountants*. Aspects covered in the code include integrity, objectivity, professional competence and due care, confidentiality and professional behaviour.
- Accountants' professional responsibility includes the ability to balance their sometimes conflicting duties to comply with rules of professional conduct and other legislation. Accountants have a responsibility to the broader public interest, not just to individual clients or employers.
- Accountants must exercise integrity, which means that they must be honest when exercising their professional judgement according to culture and ethos. They must also be objective and independent and should be, and be seen to be, free of any external interest. Furthermore, particular attention should be paid to the situations in which independence may be compromised.

Evaluate taxation standards and aspects of professional conduct for tax agents.

- Taxation standards' overriding objectives are to inform the client to make his or her decisions about future tax planning.
- The accountant should take measures to minimise the risk for noncompliance and subsequent litigation. Keeping necessary documentation and adhering to professional requirements will protect the tax agent.
- Estimates and tax transactions should be tackled with care.
- Tax agents should avoid suspension or cancellation of their licence.

Evaluate quality control in the public practice.

- Accountants are responsible for designing, developing, implementing and monitoring mechanisms for quality control, which must be tailored to the circumstances of each individual accounting practice.
- When designing quality control, accountants should consider amongst others the philosophy of the practice, organisational structure and the types of clients the practice deals with.
- A list of steps must be followed when developing and implementing a quality control system, together with the documentation of various areas of quality control.

Evaluate quality control for financial reporting and compilation.

- Quality control for specific practice areas such as financial reporting and compilation should be considered to avoid litigation.
- Accountants should be familiar with the client's business structure, industry characteristics, and history and background before accepting an assignment to prepare financial reports.

- Careful consideration should go into the provision of adequate initial engagement procedures, work program and staff planning, and control and review procedures.

Evaluate quality control requirements for special purpose financial reports.

- Special purpose financial reports require an understanding of the client and its industry, together with a need to differentiate the difference among compilation, audit and review engagements, which require different quality control and review procedures.

Identify new areas of professional responsibility.

- Accountants can find themselves in litigation over new areas for which they could not predict their responsibility. A letter setting out the rules of engagement, together with professional indemnity insurance cover, can protect them if they have acted in good faith.
- Several pertinent new areas of practice include social responsibility reporting, the provision of financial advice and antimoney-laundering legislation requirements.

Key terms

compilation report   349
ethics   335
general purpose financial report   349
profession   333
professional responsibility   334
quality control   344
special purpose financial report   349

Review questions

11.1   What are the roles and relationships that an accountant may take? Is there an inherent possibility of conflict?

11.2   Discuss the application of professional judgement in accounting decisions.

11.3   What is professional independence and what are the main threats to professional independence? How can the threats to independence be minimised?

11.4   Discuss the five objectives of the accounting profession as they are set out in *APES 110 Code of ethics for professional accountants*.

11.5   Evaluate the rules of ethical compliance as defined in *APES 110 Code of ethics for professional accountants*.

11.6   Discuss the overriding objective of a professional tax adviser and explain how this objective, in certain circumstances, may conflict with relevant legislation.

11.7   What should a tax accountant consider when starting to work with a new client?

11.8   Outline the checklist used to avoid noncompliance with taxation standards.

11.9   What is required when providing written or verbal advice to clients to avoid or minimise potential litigation?

11.10 Explain the meaning of a fit and proper person for taxation purposes.

11.11 Outline the legal liability and negligence issues surrounding a tax agent.

11.12 Analyse the need for designing a quality control system in a public practice.

11.13 Outline the ten elements of quality control that protect the accountant's professional liability.

11.14 Explain the confidentiality relationship between an accountant and a client.

11.15 Briefly outline the necessity of accountants being aware of their professional independence, skill, competence and reasonable care.

Application questions

11.16 Peter attended an ethics subject in his undergraduate course, in which he learned an ideal code of professionalism. Furthermore, during his first five years of accounting practice in a big reputable firm, he learned to comply with a variety of professional standards and laws such as the Australian accounting standards and, in particular, *APES 110 Code of ethics for professional accountants*. In his line of work with an overseas stockbroker, Peter also has a working knowledge of the international accounting reporting standards, Australian securities and the ASX. His onshore clients require him to deal with solicitors and review various contracts with them. He has a portfolio of taxation clients, which operate in both Victoria and New South Wales. Does Peter need to exercise any additional professional care in the performance of this work?

11.17 A formal complaint was submitted by an officer of professional conduct to a one-person tribunal. In her opinion, there was a breach of the constitution, by-law or standard of practice or professional conduct, or the technical or ethical standards of the professional bodies, or code of conduct professional scheme or joint statement. G Green, the alleged contravener, failed to undertake and submit to the CPA Australia a quality assurance review as directed, contrary to By-Law 706.2.6. Green also failed to reply to the required professional conversation contrary to CPC Statement D.10 (CPA one-person tribunal, 7 March 2006). You are the one-person tribunal. Present your outcome and the reasons for your decision.

11.18 Brown has a small practice in Carlton, Melbourne. For the period ending March 2006 and 2007, Brown has failed to have the trust account audited within the required period. This is contrary to paragraph 34.1 of *APS10 Client money and the maintenance and audit of member trust account*. Furthermore, for the audit period 1 April 2006–07, government duties were debited to the account contrary to paragraph 18 of the same standard. In your opinion, what are the imposable penalties?

11.19   Smith is a sole practitioner, who has a client who keeps minimal records. The barrister who is representing the client in a case of loss of income requires Smith to change the disclaimer or to sign an affidavit supporting the accounts as being true and fair. If Smith does not agree to change the disclaimers, then the client stands to lose more than $500 000. Discuss this request in line with the ethical compliance of *APES 110 Code of ethics for professional accountants*.

11.20   Erguz, a registered tax agent, was convicted of sexual harassment of male employees in her successful tax agent practice. Erguz had been very successful because she always agreed with the clients' demands. She tried to minimise their taxation obligations even if this meant ignoring certain actions of the clients that did not fall within the strict requirements of the taxation law. Furthermore, Erguz failed to disclose the convictions on her re-registration application even though there was wide media coverage of the offences. What are the possible consequences?

11.21   Barkiz, a bank officer, prepares his own income tax return after carefully reading all relevant information in the Tax Pack. In addition to his salary, Barkiz owns rented properties and has a small investment portfolio of shares. He requests a local tax agent peruse the return and lodge it under the electronic lodgement service. The ATO raises an assessment and issues an adjustment sheet increasing the taxable income by $6000 as a result of an arithmetical error in calculating assessable income. No penalty for incorrect return was imposed by the ATO. Discuss whether Barkiz has any redress against the local agent.

11.22   Dragos, a successful property developer, engaged an accountant and solicitor to advise in relation to tax matters. The professional tax advisers devised a scheme by which Dragos could minimise tax by borrowing funds to prepay expenses and then claim a deduction for the prepayments. The commissioner of taxation conducted an extensive audit, which resulted in disallowing the deduction for the prepayments. Discuss whether Dragos has any redress against the professional tax advisers.

11.23   Timothy's father has been a client of yours for 23 years. Timothy has $135 000 in the bank and he has borrowed another $100 000 from the same bank to buy a house in Melbourne's western suburbs. However, he did not budget for the legal costs and stamp duties. He needs another $11 000 for the house settlement. His father has an investment deposit of $100 000, which matures in two months from the date of settlement. If they cash in the investment before it matures, they would lose any additional interest. Therefore, being clients and friends for so many years they assume that you will provide them with $10 000 till the date of the investment maturity. Explain your course of action.

11.24 Anna is the new assistant accountant in a public practice comprising three accountants. She attended all training to use the software of the practice. She has mastered most of the modules but has trouble with billing costing of clients. When she transferred the work from the timesheets to bill the clients, she rolled over the work by mistake, all billings disappeared and she could not trace any of her transactions. Her supervisor and she spent a whole week trying to solve the problem but had no success. The numbers did not add up to the manual work. The accounts needed to be issued, so in an act of desperation, her supervisor requested her to zero all balances. They issued the new accounts based on the previous year's invoice, increased by inflation. What is the professional responsibility of the supervisor and why?

11.25 Romanio has requested you provide a quote for the preparation of projected estimated figures. Romanio wants to apply for a grant of $30 000 from the federal government. Romanio is the director of a big clothing factory that employs 110 employees. Romanio was a client of your practice ten years ago but became bankrupt. Romanio then restarted the clothing factory and has a part-time bookkeeper, who does the business activity statements on the weekends. During the week, the bookkeeper works as an accountant in another public practice. For the past two years, the bookkeeper has prepared the taxation returns and lodged them through the practice. However, the bookkeeper does not want to prepare any estimates. You have made your enquiries and you have understood that invoices and other primary source papers are kept on the business premises. You cannot rely on past financials and you must visit the factory to extract some information in reference to the preparation of past financials. What would be your professional responsibility if you accept this appointment?

11.26 You are about to go out for lunch. One of your clients, Mr Youssef, comes in and requests the savings account details of his wife, so she can withdraw some money they need immediately to pay their gas bill with. He is holding a gas account final notice. You quickly find what he requested and you hand it over to him. Next week, you receive a letter from Mrs Youssef's solicitor, requesting an explanation why something that was given to you in confidentiality was handed over to Mr Youssef. Mr and Mrs Youssef were separated and they were in the process of a divorce. Unfortunately, you have not being informed of their separation. What is your professional responsibility?

11.27 Leoni is a public accountant who has been a sole practitioner for six years. Leoni has recently employed two university students. They have been recommended by a friend who lectures at the local university. Leoni really needed some extra assistance because of being very busy with a new contract that requires travelling to New South Wales regularly. After initial practical training of three months, the two trainee accountants were given their own clientele portfolios and are now responsible for those clients. They assist each other when Leoni is away, but in some instances they cannot help each other. Give advice about Leoni's professional responsibility if the trainee accountants err because of their lack of knowledge.

11.28 You are the accountant of a very busy practice. You have been working for 20 years and you are very proud of the quality of work you provide to your clients. You have always entrusted your memory and you believe that you make minimal errors in your work. That is why you do not keep records of discussions with clients: you consider them a waste of time. In addition, you do not like keeping records of any advice provided for tax minimisation, even within the letter of the taxation law. This is in case someone later considers them as illegal advice to minimise tax. Nick, however, has pointed out that you have advised giving a client unsecured finance instead of a mortgage. This is not something that you would normally advise any client. You remember that you advised providing the customer with a mortgage loan but Nick chose not to. You cannot find anything in writing in Nick's files. Nick is very angry with you and is threatening to sue you for wrong advice if the client does not honour the unsecured finance. What is your professional responsibility if Nick's client does not honour the unsecured finance?

11.29 Mary has been a tax agent for five years. Mary has a very good reputation among clients, possessing proper knowledge of taxation laws. Mary is able to prepare income tax returns competently and can deal competently with any queries raised by ATO officers. Mary had borrowed heavily on the building purchased to expand the tax agent business in Footscray. Unfortunately, interest rates have increased and Mary could not pay the instalments. The bank declared Mary bankrupt. Can Mary be a tax agent when an undischarged bankrupt and why?

11.30 Louie was repairing photocopiers, using a certain type of thinner that affected his health. Louie had to stop working and because of his condition he retired on an invalid pension. Unfortunately, the invalid pension was not enough and he had to start supplementing his income by repairing photocopiers part time. For this job, Louie was paid approximately $100 weekly in cash. Ms Estelle is his sister and she is a tax agent. She has always prepared her brother's taxation returns. The invalid pension is untaxable and this did not need to be declared because the other income was below the taxable threshold. Recently, Centrelink requested information about her brother's repairing activities. Ms Estelle was placed in a position of conflict because of her relationship with her brother. Explain the professional liability of Ms Estelle if she does not inform Centrelink of the additional income of her brother.

11.31 Danny has an accounting practice in the city. Danny employs six other accountants. On employing a new accountant, Danny provides them with a folder that has several standardised forms and formats indicating the policies and procedures of the firm. Danny insists that everyone at the office should use them. Danny claims that when the practice began eight years ago, they were really helpful. Other forms are also available to accountants at their request. What is the responsibility of Danny and why?

11.32   Dion is an accountant who offers a competent professional service, which will integrate current developments in practice, legislation and techniques. This is evident from Dion's attendance at several seminars and conferences. The accounting bodies are satisfied with the level of professional development. Unfortunately, Dion has problems concentrating during the seminar sessions. Dion could not stay awake when the lectures on consolidations were delivered. As a result, Dion has failed to maintain the knowledge and level of skill necessary to achieve competency. However, Dion believes that he has shown a high level of due care. Comment on this.

11.33   Maria was recently awarded a certificate of excellence at her job in the accounting department. Maria's instructors congratulated her because she had an excellent understanding of the written rules of conduct of the business. This was ironic, because Maria had no previous exposure to ethics. Therefore, Maria had significant problems in making decisions on ethical issues. For example, staff in the warehouse never reported damage made to stock because of human error because the person who made the error had a sick child. In Maria's opinion, she had to report this because otherwise she would not be objective. Comment on this.

11.34   Alex prepared the work program for a client. Alex requested data relating to the client's recording of transactions, controls and systems and specific financial information, in particular sales, journals, aged debtors listing, accounts payable listings and valued stock counts. However, Alex failed to take into account the areas of risk. Determine Alex's professional responsibility.

11.35   White has requested a meeting with you to discuss the most effective way to acquire equipment in White's new business. White wants to discuss which option is better (gearing, lease, hire purchase or bank loan). You hesitate because you are not sure of your professional responsibility under the FSRA. Outline your responsibility under that act.

case**study**   **11.1**

You have been Mr Black's accountant for many years. He is one of your biggest clients. He has several private companies and trusts, which comprise about 20 per cent of your revenue base. In 2001, one of his companies, Colour Pty Ltd bought rural land. He then formed a unit trust 'The Colouring', with Mr Red's trustee company, which is called Red Pty Ltd, paying $250 000 each to start farming on Colour's land. Colour Pty Ltd has 49 units, Red Pty Ltd has 49 and you have two. Then you signed over the two units to Colour Pty Ltd without informing Mr Red. The time of the transfer and any stamp duties were to be arranged later, when Mr

Black decides to do so. Colouring is in the business of farming. Mr Red would receive $45 000 a year for managing the farm. The farming business would pay Colour Pty Ltd an amount of $120 000 a year for rent on the land.

During this time, you have grown to like Mr Red. He seems to be a trustworthy and hardworking individual, who is trying his best to promote the farming business and keep the farm in an immaculate condition. His $45 000 a year is not enough to sustain him and he relies heavily on his wife's income to meet his commitments. On the contrary, you have lost your patience with Mr Black, who does not get involved in everyday business of the farm but always finds petty faults and is constantly complaining.

The business is estimated to have assets worth about $1 million. Unfortunately, the farming business is not making any profits and Mr Black wants out. At the beginning of this year, Mr Black approached you. He says that he has two options:

- Sell the land only for $5 million. This would mean that Mr Red will receive nothing because the land belongs to Colour Pty Ltd.
- Sell both the land and the business for $6 million and pay Mr Red his share of the business. However, he considers that this option is a much more difficult alternative.

1. Advise both your clients on the consequences of the first option.
2. Advise both your clients on the consequences of the second option.
3. What is your responsibility on the acceptance and signing-off of the two units?
4. What is the problem with Mr Black being nearly 20 per cent of your fee revenue base?
5. What is the correct course of action to avoid any conflict of interest and breach of your professional responsibility?

casestudy   11.2

Bella was working for her cousin as a junior accountant for four years. She is very happy there because her cousin has a high degree of technical competence in public practice. She believes that as a professional accountant she has a duty of care to her clients, to the community, to other accountants and to herself. Therefore, she requires Bella to study professional journals and other Internet resources to assist clients who are looking for service. Bella finds this demanding because she is engaged and her time at home is limited. During her employment with her cousin, Bella made a lot of friends from the base of her cousin's clientele. Bella was then married. She had the choice to stay there under the minimum wage from which she had to pay all her expenses, including the hefty mortgage on her new home.

However, she left to join another accounting firm as a junior partner. She brought with her a portfolio of clients that mostly consisted of her cousin's clients who she solicited to enable her to join the new accounting firm as a partner.

Barb is a senior partner in the new accounting firm who believes that increased regulation is protecting the accountant so that he or she can make informed judgements. She believes that regulation helps accountants to make their own decisions. Bella works under her instructions and she provides her with advice on how to act. Barb is dealing with the most complex issues of the firm. Although Bella has not mastered enough technical skills to deal with such complex issues, she has the capacity and the opportunity to look below the surface and choose between alternatives. Unfortunately, her boss often has situations in which the choice is between similarly 'immoral' options. Bella is not happy with the way Barb is handling certain situations. Barb sometimes adopts minimum standards to satisfy clients' requests. She thinks that clients can always shop around to find an accountant who is prepared to do what they want. She believes that the most important thing is to ensure the survival of the business and the securing of their income within the letter of the law. The clients should be able to decide what they want. Bella, who was trained differently by her cousin, is now facing a dilemma whether it is better to adjust to this new way of working and pursue her career or be truthful and live without any substantial income.

1. Comment on Bella's cousin's work ethics.
2. Discuss the demand on accountants for constant professional development.
3. Comment on Bella's decision to solicit clients from her cousin's clientele.
4. Discuss Barb's belief that the most important thing is to ensure the survival of the business and the securing of one's income within the letter of the law.
5. Discuss Bella's options.

Recommended readings and websites

Accounting Professional and Ethical Standards Board 2006, *APES 110 Code of ethics for professional accountants*, www.apesb.org.au.

—— 2006, *APES 320 Quality control for firms*, www.apesb.org.au.

Australian Taxation Office, www.ato.gov.au.

Australian Securities and Investments Commission, www.asic.gov.au.

Australian Transaction Reports and Analysis Centre, www.austrac.gov.au.

CPA Australia, www.cpaaustralia.com.au.

Institute of Chartered Accountants Australia, www.icaa.org.au.

Taxation Institute of Australia, www.taxinstitute.com.au.

References

Accounting Professional and Ethical Standards Board (APESB) 2006a, *APES 110 Code of ethics for professional accountants*, www.apesb.org.au.

—— 2006b, APES 320 *Quality control for firms*, www.apesb.org.au.

Brown R 2002, 'Managing regulatory change in life insurance and pensions', *The role of the independent professional*, session 7.5.

CPA & the Institute of Chartered Accountants in Australia (CPA & ICAA) 1997, *Quality control management in the accounting practices*, Sydney.

Henderson, S, Peirson, G, Herbohn, K & Ramsay, A 2006, *Issues in financial accounting*, 12th edn, Pearson–Prentice Hall, Sydney.

Leung, P, Dellaportas, S & Cooper, B 2005, 'Accounting as a profession', *CPA program reporting and professional practice manual, module 1*, CPA, Melbourne.

Shirvington, V 2001, 'Turning a blind eye: professional liability and responsibility: dealing with clients: what are the limits', www.lawsociety.com.au.

Tax Agents' Board n.d. , 'Responsibilities and obligations of tax agents', www.tabd.gov.au.

Warnock, J 2006, *Emotional intelligence*, Women in Leadership, Melbourne.

12 FUTURE DIRECTIONS IN ACCOUNTING

LEARNING OBJECTIVES

After reading this chapter, you should be able to:

- outline the historical influences on current financial accounting theory
- evaluate the emerging role of standards regulators
- identify future directions of social and environmental reporting and intellectual capital management
- understand the influence of merging markets on the role of the accountant
- evaluate potential directions for the accounting profession.

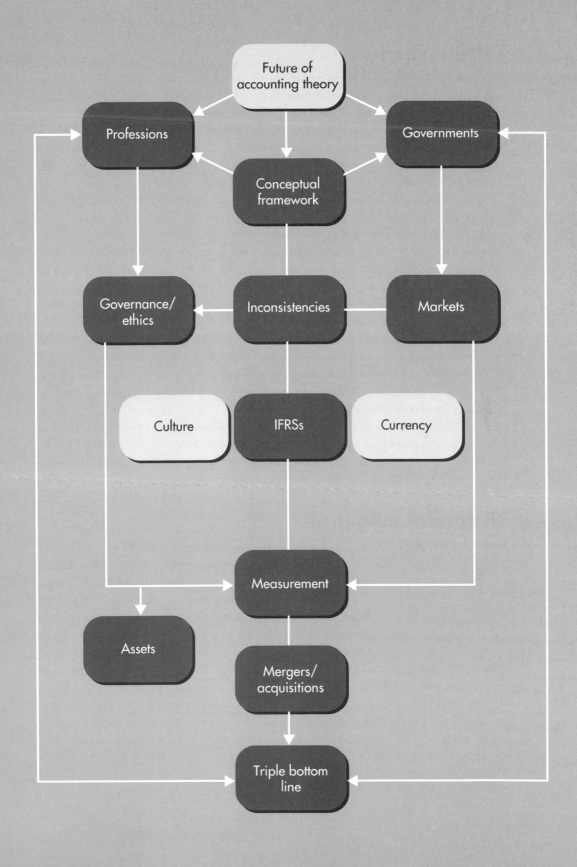

Introduction

The general globalisation trend across the globe has enormous implications for the accounting profession. Business transactions and activities are constantly evolving, becoming ever more international and complex; community expectations of business activities are shifting and the amount and complexity of regulation are growing steadily. The public information provided about an entity's activities, produced and mediated by financial accountants and auditors, is relied upon as an accurate and transparent assessment of a company's financial performance.

However, financial accounting is by no means an exact science, and accountants are constantly faced with questions that challenge their knowledge and experience. The previous 11 chapters discuss some of these issues confronting accountants in their daily practice, and some that challenge the profession as a whole. They examine some solutions to these questions, as well as some more general approaches that serve to support the decisions of accounting as a whole. As the business world is constantly evolving, however, so is the nature of the accounting practice that supports it.

This chapter examines some of the predictions for accounting as a profession. As are all professions, accounting is subject to political, social and cultural changes, and some of the influences operating at the present time have implications for the directions of accounting. Political forces seem to be encouraging greater governmental control over accounting regulation; social expectations are demanding more responsibility and ethical behaviour from corporations and the profession itself is moving to integrate and cement strong internal and external partnerships across the globe. The accountant of the future faces a challenging, exciting and fast-paced career, with enormous diversity and opportunities.

Historical influences

Before considering new directions for the accounting profession, it may be useful to evaluate its historical influences. The current approaches to financial accounting theory have evolved over many hundreds of years. The modern **corporation** emerged from the Industrial Revolution, as small agricultural industries changed to the railroads and large manufacturers of today. Even today, corporations are still based on manual labour,

corporation: A large company or group of companies authorised to act as a single entity and recognised as such in law

whether farming, manufacturing or bookkeeping. The emergence of knowledge and the knowledge worker, however, has created a profound shift in the machine-driven economy as a new technology becomes even more effective and efficient. Transactions are no longer manually tracked; the performance of global corporations rests on ethereal futures transactions and the value of a company relies on the intangible skills and experience of its workforce. This shift is fundamental to the financial accounting practices of today.

In the eleventh century, the Maghribi merchants of North Africa wanted to expand their business to the Mediterranean region — a move generally free and unrestricted, yet fraught with uncertainty and the risk of venturing into unknown territories. Merchants had to travel with the goods to guarantee the arrival of the goods at foreign ports, and to personally negotiate a good price. Eventually, the Maghribi merchants established agents around the Mediterranean trading centres. These agents were eventually entrusted with the receiving and sale of the goods, freeing the Maghribi from travelling with their goods. An informal institution enabled the agent system to operate successfully: merchants required knowledge of potential markets from their agents, while the agents were supplied with information regarding the availability and quality of the merchants' produce. The Maghribi recognised the importance of this free flow of information to the successful operation and growth of their markets and subsequent wealth. The global market of the future needs to explore how governments can build better institutions to support the free flow of information to aid capital-market development. Simple solutions need to be applied in developing economies for these countries to find a way forward (Islam 2002).

The growth of any corporation is fundamentally connected to the highs and lows of the economic cycle. While times are good and the economy booming, corporations chase further investment through an unprecedented level of accurate and mostly voluntary information about the financial position of the company. When troughs

corporate failure: The dissolution of a company, in which it is unable to continue in business because it cannot meet its financial obligations to suppliers or creditors

appear, however, governments need to focus on the problems associated with **corporate failure**.

This is inevitable in today's fast-paced economy. Despite advances in technology, the decision making of a company ultimately rests with its human management. No country is isolated from corporate failure and often the true impact is masked by the size and relative insignificance of smaller, unregulated enterprises.

Equally mysterious are the qualities of success that enable some enterprises to leapfrog their competition, sustaining exponential growth and expansion at a furious pace. With easier access for smaller stakeholders, whether supplying or demanding investment opportunities, global markets are slowly becoming more open and accessible than ever before.

With the growth in small and medium-sized enterprises now forming the backbone of many of the world's economies, both developed and developing, newly flexible and simplified financing options need to be explored to provide capital and investment to this important economic resource. And with this shift comes the need to simplify the reporting, control and transparency of information between investors and businesses; as for the Maghribi before us, the free flow of information will enable the success of capital-market development. Ensuring the transparency and reliability of the processes through which this information is supplied, used and regulated will be the purvey of accounting regulatory authorities. The past decade has seen a fundamental shift in how the world's regulators approach accounting controls, with the focus now squarely on the demise of national standard-setting entities, and the rise of a single, truly international set of accounting regulations.

Regulators of accounting standards

The most fundamental shift in accounting regulation, and the one likely to remain the focus of the accounting profession for some time to come, is the implementation of a single, international set of accounting standards across the world. With the communication of information the key to the future growth of capital markets, the better use of technology offers the potential to provide data faster and at a lower cost than ever before. Without reliable communication, there will be limitations. Nicolaisen included in a conversation that a single international system of accounting regulation has the potential to improve the quality of accounting in developing nations, and to improve the transparency of corporate disclosures across borders. Some of these improvements and innovations will originate in the standard-setting and other regulatory processes, while others will be driven by investor demand (*Journal of Accountancy* 2005).

In the largest capital market in the world, the Financial Accounting Standards Board (FASB) in the United States has set a challenging agenda for the future of accounting standards in that country. Convergence between United States and international accounting standards continues as the ultimate goal. With the rest of the world watching, the shift to international accounting standards in the European Union and Australia has so far avoided the catastrophic predictions of the doomsayers, and the transition in both markets appears to have gone smoothly and quickly. As the international standard-setting process continues to evolve, the European and Australian example will continue to provide ongoing feedback on the impact of any new directions.

Political implications

The level of political interference in the regulation of accounting standards differs from country to country. Where **corruption** is already widespread and entrenched, ineffective support mechanisms can facilitate further fraud. Access to swift, fair and inexpensive justice can profoundly affect the functioning of an emerging economy (Islam 2002). For example, procedural complexity in the collection and recovery of small debt claims has a major impact on the survival and growth of small enterprises. Overly complex and convoluted regulations may create further opportunities for bribery and corruption. Litigation takes longer in countries with procedurally complex court systems, where expected benefits may not materialise and hinder progress. And, while technology innovation can grow either in the government or private sector, the government of a country can stifle technological growth by neglect.

Bankruptcy law can also go a long way to making it easier for smaller businesses to survive and levelling the playing field. Bankruptcy laws are often contentious

corruption: Offences relating to the improper influencing of people in positions of trust, such as politicians, civil servants and other officials, through bribes that may be in cash or in kind, for an official action or inaction

bankruptcy: The state of an individual who is unable to pay his or her debts, where legal orders are issued to deprive him or her of his or her property, which is then used to pay their debts

and need to accommodate cultural expectations and social attitudes towards the roles of creditors and debtors. In Australia, recent reforms to the bankruptcy and **insolvency** laws are aimed at further protecting the employees of failed businesses, and at reducing the loopholes available for hiding assets under bankruptcy laws. In other countries, reform is happening but it is beset with difficulties. The In Focus vignette that follows examines the difficulties faced by law reforms in China.

> **insolvency:** The inability of a company to pay its debts when they fall due. Insolvency leads to liquidation, in which the assets of a company are used to repay creditors.

 ## The great Chinese robbery

It is a smart businessman who heads for a remote tax haven and keeps more of his own money. But a smarter businessman heads to China, to keep other people's money for himself.

China has a bankruptcy law with holes so large that it pays to borrow as much money as possible from as many people as possible, and then declare insolvency. Creditors are lucky if they get anything back — the law does not give any protection, meaning that a creditor has no legal recourse to fall back on if commercial negotiations break down or the debtor simply rolls over. The law was promulgated 18 years ago and came into effect in 1988, when China was in the early stages of giving up its monopoly on the ownership of businesses. Understandably, it applies to state-owned enterprises only. Whether a privately held or foreign joint venture can 'go bankrupt' is not addressed. Even so, the law says that a state-owned company needs pre-approval from its 'superiors', namely, the government, before it can file for bankruptcy.

In a political culture where the government is portrayed as infallible, bankruptcy would be an admission of incompetence.

It is no wonder, then, that in the first year after the law came into force, there were only 98 bankruptcy cases in the whole of the mainland. That number declined further, to 32, in 1990, and never exceeded more than 1000 annually in the next few years. Then, some wise men thought outside the box, and outside their conscience: because the law says that a debtor is no longer obligated to repay the loans, why not take advantage in order to keep other people's money?

Fraudulent bankruptcy caught on like wildfire, and the number of cases exploded tenfold in 1996. The fraud became so rampant that the government started work on a new bankruptcy law in 1994 in a bid to plug the loopholes. Ten years later, it is still in the delivery room.

What makes an up-to-date, operable and fair law so hard to produce? The fact that it is too painful to choose between the two evils. The first option is to let the failing businesses — most of which are state-owned — go under, meaning that workers will be laid off en masse. With no meaningful welfare scheme, that is a recipe for street demonstrations, which will disrupt economic stability.

The other choice is to keep bankrolling the losers. But the banks will watch in horror as bad debts accumulate, threatening to drag down the whole financial system. Either way, the prospect is equally destabilising to the economy. Under increasing pressure, China is now accelerating the amendment of its bankruptcy law. On October 24, the National People's Congress reviewed a new draft of amendments. The proposal is likely to become law early next year. It is expected to cover all businesses, regardless of their ownership structure, and ensure that priority is given to affected employees, rather than creditors, during the allocation of assets.

Whether the new measures will minimise fraud, punish deadbeats and protect the public is dubious, at best. To get rid of the headache once and for all, one option would be to sell the state-owned enterprises in a nation-wide privatisation. Short of that, any amount of repairs to the law will remain ineffective.

Source: This article appeared in the *South China Morning Post.*

International standards in national jurisdictions

Although the IASB attempts to set up a 'best practice' set of standards for optimal accounting quality, the implications for using a 'one size fits all' solution to such a multifaceted problem are revealing themselves with each new adoption. In each country where International Financial Reporting Standards (IFRSs) are introduced, the local regulators face a complex integration process. In Russia, for example, where IFRSs will be introduced by law in 2010, regulators are facing enormous resistance from the accounting profession itself. Sergey Moderov states that:

> Many Russian accountants have settled into the habit of relying on existing laws, as opposed to exercising professional opinion. It will be a challenge to alter the mindset of bookkeepers and accountants in this country, especially those from the older generation (*Accountant* 2004).

In Ireland, too, with its unique tax system, regulators are aware that the tax implications of each IFRS need to be carefully examined. Examples from the experience of other jurisdictions with similar tax principles have demonstrated some contentious issues to be dealt with up front to minimise conflict and reduce the level of uncertainty that can otherwise prevail among the business community.

The great challenge for accounting regulators across the globe for the future will be to curb blatant '**creative accounting**' practices, which are so damaging to the goodwill and trust of the general community. The way forward appears to be to reduce the sheer choice of permitted accounting methods and minimise the use of judgement. Although this sounds as though it is a step backwards, rescinding all the choices that have been acquired over the past 30 years, empirical evidence suggests that having choice in accounting methods brings exploitation,

creative accounting: Misleadingly optimistic, though not illegal, forms of accounting. This can occur because some accounting transactions are not subject to regulations or the regulations are ambiguous.

and is never totally unbiased. With markets, investors and analysts relying heavily on the market value of enterprises for decision making, agency theory suggests that accounting choices will continue to be directed to maximise the value of the firm, whatever the cost (Dellaportas et al. 2005).

Accountants are generally very good at their job and will find ways to maximise opportunities for their corporation or clients. Accounting regulators to date have only tackled the tip of the iceberg. Although they have gone some way to dealing with presentation and disclosure, they have not yet tackled serious recognition and measurement issues. Until the accounting regulators realise their importance, the opportunities for creative accounting will continue to increase and the result will be more corporate collapses.

Social and environmental reporting

One of the growth areas of corporate governance, and consequence the accounting profession, is corporate social responsibility (CSR), which concerns the more general impact of an entity on the community and its surroundings. It is no longer acceptable for a corporation to ignore its responsibilities to the environment, its employees and the greater community. Over the years, voluntary reporting activity has followed an earlier trend of companies including environmental disclosures in their annual reports. This has been seen as a way for companies to manage public impressions of organisation's operations, and to establish and maintain organisational legitimacy. The use of these unregulated voluntary disclosures as a marketing tool unfortunately compromises any legitimate environmental or social reforms made, further eroding community confidence in the legitimacy of corporate reporting and the transparency of their governance. Figure 12.1 outlines the interrelationships between the factors that influence the disclosure of social, ethical and environmental information by corporations.

Corporate environmental reports have unfortunately become a communication tool for companies in disclosing their positive environmental performances, but not the negative. Guidelines, such as the Global Reporting Initiatives (GRI) attempt to provide a generally accepted standard or framework to lend credibility to the process. These provide companies with a rigorous and fair structure for their reports, providing indicators and measurement techniques for areas new to companies reporting intangibles, as well as safeguards on the reporting of transparent information. Guidelines such as these go a long way to improving the credibility of corporate social reporting but they are voluntary and are only useful if management use them to provide a useful overview of company performance from both good and bad perspectives.

Triple bottom line, the reporting of social, ethical and environmental information alongside financial information, is not always considered as a part of the ordinary day-to-day processes of a business, which is a matter that needs to be overcome. Expanding the organisation field to include the local community and other undefined stakeholders by incorporating triple bottom line into the operational framework of the organisation can only ease the availability of reliable information regarding the financial impact of social and environmental decisions made by management.

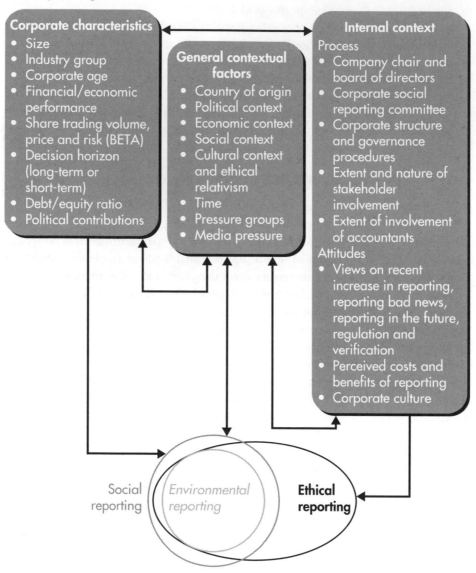

FIGURE 12.1 Diagrammatic portrayal of the influences on corporate 'social' reporting

Source: This figure appeared in the *Accounting, Auditing & Accountability Journal.*

If improvements in the extensiveness, quality, quantity and comprehensiveness of social and environmental reporting are to be achieved, some suggest academic researchers need to engage more with companies that currently attempt to provide this kind of disclosure. The idea is to gain a better understanding of their internal processes and attitudes to communicating this type of information, and how the conduct of management can influence the reporting of social and environmental issues. Few attempts have been made to combine research methodologies with content analysis, although some limited investigation into aspects of social and environmental reporting has proven fruitful.

The further improvement of reporting transparency in this field depends on the development of the reporting process, including sound governance structures involving independent and comprehensive audit guidelines. The attitudes of management stem from the culture of the corporation and their standards of ethics, and are part of a wider corporate social culture.

Corporations of the future may have objectives that move the culture of the organisation to new levels. Culture affects people's behaviour; a shift in the broader expectations of employees will see the corporation's objectives encouraging employees from the top to the bottom and vice versa to be aware of the risks relevant to the organisation's goals and to take ownership and responsibility to manage them (Kwan 1999, p. 21).

Governance and ethics

Corporate governance directives related to the settlements in the Enron and WorldCom cases, with enforcement actions by the Securities and Exchange Commission (SEC), and the new remedies available under the Sarbanes–Oxley Act of 2002 in the United States, indicate that independent directors will face very real financial, regulatory and criminal liability if they fail to execute their duties ethically and with integrity. Sowing the seeds of ethics does not come easily. It must be planned or developed over time for this ethical behaviour to surface for the good of the company. One problem facing corporate governance improvements is the frequent use of stock options to reward board members. Options provide incentives not to face up to setbacks in a corporation's performance. When bad news is revealed, the corporate board must be encouraged to advocate for transparency and full disclosure in financial reporting. The reality is, that in the United States now, corporate governance fails to tackle major problems with the system of check and balances with regards to stock options.

Government involvement in social and environmental reporting

> What is the appropriate role for government? Is it, as Adam Smith urged, to construct a system of natural liberty in which people are free to pursue their own ends, in which the invisible hand will lead people who seek to pursue only their own interests to promote the social interest? Or is the appropriate role of government... to serve as a benevolent parent to ensure that its wards act in a way that is in their own best interest? (Friedman 1981, p. 4 cited in Dellaportas et al. 2005)

Traditional accounting and economic models focus on the production and distribution of goods and services to society, while social accounting can be seen as a useful approach for measuring and reporting a firm's contribution to the community in a broader, more holistic sense.

UK legislation on environmental issues has stemmed from mainly the *Environmental Protection Act 1990*, the *Water Act 1990* and the contaminated land register. Under these regulations, corporations need to:

- invest in pollution protection
- invest in cleaner technologies
- change processes and products
- review asset values
- spend on waste treatment and its disposal (Gray, Bebbington & Walters 1993).

In the wider European Union, regulations cover a wider range of environmental legislation instigated in the mid-1990s. Some of the business implications are:

- the nature of packaging is changing
- packaging recovery or recycling schemes are needed
- cost of waste treatment or disposal is rising
- corporations need to make more information available to the public
- heavier industrial processes need to adopt environmental management practice.

In Australia, the government has been particularly active in legislating on social issues. Regulatory instruments such as occupational health and safety, equal employment opportunity and workers compensation, allow greater protection for employees, contractors and other citizens involved with corporations. Environmental governance is enforced through the *Environmental Protection Act 2000*.

Arguments for social and environmental legislation

Traditional accounting takes place within a fairly tightly defined framework. Its emphasis tends to be on reporting to shareholders and other market-oriented users. Social accounting requires a broader perspective to be taken, with recognition that there are other stakeholders besides shareholders and investors to be considered. Although there is no standard way of satisfying these needs, the literature on social accounting generally focuses on certain kinds of issues, notably such things as:

- the impact of corporate activities on the environment
- employees and employment prospects
- consumers and products
- the impact of corporate activities on the community.

Those advocating legislative action see instruments such as the proposed carbon tax, the limiting of greenhouse gas emissions and the polluter pays principle as imperative to bringing about change in the attitudes of corporations.

Arguments against social and environmental legislation

Arguments against legislative change to reporting requirements generally revolve around the perceived costs of disclosure, both financial and institutional. Given the evidence that suggests that the main motivation for social and environmental disclosure is related to corporate image and credibility, it is unsurprising that these disclosures are carefully orchestrated to maximise the positive image of the company. Although some bad news is seen as increasing the appearance of transparency and responsibility of the company, the full disclosure of bad news, such as the payment of large fines for environmental damage, is generally regarded as detrimental to corporate credibility (Adams 2002).

Professional involvement in social and environmental reporting

Although accounting academicians and practitioners had discussed how their profession could contribute to CSR before the movements of the 1960s, major progress in this area was made from the late 1960s to the middle 1970s.

Over the past 30 years, we have waited for the accounting profession to provide leadership in the corporate social reporting field. It is not enough for the professional bodies to help set accounting standards on financial matters; standards relating to social issues are also needed. The inclusion of socially oriented material in reports would provide useful information for investors as well as increasing the credibility of the corporate reporting regime. Corporations that include this kind of information are likely to be seen as good corporate citizens.

Gray, Owen & Adams (1996) summed up why the accounting profession should not be looked to for leadership in the field of social and environmental issues. His conclusions are as follows:

- Theory suggests accounting acts on behalf of corporations and capital (Lindblom, 1984).
- The accounting profession has had golden opportunities to introduce social and environmental accounting but chose not to follow them through
- The accounting profession is not widely renowned for its innovation and originality. Why might the accounting profession choose to be innovative in this field where it never has before (Bebbington et al. 1994).

The development of social and environmental reporting requires the abilities and experience of accountants. Professional bodies are committed to work with centres of excellence, discussion groups and other forums because they realise that regulation lacks both in Australia and internationally. To have guidelines so as to have organisations publicly disclose information on their performance on sustainable development issues would be a step forward for the accounting profession. This was started with the University of Sydney and CPA Australia obtaining funding from the Commonwealth government's Australian Research Council to develop a framework for managing and reporting nonfinancial information.

The International Federation of Accountants (IFAC) should be aiming to strengthen the international accounting profession in developing countries, tackle professional responsibility in financial reporting and clarify the role of accountants in corporate governance. This effort needs to consider social and environmental reporting in an integrated fashion, not merely as a desirable add-on.

The challenges and opportunities for the accounting professional internationally in the future are both daunting and exciting (Gorman & Hargadon 2005).

Growth opportunities in investment accounting as the baby-boomer generation ages will need accountants to be able to provide sound advice on the social responsibility of enterprises. The job of these accountants will be comparable with that of the controller of a corporation: they will have to coordinate, process and report on a myriad of financial activities. The future accountant will have significantly increased 'soft skills', with technical knowledge in forensic accounting, increased scepticism and a comprehensive understanding of business ethics. The accountants of today will need to lift their game to meet the challenges and opportunities that await them in the future.

Internal auditing worldwide has changed forever with the corporate accounting scandals of Enron and WorldCom. Falsifying corporate financial reports is only one area of concern for the internal auditor. The role of the internal auditor is twofold: computer and business system integrity, and transparency of financial reports, which should accurately reflect the corporation's activities. The importance of having strong, ethical internal auditors is set to grow exponentially.

Members of the accounting profession bodies should continue to learn from and share their experiences with members of other professional organisations around the globe. The global recognition and standing of the profession should mean that they are available to lend a hand and support the experience of developing countries to strengthen the credibility and integrity of accountancy. The In Focus feature that follows demonstrates the attempts by one professional organisation, CPA Australia, to educate its members, and consequently the corporations they work for, in maintaining an ethical culture.

 infocus *Surviving the whistle blowback*

Ethical dilemma: An environmental cover-up in a publicly listed company. CPA Australia's Professional Standards Board Committee proposes a solution.

The situation

You are a junior manager on the finance team in a large public-listed company. In the fine print of an obscure report you discover a huge environmental mismanagement cover-up which could cost the company millions in environmental protection fines and a serious loss in share price. However, after initial enquiries you find that senior management is involved in the cover-up. What do you do?

Recommended action

It's possible to build a work environment and culture which encourages people to do the right thing and to have mechanisms to deal with issues when some staff do the wrong thing. Regulatory authorities are more likely to look favourably on a voluntary disclosure from a workplace with an ethical culture, than on a result where the truth was involuntarily obtained from the organisation only after an expensive investigation.

If our junior finance manager's employer has installed an ethical culture throughout the organisation, it probably includes a mentor at executive level (supported by someone at board level), with whom people can discuss their concerns in the knowledge that the conversation will be confidential and that the information will be acted on. The board appointment is a necessary part of the framework to handle conversations when staff are nervous (for whatever reason) about dealing with senior management. The choice for our concerned employee will then be an easy one — use the mentoring option available and be confident that the company will deal with the improper behaviour voluntarily and in accordance with the regulatory requirements including market disclosure if that is required.

However, if no such culture exists, there could be real fears that the matter will become public knowledge in any one of a number of ways. But if the junior manager decides to report the findings and there are legitimate fears about the confidentiality of any such discussion. A letter to the board's audit committee chair would be the best option. That group should be exercising independence of thought and action about the operations of the organisation and the activities of senior management and should take the necessary steps to establish the full extent of the problem which has been identified and initiate whatever corrective action is necessary. If reference to the audit committee does not bring a result, a confidential discussion with the external auditor or a mentor provided by CPA Australia will help to identify any other options available.

Where an ethical culture does not already exist in an entity, the junior finance manager could raise the need for one in the various internal forums they are involved with, regardless of any other action decided upon. Discussion of this nature might eventually lead to the adoption of one.

Source: This article appeared in *INTHEBLACK*.

Intellectual capital management

Contemporary management refers to the notions of 'intellectual capital', 'intangibles' and 'knowledge management', long proclaimed as the advent of a 'knowledge age' or 'knowledge economy', in which the economic and productive capital of organisations derives from intellectual capital rather than the conventionally privileged modes of financial and physical capital. Intellectual capital is currently drawing the attention of governments and policy formulators and organisational practitioners globally.

The current measurement of 'intangible capital' has developed with inherent misclassifications and cobbled-together accounting approaches developed to supplement their limited consistency and comprehensiveness. To move forward in this area needs a back-to-basics costs approach, which classifies investments in intangibles as assets based on management intent at the time they are made.

Scorecard approaches now dominate the field of intellectual capital. The use of the balanced scorecard in reporting intangible assets will, over time, provide more detail on how the balanced scorecard facilitates the management of innovative processes as well as human resources and organisational capital management. Voluntary intellectual reporting raises some concerns about the potential lack of comparability and consistency between disclosures. This has important ramifications for external stakeholders of organisations, both shareholders and investors and the wider community. As with the benefits of social and environmental reporting, incentives for corporations to engage in intellectual capital disclosures are limited as they are now. Empirical investigation, and the involvement of the accounting profession in the development of consistent and reliable reporting procedures, will be an improvement.

Learning tips
Do you know...

12.1 *The implementation of international accounting standards will continue to occupy the attention of regulators and accountants in the near future.*

12.2 *Environmental and social information disclosure by enterprises will continue to grow in importance in correlation with community expectations and regulatory requirements.*

12.3 *It will become increasingly important to develop a reliable and accurate measurement system for intangibles to allow companies to more accurately represent their true value.*

Merging markets

Past experience has demonstrated that faith in open markets and economic liberalisation can be overwhelmed by big economic shocks. If the events of 11 September 2001 were to happen again, some feel that the **globalisation** process would grind to a halt. The major economic powerhouses of the United States and Europe might be tempted to retreat into a protectionist mode, and the international process of open markets and free trade may go forever.

globalisation: The process that has enabled investment in financial markets to be carried out on an international basis as a result of improvements in technology and deregulation

The US capital market is considered the largest in the world and the effect it can have on the world economy has been seen in the past. That capital market is also regarded as the most liquid and most sophisticated. The SEC is generally regarded as responsible for historical improvements to the governance process in the US. It initiated changes to independence and financial awareness of audit committees before the Enron collapse.

The SEC has the potential to be the most influential party in the world in the process of improving the quality and integrity of the financial reporting system and issues relating to governance. It is surprising to note that the SEC is underfunded and understaffed, yet it has been responsible for the enforcement of securities and financial reporting. Some of SEC initiatives for the future are:

- prohibit the CEO or any other past or current top manager of the corporation from acting as chairman of the board of directors, from being involved in any way in the nomination of directors or from being responsible for setting the board's agenda and meeting requirements
- prohibit all outside directors from holding stock options in any entity of whose board of directors they are a member
- with one exception (CEO or other), make the board members consist of outside directors who have not been employed or had significant business relationships with the corporation or its top executives
- establish a continuing education requirement for all outside board members, calling for 30 hours per year of corporate-funded continuing education coursework form accredited programs of study (Imhoff 2003, pp. 122–3).

Too few senior business leaders take the time to keep abreast of current developments in finance, financial reporting, governance and changing trends in business and industry. Therefore, by mandating a continuing education requirement, the SEC aims to increase the independence and competence of corporate boards of directors to effectively represent the shareholders' interests.

Among the biggest benefits of globalisation touted are open, free and unrestricted trade markets. Removing barriers to trade is one of the most powerful things that governments can do to give the poor a bigger stake in global prosperity. The World Bank released a report in 2001 stating that globalisation can lead to faster growth and poverty reduction in poor countries.

Free-market reforms, along with openness, hold the key to globalisation working for the poor. There is a belief that globalisation is detrimental to poorer communities, and that the integration of global markets will inevitably cause more poverty and inequality. The real issue, however, is that global inequality is inconsistent not just with civilised values but also with the international commitment to halve poverty by 2015. There is enormous potential for international trade to act as a catalyst for poverty reduction. It can provide poor countries with access to markets, technologies and resources, allowing faster and more equitable growth (Watkins 2002).

At present, however, international trade is reinforcing income inequalities.

> [W]orld trade shares mirror income distribution patterns. Thus, for every $1 generated through export activity, $0.75 goes to the world's richest countries. Low-income countries receive around $0.03. Unless developing countries capture a far larger share of exports, trade will continue to fuel widening gaps in absolute income (Watkins 2002, pp. 1–2).

In the immediate future, with the rapid growth of globalisation,

> Asia will need to continue to reform to reduce vulnerabilities to crises; deepen regional integration while remaining open to multilateralism; strengthen financial systems and enhance the flexibility of its economies in order to benefit from the emergence of China and India; and

rebalance demand to achieve more sustainable growth (Burton, Tseng & Kang 2006, p. 13).

Mergers, acquisitions and takeovers

Mergers, acquisitions and takeovers have been, and will continue to be, a feature of the global economy, especially with the cost of labour being inexpensive in developing countries. With the growth of multinational corporations, there has to be consistency and uniformity in the standardising of accounting principles and practices. They are particularly important when the information is used to compare one subsidiary's performance with another's.

mergers, acquisitions and takeovers: A combination of two or more businesses that results in the creation of a new reporting entity. Mergers involve the consent of the target company; acquisitions occur when one company purchases another or a controlling stake of its shares; while takeovers are usually taken to be of hostile intent.

Two extraordinary changes have taken place in corporations in recent years, as follows.

• People who work for organisations are no longer the traditional employees of those organisations.

• A growing number of corporations have outsourced employee relations; they no longer manage major aspects of their relationships with the people who are their formal employees.

This trend seems to be accelerating and represents a grave danger to corporations. Corporations will take advantage of the long-term freelance talent or outsource the tedious aspects of human resources management. Yet by offloading employee relations, corporations are going to lose the capacity to develop people and with them their skills and experience (Drucker 2002, p. 49).

One of the biggest limitations of the current corporate structure that will need to be overcome involves the make-up of the board of directors. The role of the corporation's board has to change to meet the needs of the shareholders first and foremost. Normally, the board of directors is made up of outside directors, designed to add value to the quality and integrity of management's financial reports by serving as a liaison with the independent professional accountants, and eventually the internal auditors. It also makes sure managers receive the appropriate compensation for their efforts. In doing so, it sees that incentive plans properly reward managers for their efforts to maximise shareholders' wealth (Imhoff 2003).

In identifying the causes of corporate disasters, you only have to look at how the corporate boards were put together. They are not really nominated by shareholders. Shareholders may have the vote but they are prescribed a limited choice on the ballot paper. In essence, the CEO can significantly influence the membership of the board, with former chairmen or CEOs of the corporation often nominated to new boards. This is intuitively contrary to effective corporate governance. Why does management sit in such a position of importance on the board of directors? How can the CEOs nominate people to serve on their own oversight boards, and still maintain the boards' independence and credibility? This practice will need to change to restore the public's confidence in the ability of a board to oversee a corporation.

While board independence is a problem in many Western organisations, in other countries, social and cultural norms can have a significant effect on the structure of a company. Multinational organisations struggle to integrate the different elements of their corporations. Whether it is the culture, development of technological advances or legal and political barriers to the communication of information from subsidiaries to the parent company, these differences cannot be disregarded. For example, Japanese managers and employees are used to working in teams and use team performance evaluation measures to increase cooperation. American workers and managers, on the other hand, are used to being evaluated as individuals. Even the incompatibility of computer systems can cause difficulties.

With rising globalisation of the marketplace, international investors need comparable financial reports to help them make better economic decisions. By providing harmonised reports, accounting practices can play a pivotal role in facilitating international investment. The shift to computer-assisted harmonisation will have embedded features for ease of use, functional modularity, expandability and network connectivity, which will spur on the international accounting community in its advocacy of harmonisation (Sankaran & AlHashim 2006).

Creative accounting

Many corporations practise creative accounting, although to what extent is not fully known. Changes in the accounting standards further increase the possibilities for manipulation of accounting numbers, especially with the use of 'fair value'. Smith (1992) lists several techniques that have been applied to the balance sheet and income statements to change the impact of the results. They are:

- writing down of assets before an acquisition
- disposals: profits on sales of assets taken 'above the line' and deconsolidation of subsidiaries in expectation of a sale
- deferred consideration on acquisition
- extraordinary and exceptional items
- off-balance-sheet finance
- contingent liabilities
- capitalisation of costs such as interest, and research and development
- brand accounting: capitalisation of assets
- changes in depreciation policy, both in method and in the period
- convertibles, with premium put options or variable-rate preferred stocks
- use of pension fund surplus to reduce annual charge
- currency mismatching between borrowing and depositions.

The practice of manipulations seemed commonplace across several countries. Smith (1992) reported that in the UK, 208 of the largest quoted corporations applied manipulations. In Australia, Smith, Fiedler & Kestel (1997) found 274 corporations had made 185 policy changes over the period 1987–88, with a further 78 changing the income impact. Davis (1999) reported how WR Grace & Co. in the United States, along with PricewaterhouseCoopers LLP, had been accused of earnings manipulation through creative accounting techniques. It was found that WR Grace & Co. had created corporate reserves to give the illusion of consistent profits.

Problems with manipulated accounts

Accountants manipulate the accounts for several reasons, including a desire to:

- enhance the earnings and the profit figures
- improve the appearance of the balance sheet
- be seen as successful in a political and social climate that demands it
- show a steady gradual annual increase in their annual profits
- avoid failure
- satisfy investor demands (Dellaportas et al. 2005, p. 192).

In the aftermath of Enron, the importance of audit credibility looms large. The consequences of another Enron would be disastrous not only for the corporation but also for the accounting and auditing profession. The outcomes would benefit no one and irreparably harm many. In the best interests of the community, placing public audit responsibility in the hands of a government agency seems the only option.

Solutions to 'creative accounting'

IFAC put forward its extensive study entitled *Rebuilding public confidence in financial reporting: an international perspective* (2003), which made recommendations to reduce the possibility of creative accounting. They stated that all participants in the accounting and reporting process were to be held accountable, and that with a positive attitude to ethics in business, the instances of creative accounting would cease. IFAC recommends ten steps to reduce 'creative accounting':

1. Effective corporate ethics codes need to be in place and actively monitored.
2. Corporate management must place greater emphasis on the effectiveness of financial management and controls.
3. Incentives to misstate financial information need to be reduced.
4. Boards of directors need to improve their oversight of management.
5. Threats to auditor independence need to receive greater attention in corporate governance processes and by the auditors themselves.
6. Audit effectiveness needs to be raised primarily through greater attention to audit quality control processes.
7. Codes of conduct need to be put in place for other participants in the financial reporting process and their compliance should be monitored.
8. Audit standards and regulation need to be strengthened.
9. Accounting and reporting practices need to be strengthened.
10. The standard of regulation of issuers needs to be raised.

The most important solution is in the process of education, as mentioned, to discourage the notion that accounting is objective, precise and reliable because of its arithmetical neatness. Users can be alerted to what the figures actually represent by being in a better position to make judgements about the accounting methods used.

Finally, the hardest solution to achieve would be to apply one single accounting standard globally, based on a single global currency (Dellaportas et al. 2005). The possibility of seeing this in our lifetime is very remote. If this does take effect, maybe the accounting profession will become a 'watchdog' for the government!

Taxation

Multinational enterprises claim that the job of preparing for taxes is complex, expensive and forever changing. Taxation effects have a pervasive effect on multi-nationals. This creates an in depth decision-making processes for internal management. Tax systems are used globally to affect economic policy and social and environmental issues, and this use will grow.

Tax advisers in Australia will need to carefully determine whether the adoption of IFRSs causes an inadvertent breach of the thin capitalisation provisions. The provisions of Div. 820 of the *Income Tax Assessment Act 1997 (Cth)*, which became effective on 1 July 2001, represented a significant change in thin capitalisation rules. An important aspect of the change is the reliance on the measurement process prescribed in Australian accounting standards in the valuation of assets. These substantial changes not only affect how assets are identified, measured and valued, but also how profit is determined.

Denning (2004) reported that the adoption of IFRS in the preparation of the general purpose financial statements is critical for taxation purposes, because in practice these same financial statements normally form the basis on which income tax computations and tax returns are prepared. Where IFRSs require a treatment of a particular matter that conflicts with its underlying tax treatment, an adjustment to an entity's income tax computation will be required. There is enormous potential, in this period of adjustment, for conflict between the tax authorities and taxpayers (and their advisers) as well as the taxation treatment of any cumulative adjustments to a corporation's reserves arising from IFRSs.

Key differences between tax law and principles and IFRSs are:

- The timing of income and expense recognition for tax purposes may differ from that required by the relevant IFRS, for example, where profits and losses are recognised on a realised basis for tax purposes versus on an accruals basis under the IFRS.
- Amounts and transactions may be recorded or carried otherwise than at historical cost under IFRS (e.g. asset revaluations, impairment write-offs or the use of discounting), while tax rules generally follow historical (i.e. actual) cost.
- IFRS requirements regarding classification, presentation and disclosure generally follow substance over form. Tax rules continue to rely primarily on the legal form of transactions when determining their tax consequences.
- Some items have an income tax impact but are dealt with otherwise than through the profit and loss account under IFRS (e.g. directly through equity).
- First-time adoption of IFRS and adjustments or restatement of prior years may have a tax effect that needs to be determined.

Learning tips

Do you know...

12.4 New and effective solutions to 'creative accounting' manipulations will need to be explored to restore community faith in the accounting profession.

12.5 Accountants will need to be aware of the constantly shifting interface between international accounting requirements and other national laws, such as tax law, in Australia and in other jurisdictions.

■ Communicating the way forward

Accounting professionals of the future will be required to have greater knowledge skills than ever before. They will be required to have insight, good professional judgement, project management skills, integrity and ethics. Their leadership qualities must include strategic thinking, planning and have a good understanding of their corporation and industry, **risk management** and organisational systems and processes.

risk management: A process that aims to help organisations understand, evaluate and take action on all their risks, involving identifying and evaluating the trade-off between risk and expected return

Although traditional technical skills such as taxation and financial analysis will be important, they will become specialisation areas. The sheer complexity of the taxation act will push some accountants to specialise. Accountants face more challenges today and there is a need for specialisation to keep up to date with the current legislation, especially on social and environmental issues. This will result in single accountants merging with others to be able to give the detail to the clients' financial statements.

However, the role of the generalist will continue to be important and will still be underrated. There will continue to be ongoing special projects that require an understanding of accounting and will rely on individuals with a wide understanding and a broad base from which they can synthesise a solution. In the short term, however, the IFRS reviews will continue to characterise the immediate future of the accounting profession.

New frontiers and challenges confronting the accounting profession in the future will include:

- risk management skills
- increased responsibility of the designated accountant
- increased 'nontraditional accounting', covering the triple bottom line
- the need for good accountants to be interpreters of information
- the loss of the last of the generation who have a good understanding of double-entry bookkeeping and not just computer spreadsheets.

Risk management skills

The release of the COSO risk management standard and Australian standard has helped define some of the questions within this framework and some discussion has put the topic on the map. There is also a recognition that the initial training of the accountant is in financial risks (if from an audit background), with the possibility that the accountant will be asked to cover this area. Sometimes the failure to report these issues will be reflected back onto accountants regardless whether they have any knowledge of this topic. There will be a transfer of a lot of internal auditors (and others) into the review of risks.

Responsibility of the accountant

The influence of the Sarbanes–Oxley Act 2002 has seen the accountant being asked to certify more information as being accurate. The accountant or financial controller is being asked to confirm more, both independently and by the directors, in undertaking their due diligence requirements.

Directors and regulators will push for certification from accountants. There has been a loss of faith in the external audit process, requiring others to sign off on accounts to support their overall integrity. Part of this is because items cannot be consistently identified without being involved in the business.

Future accountants or business advisers must have a strong focus on resource deployment and analysing financial and other information to develop total business solutions. In doing so, they have to be able to identify new market openings, maximise shareholder wealth and build an innovative strategic management.

'Nontraditional' accounting

With the changes in the reporting of information other than financial performance, there is an increasing need to be able to obtain and use nonfinancial data, particularly given a triple bottom line focus. Even the production of reports such as a balanced scorecard requires the knowledge of a wider reporting framework. Some of these areas are verging on being part of the accountant's role, such as payroll, which is either under finance or human resources. This information is not yet available in a manner that can be standardised and prepared and will require analysing to provide a meaningful and consistent story.

Communication for accountants

Quite often accountants do not communicate with their clients nor other accountants within their region very much. This is one aspect of the profession that will need to change dramatically. Accountants need to follow simple rules of effective communication and apply these strategies not only to communicate to partners but to clients and other accountants in their own region:

- Accountants should focus on frequent, quality electronic communications, using all available means from email to Internet.
- Regular face-to-face contact is important — even it is in a video conference.
- There is real value in spending time and money getting regional and head-office workers together.
- Accountants should understand the need to be globally integrated but locally responsive, and hire locals.
- Accountants should practise two-way feedback so that everyone can see the big picture.

- Head-office decision makers need to trust the expertise and advice of regional members.
- Accountants should listen and be tolerant of the practices required to be productive in different markets and cultures. One size probably will not fit all.
- Accountants should develop a culture that allows people to learn from their own mistakes, and give credit when it is due.
- Common corporate goals should be developed for head and regional offices (Tarrant 2005, p. 29).

Good accountants need to be interpreters of information. A useful example is the changing role of library staff. The rise of the Internet was at one stage touted as a death knell for librarians. However, although the role has changed a little, from a library technician to more of an information management role, the demand for good librarians is as high as it has ever been. This is also the case in accounting, where the mechanical processing has changed but good accountants are still able to tell the story that goes with the mechanically processed data.

The last of a generation

The last of the generation of accountants with a good understanding of double-entry bookkeeping and not just computer spreadsheets will soon be gone forever. There is a general concern in the profession that many accountants do not have a good basic grasp of how accounts are put together. Moreover, they are increasingly conservative and lack innovative thinking strategies. Deakin University has been conducting research into the personality traits of accountants using the **Myers–Briggs system**. They have found:

Myers–Briggs system: A personality inventory for measuring personality traits, and using them to identify a person's overall personality type

- 50 per cent are (E)xtraverts, 50 per cent (I)introverts.
- 68 per cent are (S)ensing types, 32 per cent i(N)tuitives.
- 80 per cent are (T)hinking types, 20 per cent (F)eeling types.
- 73 per cent are (J)udgemental, 27 per cent (P)erceptives (Aaron 2005, p. 49).

About half of business advisers are either ESTJs (extroverted, sensing, thinking and judgemental) or ISTJs (introverted, sensing, thinking and judgemental). The ITSJs' orientation to the world is practical adaptation, building on what others have done and fine tuning. Generally, they learn to think inside the box. The implementation of a chosen solution is achieved through organisation and planning, whereas the ESTJs make decisions and have things settled. They tend to work on the first workable solution to resolve a problem. With all the changes occurring in the profession, and constant evolution of accountants' role and responsibilities, what will be the personality characteristics of future accountants?

Summary

Outline the historical influences on current financial accounting theory.

- History plays an important role in providing directions for the future of accounting by providing an explanation of how markets and agency systems have evolved over time. It also helps to explain how communication through the involvement of the professional bodies and governments is important.

Evaluate the emerging role of standards regulators.

- The most fundamental shift in accounting regulation, and the one likely to remain the focus of the accounting profession for some time to come, is the implementation of a single, international set of accounting standards across the world.
- Some innovations will originate in the standard-setting and other regulatory processes. The role of the IASB, and that of other national regulators, such as the SEC and FASB in the United States, will continue to evolve as the globalisation of open markets increases.
- The role of regulators and other judicial and governmental systems in developing countries will continue to influence the expansion and growth of poorer economies.

Identify future directions of social and environmental reporting and intellectual capital management.

- It is no longer acceptable for a corporation to ignore their responsibilities to the environment, their employees, and the greater community. Guidelines for the transparent and accurate disclosure of social and environmental information will need to be enforceable and accountable.
- Cultural shifts in corporations, including the integration of triple bottom line reporting and high ethical standards, and the involvement of experienced accounting professionals and professional associations, will improve the quality and availability of information.
- A comprehensive and reliable system of intangibles measurement needs to be developed to allow corporations to better represent the true value of their knowledge and employee-based capital.

Understand the influence of merging markets on the role of the accountant.

- The rising globalisation of the marketplace and the constantly shifting business environment resulting from mergers and takeovers mean accountants will need to facilitate harmonisation on an international scale.
- New and effective solutions to 'creative accounting' manipulations will need to be explored, and accountants will need to be aware of the constantly shifting interface between international accounting requirements and other national laws, such as tax law.

Evaluate potential directions for the accounting profession.

- Accounting seems to be headed in two divergent directions. The role of the specialist in particular areas of accounting law will become even narrower and more expert. Similarly, the knowledge of generalist will need to become even further diversified, with broad-ranging skills from many perspectives.

- New opportunities in risk management and 'nontraditional' accounting, such as social and environmental accounting, will provide further growth and responsibility.
- All accountants will need increased communication and other 'soft' skills, and will face added responsibility and accountability in all areas of their practice.

Key terms

bankruptcy   366
corporate failure   365
corporation   364
corruption   366
creative accounting   368
globalisation   376
insolvency   367
mergers, acquisitions and takeovers   378
Myers–Briggs system   384
risk management   382

Review questions

12.1   Outline how historical influences have affected the understanding of market and agency systems.

12.2   Identify some of the major regulatory bodies involved in accounting regulation around the world.

12.3   How can the profession contribute to regulatory reform?

12.4   How has the role of the accountant changed over the past 20 years?

12.5   How have community expectations changed how corporations operate?

12.6   Explain what is meant by an intangible asset. Give examples.

12.7   Are there any problems associated with multinational enterprises reporting worldwide operations?

12.8   How important is social and environmental reporting?

12.9   What role will governments play in legislating on social and environmental issues?

12.10   Explain risk management.

12.11   What is creative accounting?

12.12   What are some solutions for creative accounting?

Application questions

12.13   The annual reports of many entities are now available on the Internet. Find a company listed on the Australian Securities Exchange that has published its annual reports on the Internet over a five-year period.

(a) Identify any changes to the information provided in the first half (non-financial) of the annual reports over the five years.

(b) What might be the reasons for any changes or lack of change in this kind of information?

12.14 Visit the websites of accounting professional organisations in Australia, such as CPA Australia (www.cpaaustralia.com.au), the Institute of Chartered Accountants of Australia (www.icaa.com.au) or the National Institute of Accountants (www.nia.org.au). Do any of them provide information about the changing role of accounting in the future? What material, (if any) do they provide on the topics discussed in this chapter?

12.15 Visit the Department of the Environment and Heritage website (www.deh.gov.au). What advice does the site give regarding corporate sustainability guidelines for enterprises? What kind of research does the department conduct into the sustainability reporting activities of Australian companies? What are the results reported in the latest study?

12.16 Search the Internet for any information regarding mergers or takeovers of companies in the past few years. Try searching for terms such as 'corporations merger', 'corporations acquisition' and 'company takeover' and investigate the results.

12.17 Investigate national standard-setters' websites from other countries and report on their current response to the international accounting standards process.

12.18 Access the IASB website and report on at least one 'current project' and its potential implications.

12.19 Compare the annual reports of three multinational enterprises with those from three domestic companies. How do their accounting practices differ?

12.20 Investigate the reporting of intangible assets in one of the companies from question 12.19. How important are intangible assets to the company? What accounting approach do they use to value them?

12.21 Find information regarding the social and environmental reporting regulations from two countries other than Australia. How do they compare with Australia's requirements?

12.22 From the ASIC website (www.asic.gov.au), access the 'Principles of good corporate governance and best practice recommendations' guidelines, and compare them with the corporate governance statement of compliance produced by ASIC itself. How many guidelines from the recommendations does the statement follow? What kinds of disclosures are made in the statement? Where is corporate governance information reported?

12.23 Investigate the websites of the professional organisations in question 12.17 for ethics guidelines for accountants. What issues are covered in these guidelines? What services (if any) do these organisations provide for members faced with ethical dilemmas?

12.24 Investigate the job opportunities for Australian accountants travelling overseas. What kinds of skills are employers looking for?

12.25 Investigate job ads for accountants in Australia. How do the skills and requirements differ from the overseas employers in question 12.24?

12.26   The Westpac banking corporation claims to have excellent social and environmental credentials. How does it support these claims? What kind of information does it supply on this topic in its annual report? What guidelines (if any) does it follow in the reporting of this information?

12.27   Investigate the annual report and website of an enterprise operating in an industry known for its detrimental effect on the environment. Consider mining operations, power suppliers, petrol companies and the like. Does the company make any claims about their environmental activities? If so, how are these claims reported? Do you think they are legitimate claims, or merely a marketing ploy?

case**study**   **12.1**

Property bosses earn top dollar

Executive salaries have become the latest battleground in the consolidation of the property trust sector. The new and prospective entrants to the property index, who bring with them large offshore operations and staff paid salaries set at international levels, are leading the charge higher.

But the new giants of property — one will be formed as Stockland and Lend Lease square off for GPT — have a long way to go before closing the gap to Westfield Group executive chairman Frank Lowy's $14.7 million package.

This year will be the first in which Mr Lowy is paid a salary from an entity in the index rather than receiving a salary from a holding company that sits outside it. As part of the $26 billion merger of the Westfield trusts and parent company, he will restrict his famous bonuses for at least the next two years.

His bonuses for 2004–05 and 2005–06 will be $4 million and $5 million respectively if distributions of $1.03 and $1.10 are achieved. One of the biggest potential pay packets hangs in the balance. If Lend Lease succeeds in taking over GPT, Lend Lease CEO Greg Clarke will receive a $1.375 million merger bonus, taking his potential package to $7.2 million this financial year.

By contrast, Stockland managing director Matthew Quinn stands to receive a comparatively modest $2.4 million this year. Mr Quinn's actual remuneration for 2005 will be $2 079 000. He will have access to 160 000 Stockland stapled securities valued at $374 400. Stockland said Mr Quinn would not receive a merger-related bonus if it wins GPT. But part of the group's pitch is that it will not engage in the high-risk offshore business that is associated with bigger pay packets.

The latest confirmed entrant to the property index, Multiplex Group, is experienced in this area. In its first year, CEO Andrew Roberts was paid $1 050 000. But the deputy managing director of Multiplex and chairman of the development division, Ross McDiven ($1 175 483), was better paid. Group founder John Roberts took just $112 943.

Salaries at the smaller end of the scale have also been lifted by merger activity. Macquarie Bank's Simon Jones received $618 385 for his role as CEO of the manager of Macquarie Office Trust. Almost $500 000 was in the form of the Macquarie Bank profit share and he could also be line for a bonus this year after taking over the Principal America Office Trust. The near $1 billion deal generated a healthy $14 million in fees for the bank.

James Fielding Group's Greg Paramor is in line to become CEO of the Mirvac Group as part of another takeover. Mirvac is offering script for James Fielding securities to form a $3.8 billion entity. Mr Paramor owns 6 471 260 shares, a stake of about 4.5 per cent.

Unlike the new class of managers, he will be aligned to the fortunes of the new group through this stake. Mirvac Group founder and managing director Bob Hamilton owned more than 13 million securities at the end of June but was criticised for selling 10 million securities for $44.8 million last month.

Source: This article appeared in *The Australian Financial Review.*

1. Investigate the salary levels of CEOs in Australia, Japan and the United States. How do they compare?
2. The details of directors' salary agreements appear in the annual report. Check the annual report of any one of the companies in the article. What kinds of conditions (if any) are attached to the CEO's salary package? Are CEO bonuses paid in cash or stock options?
3. How does merger activity affect the salaries of the CEOs involved?
4. Large CEO salaries and bonus packages are often a source of contention in the general community, especially when workers are made redundant or jobs outsourced. Investigate the concerns raised when this situation arises. Have any of the companies mentioned in the article been involved in a scandal of this nature?
5. Shareholders can also object to high directors' salaries, especially when the performance of the company (and its share price) appears to be struggling. Investigate reports of a company dealing with this kind of situation. See whether you can find any statements detailing the shareholders objections. What reasons do they give for their objections to the salary package? Do you think shareholders' concerns are legitimate?

case**study**   **12.2**

New standards to lift investor confidence

On February 15 the Chinese Ministry of Finance announced that it would bring its accounting and auditing standards in line with international rules.

The move, which follows a decade-long review of local accounting practices, is aimed at bolstering foreign investor confidence in the financial information issued by Chinese firms.

Vice-Finance Minister Lou Jiwei said China would adopt 'one basic accounting standard' — similar to the International Accounting Standards Board's Framework for the Preparation and Presentation of Financial Statements — and 38 accounting standards dealing with specific accounting issues, all these being largely based on International Financial Reporting Standards (IFRS), which are used in almost 100 countries.

...

The government's move, which signals the mainland's continued integration into the global economy, extends the nation's approach to accounting and allows it to keep up with other Asian countries such as Malaysia and India, which are more advanced in aligning their national standards with IFRS.

...

The transition is being spread over several years, which should create less strain on the available pool of skill and expertise. But it will be a challenge for local accounting firms struggling to compete with the Big Four, all of which have a strong presence in the mainland.

The magnitude of the training challenge facing the Chinese accounting market should not be underestimated.

The Association of Chartered Certified Accountants (ACCA) has trained thousands of Chinese accountants in IFRS in recent years — there are 135 000 qualified accountants in total.

The revisions bring Chinese standards closer to the IFRS benchmark but will not be word-for-word translations of the IFRS. Differences include the application of 'fair value', which will have to be tailored for a country such as China, where the government retains significant influence and free markets are not fully developed.

...

Apart from education and training, the key issues for China will be: applying the new rules, including any new data collection and restatements of prior-year figures; ensuring users have a clear understanding of accounts on the basis of the financial information they are being given; having systems in place to encourage conformity with the new standards; and correcting issues arising from the application of the standards in practice.

China has also pledged to adopt International Standards of Auditing.

This move is also welcome although there has been less international agreement on auditing than on accounting.

The original auditing standards were, ACCA believed, aimed mostly at larger firms and were not suitable for smaller enterprises. But the recent 'clarity project' instigated by the International Auditing and Assurance Standards Board has been a big step forward.

China has a huge influence on the regional and world economy, and serves as a guiding example for developing countries.

Its endorsement of international standards in financial reporting and auditing is therefore likely to be widely influential.

Source: This article appeared in the *South China Morning Post.*

1. How are international accounting standards important to the success of an emerging economy like China?
2. What ethical and governance issues will be need to be addressed by the Chinese regulators?
3. What issues regarding the implementation and application of IFRSs do Chinese accounting regulators face? Are these concerns echoed elsewhere in the world?
4. China has a significant economic influence in the Asian region. Research the economic status of other regional economies, including the implementation of IFRS. How is the Chinese adoption of international standards likely to influence the decisions of other nations?
5. Can you find similar reports on other developing nations where accounting initiatives are gaining importance? What kinds of support and education mechanisms are being implemented in these countries, and how do they compare with those identified in the article?

Recommended websites

AusIndustry, www.ausindustry.gov.au.

CPA Australia, www.cpaaustralia.com.au.

Department of the Environment and Heritage, www.deh.gov.au.

Institute of Chartered Accountants of Australia, www.icaa.com.au.

References

Aaron, M 2005, 'Imagine: Research into business and finance professionals reveals most are closed to new ways. It's time to start thinking differently', *INTHEBLACK*, March.

Accountant 2004, '2010 total compliance deadline is "wishful thinking"', October, p. 14.

Adams, CA 2002, 'Internal organisational factors influencing corporate social and ethical reporting: beyond current theorising', *Accounting, Auditing and Accountability Journal*, vol. 15, no. 2, pp. 223–50.

Bebbington, KJ, Gray, RH, Thomson, I & Walters, D 1994, 'Accountants' attitudes and environmentally sensitive accounting', *Accounting and Business Research*, vol. 94, Spring, pp. 51–75.

Burton, D, Tseng, W & Kang, K 2006, 'Asia's winds of change', *Finance and Development*, June.

Dellaportas, S, Gibson, K, Alagiah, R, Hutchinson, M, Leung, P & Homrigh, DV 2005, *Ethics, governance and accountability: a professional perspective*, John Wiley & Sons, Brisbane.

Denning, B 2004, 'Adopting International Financial Reporting Standards: the tax implications', *Accountancy Ireland*, vol. 36, no. 4, pp. 19–20, 22.

Davis, A, 1999, 'SEC and WR Grace are near accord over alleged earnings manipulation', *Wall Street Journal*, 25 June, p. B5.

Drucker, PF 2002, 'Future firm', *Human Resources*, March, pp. 42–9.

Gorman, JF & Hargadon, JM 2005, 'Accounting futures: Healthy markets for a time-honored profession', *Journal of Financial Service Professionals*, vol. 59, iss. 1, pp. 74–9.

Gray, R, Bebbington, J & Walters, D 1993, *Accounting for the environment*, Paul Chapman, London, pp. 3–15.

Gray, R, Owen, D & Adams, C 1996, *Accounting and accountability: changes and challenges in corporate social and environmental reporting*, Prentice Hall, Sydney.

Imhoff, Jr, EA 2003, 'Accounting quality, auditing, and corporate governance', *Accounting Horizons*, vol. 17, pp. 117–28.

Islam, R 2002, 'Institutions to support markets', *Finance and Development*, March, pp. 48–51.

Journal of Accountancy 2005, 'A conversation with the chief accountant of the SEC: in the public interest', January, p. 63.

Kwan, W-K 1999, 'Risk management — needed: an integrated approach', *Australian CPA*, June, pp. 20–1.

Lindblom, CK 1994, 'The implications of organisational legitimacy for corporate social performance and disclosure', paper presented at the Critical Perspectives on Accounting Conference, New York.

Sankaran, S & AlHashim, DD 2006, 'An accounting information system for harmonization', *Journal of American Academy of Business*, vol. 9, no. 2, pp. 250–6.

Smith, M, Fiedler, B & Kestel, J 1997, 'Structure versus judgement in the audit process: a test of Kenney's classification', University of South Australia seminar series, Adelaide.

Smith, T 1992, *Accounting for growth*, Century Business, London.

Tarrant, D 2005, 'The evil empire: why can't head office and its regional satellites get along? Perhaps a little TLC is needed to build good relationships', *INTHEBLACK*, March.

Watkins, K 2002, 'Making globalization work for the poor', *Finance and Development*, March, pp. 24–7.

GLOSSARY

accountability (stewardship): The responsibility of providing information to enable users to make informed judgements about the performance, financial position, financing and investing and compliance of the reporting entity *p. 195*

accounting conceptual framework: A coherent system of concepts that underlie financial reporting *p. 27*

accounting standards: Authoritative statements that guide the preparation of financial statements *p. 65*

Accounting Standards Board: The accounting standard setter in the UK *p. 231*

accounting theory: Either a description, explanation or prediction of accounting practice or a set of principles on which to evaluate or guide practice *p. 5*

accrual basis: Where the effects of transactions and other events are recognised when they occur (and not as cash or its equivalent is received or paid) and they are recorded in the accounting records and reported in the financial statements of the periods *p. 35*

active market: A market in which the items traded are homogeneous, willing buyers and sellers can be found at any time and prices are available to the public *p. 128*

agency relationship: A relationship in which a principal delegates decision-making authority to an agent *p. 155*

asset: A resource controlled by the enterprise as a result of past events and from which future economic benefits are expected to flow to the entity *p. 39*

associate: An entity, including an unincorporated entity such as a partnership, over which the investor has significant influence, which is neither a subsidiary nor an interest in a joint venture *p. 318*

association: A suggestion of a relationship between two or more sets of numbers when regressed *p. 271*

association study: Research method that looks for correlation between an accounting performance measure and share returns *p. 267*

Auditing and Assurance Standards Board: The body that has the responsibility to set auditing standards in Australia *p. 246*

Australian Accounting Standards Board: The body responsible for setting accounting standards in Australia *p. 232*

bankruptcy: The state of an individual who is unable to pay his or her debts, where legal orders are issued to deprive him or her of his or her property, which is then used to pay their debts *p. 366*

basis for conclusions: A part of a standard that outlines the reasons the standard setter chose particular accounting treatments of one kind over others *p. 240*

bonding costs: The restrictions placed on an agent's actions deriving from linking the agent's interest to that of the principal *p. 156*

bonus plan hypothesis: A prediction of agency theory that if managers' remuneration is tied to accounting profit through a bonus plan, they will adopt accounting policies that shift reported income from future periods to the present period *p. 160*

compilation report: A report that makes specific reference to the purpose of the financial report, including clarification of whether it is a general purpose or special purpose financial report *p. 349*

conceptual framework: A set of broad principles that provide the basis for guiding actions or decisions *p. 26*

consolidated financial statements: The financial statements of a group of entities consisting of a parent and one or more subsidiaries *p. 318*

corporate failure: The dissolution of a company, in which it is unable to continue in business because it cannot meet its financial obligations to suppliers or creditors *p. 365*

corporate governance: The system by which business corporations are directed and controlled *p. 153*

corporate social responsibility: Term referring to management's choosing to voluntarily disclose noncompulsory information in the front section of annual reports *p. 138*

corporation: A large company or group of companies authorised to act as a single entity and recognised as such in law *p. 364*

corruption: Offences relating to the improper influencing of people in positions of trust, such as politicians, civil servants and other officials, through bribes that may be in cash or in kind, for an official action or inaction *p. 366*

cost: Something that is given, needed or lost to obtain a particular thing *p. 99*

creative accounting: Misleadingly optimistic, though not illegal, forms of accounting. This can occur because some accounting transactions are not subject to regulations or the regulations are ambiguous. *p. 368*

current cost: The lowest amount that would be paid at the current time to provide or replace the future economic benefits expected from the current item *p. 101*

deduction: The process of reaching a conclusion about particular instances from general principles *p. 9*

deprival value: The loss that a rational businessman or businesswoman would suffer if he or she was deprived of the asset *p. 105*

differential reporting: The notion that different categories of entities should be subject to different accounting and reporting rules *p. 309*

discussion paper (invitation to comment): The first phase in the development of an international standard, in which the International Accounting Standards Board engages its constituents in considering a range of issues on a topic *p. 240*

draft interpretation: A document proposing an interpretation of an accounting standard or accounting standards that is released for public comment *p. 241*

due process: The consultation and decision-making process of a standard setter *p. 239*

earnings management: A manager's use of accounting discretion through accounting policy choices to portray a desired level of earnings in a particular reporting period *p. 124*

eco-efficiency: A focus on the efficiency of activities to minimise their effect on the environment, which is short term *p. 205*

eco-justice: Intergenerational and intragenerational equity and social equality *p. 205*

efficient market hypothesis: A market in which all share prices reflect fully all the available information, so that investors cannot make excessive returns by exploiting information *p. 266*

empirical research: Research based on observation or experience *p. 13*

equity: The residual interest in the assets of the enterprise after deducting all its liabilities *p. 39*

ethical investment funds: Investment funds that screen potential investments for not only economic performance, but also social and environmental attributes; for example, whether the company conducts experiments on animals or is involved in armaments *p. 208*

ethics: The standards of conduct that indicate how one should behave based on moral duties and virtues; also, compliance with the written rules of conduct of a profession, together with adherence to individual attitudes and origins, taking into account differences in background, culture and philosophy *pp. 177, 335*

European Commission: The authority in Europe that deals with regulatory issues affecting the single European market *p. 244*

European Financial Reporting Advisory Group: A body based in Europe consisting of accounting experts that drafts responses on technical issues to the International Accounting Standards Board *p. 244*

event study: Research methods that examine the changes in level or variability of share prices or trading volume around the time new information is released *p. 267*

exclusion approach: The process by which firms are excluded from a socially responsible investment fund on certain criteria *p. 215*

expenses: Decreases in economic benefits during the accounting period in the form of outflows or depletions of assets or incurrences of liabilities that result in decreases in equity, other than those relating to distributions to equity participants *p. 39*

exposure draft: A proposed accounting standard issued for public comment *p. 240*

fair value: The amount for which an item could be exchanged between knowledgeable, willing parties in an arm's length transaction *p. 102*

falsification: The method of testing theories by attempting to find observations that conflict with the conclusions or predictions of the theory *p. 13*

financial accounting: The regular reporting of the financial position and performance of an entity through financial statements issued to external users *p. 4*

Financial Accounting Standards Board: The accounting standard setter in the United States first created in 1973 *p. 230*

financial instruments: Contracts that give rise to a financial asset of one entity and a financial liability or equity instrument of another entity *p. 315*

Financial Reporting Council: The oversight body that has among its various responsibilities the task of reviewing the operations and performance and strategies of the Australian Accounting Standards Board and the Auditing and Assurance Standards Board *p. 245*

general purpose financial report: A report that complies with the Australian conceptual framework (see chapter 2) and accounting standards and meets the common information needs of users who are unable to request the preparation of a report to satisfy their needs

general purpose financial statements: Financial reports intended to meet the information needs common to users who are unable to command the preparation of reports tailored to satisfy, specifically, all of their information needs *p. 31*

Generally Accepted Accounting Principles (GAAP): Accounting principles that are in most cases embedded in a conceptual framework and accounting standards. Sometimes, GAAP are represented by evolving practice. *p. 253*

globalisation: The process that has enabled investment in financial markets to be carried out on an international basis as a result of improvements in technology and deregulation *p. 376*

going concern basis: Where the financial statements are normally prepared on the assumption that an enterprise is a going concern and will continue in operation *p. 35*

Group of Four plus One: A group of national standard setters from Australia, Canada, New Zealand, the UK and the United States that met along with the IASC to develop joint views on accounting matters *p. 233*

harmonisation: The adoption of the content and wording of IASB standards, except where there is a need to change words to accommodate Australia's legislative requirements *p. 79*

heuristics: Rules of thumb derived from past experience that are used in decision making *p. 281*

historic cost: The amount of money (dollars) sacrificed or given up to obtain an item *p. 100*

hypothesis: A tentative assumption or prediction of a theory *p. 8*

income: Increases in economic benefits during the accounting period in the form of inflows or improvements of assets or decreases of liabilities that result in increases in equity, other than those relating to contributions from equity participants *p. 39*

induction: The process of inferring general principles from particular instances *p. 9*

insolvency: The inability of a company to pay its debts when they fall due. Insolvency leads to liquidation, in which the assets of a company are used to repay creditors. *p. 367*

intangible assets: Identifiable nonmonetary assets without physical substance *p. 127*

intellectual capital: An umbrella term encompassing capital created by employees (such as patents), relationships with customers and suppliers (such as brands, trademarks) and capital invested in employees (such as in training or education) *p. 129*

intergenerational equity: A concept that, consistent with the definition of sustainable development, recognises that the Earth is a finite planet and all humans require its natural resources. It has a longer-term focus; that is, in future generations. *p. 205*

interim financial reports: Reports issued between annual reports *p. 136*

intermediaries: Financial analysts, auditors, managers and others who examine primary data and send a message about that data to investors *p. 273*

International Accounting Standards Board: The London-based standard setter developing accounting standards for worldwide use *p. 230*

International Accounting Standards Committee: An accounting standard setter overseen by the International Federation of Accountants that existed between 1973 and 2000 *p. 231*

International Accounting Standards Committee Foundation: The organisation that houses the board of trustees of the International Accounting standards Board, the standard setter and associated committees and operational and technical staff *p. 234*

International Auditing and Assurance Standards Board: A committee overseen by the International Federation of Accountants that sets standards for auditors *p. 246*

international convergence: The adaptation of national accounting standards to align with the international accounting standards administered by the International Accounting Standards Board *p. 311*

International Federation of Accountants: The representative body for professional accounting organisations worldwide *p. 231*

International Financial Reporting Standards: A single set of enforceable global accounting standards that require transparent and comparable information in general purpose financial statements, produced by the International Accounting Standards Board *p. 237*

International Organisation of Securities Commissions: The umbrella body for securities regulators across the world *p. 231*

International Public Sector Accounting Standards Board: Body overseen by IFAC that sets accounting standards for the government sector *p. 246*

legitimacy theory: The theory that suggests society will penalise firms that fail to conform to community expectations and values *p. 195*

liability: A present obligation of the enterprise arising from past events, the settlement of which is expected to result in an outflow from the enterprise of resources embodying economic benefits *p. 39*

manipulation: The use of management's discretion to make accounting choices or to design transactions to affect the possibilities of wealth transfer between the company and society (political costs), funds providers (cost of capital) or managers (compensation plans) *p. 124*

materiality: The quality of information if its omission or misstatement could influence the economic decision of users taken on the basis of the financial statements *p. 36*

measure: The quantity, weight, height and so on of something or a unit used for stating the size, weight and so on, of something or the extent or dimensions of a thing as determined by measuring *p. 91*

measurement: The act or process of measuring *p. 91*

mergers, acquisitions and takeovers: A combination of two or more businesses that results in the creation of a new reporting entity. Mergers involve the consent of the target company; acquisitions occur when one company purchases another or a controlling stake of its shares; while takeovers are usually taken to be of hostile intent. *p. 378*

monitoring costs: Costs incurred by principals to monitor the behaviour of the agent *p. 156*

Myers–Briggs system: A personality inventory for measuring personality traits, and using them to identify a person's overall personality type *p. 384*

net realisable value: Fair value less the costs of sale or disposal *p. 103*

normative theories: Theories that provide prescriptions about what *should* happen *p. 11*

positive theories: Theories that describe, explain or predict what is happening in the world (such as describing, explaining or predicting current accounting practice) *p. 8*

post-earnings announcement drift: The finding that prices adjust gradually to new information *p. 270*

present value: The present discounted value of the future net cash flows associated with an item *p. 104*

prices lead earnings: The finding that earnings lag prices because prices contain information about future earnings *p. 268*

principles-based standards: Standards that contain a substantive accounting principle that focuses on achieving the accounting objective of the standard. The principle is based on the objective of accounting in the conceptual framework. *p. 66*

proactive management strategies: Preventative measures involving risk management to predict and avoid breaches of legislation; for example, pollution prevention, recycling and cleaner processes *p. 197*

profession: A disciplined group of individuals who are accepted by the public as possessing special knowledge and skills in a widely recognised body of learning derived from research, education and training *p. 333*

professional responsibility: Ability to balance the various duties owed by accountants to the users of accounting information, such as the public, clients and the profession *p. 334*

pro-forma results: Financial statements for a period prepared before the end of the period, which therefore contain estimates *p. 125*

prospect theory: The theory that suggests that the pain associated with a given amount of loss is greater than the pleasure associated with an equivalent gain *p. 278*

prudence: The inclusion of a degree of caution in the exercise of the judgements needed in making the estimates required under conditions of uncertainty, such that assets or income are not overstated and liabilities or expenses are not understated *p. 37*

quality control: A system of policies and procedures to deal with leadership responsibilities for quality within the firm, its ethical requirements, acceptance and continuance of client relationships and specific engagements, engagement performance and monitoring *p. 344*

reactive management strategies: Compliance with legislative requirements after the event; for example, clean-up, compensation or the payment of penalties for breaches of legislation *p. 197*

recognition: The process of incorporating an item in the balance sheet or income statement. It involves depiction of the item in words and by a monetary amount and that inclusion of that amount in the balance sheet or income statement totals. *p. 40*

regulation: The policing, according to a rule, of a subject's choice of activity, by an entity not directly party to or involved in the activity *p. 69*

relevance: The quality of information when it influences the economic decisions of users by helping them evaluate past, present or future events or confirming, or correcting, their past evaluations *p. 36*

reliability: The quality of information when it is free from material error and bias and can be depended upon by users to represent faithfully that which it either purports to represent or could reasonably be expected to represent *p. 36*

replacement cost: The amount that would be paid at the current time to acquire an identical item *p. 101*

reporting enterprise: An enterprise for which there are users who rely on the financial statements as their major source of financial information about the enterprise *p. 32*

research: Diligent, systematic enquiry into a subject to discover facts or principles *p. 13*

residual loss: The reduction in wealth of principals caused by their agent's non-optimal behaviour *p. 156*

risk management: A process that aims to help organisations understand, evaluate and take action on all their risks, involving identifying and evaluating the trade-off between risk and expected return *p. 382*

rules-based standards: Standards that contain specific details and mandatory definitions that attempt to meet as many potential contingencies and situations as possible *p. 66*

scientific method: The process in which a theory is derived from observations and then makes predictions. Further observations are then made to test these predictions. *p. 10*

Securities and Exchange Commission: The securities regulator in the United States, which has the power to set listing requirements for entities seeking to source debt or share capital from American companies or individuals *p. 230*

segment information: Financial information related to the different types of products and services an entity produces and the different geographical areas in which it operates *p. 317*

small and medium-sized entities (SMEs): Entities that do not have public accountability and do not publish general purpose financial statements for external users *p. 295*

social and environmental reporting: The disclosure of information on social- and environmental-related issues and performance; for example, the reporting of policies on equal opportunity and minorities, disclosure of emissions targets *p. 194*

social costs (externalities): The costs of a company's activities on the environment and society that are met by the general community *p. 194*

socially responsible investment (SRI): Investment concerned with socially and environmental criteria or benchmarks, together with financial performance of a firm. Groups of firms meeting the specified criteria of research analysts combine to form an SRI fund. *p. 215*

special purpose financial report: A report that is prepared for a specific user, for example, the ATO *p. 349*

stakeholder theory: The theory that incorporates the interests of a broader range of stakeholders in an entity, not just the shareholders *p. 196*

sustainability: Equitable consumption of resources that does not compromise the needs of future generations *p. 194*

sustainable development: Development that meets the needs of the present without compromising the ability of future generations to meet their own needs *p. 195*

triple bottom line: A practice that reports on the economic, social and environmental management and performance of a firm *p. 199*

understandability: The quality of the information that means it is readily understandable by users *p. 36*

value: The importance or worth of something for someone; utility or merit *p. 99*

value in exchange: The benefits from selling an item, usually considered as fair value or net realisable value *p. 100*

value in use: The benefits from using an item, usually considered as the present value of the future cash flows associated with the item *p. 99*

value relevance: An item of accounting information that makes a difference to the decisions made by users of financial statements *p. 270*

Index